Gentry Life in Georgian Ireland
The Letters of Edmund Spencer (1711–1790)

LEGENDA

LEGENDA is the Modern Humanities Research Association's book imprint for new research in the Humanities. Founded in 1995 by Malcolm Bowie and others within the University of Oxford, Legenda has always been a collaborative publishing enterprise, directly governed by scholars. The Modern Humanities Research Association (MHRA) joined this collaboration in 1998, became half-owner in 2004, in partnership with Maney Publishing and then Routledge, and has since 2016 been sole owner. Titles range from medieval texts to contemporary cinema and form a widely comparative view of the modern humanities, including works on Arabic, Catalan, English, French, German, Greek, Italian, Portuguese, Russian, Spanish, and Yiddish literature. Editorial boards and committees of more than 60 leading academic specialists work in collaboration with bodies such as the Society for French Studies, the British Comparative Literature Association and the Association of Hispanists of Great Britain & Ireland.

The MHRA encourages and promotes advanced study and research in the field of the modern humanities, especially modern European languages and literature, including English, and also cinema. It aims to break down the barriers between scholars working in different disciplines and to maintain the unity of humanistic scholarship. The Association fulfils this purpose through the publication of journals, bibliographies, monographs, critical editions, and the MHRA Style Guide, and by making grants in support of research. Membership is open to all who work in the Humanities, whether independent or in a University post, and the participation of younger colleagues entering the field is especially welcomed.

ALSO PUBLISHED BY THE ASSOCIATION

Critical Texts
Tudor and Stuart Translations • *New Translations* • *European Translations*
MHRA Library of Medieval Welsh Literature

MHRA Bibliographies
Publications of the Modern Humanities Research Association

The Annual Bibliography of English Language & Literature
Austrian Studies
Modern Language Review
Portuguese Studies
The Slavonic and East European Review
Working Papers in the Humanities
The Yearbook of English Studies

www.mhra.org.uk
www.legendabooks.com

Gentry Life in Georgian Ireland

The Letters of Edmund Spencer (1711–1790)

Edited by
Duncan Fraser and Andrew Hadfield

Modern Humanities Research Association
2017

Published by Legenda
an imprint of the Modern Humanities Research Association
Salisbury House, Station Road, Cambridge CB1 2LA

ISBN 978-1-910887-14-1 (HB)
ISBN 978-1-78188-357-0 (PB)

First published 2017

Copy-Editor: Charlotte Brown

CONTENTS

Acknowledgements ix
List of Abbreviations xi
Dating and References xii
Historical Maps xiii
Introduction: Edmund Spencer and His Times 1
The Letters 47
Appendix I: Additional Letters from the Puleston Collection 219
Appendix II: Index of People Mentioned in the Correspondence 231
Appendix III: Index of Places Mentioned in the Correspondence 259
Appendix IV: Places Given as Addresses of Origin 274
Bibliography 275
Index 281

ACKNOWLEDGEMENTS

This has been an especially enjoyable book to produce and we have gathered numerous debts along the way, with many people and institutions reminding us how pleasant and constructive scholarly communities can be. Both editors are particularly grateful to the National Library of Wales, Aberystwyth, where the archival research has been undertaken, and where the staff have been uniformly courteous and helpful, as were staff at the library of Trinity College, Dublin, who responded to telephone and e-mail enquiries; to the British Library, where we have checked many references; to Catherine Packham and Hannah Field at the University of Sussex, both of whom read the Introduction and made a number of valuable suggestions; and to the many generous individuals who have supplied references or answered queries: Andrew Foster, Rev. David Child, rector of St. Mary's Church, Overton, and Rebecca Baskerville, the librarian at Overton, all helped us with Francis Price's personal history and immediate social circle, as did Siobhán O'Brien at the Chester Record Office, Will Meredith at the Wirral Archives, and Roger Hull of the Liverpool Record Office. The extensive research carried out for us by Liz Newman and Sue Copp of the Flintshire Record Office enabled us to identify Francis Price's troublesome neighbour 'Trigger'. Dr Anthony Malcolmson and Prof. David Hayton advised on some of the more obscure references to Irish history, politics, and civil governance; Christopher Whittick, Senior Archivist, East Sussex, helped with decoding some of the less legible marks made by Edmund Spencer. Angela Andreani gave timely and helpful advice at an early stage with transcription conventions and pointed us in the direction of some useful reading. Nicole Mennell provided information about the taming of eagles in the early modern period, and conversation with Prof. Andrew Gibson shone some light into the shadowy world of Irish land law. We are also grateful to Dr Jane Grogan for giving us the opportunity to air some of our early thoughts at the 2015 Conference of the International Spenser Society in Dublin. Graham Nelson at Legenda has been an exemplary series editor and has worked hard to ensure the book has been produced very much as we want it to be. We are also indebted to Charlotte Brown whose meticulous copy editing has saved us from a multitude of errors and infelicities; it goes without saying that the responsibility for any that remain lies solely at our door. The anonymous reader for the press made a number of extremely helpful suggestions which greatly improved the text and we are grateful for such valuable advice. Our wives, Lyn and Alison, have been patient and encouraging throughout, as they have learned more about Spencer, Price, Barrymore, Watkin Williams, and other characters, than they probably truly desired.

Illustrations from the Puleston archives were supplied by Llyfrgell Genedlaethol Cymru / The National Library of Wales..

D.F., A.H., Sussex, January 2017

LIST OF ABBREVIATIONS

DIB James McGuire and James Quinn, eds., *Dictionary of Irish Biography* (Cambridge: Cambridge University Press, 2009)

HIP Edith Mary Johnson-Liik, *History of the Irish Parliament, 1692–1800*, 6 vols (Belfast: Ulster Historical Foundation, 2002)

ODNB Colin Matthew and Brian Harrison, eds., *The Oxford Dictionary of National Biography*, online edition (Oxford: Oxford University Press, 2004)

OED *Oxford English Dictionary*, 2nd edn (Oxford: Oxford University Press, 2009)

Carlisle, Ireland Nicholas Carlisle, *A Topographical Dictionary of Ireland* (Bedford Bury: printed for William Miller, 1810)

Carlisle, Wales Nicholas Carlisle, *A Topographical Dictionary of the Dominion of Wales* (London: printed for the author, 1811)

Lewis, Ireland Samuel Lewis, *A Topographical Dictionary of Ireland*, 2 vols (London: S. Lewis, 1837)

Lewis, Wales Samuel Lewis, *A Topographical Dictionary of Wales*, 2 vols (London: S. Lewis, 1840)

Tilley M. P. Tilley, *A Dictionary of the Proverbs in England in the Sixteenth and Seventeenth Centuries* (Ann Arbor: University of Michigan Press, 1950/1966)

Unless otherwise noted information referenced from dictionaries comes from the entry for the word, person or place specified in the lemma.

Quotations from the works of Shakespeare, and references thereto, are unless otherwise specified, from *The Riverside Shakespeare*, ed. by G. Blakemore Evans and others (Boston, MA: Houghton Mifflin, 1974).

DATING AND REFERENCES

In January 1752, roughly in the middle of this correspondence, the Calendar (New Style) Act 1750 came into force, moving the beginning of the legal year from 25 March to 1 January and replacing the Julian Calendar with the more accurate Gregorian Calendar. Up to 1752, for letters written between 1 January and 24 March, Spencer consistently applies the Old Style; from January 1752 he equally consistently adopts the New Style. We have retained his dating throughout, and use the dates given on the letters when referencing them; thus the letter of 10 January 1743 (Old Style) is referenced '10 January 1743: folio 13'. The only place where we depart from this practice is in the chronological table that precedes the transcription, where it was felt that giving the date New Style in square brackets would help to make the table clearer for a modern reader. There, the letter dated 10 January 1743 by Spencer is listed as '10 January 1743[4]'.

There are no letters dated between Wednesday 2 September and Thursday 14 September 1752, the eleven days that were removed in that year to bring the calendar into astronomical line, and as that measure has no impact on either the dating or our discussion of these letters it has been effectively ignored.

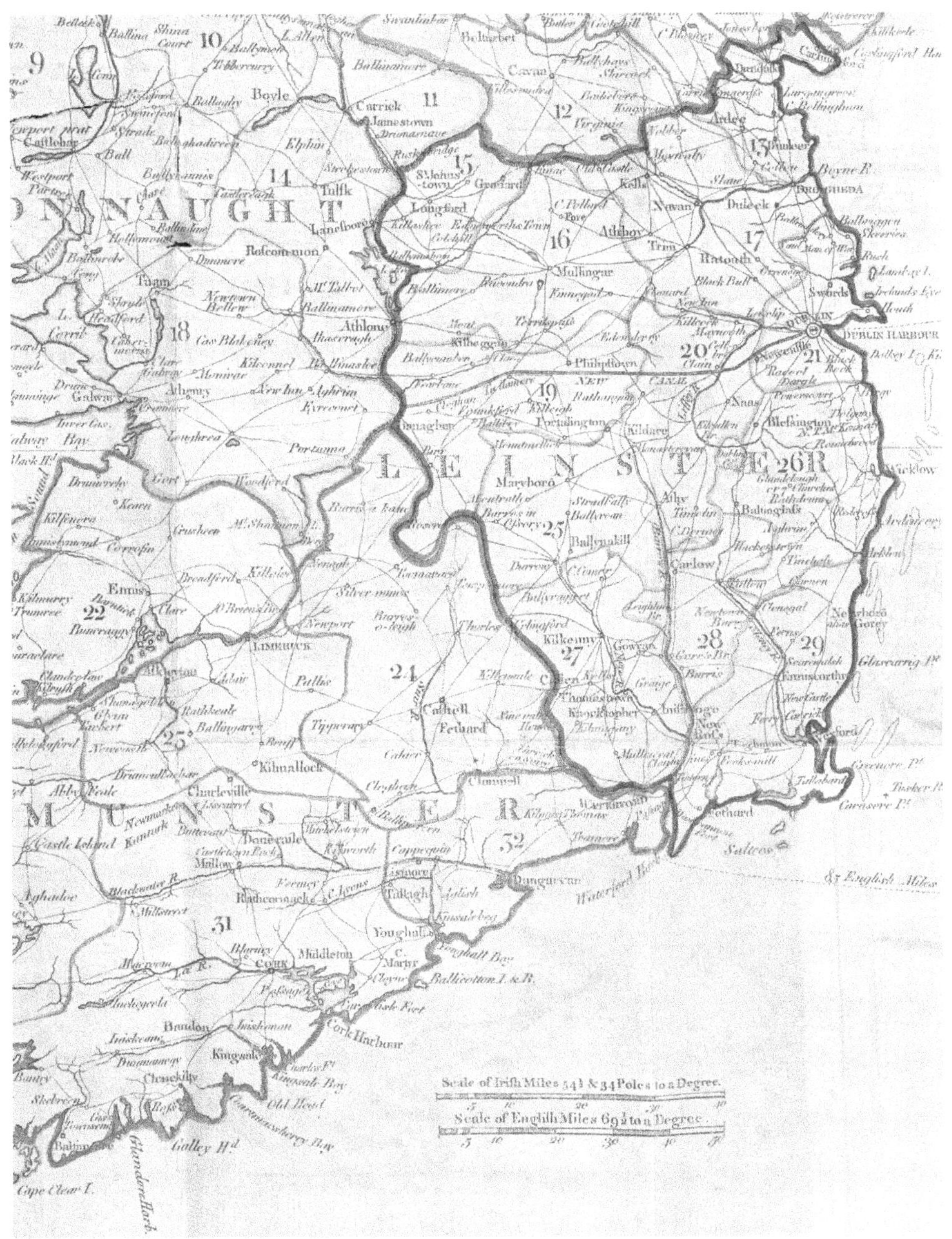

A detail of *Wilson's New and Accurate Map of the Roads of Ireland*, published in *The Post-Chaise Companion or Traveller's Directory Through Ireland*, published in London by William Faden, 1784.

A detail of *A plan of the city of Dublin* by William Senex, published in London by William Faden, 1797.

INTRODUCTION

Edmund Spencer and His Times

The Correspondence

This edition reproduces the letters of Edmund Spencer (1711–*c.*1790), the great-great-grandson of Edmund Spenser, the Elizabethan poet who settled in south-west Ireland at the end of the sixteenth century.[1] Our Edmund Spencer spent his life in Ireland, most of it in Munster (where he grew up and married, and where his famous ancestor had acquired a number of properties) though in later life he and his small family lived also in the south-east of Ireland and in Dublin.

Most of the letters were written to Francis Price, and after Price's death in 1749 the correspondence continued with his widow Alice, and, later, their son Richard.[2] Francis Price 'was born in Ballyhooly in the county of Cork and kingdom of Ireland June 4 1696', less than two miles from where Spencer grew up.[3] At the time this correspondence started, though, he was living in Overton, near Wrexham, Wales, where he was a gentleman of some considerable standing: he had land in Birkenhead and Liverpool, where he possibly also had financial interests in businesses such as shipping.

The letters are preserved in the Puleston archives (now held in the National Library of Wales).[4] There are 117 of them altogether, along with some additional associated papers, and they were written between February 1732 and June 1762.[5] However, the last document in the archive (an account sheet that goes up to November 1774) would have been sent to the Prices in that year or early in 1775 so we can be fairly certain that some correspondence between Spencer and the Price family continued for another fourteen years after the last letter in this collection. There are clearly other lacunae in the surviving correspondence but on the whole the archive provides very considerable coverage of Edmund Spencer's communications with this family across three decades of the mid-eighteenth century.

1 The one letter difference in the spelling of the surname is the simplest way of distinguishing between these two, though Edmund Spencer, the letter writer, does have the unfortunate habit of spelling his ancestor's surname like his own.

2 There are also four which were written to a physician who was assisting Alice Price with her business affairs immediately after her husband's death.

3 Price's memorial tablet in St Mary's Church, Overton.

4 Llyfrgell Genedlaethol Cymru / National Library of Wales, Aberystwyth, Puleston 20: NLW MS 3580E.

5 The earlier date is more than likely 1733 as Spencer consistently used Old Style when dating his letters until the change to the Gregorian Calendar in 1752.

Spencer's correspondence with the Prices is of value because it gives us a detailed account of the life and interests of a member of the Anglo-Irish provincial gentry living in Ireland, as well as telling the story of an epistolary relationship that lasted over thirty years. Such collections are not common, as most caches of letters preserved in archives from the period were written by people of much higher social status. Unfortunately, the letters from Price to Spencer have not survived so we have a somewhat one-sided understanding of their relationship, being able to read only the communications of the rather less exalted Spencer to his social superior.[6]

The Correspondents, Their Families, and Acquaintanceships

Edmund Spenser (1552?-1599), the Elizabethan poet and great-great-grandfather of Edmund Spencer, married twice. With his first wife, Maccabaeus Childe (who died sometime between 1590 and 1593) he had two children, Sylvanus and Katherine; with his second, Elizabeth Boyle (who survived him and subsequently remarried twice) he had one son, Peregrine.[7] Sylvanus had two sons, Edmund and William, the first of whom died without issue; William, however, had a daughter, Susanna, who remained unmarried, and a son, Nathaniel, who married Rosamund Bulkeley, the daughter of the Rector of Mallow; they had four children, the eldest of whom was Edmund, the writer of these letters.[8]

Spenser spent much of his adult life in Ireland working for the Elizabethan colonial administration and as a result of and partly as a reward for the work he did, he acquired a considerable amount of property in the province of Munster, an area which the English government was keen to see occupied by English settlers (known also as 'undertakers' or 'planters') in order to replace — or at least dilute — a native population that was becoming increasingly resistant to English rule, especially after the Desmond rebellion of 1579–1583. The most significant of Spenser's acquisitions were in Co. Cork and they included Kilcolman and the castle of Renny, along with its surrounding lands, which he purchased for Peregrine, his younger son. Peregrine passed Renny to his eldest son Hugolin who, in 1694, had them confiscated after he was declared a traitor for his support of James II in the Williamite Wars of 1688–1691. The estate was then transferred to his cousin William (whose assistance had enabled King William to win the Battle of Aughrim and so defeat James) and, whilst he was still alive, he gave them to his son Nathaniel.

6 The archive does contain three rough drafts of letters written by Price (folios 124–26), but they were written on Spencer's behalf and were not actually to him.

7 Our account of Spenser's family in the next three paragraphs is heavily indebted to the work of W. H. Welply in, 'The Family and Descendants of Edmund Spenser', *Journal of the Cork Historical and Archaeological Society*, 2nd ser., 28 (1922), 22–34 & 49–61, and 'Edmund Spenser: Being an Account of Some Recent Researches into His Life and Lineage, with Some Notice of His Family and Descendants', *Notes & Queries* 162 (1932), 128–32, 146–50, 165–69, 182–87, 202–06, 220–24, 239–42 & 256–60.

8 Susanna is possibly the aunt whom William Pearde refers to in his letter to Francis Price of 26 February 1741/2 (see Appendix I: Additional Letters from the Puleston Collection) 'who was left by her father £500 on y:[e] lands of Renny as a portion in Case she married' (ll.6–8) and whose 'persecution' led to Spencer's imprisonment for debt in 1740.

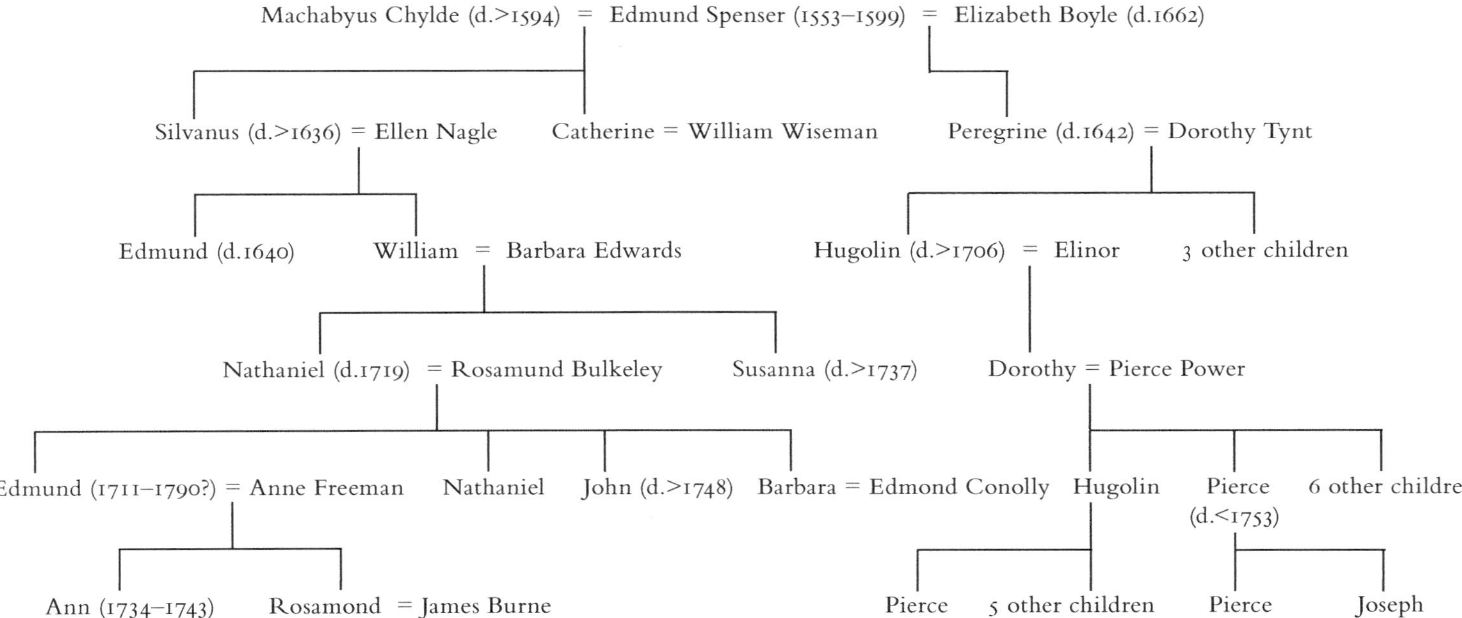

The genealogy of Edmund Spencer, based on W. H. Welply's 'Pedigree of Spenser', published in *Notes & Queries*, 162 (1932), p. 257.

Unfortunately for William and Nathaniel, Hugolin had mortgaged Renny to a son-in-law, Pierce Power, for £300, that sum to be raised to £500 if Hugolin died without male issue — which, from William and Nathaniel's point of view, he rather inconveniently did.[9] In response the father and son mortgaged Kilcolman (which William, as the son of Sylvanus, had also inherited) and remortgaged Renny, leaving Nathaniel so heavily indebted on his father's death that he had to sell off a large part of these estates. Nathaniel himself then died whilst his son Edmund was still a minor, leaving trustees to look after the inheritance, and when Edmund came of age little was left of the substantial properties in Ireland originally acquired by his great-great-grandfather. Moreover, Renny was subject to a complicated law suit still being pursued by the descendants of Pierce Power, and, to make things even worse, one of the trustees, a lawyer named Busteed, had methodically embezzled the income from Renny. Edmund Spencer arrived at the age of twenty-one to find his financial affairs in tatters, a sorry state of affairs as retaining one's position in the Irish ruling class depended on not selling one's land to meet interim financial difficulties.[10]

Some of this is explained in the first letter in the collection.[11] It is covered again, with some further details, by Francis Price in the drafts of the letters he wrote with the aim of persuading some of his influential acquaintances to help Spencer find another source of income.[12] This increasingly desperate pursuit occupied much of Spencer's energies and takes up a considerable proportion of the content of his letters to Price who, as a wealthy landowner, seems to have seen it as his duty to look after the less privileged and more unfortunate members of his family and friendship circle, as the letters reproduced here demonstrate. Price was also an assiduous keeper of records and correspondence which is why we have, preserved in the Puleston Papers, such an insight into the life of this circle.

That particular thread of the correspondence which deals with Spencer's pursuit of an income has been fully explored by Toby Barnard, who has shown how urgent were the pressures on Spencer to secure employment — the number of people he felt he had to approach, the variety of schemes he pursued, and the sheer amount of his waking life that the quest absorbed.[13] Therefore, the letters can be read to tell us a great deal about gentry life in eighteenth century Ireland, but they also have to be read as personal expressions of friendship and they clearly tell us a great deal about Spencer himself and his relationship with Francis Price.[14]

9 Andrew Hadfield, 'A Mortgage Agreement of Hugolin Spenser, Edmund Spenser's Grandson,' *Spenser Studies*, 27 (2012), 329–35 (p. 330).

10 S. J. Connolly, *Religion, Law and Power: The Making of Protestant Ireland, 1660–1760* (Oxford: Clarendon Press, 1992), p. 59.

11 6 February 1732: folio 3.

12 Folios 124, 125 & 126. In the transcription folio 124 follows the letter of 30 November 1745: folio 38; folios 125 & 126 are placed after the Memorial (folio 127) that follows the letter of 20 January 1748: folio 81.

13 Toby Barnard, *Irish Protestant Ascents and Descents, 1641–1770* (Dublin: Four Courts Press, 2004), ch. 10.

14 Compare the tone of intimate friendship in the letters of Thomas Gray to Horace Walpole, written at the same time (1730s-1770s): Thomas Gray, *The Correspondence of Thomas Gray*, ed. by

Francis Price, as has already been noted, was born in Ireland. What his parents were doing there at that point is, though, slightly puzzling as his father is given on the memorial tablet in St Mary's Church in Overton as 'Captain Richard Price of Bryn y Piece', that being the family's house near Overton in Wales. Equally puzzling is that there appears to have been some kin-relationship between Price and Spencer, but what that relationship might have been is never made explicit, the letters suggesting only that the two are related. The first letter begins with the salutation 'Dr Couz' (that is, 'Dear Cousin'), but while the term 'cousin' could at that time describe specifically the child of a parents' brother or sister, it could be used of more distant family relationships, or even just to indicate a particularly intimate friend.[15] Besides that 'Dr Couz', though, there are two clear references in the letters to this kinship: first, at the end of the letter of 19 July 1755: folio 96 Spencer apologizes to Alice Price for what appears to have been some slight from one of 'M.r Price's relations on this side the Water', and then includes himself in that group by continuing, 'nor could I wonder or complain if you shook us all off',[16] and second, he refers in an earlier letter to Francis Price's son, Richard, as 'my dear Kinsman'.[17] Disappointingly, none of W. H. Welply's detailed pedigrees of the Spenser family reveals anyone with the surname Price.[18]

There is an intriguing passage, however, in a letter from Lord Barrymore to Price dated 9th May 1732 (by which time Price was living in Wales). Barrymore, who is at his house in Castlelyons, tells Price that he is writing:

> to let you know the condition of your mother, in short, prepare! 'Black Castle Town' is the word. She is in a green-house, plaistered about 15 days, full of smoke above and below, and you must wade over shoes to get to any room below, either kitchen or parlour. She keeps her bed, as I am assured[19]

This information, alarming though it sounds, is too surreal to tell us what has actually happened to Price's mother; what it does tell us, however, is that she had stayed behind in Ireland after he had returned to Wales, and one possible reason for that could be that she was Irish. That, in turn, might explain why Price's father was in Ireland when Francis was born. It is also just conceivable that the woman Richard Price married, whose forename was Mary,[20] was related to Edmund Spencer. Welply's genealogies are not helpful here — the Marys he notes do not fit for various reasons — but he lists many unnamed daughters descended from Spenser

Frederick A. Pottle and Charles H. Bennett, rev. Herbert W. Starr, 3 vols (Oxford: Clarendon Press, 1971), letter 1, 'Gray to Walpole', 16 April 1734 (I, 1–2); letter 52, 'Gray to Walpole', 28 March 1738 (I, 83–85), passim.

15 6 February 1732: folio 3.

16 19 July 1755: folio 96, ll.33–34.

17 14 January 1752: folio 94, l.3.

18 It is now extremely unlikely, following the destruction of the Public Records Office in Dublin in 1922, that we would be able to trace any family connection through the type of contemporary records Welply had access to.

19 Historical Manuscripts Commission, Fifteenth Report, Part VII, *The Manuscripts of the Duke of Somerset, the Marquis of Ailesbury, and The Rev. Sir T. H. G. Puleston, Bart.* (London: Her Majesty's Stationery Office, 1898), p.313.

20 Price's memorial tablet in St Mary's Church, Overton.

on Peregrine's side of the family and, given that Mary is a common name in Ireland, it could just be that one was the wife of Richard Price. In the end, though, all we can say about the relationship between the two correspondents is that it must have been fairly distant.[21]

Nor do we know anything about the nature of Price's wider circle of relations in Ireland, other than that such connections existed — that reference to 'M.[r] Prices relations on this side the Water' tells us so quite definitely. Three people named Price[22] are mentioned by Spencer in the letters in relation to the Prices' property holdings in Ireland, and though none of them is explicitly defined as being a relative of Francis Price it is clear that at least one of them is, that being the person to whom Lord Buttevant sold the Mohire estate in 1692, but whether this person is a grandparent, or some more distant relative, we are not told.[23] There is plenty of evidence, then, in this collection of letters and associated documents that makes it clear that the Prices had family connections in Ireland going back to the seventeenth century, and, perhaps of more interest to us in considering his relationship with Spencer, that the family had amassed a substantial property portfolio in Munster and Dublin which Francis, and subsequently his widow and his son, inherited.

At some point, possibly after April 1729 but certainly before February 1732,[24] the year the first of the letters was written, Francis Price moved back to Overton, marrying in (or shortly after) May 1735 Alice Lloyd, a widow.[25] Through that marriage he obtained the Birkenhead Priory Estate on the opposite side of the Mersey from the burgeoning port of Liverpool, Alice having inherited the estate on the death of her brother William in 1724; he in turn had inherited it from their father, John Cleiveland, one of the most eminent Liverpool merchants of his day. Four years later, in 1740, a lease originally taken out by John Cleiveland on an area of land in Liverpool, close to the Mersey and directly opposite Birkenhead, was transferred to Francis Price, and on that land he had Price Street and Cleveland Square built.[26]

21 We might also note that Price was fourteen years old when Spencer was born, and their respective ages when Price probably left Ireland would have been thirty three and eighteen; such a difference at this early stage of their lives does seem too great for it to be likely that the relationship between the two was one of friendship.

22 They are in 23 May 1745: folio 31, 20 August 1745: folio 34, and 19 July 1755: folio 96; the first two may be the same person with a different title.

23 One further piece of evidence that the Price family had well-established property links with Ireland is provided by the entry for Francis Price in Bernard Burke's *A Genealogical and Heraldic Dictionary of the Landed Gentry of Great Britain and Ireland for 1852*, 2 vols (London: Colburn and Co., 1852): 'Francis Price, Esq. of Bryn-y-pys and of Castle Lyons, co. Sligo'. Castlelyons, some twelve miles from Price's birthplace, Ballyhooly, was where Lord Barrymore had his Irish residence.

24 In a legal bill of 21 April 1729 between himself and an Irish tenant who is given as living in Castlelyons, Price is described as being 'of the same' (Puleston 19: NLW MS 3579D) so he was presumably still living in Ireland at that date; the later date may be February 1733 if Spencer was giving the date, as he usually did, Old Style.

25 Cheshire Record Office, Marriage Licence Bonds and Allegations, EDC 8 1735 (J) — 1736 (V).

26 Lease register for Liverpool Corporation, Liverpool Record Office, 352 CLE/Con 3/2 (1672–1767), entry dated 13 January 1713; see also 20 August 1745: folio 34, note to l.3.

That relationship with the Cleiveland family may well have given Price useful business connections with the ship-owners of Liverpool, and Spencer's request that he speak to the owners of a ship called *The Thurloe* on behalf of the 'son of unfortunate Dick Chinnery'[27] (whom Price knew when he lived in Mallow) would support that conjecture. Such connections would no doubt have provided opportunities for lucrative investments in Liverpool's rapidly growing international trade.[28] One other indicator of his status is that for the year 1737–1738 he held the prestigious position of Sheriff of Flintshire.[29]

Clearly Francis Price was much more successful than Spencer, both economically and socially. He counted amongst his friends the likes of the Earl of Barrymore and Sir Watkin Williams-Wynn, the MP for Denbighshire, making him, therefore, well placed to lobby influential people who could help his humbler relative in the search for an alternative source of income, whether through speculative ventures such as his proposal to publish the complete works of his great-great-grandfather, by a commission in the army, or a salaried position in the civil administration in Dublin.

Such contacts remind us that Spencer and Price both lived, as did all the gentry in the period, as part of a wider circle. The disastrous property dealings that took place in his infancy and youth left Spencer impoverished and dependent on the more powerful members of a loosely affiliated group based in south-west Ireland and north-east Wales. As an examination of other Puleston papers in the National Library of Wales demonstrates, the most powerful figure in this acquaintanceship circle was James Barry, 4th Earl of Barrymore (1667–1748), a strange figure who, after many years of loyalty to the crown became an enthusiastic Jacobite in his seventies, conspiring with the French to help Charles Stuart's invasion in 1744.[30] Barrymore was clearly the man best situated to secure favours and opportunities for his supporters and allies and many in his circle, unless already persuaded of the Jacobite cause, may have experienced a conflict of loyalty to their patron and the crown. Barrymore was plotting to overthrow the House of Hanover at the same time that Spencer was dithering about whether to ask Francis Price to intercede with the powerful lord on his behalf. Spencer may not have known the details of the intrigues of his social superiors — and the letters provide no evidence of his knowing — but he was dependent on the favours of a Jacobite network the members of which usually refer to him as 'poor Spencer'.

Barrymore's letters to Price suggest a degree of intimacy far beyond what one would expect between a country squire and a peer of the realm. They are warm and friendly and he obviously is very fond of this man whom he usually addresses as

27 Postscript to 19 August 1744: folio 25; see also 10 April [1745]: folio 30, ll.11–14: 'I must trouble you again in Favour of Mr Chinnery [...] a letter from you $_{\wedge}^{to}$ Mr Sam: Seel woud be of singular Service'.

28 A growth that was driven, we might remind ourselves, to a great extent by the slave trade.

29 <http://www.cefnpennar.com/flint/flint_sheriff.htm> [accessed 8 October 2013].

30 See the *ODNB* entry for *Barry, James, 4th Earl of Barrymore*. On Barrymore's intrigues in the 1740s see Jacqueline Riding, *Jacobites: A New History of the '45 Rebellion* (London: Bloomsbury, 2016), pp. 19–24.

'Dear Doctor'.[31] He also takes a keen interest in Price's son, Richard, to whom he was godfather. Barrymore has a nice turn of phrase and can be amusing. Speaking of an ineffective cleric he writes, 'Hunt as usuall was out of the way, and what is worse cannot preach or pray in Welsh and if he does not get soon into some practice will forget to doe it in English' — a comment which suggests that Price and Barrymore, and probably many others in the circle, were Welsh speakers.[32] Barrymore was supported by other influential figures to whom Francis Price as an intimate of Barrymore will have had access. Many of them were clearly party to Barrymore's rather inept conspiring, which very nearly led to his execution in May 1744 when he was arrested (see Appendix I) and steering a course between friendship and loyalty on the one hand and personal safety on the other must have required a delicate balancing act for these people.

The second most significant figure in this circle is Sir Watkin Williams-Wynn (1692–1749), another close ally of Lord Barrymore and a noted Jacobite whose sympathies were also well known.[33] In *Midwinter*, John Buchan's novel of the Forty Five Rebellion, the hero, Alastair Maclean, travels to Sir Watkin's house to find out about the Welsh plans to support the Scottish and 'Old English' Jacobites. It is later made clear that the failure of the rising in 'the West' fatally undermines the rebellion.[34] Sir Watkin appears frequently in the letters reproduced here, and throughout the Puleston papers, and was a leading figure in the Cycle of the White Rose, a Welsh Jacobite society (referred to in the letter of 6 December 1743: folio 10 as the 'Cycle Club').[35] Like Lord Barrymore, Sir Watkin had his sympathies and commitment to the Stuart cause sounded out by the French in the early 1740s and his support played a part in persuading Charles Stuart to launch the Forty-Five Invasion.[36] Lord Barrymore was arrested in 1744, his enthusiastic but ill-concealed support for a French invasion making him an easy target for the government, who decided that executing him might cause more problems than it solved. When the Young Pretender landed the following year, Sir Watkin and Lord Barrymore promised support but the Prince had already turned back from Derby, the furthest south his army reached, and any chance of its success was over. Sir Watkin continued

31 The reason for the soubriquet is presumably that Price had had a university eduction: he entered Trinity College, Dublin, on 22 September 1712 (Trinity College Entrance Books/ Matriculation Registers, TCD MUN V 23/1 (1637-1725), p. 294); there is no indication, however, that he completed his degree. The entry in the Matriculation Register also tells us that Price went to school with a Mr Morgan in Tipperary.

32 Barrymore to Francis Price, 24 July 1741, Puleston 22: NLW MS 3582D.

33 See his entry in The History of Parliament online database, <http://www.historyofparliament online.org> [accessed 10 June 2016].

34 John Buchan, *Midwinter: Certain Travellers in Old England* (London: Hodder & Stoughton, 1923).

35 On the Cycle Club see Peter G. Thomas, 'Jacobitism in Wales', *Welsh History Review*, 1.3 (1962), 279–300 (pp. 287–90). The club was founded on 10 June 1710, the birthday of 'James III', the Old Pretender. It met every three to four weeks in a member's house (hence 'cycle') to toast the 'king over the water'. We are grateful to Marion Loffler for this reference.

36 Although when it did happen the invasion took Sir Watkin by surprise and, as with his fellow Jacobites in Ireland, he took no action. Charles Stuart later commented that he would help the Welsh as much as they had helped him, i.e. by toasting them (Thomas, 'Jacobitism in Wales', pp. 296–300).

his intrigues but died from a fall off his horse in September 1749.

Other figures in the circle warrant some mention. Spencer refers to Jack Coppinger, whom he encounters on a sea crossing.[37] Coppinger was another friend and ally of Lord Barrymore who leased Barryscourt Castle, in Carrigtwohill, Co. Cork, from him. The remaining group are of significantly lower status and details of them are inevitably sketchy. John Buchan was a doctor who took Francis Price's son into his home in 1749 to look after him. This was normal practice for the children of the wealthy in an era before hospitals, but the nature and tone of the letters Buchan sends the father indicates a more friendly rapport, in keeping with Price's cordial relationships with most of his correspondents. Buchan's words reassuring Price that his son is in 'perfect health' also indicate the level of the concern that the Prices, who had only one child, experienced and Buchan's desire to reassure his client and friend.[38] The four letters written by Spencer between July 1750 and April 1751 (folios 90–93) show that Buchan also took over responsibility for some of Alice Price's business affairs in the two years following her husband's death.

A whole volume of the Puleston papers (Puleston 24: NLW MS 3584E) contains letters from Thomas Kingsbury, a lawyer who looked after Price's affairs in Wales and Ireland and who also had dealings with Lord Barrymore. However, we do not get much of an impression of Kingsbury's character from his largely practical correspondence.

Another volume (Puleston 19: NLW MS 3579D) contains numerous letters from William Pearde who lived at Castlelyons in Ireland, perhaps acting for Lord Barrymore as a seneschal of one of his estates in Ireland. He was an uncle of Spencer who took an active interest in his young relation's welfare,[39] sometimes interceding on his behalf with Price, and at least once reporting to Price on one of the young man's less happy episodes.[40]

One last person deserving notice who was very much part of Price's social world, but definitely not in the circle held together by friendship, is the character whom Spencer refers to rather mysteriously as 'Trigger'. We are satisfied that this person can be identified as Thomas Lloyd,[41] usually described as being of 'of Gwernhaelod and Overton', the owner of Gwernheylod House,[42] and hence the Price's immediate neighbour on Argoed Lane, just outside and north-west of Overton.

37 See [December 1741]: folio 121, ll.9–10.

38 Buchan to Price 7 May, 11 May, 18 May 1749: Puleston 18: NLW MS 3578E.

39 Spencer identifies him as such in 25 May 1747: folio 58, l.4, but Barnard states that he is Spencer's half brother (*Irish Protestant Ascents and Descents*, p. 296).

40 See his letter to Price of 26 February1741/2 in Appendix I.

41 See 8 November 1743: folio 8, note to l.6 for the evidence that led to this identification.

42 This name occurs in a number of variant spellings in eighteenth-century documents; the modern version is 'Gwernheylod'. Francis Price is also frequently referred to in legal documents as being 'of Gwernhaelod' (e.g, Deed of Covenant to Levy a Fine, 12 Mar 1738/1739, Flintshire Record Office, D/LJ/885) and many of the letters in his archive are addressed to him there, even when he was clearly living at Bryn y Pys; this most likely indicates nothing more than the flexibility of eighteenth-century addresses, and that the name refers to an area as much as to a specific house; the house was destroyed in the late nineteenth century and only the wood that bordered it appears to have retained the name.

The fact that every one of the seven references to him in the correspondence is pejorative makes obvious Spencer's low opinion of this man. The portrait he constructs of Trigger is of a cunning, dangerous, hypocritical person whose one aim in life is to stir up trouble and annoy his neighbours. However, phrases such as 'I never coud hear that he attempted to pass for an honest man', 'the Account you give of the old Gentleman', and 'I dare say he continued troublesome to the last' suggest that this view is not based on Spencer's first-hand experience of Trigger, but rather reflects Price's attitude towards him, and hence a personal animosity on Price's part.[43]

The first mention of Trigger suggests that he and Price were, possibly, in a dispute over tithes, though the passage is so elliptical that it is impossible to say more than that it hints at some dissension in the parish and connects it with Trigger's disruptive behaviour towards those around him.[44] However, since Alice Price's first husband was also a 'Thomas Lloyd, Esq. of Gwernhaglod' we can be fairly confident that Francis Price was related to Trigger, so it is equally possible that their quarrel was over property, there being nothing quite like property to cause dissension in a family.[45] That might be implied in Spencer's speculation that Price had 'a Right to something considerable upon his Death'[46] — meaning that he was likely to be, through his wife, a beneficiary of Trigger's estate.[47]

Whatever the personal disagreement between Francis Price and Trigger might have been, though, the interesting thing about this character for us is his function in the narrative of the correspondence as the archetypical difficult neighbour. The mocking nickname makes explicit his exclusion from the social world of Overton, and he is seen off to the next one with little regret at his passing: 'I congratulate you & your Parish on the Decease of the Old Trigger,' says Spencer, 'as I know it must be a great Ease to all'.[48]

As to Spencer's social circle in Ireland, whilst he knew Lord Barrymore well enough to wait upon him at Castlelyons, his relationship with him was that of client to patron rather than one of friendship, as was the case with Price. He felt (as we will note again later) uncomfortable in the presence of such elevated company as gathered around the Earl, telling Price in one letter:

> My Lord has such a Run of grand Company that I have not been to wait on him, as I do not know ^how one in my Way may be liked among so many of the best Fortunes, but as I suppose he will have more Time to himself when most of our Members are gone up to Parliament: I will then take the Opportunity of waiting on him.[49]

43 24 July 1744: folio 24, ll.18–19, 16 December 1746: folio 54, l.1, and 5 August 1748: folio 75, l.3.

44 See notes to ll.3 & 4 of 8 November 1743: folio 8.

45 Burke, *A Genealogical and Heraldic Dictionary*, II, 1070. Thomas Lloyd (Alice Price's first husband) died sometime before 1735.

46 5 August 1748: folio 75, l.3.

47 Whether this turned out to be the case we do not know: possibly determined to be as annoying as he could be to others even from the beyond the grave Trigger left no will, and only the documentation appointing three of his daughters as executors of his estate has survived (NLW, Welsh Wills, Thomas Lloyd, Overton, 1748, C1748/6).

48 5 August 1748: folio 75, ll.1–2.

49 9 October 1747: folio 60, ll.10–16.

Spencer's personal friendship group in Ireland was more from the middling gentry to which he belonged, men like his brother-in-law William Freeman, who helped him with his financial affairs and with whom he hunted and whom he describes, after the death of another great friend and hunting companion, Mr Oliver, as his 'one Friend left in Ireland'.[50] He also seems to have been on very good terms with Mr Richard (Dick) Welsh who frequently visits Price in Wales, often carrying things back and forth between Ireland and Wales for Spencer (even, on one occasion, a live eagle for Richard Price). A friend of Price from when he lived in Ireland (Welsh lived in Ballyhooly where Price was born) he was, like Spencer, in deep financial trouble, having lost his house in 1743 and one suspects that, again like Spencer, he is the object of Price's benevolent attentions as an old Irish acquaintance who needs assistance.[51]

If Spencer is in no position to mix on equal terms with the Barrymores and Sir Watkins of Price's world, nonetheless he keeps his sardonic eye on the goings on of the younger scions of the Barry family, and the likes of his old guardian Arthur Hyde, MP for Youghal and Cork. He may also even enjoy the occasional social evening with locally powerful people such as Sir Matthew Deane of Inistiogue;[52] but for the serious patronage and assistance he needs in finding a secure position with a regular income he is very much dependent on having that wider social circle at one remove, as it were, through Francis Price.

There was, however, one other advantage that he directly enjoyed as a result of Price's connections that is pertinent to this correspondence, and that was what we might call postage avoidance.

Postal services were not cheap in the eighteenth century, letters being charged according to their size and the distance travelled, and up to 1840 the costs were borne by the recipient not the sender. A single sheet letter that had been carried from Co. Cork to North Wales would have cost Francis Price sixpence[53] (half the daily wages of a craftsman in Ireland in the 1750s)[54] and on 26 June 1772 Spencer paid the considerably higher fee of 1/6 for 'a Letter from Mr Hayman'.[55] For the not so well off, carrying on a regular correspondence could therefore be quite a financial burden, whilst even for wealthy people like Francis Price, if they carried on a frequent correspondence with a wide circle of acquaintance as he did, the costs would form a noticeable item of expenditure in their budgets.[56]

50 23 May 1745: folio 31, l.39; see that letter also for the death of Mr Oliver.

51 See 4 October 1743: folio 7, ll.13–14.

52 See 4 February [1746]: folio 42, ll.4–6.

53 A. D. Smith, *The Development of Rates of Postage: An Historical and Analytical Study* (London: George Allen & Unwin, 1917), p. 9. Sixpence is two and a half pence in decimal coinage.

54 Toby Barnard, *A New Anatomy of Ireland: The Irish Protestants, 1649–1770* (New Haven, CT: Yale University Press, 2003), p. 285; Barnard also observes that 'the poorest labourer could [in the 1750s] earn sixpence daily' (ibid.).

55 Folio 122, verso; on the basis of the rates given by Smith, this would have been a package of over one ounce that had travelled more than 140 miles. One shilling and sixpence is seven and a half pence in decimal coinage.

56 Though one wonders whether postage was regarded by the rich as, like taxation, one of those vexatious financial obligations that it was acceptable to circumvent whenever possible.

One way of reducing these costs was to bundle a number of letters up in a single packet which was then sent 'under a cover' to one address from where the individual letters would be conveyed to their addressees, and Spencer clearly did this: first, the absence of full addresses on letters to Price (there are two exceptions: the very first one in the collection and the letter of 9 October 1747: folio 60)[57] indicates this, but second, he makes specific reference to the practice on several occasions.[58]

The other way of saving money, though, was even more economical, and that was the direct result of Price's friendship with members of parliament. Both Sir Watkin Williams-Wynn, the MP for Denbighshire, and the Earl of Barrymore, who sat in the upper house, had the privilege of 'franking' their mail — that is, their signature on a letter under the word 'free' enabled it to be carried by the postal service without charge. As it was the recipient who paid, the advantage to the franker could only be obtained on letters he was sent, so people with this privilege obviously gave out pre-franked sheets to their correspondents when they wrote to them. It would appear that these correspondents then passed on these franks to their friends.

We know that Price gave sheets franked by Barrymore to Spencer because the letter of 19 November 1745: folio 37 has Barrymore's frank on the address side of the sheet (presumably, as the address has, as usual, only Price's name on it, Spencer did not realize when he started the letter that he was wasting a franked sheet). Also, when he writes to Price in June 1747 Spencer says that he would be 'be vastly obliged [...] for a few franks as I want to write to a brother in law in Scotland'[59] and there is reason to believe that these would also have been those of the Earl.[60]

57 On the address panel of the first of these letters there is part of a postmark /-VILL/ which could be, in full, /CHARLE-VILLE/, and that would fit with the address of origin given by Spencer at the end of the letter 'Ballinguile near Charleville'. The letter of 9 October 1747 also has a postmark, /DUBLIN/, and a partly legible date, /[OC] 13/ — i.e. 13 October. The first two letters he writes to Alice Price after the death of her husband have nothing to indicate how they were sent, but the two after that (27 November 1749: folio 88, and 2 December 1749: folio 89) both have the full address in the address panel — 'Brynypiece near Wrexham Chester' — and a postmark: on the first the /DUB/ of /DUBLIN/ is partially legible and there is a date, /NO 28/ — i.e. 28 November; on the second the /DUBLIN/ is mainly legible, but there is no visible date. After that, all letters to Alice and Richard Price have only the addressee's name in the address panel, so Spencer returns either to sending packets, or to using franks (or both).

58 See for example 10 September 1745: folio 35, l.12, and 9 October 1747: folio 60, l.4. A question that then arises, however, is who the other letters in the bundles were for — or, one might equally ask, who they were from; the answer to that may lie in the fact that Spencer also frequently refers to receiving 'packets' from Overton (for example, 30 November 1745: folio 38, l.3 and 2 February 1747: folio 67, ll.6 & 10) which suggests that when Price wrote to Spencer he possibly also sent letters to other friends in that district which Spencer then passed on, and then when he replied to Price he included replies from those friends in his packets; Price also had business contacts in Dublin whom Spencer could send letters through when he was staying there; we might also note that Spencer makes absolutely no mention of any other acquaintances in the Overton area except those to whom he sends his compliments via Price in postscripts (which would, of course, obviate the need to write individually to those people) but it also has to be acknowledged that we are in highly speculative territory here.

59 16 June 1747: folio 59, ll.20–21.

60 See fn. 64.

We can also, however, reasonably assume that it was normal practice between Spencer and Price to send packets of mail back and forth using Sir Watkin's franks since Spencer tells Price in October 1747, 'I suspect you did not receive either of mine [...] tho directed as usual under cover to Sir Watkin'.[61] Sir Watkin lived at Llanforda, Oswestry, about twelve miles from the Price's home in Overton, so presumably mail was carried from Llanforda to Bryn y Pys by a servant. Whilst this would have caused no extra cost to any of the parties to the arrangement, the additional complication to the business of corresponding shows how worthwhile this use of covers and franks, possible only because of the high status of Price's friendship network, was to both Spencer and Price — and this despite the difference in their economic situations.[62]

Edmund Spencer's Ireland

Edmund Spencer's life coincided with one of the most stable periods of Irish history, during which Ireland 'experienced a longer period of internal peace than it had ever known before'.[63] After the Williamite Wars, the triumph of Protestantism and the exclusion of Catholic monarchs, Ireland was established as a colonial society under the rule of a British monarch based in London.[64] Even so, threats to that stability lay not far beneath the surface. We can understand, for example, the sense of anxiety rising as Spencer notes the progress of the Forty-Five — the rebellion of Charles Stuart, Bonnie Prince Charlie, which sought to restore the exiled Stuart line.[65]

More persistent, and indeed corrosive, problems had been inherited, however, from the English government's continuation since the sixteenth century of its policy of transferring by force land from Catholic to Protestant owners, this 'period of confiscation and resettlement of Irish land by the English [...] sowing the seeds of what came to be called universally "the Irish land problem"'.[66] This had built up trouble for the eighteenth century in two ways.

First, land settlements (the Cromwellian and the Restoration settlements, for example) had been left unfinished, and made, moreover, with incomplete knowledge of the landscape so that some property was sometimes granted twice or the

61 9 October 1747: folio 60, ll.2–4.

62 We can assume that Sir Watkin's franks were being used as otherwise there would be no point in adding this extra complication to the correspondence; however, it is interesting to note that Sir Watkin's franks are not used to send mail directly from Ireland to Price's house in Overton as appears to be the case with franks supplied by Barrymore, and the answer is possibly that, as Sir Watkin has no house in Ireland, it would excite suspicion that he was abusing his privilege if letters were seen to be passing under his frank from Ireland to a house in Wales other than his own. That would not be the case with Barrymore's franks as he, of course, had an Irish residence only a few miles from where Spencer mostly lived.

63 J. C. Beckett, 'Eighteenth-Century Ireland', in *A New History of Ireland: IV, Eighteenth-Century Ireland, 1691–1800*, ed. by T. W. Moody and W. E. Vaughan (Oxford: Clarendon Press, 1986), pp. xl-lxiv (p. xl).

64 J. G. Simms, 'The Establishment of Protestant Ascendancy, 1691–1714', in *Eighteenth-Century Ireland*, ed. by Moody and Vaughan, pp. 1–30 (p. 1).

65 10 October 1745: folio 36.

66 J. C. W. Wylie, *Irish Land Law*, 2nd edn (Abingdon: Professional Books Limited, 1986), p. 6.

boundaries of grants were unclear. Consequently the Irish courts in the eighteenth century were still bedevilled by appallingly complicated suits over titles to property the validity of which was almost impossible to determine. Second, cases involving land and property could be further complicated by the practice of sub-leasing, whereby tenants holding a lease would sub-lease, and even the sub-leasers then sub-lease again, with those at the bottom of this chain being the least secure financially and the least powerful legally.

Acting as he did for the Prices as their land agent (on an informal basis for Francis Price but formally for Alice and Richard) Spencer was continually having to deal with such problems. His attempts to obtain some clarity for Francis Price about the status of Price's lease on a house in Mallow which Price has sub-let ('the Mallow affair'), and then his tenants have sub-let again to people unknown to Price, leads to his exclaiming in exasperation that 'twoud be easier to find out the Longitude'.[67] The later business of the title to the Mohire estate is even more obscure and complex: Spencer reports to Alice Price in his letter of 19 July 1755: folio 96 that he has evidence of a deed recording the sale of this property by Lord Buttevant (one of the Barrymores) to a relative of her late husband but that it also seems to be the case that a lease which still has ten years to run came with the sale; to complicate matters further, not only has the tenant, who is constantly behind with his rent, complicated the process of ejecting him by sub-leasing, but Lord Barrymore disputes the title and claims the right to levy rents on the property himself. Again, Spencer expresses his frustration: 'I beg Leave to assure you,' he writes to Alice Price, 'that the many Dissapointments I meet with about this small affair of Mohire, give me more Chagreen & Uneasiness [...] than the whole of my other Agencies'.[68]

The second problem consequent on the transference of land through the seventeenth century was that by the early eighteenth century Catholics made up 75% of the population but owned only 7% of the land.[69] To further skew this imbalance, the continual refinement of the Penal Laws throughout the first three-quarters of the eighteenth century reinforced restrictions on the religious, political, and economic activities of that Catholic majority.

Ireland had its own parliament in Dublin with an uneasy relationship to Westminster, as well as a state church, the Anglican Church of Ireland, a major landowner with relatively few clergy. But to complicate matters further, these bodies were opposed not only by many Catholics but also by more radical Protestant sects who had settled in Ulster.[70] In the first two decades of the eighteenth century Ireland was hit by an economic recession that some blamed on the Westminster government's attempts to interfere in Irish trade, culminating in the Declaratory

67 20 August 1745: folio 34, l.5. Spencer's enquiries into the Mallow lease are a major topic in the letters from 23 May 1745: folio 31 to 10 September 1745: folio 35.

68 27 October 1759: folio 113, ll.24–27.

69 Karl S. Bottigheimer, *English Money and Irish Land: The Adventurers in the Cromwellian Settlement of Ireland* (Oxford: Clarendon Press, 1971).

70 J. L. McCracken, 'The Ecclesiastical Structure, 1714–60', in *Eighteenth-Century Ireland*, ed. by Moody and Vaughan, pp. 84–104.

Act of 1720 that asserted the right of Westminster to control Irish affairs. The result was a reaction by those, such as Jonathan Swift and William King, who argued that Ireland was an independent kingdom and that its political nation, composed of the members of the Church of Ireland elite, were not colonists but had all the rights of Englishmen including the right to manage Irish affairs.[71] While this movement waned in the 1730s and 1740s it re-emerged in the 1750s as a nascent 'Patriot Party', to which Spencer obliquely refers.[72] The core of this group would provide the basis for the emergence of a liberal Protestant political movement in the late eighteenth century that produced the Volunteers and the demand for parliamentary reform in 1782. If Spencer's political world is largely one of a privileged Irish Protestantism which sees its interests served through its alliance with England, his attachment to the patriot group shows us that the political map of eighteenth-century Ireland cannot be simplistically divided into two opposed constituencies differentiated by religious beliefs.

Ireland was ruled by a viceroy, the lord lieutenant, who oversaw government and reported back to England: Spencer refers to William Cavendish, 4th Duke of Devonshire (1720–1764)[73] and Philip Stanhope, 4th Earl of Chesterfield (1694–1773),[74] and his letters frequently express the hope that his best chance of securing employment was through connections to Irish society in Dublin linked to the viceroy.[75] Fashions and practices, as Spencer's letters also often suggest, were largely English and European and many of the Protestant gentry had little contact with the native Irish. Many, of course, like Francis Price, were absentee landlords administering their estates through agents (like Spencer), and were to assume considerable notoriety in the nineteenth century.[76] Ireland's economic well-being was increasingly tied to that of Britain and its empire where it exported its raw materials (principally the products of farming such as beef, pork, butter, and cheese) and, while other nations were industrializing, that revolution had not yet reached Ireland.[77] Spencer frequently refers to the weather, in part because he lived through a period of bad weather which created sustained periods of hunger and even starvation in a society tied to its rural economy.[78] More tragically, in the following century the high population of Ireland and its limited farming methods with reliance on one crop were to lead to the holocaust of the potato famine (1845–1852).[79]

71 Swift is referred to in the letter of 14 January 1752: folio 94, l.27.

72 14 January 1752: folio 94, l.27 and 19 July 1755: folio 96, l.7.

73 14 February 1743: folio 18, ll.14–15.

74 18 January 1745: folio 28, ll.14 & 18.

75 On the office of lord lieutenant see J. L. McCracken, 'The Political Structure, 1714–60', in *Eighteenth-Century Ireland*, ed. by Moody and Vaughan, pp. 57–83 (pp. 57–61). On the individual office-holders see *ODNB*.

76 Paul Bew, *Ireland: The Politics of Enmity, 1789–2006* (Oxford: Oxford University Press, 2007), pp. 250–51.

77 L. M. Cullen, 'Economic Development, 1691–1750', and 'Economic Development, 1750–1800', in *Eighteenth-Century Ireland*, ed. by Moody and Vaughan, pp. 123–58 & 159–95.

78 As in, for example, letters of 4 October 1743: folio 7, ll.7–11 and 29 September 1744: folio 26, ll.9–13.

79 Bew, *Ireland*, ch. 5.

Spencer has a keen interest in the wider world and is acutely aware of his location. He is often nervous about the prospect of invasion and writes with keen knowledge about ships coming in and out of Cork harbour. But most of the military conflict he heard about was colonial, a long way from Cork in the Americas, and he refers to military expeditions with the curiosity of an interested spectator in a number of letters.

However, violence was moving closer to home towards the end of his life. In the second half of the eighteenth century secret agrarian societies developed, such as the 'Whiteboys', who sought to challenge the development of rack-renting landlords and defend the Irish peasantry.[80] In 1782 the Patriot Party led by Henry Grattan, and partly inspired by the challenge of the American colonies to George III's imperial aspirations, established legislative independence for the Irish Parliament which was now placed on an equal footing with Westminster.[81] Such developments were far too modest for many in Ireland. In 1791 the United Irishmen, inspired by the French Revolution as well as the American, were established as a debating society that connected Catholics and Protestants eager to establish an independent Ireland; they were opposed by aggressive Protestant societies such as the 'Peep O'Day Boys' whose aim was to terrorize Catholics, as well as the Orange Order (founded in 1795) established to protect Protestant interests.[82] Ireland was a country of relative calm but the seeds of more dramatic change were sown during Spencer's lifetime and it was not long after his death that Wolfe Tone's Rebellion (1798) established the nature of nineteenth-century Irish nationalism and more vigorous conflict with Britain.[83]

Gentry Life in Georgian Ireland

These letters provide us with a number of insights into the interests and concerns of the insecure lower end of the property-owning classes in eighteenth-century Ireland, the Protestant settlers of whom Toby Barnard, one of the few historians to have explored Spencer's letters, has written with such great distinction.[84]

Defining the 'middling sort' is a notoriously difficult and often fruitless exercise and, all too often, historical analysis descends into unsustainable generalizations linking disparate individuals who have little in common. What can be agreed is that the category of 'gentility' was an important factor in eighteenth-century Britain and Ireland and that it describes the desire to appropriate 'the material signifiers of gentility'. An exact definition matters less than an understanding that socially aspirant and socially anxious individuals above and below what they perceived as the dividing lines placed 'their continued faith in its existence as a social category'.[85]

80 Bew, *Ireland*, pp. 11 & 106.

81 R. B. McDowell, 'Parliamentary Independence, 1782–9', in *Eighteenth-Century Ireland*, ed. by Moody and Vaughan, pp. 265–88.

82 Bew, *Ireland*, pp. 33 and 40–44, *passim*.

83 See Roy Foster, *Modern Ireland, 1600–1972* (Harmondsworth: Penguin, 1988), ch. 12. See also J. A. Froude, *The English in Ireland in the Eighteenth Century*, 3 vols (London: Longmans, 1882), III, Bks. 9–10.

84 Barnard, *Anatomy* and *Irish Protestant Ascents and Descents*, ch. 10.

85 H. R. French, *The Middle Sort of People in Provincial England, 1600–1750* (Oxford: Oxford Univ-

Edmund Spencer started above the line: he was, Price states in one of his draft letters 'born to above twelve hundred pounds a year'.[86] Unfortunately, as Price continues, 'three parts of [it] his father privatly sold for not half its worth [...] dyed and left the remainder mortgaged' with the result that Spencer spent his life fearing that he would fall below that line.[87] He constantly battled with the fear and reality of losing his wealth and status and in one sad letter laments to Alice Price: 'I was unfortunately not educated in a Way of understanding Trade by which I might improve my Principle'.[88]

Spencer reveals a great deal about his personal anxieties in these letters. He was always short of money, both in terms of immediate ready cash and longer term investments to secure the future of his family, having suffered from bad financial advice and embezzlement from his guardian, as well as — possibly — reckless over-indulgence in his youth.[89] He worries about his health, as many did in the period, and, even though he lived to a good old age, he suffered a number of bouts of ill-health which he describes in his correspondence. As Susan Whyman has pointed out in her study of post-Restoration letters, 'Health, money, and favours were mentioned most often' in personal letters, making Spencer's letters typical examples of the genre.[90]

He is eager to write about current events and he frequently refers to events in what became known as the War of Jenkins' Ear (1739–1748), a colonial conflict between Britain and Spain over trading rights in the Caribbean which was relatively hot until 1742, then became a series of minor disputes and engagements merging with the War of the Austrian Succession (1740–1748) and the Seven Years War (1756–1763). He has a pronounced interest in ships and shipwrecks, noting the famous wreck of *HMS Victory* off the Channel Islands in 1744, and constantly commenting on which privateers have docked in Cork Harbour.[91] On one occasion, having written and sealed a letter, he reopens it to add the story of the taking by a French privateer of a ship in which he seems to take a particular interest, *The Old Noll*.[92]

He worries, too, about the prospect of a naval invasion, principally from the French attempting to secure an entry into the British Isles via south-west Ireland, though he does balance this with the comment that 'I [...] am not a bit uneasy for

ersity Press, 2007), p. 200. Paul Langford points out that the issue was about distinguishing oneself from the social group below rather than accurately defining one's rank, which is why it is so hard to reconstruct the middle class with any degree of accuracy (*A Polite and Commercial People: England 1727–1783* (Oxford: Clarendon Press, 1989), pp. 61–62).

86 Folio 125, ll.28–29.

87 Folio 125, ll.29–33.

88 25 September 1749: folio 86, ll.7–9.

89 Barnard quotes from other correspondents of Price who suggest that Spencer was a spendthrift in his youth, and that his wife encouraged mismanagement of his financial affairs (see *Irish Protestant Ascents and Descents*, pp. 292 & 293).

90 Susan Whyman, 'Paper Visits: The Post-Restoration Letter as Seen Through the Verney Family Archive', in *Epistolary Selves: Letters and Letter-Writers, 1600–1945*, ed. by Rebecca Earle (Farnham: Ashgate, 1999), pp. 15–36 (p. 18).

91 5 November 1744: folio 27, ll.18–22.

92 29 September 1744: folio 26, verso.

any Consequences, as let what will happen. I have nothing to lose'.[93] His letters register the shock of the 1745 Jacobite invasion of England from the north, hearing belated news of Bonnie Prince Charlie's capture of Edinburgh after his victory at the battle of Prestonpans (21 September 1745) and fearing the worst as his large army headed south, demanding loyalty from other Scots and ordering them not to maintain links with London.[94] The rebellion ended soon enough and the Jacobites were forced to retreat from Derby, but we understand the tension and fear in the brief period before it became apparent that the uprising was not going to succeed. Spencer's reactions are all the more interesting because there are hints in some of the letters that he may have harboured some sympathy for the Jacobite cause: Francis Price, as has already been noted, certainly did.[95] It is possible that the suggestions that Spencer is in agreement may be simply the result of deference towards the person he depended on so much for support. On the other hand he may have had a lukewarm, albeit genuinely held, attachment to the Stuarts but, in the end, fear of chaos and uncertainty won out over loyalty to the monarchy's bloodline.

The letters show Spencer to have had a keen interest in contemporary life and culture. Like many eighteenth-century gentlemen he is eager to impress on Price, his social superior, that he takes note of a range of substantial and fashionable topics. He comments on political scandals and events, such as the trial for murder of Nicholas Netterville, 5th Viscount Netterville,[96] and the campaigns of Admiral Vernon in the West Indies, which he fears have little chance of succeeding.[97] He comments frequently on the weather and its effects. This is principally because he held significant farmlands and was eager to see them prosper,[98] but his comments also suggest that he was eager to represent himself as man of science, up-to-date with the latest developments and in tune with the Enlightenment ambition eventually to control nature.[99] He also has a notable interest in plants and stock breeding, acquiring fashionable plants such as white strawberries[100] and keenly following, like many Irish gentry, horseracing.[101]

But the letters are also full of gossipy jokes that were clearly important to the two men. They laugh at the failings of priests and their inability to maintain their principles, as well as the aggressive pugnaciousness and shifty behaviour of prominent local figures. This particularly familial aspect of the correspondence tells us that receiving letters from Price was clearly important to Spencer, who seems to have felt acutely isolated when remaining in the Cork area, and he frequently complains to Price that he has not received a letter as he had hoped. Similarly, his visits to Dublin were of great comfort to him, connecting him to a wider world as

93 14 February 1743: folio 18, ll.21–24.

94 See Riding, *Jacobites*, pp.151–201.

95 See also below, 'The Letters and the Man', for further discussion of this question.

96 21 January 1733: folio 14, ll.11–14.

97 4 October 1743: folio 7, ll.20–21.

98 See, for example, 4 October 1743: folio 7, ll.7–11, and note to l.9.

99 Other contemporary writers also showed a keen interest in the weather in their letters: see Gray, *Letters*, ed. by Pottle & Bennett, rev. Starr, I, 644, and II, 652 & 681–82.

100 26 July 1745: folio 33, ll.16–18.

101 24 June 1746: folio 49.

he stayed in the fashionably literary Dick's Coffee Shop, even if they were associated with the anxiety of trying to secure some form of remunerative employment (usually a commission in the army or a post in the lord lieutenant's administration), or to further schemes such as his plan to publish a new subscription edition of his famous ancestor's works (stymied by the Forty-Five).[102]

Spencer's letters tell us a great deal about life in Ireland for a man at his social level: he was able to attend grand events such as a ball at Dublin Castle, but constantly worried about money and his future prospects until well into middle age when he secured, at the age of forty, a position in the Registry Office in Dublin in 1752, then a salaried post in the Revenue Office in Wicklow (1755), whilst simultaneously acting as the agent for the Prices in Ireland (a job which perhaps had more than a hint of charity).[103]

The Letters and the Man

When asking what letters might tell us about their writer as an individual, we must first remind ourselves that such documents should never be read as simple testimonies, unmediated expressions of the author's mind. Letters are a specific form of writing, a genre with rules and regulations that could be learned either through practice or through reading the manuals available to guide the apprentice writer into the mysteries of epistolary culture.[104] Such works were purchased in the eighteenth century throughout the literate classes, and servants were often eager to learn how to write letters properly, either to serve their masters better or through social aspiration, probably both.[105]

These manuals gave instructions for writing, amongst other types, the 'familiar' letter;[106] the result was, as Rebecca Earle has observed, that the writing of that type of letter became a performance, with all the consequent suggestion of ludic pretence, and in particular the assumption of a persona or a constructed, fictionalized self on the part of the writer.[107] So how much can letters — especially the 'familiar' type that make up this correspondence — actually tell us about their writer?

102 10 October 1745: folio 36, ll.8–9.

103 Barnard, *Anatomy*, pp. 182–83, and *Irish Protestant Ascents and Descents*, p. 296.

104 There is now a significant literature on letter-writing in early modern England: see, for example, James Daybell, *The Material Letter in Early Modern England: Manuscript Letters and the Culture and Practices of Letter-Writing, 1512–1635* (Basingstoke: Palgrave, 2012), and Clare Brant, *Eighteenth-Century Letters and British Culture* (Basingstoke: Palgrave Macmillan, 2006).

105 Jan Fergus, 'Provincial Servants' Reading in the Late Eighteenth-Century', in *The Practice and Representation of Reading in England*, ed. by James Raven, Helen Small and Naomi Tadmor (Cambridge: Cambridge University Press, 1996), pp. 202–25 (p. 215).

106 This term refers more to the style of the letter than the content, and perhaps also implies the relationship between the correspondents; whilst content could range from the highly personal to matters of business, the style that was to be aimed at was that of easy, but intelligent, conversation between friends or close acquaintances. See 'Introduction' in Bruce Redford, *The Converse of the Pen: Acts of Intimacy in the Eighteenth Century Familiar Letter* (Chicago & London: University of Chicago Press, 1986).

107 Rebecca Earle, 'Introduction: Letters, Writers and the Historian', in *Epistolary Selves*, ed. by Earle, pp. 1–12 (pp. 1–2).

Archival collections of letters can be divided into two basic types. First, there are those written by someone we already know from another, wider sphere — an author, for example, or politician; such letters are immediately situated for us in the context of that person's life and work, and the letters are of interest because we hope they will throw additional light on that life and work, on the writer's relationship to it, and on the character of the writer. Second are those written by people who are completely unknown to us, but whose letters illuminate an aspect of life we might be curious about — what it was like, for example, to be a chambermaid in a great Victorian house, an ordinary seaman who fought in the Battle of Trafalgar, or, indeed, as in this case, a member of the middling gentry in Ireland in the eighteenth century.[108]

While with the first type of collection there is inevitably a dynamic interplay between documents and writer, the converse is not necessarily the case with the second type. That is not to say, however, that these writers do not become personally interesting to us through their letters. Both the world they evoke and the context that they create for themselves in that world is what makes the writer of the letter represented in the text interesting for modern readers. But we cannot just assume that we can extract both easily from the letters: we have to make a more positive effort to read that person out of their letters, since that person exists for us nowhere else.

However, precisely because this type of writer exists only in the letters we have no external frame of reference against which to test our sense of the person. Hence the very real possibility exists that we might simply invent the writer on the basis of assumptions or even misreadings. Secondly, it is questionable whether letters can actually 'speak the person' in this unproblematic way, that they really are unmediated documents, a transparent window into the inner person. Given the extensive and complicated rules that govern letter-writing, we need to ask whether a series of letters by Spencer to another correspondent would show us an entirely different person to the one 'demonstrated' in this collection.

We also have to bear in mind the relationship between the letter-writer and the addressee: is the writer addressing someone of a lower or higher social status, a social equal, or a friend? Friendship correspondence had an important significance in early modern Britain and Ireland, the model for most writers being the Roman Republican hero, Marcus Tullius Cicero (106–43 BCE), who wrote not only a large number of letters to family, friends, superiors, inferiors, and equals, but also a treatise on friendship as a particular virtue that could unite people in times of hardship.[109] Writers were eager to perform the virtues of friendship in their letters, to show their correspondents that they were good friends who understood the value and rules of friendship, just as they knew how to address a superior with due deference and an inferior in an appropriately friendly or stern manner according to the situation. The subjects of letters may look innocent to us but they were often

108 For examples through the ages see *Epistolary Selves*, ed. by Earle.

109 Cicero, *Selected Letters*, trans. by D. R. Shackleton Bailey (Harmondsworth: Penguin, 1986); Cicero, *On Old Age, On Friendship, On Divination*, trans. by W. A. Falconer (London: Heinemann, 1923).

11

near Charleville December the 13th. 1743

Dear Sir

Since my last I have settled a Scheme, by which
(if it hits) I expect to procure some pence, it's this; I have consulted
with sev.ll acquaintance about reprinting Spencers Works, by whose
Means I have got acquainted & agreed with Grierson the Kings Printer
who has advised me to publish by Subscription, & if I can procure
500 Subscribers 'twill be very well worth my while to undertake it, the
Price must be One Guinea for every Subscriber half to be paid in hand
& the remainder at the Delivery of the books which are to be Six Volumes
& which shall be put to the Press as soon as the Subscription is
full. As you have a numerous Acquaintance I believe upon your
solicitation a Number of Subscribers may be procured among them, &
therefore beg you will be so kind to inform me how many I may
expect from that Quarter. If my Lord Barrymore & Sir Watkin were
applyd to, I believe they coud procure a good many especially as they
are now in London. I sett out to Morrow to try my interest among the
Gentlemen in the Country & shall give my self no Rest till I try to
compleat the Subscription, or at lest till I know if 'twill be worth while
to sett about it in earnest, which as soon as I can fix I will publish
Proposals. I intreat the Favour of your Animadversions on this
Scheme as soon as your Leisure will admit. My Wife joins in our
best Respects to you, Coz.n Price & Dear Mr. Richard, Dear Sir

Your most affectionate Kinsman
& obliged humble servant

Edm Spencer

P.S.
I fear you have not seen Mr. Trevor
since you mentiond him to me
my Service to Mr. Smith & all friends

The letter in which Spencer first mentions his proposal to publish an edition of his great-great-grandfather's works, 13 December 1743: folio 11.

carefully chosen to represent the writer in a particular way, as a person of integrity, charm, self-sufficiency, in need of the addressee's help, and so on. The style adopted would vary accordingly. It is with these caveats in mind that one has to approach the business of reading 'Edmund Spencer' out of this correspondence and deciding what he meant when he communicated with Francis Price.

We might start this enquiry with some very basic observations: what the letters actually look like. What might be the first impressions one would have of this writer from his hand and other literary traits such as punctuation and orthography?

Spencer has a strong, regular, clear, and slightly ornamented hand: note, for instance, in the letter of 13 December 1743 illustrated on the preceding page, the capital /Ps/ and /Ds/ of /Printer/ in l.4 and /Delivery/ in l.8, and the flourished /ds/ at the ends of /acquainted & agreed/ in l.4. Spelling is mildly inconsistent: throughout the correspondence third person past tenses of verbs ending /-ed/ are sometimes given the /e/, sometimes not, and he switches quite early in the correspondence from always putting the /l/ in /could, should, would/ to regularly leaving it out, and then later switches back to consistently putting it in. On the whole, though, his spelling largely confirms to modern orthographic practice, which is interesting given that the drive to achieve a consistent orthography throughout the British Isles was in its infancy.[110]

Punctuation, on the other hand, does not at all follow modern rules and has no obvious internal consistency; this, however, is no more than one would expect at a period when punctuation was undergoing a shift from an elocutionary system based on breathing, to one based, as it is now, on syntactical or grammatical principles.[111] What is perhaps surprising, though, is that just as he seems to be in the vanguard for his period in terms of orthography so Spencer seems to favour the newer approach to punctuation, using his stops to guide a reading in terms of the syntactical combination of words rather than for rhetorical effect. So, whilst full-stops, commas, and dashes are used interchangeably and without any clearly consistent method, they nonetheless effectively work to enable the reader for the most part to see easily how the individual words and phrases that make up discrete statements hang together or how they might be separated. That said, there also seem to be elements of the elocutionary system in play, especially in his use of the dash.[112]

We must not make too much of these observations, but such technical characteristics would suggest — as one might expect for someone of this class at this period — a person with a solid basic education and perhaps, more interestingly, that he has not just been educated but is intelligent enough to have benefitted

110 Standardization of spelling across the United Kingdom began, according to Eve Bannett, 'during the second half of the eighteenth century' (Eve Tavor Bannet, *Empire of Letters: Letter Manuals and Transatlantic Correspondence, 1680–1820* (Cambridge: Cambridge University Press, 2005), p. 16).

111 Ephraim Chambers was moved to complain in the fourth edition of his *Cyclopaedia* (London, 1741) that 'there is scarce any thing in the province of the grammarians so little fixed and ascertained as [punctuation]. The rules usually laid down are impertinent, dark, and deficient; and the practice, at present, perfectly capricious, authors varying not only from one another, but from themselves too', quoted by Park Honan in 'Eighteenth and Nineteenth Century English Punctuation Theory', *English Studies*, 41:1–6 (1960), 92–102 (p. 95).

112 See the discussion of the use of dashes in the section on the transcription below.

from that experience. We should note here, though, that we do not know what access Spencer had to education.[113] He certainly does not lard his letters with Latin tags as more educated gentlemen were wont to do — and as Price's letters may have done.[114] He presumably had read his great-great-grandfather's works, as he intended to publish them, and he does occasionally refer to contemporary literature — Swift, Orerry's translation of Pliny — but not the classics, and it is most likely that he was an intelligent man who had not had the opportunities of others in metropolitan centres. However, he had quite likely studied one of the letter-writing manuals that were becoming popular at the turn of the seventeenth century, and so would have known that a good letter should read like a conversation.[115] It is clear that this is an ideal that Spencer adopted in his chatty, friendly correspondence, varying the subject matter and tone from high to low to prevent tedium.[116] He writes well and has a nice turn of phrase, as well as a sly sense of humour, giving the impression throughout that he is keen to have Price treat him as a serious equal as well as someone who is able to entertain him with the pleasant and sophisticated intercourse vital for conversation through familiar letters.

In asking what sort of an individual emerges from the letters, we should start, then, with Spencer's 'familiar' style — how he conveys that sense of candour and self-performance required in the familiar letter. The three most important characteristics to consider are, according to Kate Teltscher: power of invention, the

113 In the first letter Spencer complains that during his early years his guardian 'left [*me*] to my self' and failed to 'place me any where to [*keep me*] out of [*bad*] Company' (6 February 1732: folio 3, ll.11 & 12), but that may well refer to his post-school years and it is just possible that Arthur Hyde, one of the trustees of the Spencer estates (Barnard, *Irish Protestant Ascents and Descents*, p. 293) arranged for the young Spencer to attend the school to which he went himself and to which he sent his own son (born very shortly after the decease of Nathaniel Spencer) which was with a Mr Chinnery in Charleville, not far from Renny (see entry for *Arthur Hyde (1062)* in *HIP*). One tiny detail that supports that idea is that the name 'Chinnery' is mentioned in the postscript to the letter of 19 August 1744: folio 25, where Spencer asks Price to speak to some ship owners in Liverpool on behalf of a son of the 'unfortunate Dick Chinnery', and one is bound to wonder whether this desire to do a good turn for one of that man's children derives from the particular affection and sense of loyalty that sometimes develops between a pupil and teacher. We must also acknowledge, however, that the Chinnery who kept a school may well not be the same Chinnery who had a son who went to sea, especially as 20 August 1745: folio 34 makes it clear that there was a family of that name in Mallow (it refers to a John Chinnery in relation to the property in that town that Price has an interest in). (We should note here that it is possible that Spencer's guardian was not this Arthur Hyde, but his father, also called Arthur Hyde (see 6 February 1732: folio 3, note to l.10), but as he sent his son to the same school it is equally likely that he could have sent Spencer to be educated by Mr Chinnery).

114 Having been educated to university level (see fn. 31) Price would certainly have known Latin, and one of his correspondents, George Dickins, was prone to quoting Latin, suggesting that his friends knew he was able to read it (letters from Dickins to Price are included in Puleston 21: NLW MS 3581E).

115 John Hill's very popular *The Young Secretary's Guide* was published in Dublin in 1708, so may well have been a work in his family's possession. There were, however, other, more informal ways in which people learnt the conventions of letter writing (see Susan Whyman, *The Pen and the People: English Letter Writers, 1600–1800* (Oxford: Oxford University Press, 2009), ch. 3, 'Letters and Literacy') and there is no evidence in the letters that he wrote that Spencer knew of or used this particular manual.

116 Earle, *Epistolary Selves*, p. 5.

impression of an easy, natural, and sincere style, and vivacity or 'immediacy of voice'.[117] There are many moments in these letters where Spencer demonstrates these qualities. For example, on the late arrival of summer in 1745 he writes:

> Never was seen such unseasonable Weather as we have from the beginning of April, which still continues so, not a Day or night without Rain, & so cold that Fires are still kept, & not an hour of summer has yet been seen.[118]

Elsewhere he jokes about a mutual acquaintance who visits the Prices in Wales, noting the beneficial effects on him of the superior food provided there:

> Welsh [...] has slipd his Skin / like the Serpent / & seems young again; I fear the Food of Ballyhooly will so ill agree with his Constitution after Brynypiece that the poor fellow will be reduced in a few Weeks to his pristine Appearance.[119]

In his letter of 15 May 1744 he concludes the news that two young men have recently died with a somewhat darkly humorous quip:

> Young Causabon died last Week at his Seat at Carrick, he was a very honest young Fellow & was lately married to one of Sir John Rogerson's Daughter's, another of them was married to Col Jephson's eldest Son who she buried within the year, dangerous Women to attack![120]

We get to know some people quite well as they crop up in various different events, rather like characters in a soap opera. One such is that same Col. Jephson just referred to, and whom Spencer clearly disliked. On 1 July 1745 he gives a rather laconic description of the military gentleman's behaviour, with its end left hanging but full of anticipated pleasure at the assured outcome:

> Our worthy Colonel Jephson is at present in the Dumps, for being the eldest Cap.[t] in the Regiment he was orderd to Flanders with the Draughts, but as he does not care to venture his sweet person on the Water when he had marchd the Men to Cove & shipd them, he there pretended to have been taken violently ill & had himself bled & blisterd, but as soon as the Transports sail'd he returnd to Mallow in as good a Condition as he left it: how twill be taken to send off the Men without an Officer, a little Time will discover.[121]

There is, though, at times, another side of Spencer revealed — still through a certain candour, but perhaps slipping out of that urbane ease that the properly performative familiar letter might aim to maintain. The very first letter in the collection suggests a somewhat sensitive, possibly personally insecure character with its hint that there might have been some strain in the relationship between the two correspondents: 'I should have troubled you long e'er this with a Letter but feard it

117 Kate Teltscher, 'The Sentimental Ambassador: The Letters of George Bogle from Bengal, Bhutan and Tibet, 1770–1781', in *Epistolary Selves*, ed. by Earle, pp. 79–94 (p. 83). See also Toby Ditz, 'Formative Ventures: Eighteenth-century Commercial Letters and the Articulation of Experience', in *Epistolary Selves*, ed. by Earle, pp. 59–78 (p. 69).

118 1 July 1745: folio 32, ll.10–14.

119 2 February 1747: folio 67, ll.1–5.

120 Folio 21, ll.10–15.

121 Folio 32, ll.14–23.

may not be taken as [*well as I*] hoped'.[122] And we observe a similar tone in a letter written some twelve years later, where he wonders why he has not heard from Price for so long:

> As I never did any Thing / even in Thought / to deserve your Slighting me, I cannot lay any Thing to my own Charge that shoud Occasion this Neglect of me, & therefore must impute it to some other Cause as yet unknown to me.[123]

He returns, yet again, to this theme in July 1749: after a five-month interval since his last letter from Price, Spencer worries that he is being unfairly neglected:

> Tis so long since I had the Satisfaction of a Letter from you, that I begin to despair of another, & dread that by Some / unforeseen at least undesignd / accident I might be unhappy enough to provoke your Slighting me, or else, sure, you wou'd before now have favourd me with a Line or two to inform me how you & yours are.[124]

On this occasion, however, there is a good reason why Price has not informed him how he is: he has, in fact, been dying, yet none of the family in Wales seems to have thought fit to tell Spencer about that state of affairs.[125]

A later letter evidences the same neglect of reciprocity on the Welsh side: Richard Price, Francis Price's son and a young man for whom Spencer clearly had a considerable affection, has married, but they write to tell him this only after the Irish papers have published the fact:

> I return Thanks for your kind Information of M.r Price's Intention to alter his Condition, our News Papers inform us that he is marryed, & I sincerely wish him and you all the Joy imaginable on the Occasion; as tis some Years since I had the Pleasure of his Correspondence, I take the Liberty to intreat you'll please to present him with my Congratulations & those of my Wife & Daughter.[126]

Is there a touch of chagrin in the straight formality here, and of reproach in that 'tis some Years since I had the Pleasure of his Correspondence'?[127] On this occasion, if not before, Spencer could be forgiven for thinking that he had been slighted.

Perhaps Spencer was less important to the Price family than they were to him. It is a great shame that we do not have Price's letters to Spencer so that we can see whether Spencer's warm affection for Price and desire to maintain an intimate friendship with him was reciprocated. But is what we are seeing here simply a matter of everyday family dynamics? Certainly Spencer represents himself as the

122 6 February 1732: folio 3, ll.2–3.
123 10 September 1745: folio 35, ll.13–17.
124 21 July 1749: folio 85, ll.1–6.
125 He died on 27 July, six days after Spencer wrote this letter.
126 31 December 1759: folio 115, ll.3–9.
127 One wonders whether Richard Price was a kind of substitute son for Spencer (he had two daughters and lost one of those in her early childhood) for though he clearly very seldom saw the boy he continued to maintain the relationship vicariously through the letters to the father (unless he also wrote now lost letters to the son), and took great pains to do things for the boy such as finding him a pet eagle and then having it carefully transported to Wales (see 29 May 1744: folio 22, ll.8–13, and 26 January 1746: folio 55, ll.1–9).

poor relation who has got into debt and needs to be rescued, and whose difficult circumstances (whether self-inflicted or not) lead to his continually seeking help from his wealthier, more influential and hence more successful relative.[128] However, a letter of December 1747 suggests that another factor is in play. Here Spencer first reiterates his gratitude to 'cousin' Price for all his 'favours', but then expresses uneasiness about his powerlessness in relation to great men. He requests his cousin *not* to intercede on his behalf with Lord Barrymore concerning a dispute he has with the Power family (with whom he is in dispute over his Renny property). They have, he says, 'used me basely' but Barrymore has them 'greatly at heart'.[129] Here the diffidence stems, clearly, from Spencer's acutely-felt impotence in these situations: 'as he [Lord Barrymore] is a very great man: I woud not choose to deal with him; for shoud he at any Time take it into his head he woud crush me to Atoms'.[130] Does this suggest another explanation for his uneasy relationship with Price — that because of his painful awareness of his position of dependence on Price, he recognizes all too clearly the imbalance in social status between the two of them? Is Spencer's uncertainty, in other words, more strictly a matter of class, which is why he performs the nature of friendship so often in the correspondence? Is he a relation whom the Prices regard as socially inferior, excluded from their close personal affairs, so that writing letters is on his part an obligation but on theirs a favour?

Here we might usefully return to the letter-writing manuals. One of the niceties they taught was that salutations and valedictions were a major signifier of the hierarchical relationship and the degree of familiarity in which correspondents believed they stood relative to each other. Within a family, for example, specifying the familial relationship in the salutation indicated social superiority or equality, while the hierarchically inferior correspondent named it only in the valediction.[131]

Thus we might note that in only one letter does Spencer address Price as family, and that is in the very first one which starts, 'D[ea]r Couz'. In the next letter and for the rest of the correspondence he addresses him consistently as 'Dear Sir'. The explanation for this change (and we must remember that there is a gap of some nine years between these two letters) could well be that in the earlier one Spencer was basking in his apparent success in lifting himself out of the poverty he seemed destined for by his loss of the family wealth, whilst in the second he has clearly returned to a state of financial embarrassment and is seeking his relative's help in escaping from it. In other words, he has sunk back to the status of a suitor for patronage rather than being a relative on an upwardly mobile path towards social and economic equality.

Similarly, as regards the valedictory subscriptions, with the exception of that first letter, which ends 'I am D^{r}Couz Your Affectionate Kinsman', Spencer regularly signs off with a close variant of: 'I am, dear sir, your affectionate kinsman & most obliged humble Servant', thereby minimizing the *familial* relationship with the

128 See 30 November 1745: folio 38, ll.11–12: '[I] do assure you I never contracted a Debt since I left Wales but w.^{h} was occasiond by my long Illness and which I have already dischargd'.

129 5 December 1747: folio 63, ll.22–23.

130 Ibid., ll.23–25.

131 Bannett, *Empire of Letters*, p. 65.

generic 'kinsman' and stressing the *social* distinction with the more specific and subservient 'most obliged humble Servant'.[132]

However, running alongside Spencer's rather morbidly introspective sensitivity there are signs of an outward looking generosity of spirit in many of the letters. For example, despite his own increasingly desperate search for a way of bringing in money he still finds time to ask Price to exert his influence on behalf of a young sailor called Chinnery.[133] At a point when he himself was desperate to find gainful employment, he helps his brother Nathaniel find work in the Excise in Dublin.[134]

Elsewhere, having explained to Alice Price his procedure for ensuring that tenants pay their dues on time, he then shows a touching sympathy for the plight of those dealing with genuine financial difficulties:

> On my first being appointed [Mr Deane's] Agent I obliged [his tenants] to pay a years rent the beginning of May which was due at Ladyday, by which I have them now so punctual that there is not this day a shilling due of last Michaelmas Gale in that County, tho' I cant say so much for the County of Kilkenny Tennants, as I must forbear with them being poor & a great Distance from Market.[135]

And in the autumn of 1743, when market prices have fallen badly enough to cause general hardship and many landlords are dunning their tenants for rent, he clearly has not the heart to follow suit, telling Price: 'where I expected to have reced a little money upon Demand, I was obliged to be content with a putt off, & coud not in conscience press too home as marketts go'.[136] Spencer may have been needy and insecure but he was certainly imaginative and empathetic enough to understand how things might be for others.

Spencer's letters are also distinctive as much for what they do not say or reveal as for what they do tell us. Concerning his religious affiliation the letters are remarkable for their almost complete silence; there is not one comment that gives us a definite answer to the question, 'was Spencer a Protestant or a Catholic?'

That he was a Protestant is the natural assumption since, were he a Catholic, he would not, under the Penal Laws prevailing in Ireland at that time, have been able to obtain any employment in the administration.[137] But that is only part of the story. Many of Edmund Spenser's direct descendants had reverted to Catholicism, including Hugolin, the grandson who inherited Renny. William (the grandson through Maccabaeus Childe's line, and Edmund Spencer's grandfather) seems to have adopted a fairly flexible religious position, having apparently converted from Catholicism to Protestantism in order to recover lands confiscated by Cromwell's

132 Ibid., p. 66.

133 See 19 August 1744: folio 25, postscript, and 10 April 1745: folio 30, ll.14–15.

134 See 16 July 1746: folio 50, ll.13–15. Barnard, we should note, gives a rather different account of this, one in which Spencer does not figure as an influential actor (see *Irish Protestant Ascents and Descents*, p. 299).

135 March 23 1757: folio 108, ll.21–26. We might note also the thoughtful sensitivity revealed in: 'I woud have askd for the Lease but that I feard your Agent might have taken it unkind, as he is but a young Gentleman' (November 27 1749: folio 88, ll.32–33).

136 4 October 1743: folio 7, ll.29–30.

137 On the penal laws see Simms, 'The Establishment of Protestant Ascendancy, 1691–1714', pp. 16–21.

administration.[138] He seems to have had no problem with the restoration of the Stuarts, but on the Hanoverian succession he supported William of Orange. Such facts might suggest that William Spenser was something of a pragmatist, his actions determined by political considerations and the need to maintain possession of his property, rather than by religious conviction, but in that respect he was in line with most Christians in post-Reformation Europe who had to make a living and had no particular desire to be martyrs whatever their confessional allegiance.[139] Wealth was acquired through land rather than salaries so marriage to the sons and daughters of neighbours was especially important as it enabled families to accumulate more property and so secure their future. One suspects that many religious principles and beliefs were sacrificed for such hope of earthly gain, especially in religiously divided Ireland.

In line with his silence on his own religious convictions, Spencer has little to say about those of other people. One noteworthy exception, though, is his comment on the death of the vicar of Castlelyons. This is reported with a subtly sarcastic suggestion that the vicar's charitable behaviour is more in line with Catholic belief concerning good works and salvation rather than the Protestant rejection of that in favour of dependence on God's mercy and grace:

> Harry Harrison who has lived like a Hermit for many y.ͤ & still continues to do so, has last Week remitted to the Society for promoting Protestant Schools, one thousand pounds in a Lump, by w.ᶜʰ Charity I believe he expects to pave the way to wipe off his Extortions &-- with w.ᶜʰ he might be hereafter chargd.[140]

It would be foolish, of course, to make any more of that than to note Spencer's ability — and willingness — to make a theologically inflected joke, but what do we make of his comment in the letter of 12 March 1760, that 'our Militia is not arrayed nor the Act yet passd, it seems votes of Credit are of greater consequence than arming the Protestants to defend themselves'?[141] Does that rather detached phrasing suggest that 'the Protestants' are a group that the writer does not feel a part of, and that their need to 'defend themselves' is not his need? It is hard to tell.

There is no decisive evidence here, only a sense of veiled disaffection towards the established church, one that does not hint at overtly opposed views but rather a resigned dissatisfaction. Perhaps Spencer, if not a secret Catholic, had sympathy for the Catholics, and seeking work in the administration, under the Penal Laws, felt he had to be particularly cautious when using a postal system that was, as Paul Langford writes, 'notoriously open to inspection for Reasons of State', these reasons including 'party politics as well as national security'.[142] James How notes that 'during this period the Post Office quickly earnt itself a malign character and the

138 See 'Appendix I: Spenser's Descendants' in Andrew Hadfield, *Edmund Spenser: A Life* (Oxford: Oxford University Press, 2012).

139 For the phenomenon of 'Nicodemism', whereby Christians knew the truth but refused to declare their belief for fear of persecution, see Diarmaid MacCulloch, *Reformation: Europe's House Divided, 1490–1700* (Harmondsworth: Penguin, 2004), pp. 268, 290–91 & 371–72.

140 1 December 1748: folio 79, ll.10–16.

141 Folio 116, ll.30–32.

142 Langford, *A Polite and Commercial People*, p. 408.

betrayal of trust and interception of letters by it came almost to be seen as a given', letters being systematically 'subject to stops and checks by anonymous officials employed for just that purpose'.[143]

We might consider here whether Spencer's use of franks was a strategy for circumventing the unwelcome attentions of the Post Office, but it has to be said that one suspects the reverse was actually the case: members of parliament would have been of particular interest to the state surveillance services — especially those like the Earl of Barrymore and Sir Watkin Williams-Wynn who were both well-known Jacobites in regular contact with the agents of the Pretender in France. More likely is that saving money was a higher priority that avoiding interference with the correspondence (which may well have been seen as more or less inevitable anyway) and if that was the case we should be that much more more sensitive to Spencer's need to be circumspect concerning his personal political and religious sympathies.

But the issue is not just one of censorship or surveillance by the authorities: until relatively recent times letters were not considered to be private communications. They were not always composed in isolation,[144] were likely to be read out to others, and were often imagined almost as public documents.[145] So perhaps, finally, he is reticent on this subject because his views are being tailored to his addressee and others of his acquaintance who may have had views at odds with Spencer's own but which the poor relation felt obliged to respect if not endorse.

In *Letters from Georgian Ireland: The Correspondence of Mary Delaney 1731–68*, Angélique Day notes another, more socially influenced practice that might have been a consequence of this broad dissemination of letters when she comments on the use by Mary Delaney and her correspondents of 'petnames, and sometimes classical names to disguise some of their subjects of gossip', this habit being prompted by the fact that the letters might well be inadvertently heard or read by friends of those subjects — even, in some cases, the subjects themselves.[146] Such nicknames, both familiar and derogatory, occur frequently in Spencer's letters. The otherwise unidentified 'Alderman' is an example of the former type, as is

143 James How, *Epistolary Spaces: English Letter Writing from the Foundation of the Post Office to Richardson's Clarissa* (Aldershot: Ashgate, 2003), p. 5.

144 We might note in this respect Spencer's habit of frequently including in the valedictions some such phrase as 'My Wife joins me in our best Respects to You, Coz^{n} Price and Dear Mr Richard' (8 November 1743: folio 8, ll.37–38) as though she were actually present when he was writing (as quite possibly she was) and almost as though she had participated in the composition of the letter he had been engaged upon (as, again, she quite possibly did); it is interesting to note that this phrase (or a close approximation of it) is included only when he is at the family home, wherever that might be at the time of writing; when he is away from home the phrase is always omitted.

145 One indicator of this in Spencer's letters would be the regular postscripts tagged on alongside the valedictions in which he presents his 'service' to mutual friends in the Price circle (see, for example, 8 November 1743: folio 8 where he sends 'My Service to Mr Smith & the rest of my Sober Acquaintance'); the passing on of these complimentary notices by Price would no doubt have given occasion for the transmission also of much of the news contained in the letter so that Mr Smith and those other 'sober acquaintances' could participate in the social event that the letters constitute. See also Ylva Hasselberg, 'Letters, Social Networks and the Embedded Economy in Sweden: Some Remarks on the Swedish Bourgeoisie, 1800–1850', in *Epistolary Selves*, ed. by Earle, pp. 95–107 (p. 103).

146 Mary Delaney, *Letters from Georgian Ireland: The Correspondence of Mary Delaney 1731–68*, ed. by Angélique Day (Belfast: Friar's Bush Press, 1991), p. 6.

Barrymore's soubriquet 'The Doctor' for Francis Price.[147] Those examples might carry a slight irony, but if so it is the good-humoured, bantering irony of close familiarity and mutual respect. On the other hand, 'Trigger', the nickname Spencer uses for Price's neighbour, Thomas Lloyd, is a clear example of the derogatory type which reinforces their shared distaste for the man and functions to underpin their alliance against him.[148] Another factor in the use of nicknames by Price's correspondents might lie in the fact that this circle was to some extent drawn together by their shared Jacobite sympathies, which could well have given the propensity an additional pleasantly conspiratorial flavour.

The evidence in the letters of Spencer's political affiliation is similarly tantalizing and elusive, albeit a little more substantial. On 6 December 1743 he writes to Price: 'I congratulate you on the Addition of so many worthy new Members to your Cycle'.[149] This confirms quite definitively where Price's political sympathies lay as the Cycle was a Jacobite club — but do the approbatory 'congratulate' and 'worthy new Members' indicate Spencer's concordance with his correspondent?[150]

Spencer then rather cryptically continues:

> We have our own Clubs here too, /but such Clubs!/ I have not the Honour of being a Member to any one of them, /unfortunate [*!*] — the grandest is our Dettingen Club, which has a great many Members as it is the newest, & by their Excess in Drinking will, I believe, be of short Duration.[151]

The Dettingen was named after the battle in which the French were defeated by an allied force under George II earlier in 1743 so it is clearly a Hanoverian club. Does that 'unfortunate [*!*]' carry a suggestion that he would like to join but laments that his Jacobitism prevents him, or even that because of those sympathies he feels a need to try to camouflage them through membership of such a club? And if that is the case, is the 'unfortunate [*!*]' ironic, carrying, along with the prediction that the heavy drinking will lead to the club's early demise, a hint of *Schadenfreude*? Or has it nothing to do with political leanings at all, but simply signifies, as Toby Barnard suggests it does, that his 'meagre resources excluded [him] from the swells gathered in the Dettingen Club'?[152]

Moreover, if he were a Jacobite, surely he would not be angling for a commission in the Hanoverian army: that would be an ideological step too far, even for a man desperate for a secure salary. One suspects that Barnard is right, and that in the reference to the Cycle Club he is simply indicating respect for his relative's views by politely acknowledging them, then following that up with a humorously conspiratorial and negative commentary on his local Hanoverian club.

147 See 27 December 1743: folio 12, l. 6 and n. 31 above.

148 Which category George Ross's bizarre nickname for Spencer — 'Sucking Pendergrass' (George Ross to Francis Price, 20 February 1741/2, Historical Manuscripts Commission, Fifteenth Report, Part VII, 324) — fits into is another matter; Ross affects an extraordinarily elliptical style of comic writing so it may simply be intended as funny.

149 Folio 10.

150 The club was formed in Wrexham in 1710 and at its head was, as has been noted, Sir Watkin Williams-Wynn, Price's neighbour, friend, and correspondent.

151 6 December 1743: folio 10, ll.24–27.

152 Barnard, *Irish Protestant Ascents and Descents*, p. 296

A letter he writes to Alice Price in July 1755 is, however, a different matter. Here he explains that he has been distracted from writing to her:

> On Account of a disputed Election for Portrive in M.r Deanes Corporation, where the C--t party has seduced some of our Voters and tryd to force others on us who have no right to vote ... they also have returnd for themselves, which will make it a Kings bench Affair where I make not the least Doubt of invalidating such a Number of their poll as will [...] preserve to us our Patriot Borough.[153]

Barnard describes this passage as 'a cryptic expression of Irish patriotism', but the phrase 'our Patriot Borough', and the following explanation of the action to overturn the vote, must surely indicate quite unambiguously that Spencer is an active member of that group (still in its infancy at this point as a formal political party) which desired greater independence for Ireland and reform of the anti-Catholic Penal Laws.[154]

So if he is not a Jacobite, he is hardly the fully paid-up pro-Hanoverian described in the draft letters and notes that Francis Price wrote in preparation for lobbying possible patrons or employers on Spencer's behalf.[155] Price presents him there as a man 'verry well affected to the present establishment';[156] he takes care to mention his 'constant adherence ... to the revolution & ye Protestant line in the illustrious house of Hanover', and that his grandfather did 'great Service ... to King William & his army at the battle of Achrim by shewing them the difficulties, defiles & passes, which saved the Protestant army from beeing destroyed'.[157] Is there a

153 19 July 1755: folio 96, ll.2–7. The borough is almost certainly Inistioge, Co. Kilkenny; the Deane family was very powerful in Inistioge, both in local politics (the portrive was a local official similar to a mayor) and in national politics; their main opponents were the Fownes, another powerful local family, and the parliamentary seat for the borough was successfully wrested by Sir William Fownes of the Court Party from the Patriot Deanes in this period. The 'Patriots' at this juncture were the followers of the Speaker, Henry Boyle of Castlemartyr, Co. Cork, and other MPs opposed to the ambitious Primate Stone and Stone's allies, who included, interestingly, John Ponsonby, chief commissioner of the revenue, who was not just Spencer's employer at this point but also an in-law of Fownes. These alignments were formed in the early 1750s and hardened in December 1753 when the Patriots defeated the government on a form of words in the principal Money Bill of the session. A compromise was painfully hammered out between 1755 and 1756, after the recall of the Lord Lieutenant, the Duke of Dorset; Stone was temporarily sidelined, and Boyle was persuaded to retire very remuneratively from the Speakership, to which Ponsonby was elected; a Patriot 'rump' was left angrily out in the cold. Being a Patriot in this temporary 1752–1756 sense would have well-nigh ruled someone out of appointment to or promotion in the revenue and in most government jobs, but Spencer was now firmly ensconced in such a job, and so may well have felt freer to speak and act more openly; the aftermath of the Inistioge election for portrive, however, may have left him feeling exposed again.

154 Barnard, *Irish Protestant Ascents and Descents*, p. 303.

155 See folios 124, 125 & 126. Spencer would not have been alone in the epistolary community in demonstrating such an unenthusiastic attitude to the Hanoverian dynasty: Thomas Gray writes to William Mason on 29 November 1759 about George II's death: 'it is an odd contemplation, that somebody [i.e., George II] should have lived long enough to grow a great & glorious Monarch' (Gray, *Letters*, ed. by Pottle and Bennett, rev. Starr, II, 655).

156 Folio 125, ll.23–24.

157 Folio 124, ll.48–58.

hint here of the gentleman protesting too much? Might Price's concentration on Spencer's loyalist credentials be on a par with that possibility floated earlier — that membership of the Dettingen Club would have operated as camouflage — though here to disguise the somewhat less marginalizing political position of being an Irish patriot rather than an outright enemy to the established power?[158]

Whatever we make of this isolated declaration of Spencer's personal convictions, it certainly sheds some light on the difficulties he experienced in finding employment, and does so more effectively than Barnard's suggestion that he lacked the backers or the money to get a military commission or a post in the administration:[159] 'being a Patriot in this temporary 1752–56 sense would have well-nigh ruled you out of appointment to or promotion in the revenue and in most government jobs, and impeded your progress in the army'.[160] And yet, he still pursued such a post, precisely the sort of difficult negotiation than many must have been making regarding these complex intersections of the political and the personal in mid-eighteenth-century Ireland. Underlying all this is, of course, a simple, stubborn fact: he had a family to support and he needed to secure some form of income.

A third puzzling absence in this correspondence is death. Sometime in 1743, in the tenth year of her life, Spencer's elder daughter Ann died, but there is no mention of this dreadful event in any of the surviving letters from that year. Whilst it is striking that he generally has little to say about his children, it would seem extraordinary that such an occurrence would pass without notice in a letter to a member of the family. This seems the more surprising given that one of the few mentions of them is when he tells Richard Price on 27 February 1761 that 'my Wife's & my Daughter's Illness who is not yet well enough recoverd to leave her Chamber [...] hinderd my being able to meet in Dublin the Gentleman I so much wanted to settle with',[161] suggesting that he has sufficient affection for his daughter to prioritize her care above his business affairs.[162]

158 It is interesting to observe here, with reference to the surveillance of letters by the authorities, that Spencer is slightly less reserved about political matters than religious, with regard to both his and Francis Price's convictions. Price, of course, was very much more socially and economically established than Spencer so may well not have needed to conceal his preference for a Stuart succession (which he most likely saw, moreover, as being best achieved through constitutional rather than military means); as to Spencer, he had, as has been noted, attained his objective of finding a post in the administration in Dublin and at some point in 1755 had secured a salaried position in the revenue at Wicklow, so may therefore have felt he could afford to be more open about his political sympathies at this point in his life.

159 Barnard, *Irish Protestant Ascents and Descents*, p. 294.

160 We are grateful to Dr Anthony Malcomson for this observation, made in an e-mail, 3 June 2015.

161 Folio 118, ll.15–17. The other mentions of the surviving daughter Rosamond are in the letters of 5 December 1747: folio 63, 28 February 1748: folio 83, and 21 October 1761: folio 119; this last refers to Rosamond's husband, so she has obviously married at some point, possibly between this letter and the previous one of 27 February 1761: folio 118 (when she was confined to her chamber by illness and so presumably still living in her parent's house); as Spencer was working for the Prices at this point there must have been several letters between them during these eight months which have not survived, and that could include the one in which he one announced this marriage.

162 A similar affection for his family is suggested in the letter of 14 January 1752: folio 94, in which, writing from Dublin, Spencer tells Alice Price that 'I was debarrd of the Satisfaction I flatterd

After Price's death in late July 1749, there is a gap in the archive of some two months before the first letter that we have from Spencer to Alice Price; that letter contains nothing by way of condolences for her loss, suggesting strongly that a letter marking the death was written earlier.[163]

In both these cases of bereavement it is inconceivable that such significant events were not mentioned in the correspondence; far more likely is that they were the sole subject of specific communications. But it seems equally unlikely that such letters were destroyed or carelessly misplaced (as, for example, was possibly the fate of some of the letters from Spencer written during Price's final illness). On the contrary, it might be argued that their absence from this collection is mute testimony to the higher valuation of such letters, and that they were kept separately with other mementos of a person's passing, as we now might gather up and keep together the condolence cards received after the death of a loved one along with a funeral order of service and such other documents as press notices of the occasion.

However, while this might explain the absence from this collection of Spencer's letter of condolence on Price's death, it would not really explain the absence of a letter informing the Price family of Rosamond's death — she, after all, was not one of their immediate family. That may suggest in turn that there are other reasons in play which separated off 'death' letters from others, possibly to do with taboos around death, and possibly specific to this family. Whatever cultural or personal habits are at work here, though, we can be sure that these absences were not the result of those insecurities about the mail service that may well have steered Spencer towards caution about exposing his more personal beliefs and convictions.

Conclusion

In conclusion, what we might see through these letters is a fascinatingly conflicted individual. Spencer is easy to like: he is genuinely funny in a dry, understated manner, and is capable of warm, generous feelings towards others, maintaining in adversity his sympathy for those even less well off than himself; he emerges from his letters as a dedicated family man, concerned to do the best for his wife and children in trying circumstances; he is astute, observant, and an eloquent correspondent able to continue a long-distance friendship through the means he had available. On the other hand, he is also a rather needy man, somewhat self-deprecating and unsure of having enough culture and learning to distinguish him from his fellows; understandably perhaps given his birth, he feels keenly the humiliations of his unfortunate economic situation, so is constantly anxious about his status. Most interestingly of all, though, he emerges as someone who is negotiating, as best he can — and as so many others of his socio-economic position in Ireland at that time must also have been doing — the uneasy intersection of his personal political sympathies with the wider constitutional situation in the face of an all too real but

my self with of seeing my little Family, these holydays, by a treaty I am on about the purchase of a small Employment' (ll.43–45).

163 25 September 1749: folio 86.

unacceptable possible outcome: complete impoverishment and ruin for himself and his family.

There are, of course, other Edmund Spencers that might be read out of these letters: one, perhaps, with a rather spiteful sense of humour, or a snob obsessed with presenting himself as one who moves in the better circles; a man with enough education to write well, craft nicely constructed letters and engage with others; someone clearly capable of gainful employment, yet who was too keenly aware of his precarious status in both financial and social terms, fearing that if he did not perform the roles assigned to him well enough he and his family might plunge into a terrifying abyss.

It is true that Spencer is no Dorothy Osborne, who was among the most fluent and sophisticated English letter-writers of the previous generation, but his letters are engaging, informative, amusing to read, and fascinating for what they tell us about status and class in Irish, and British, society in the eighteenth century, and however one reads the man we have in these letters both a case study which tells us much about the pleasures and pains of gentry life in the mid-eighteenth century and a rounded self-portrait of an interesting character in his own right.[164]

Postscript

After the death of Francis Price in July 1749 Spencer continued to correspond with Price's widow, Alice, until late 1760, at which date he was living in Waterford and probably still working for the revenue as supervisor of the Wexford hearth money district. At around the end of that year Richard Price, the son, appears to have taken over management of the family's affairs, the last three letters in the collection being written to him, also from Waterford. All three of those letters reveal that Spencer, besides transferring sums of money from Ireland to Wales, was acting for the Price family concerning a dispute with Lord Barrymore over the title to the Mohire estate. It is clear from the final letter (28 June 1762: folio 120) that Spencer was still enmeshed in this complex legal business, so it seems reasonable to assume that, although we have no further letters, he continued to act for Richard Price for some time after June 1762. That would be confirmed by the accounts he sent Richard Price in 1774 (folio 122), but the scribbled note on the verso side of the sheet complaining that this was 'Mr Spencers last Acc$^{\underline{t}}$ sent to England of his Rec$^{\underline{ts}}$ in Ireland tho repeatedly solicited to$\wedge^{\text{send}}$ th[*e*] succeeding one[*s*] by M$^{\underline{r}}$ Price in his Life Time' surely marks the termination of his working for the Prices.

Of his life after 1774 we have only one small definite detail. W. H. Welply, in his article 'The Family and Descendants of Edmund Spenser (contd)', notes a legal document dated 20 May 1779 in which 'Edmund Spenser [sic] and his wife Anne, are described as "now of Mallow"'.[165] The correct correlation of the forenames of Spencer and his wife along with the clear connection of the document, 'Freeman

164 Dorothy Osbourne, *The Letters of Dorothy Osbourne to William Temple*, ed. by G. C. Moore Smith (Oxford: Clarendon Press, 1928).

165 Welply, 'The Family and Descendants of Edmund Spenser (contd)', p. 58, fn. 94.

v. Freeman', with his wife ('Freeman' being her maiden name) give authority to this piece of evidence. What he was doing in Mallow and why he had moved from Waterford we do not know, but the word 'now' suggests that the move was a recent one.

Less straightforward evidence concerning the place and date of Spencer's death is offered by Rev. Charles Gibson, a nineteenth-century historian of Cork, who tells us that 'Edmund Spenser [sic] died about 1790 at Mallow, leaving this sad epitaph for his tomb: — "Here lies the body of Edmund Spenser, great-great-great grandson of the poet Spenser, unfortunate from his cradle to his grave"'.[166]

As Welply rightly points out, the addition of a generation in the epitaph suggests that this could be the son of the writer of these letters — that is, the fourth Edmund Spencer of that name in the lineage of the poet and not the third. He proposes, though, that the 'slight error in the number of greats [...] would, if rectified, make him out to be Edmund the third himself'.[167] But Gibson is quite clear that he is talking about a son of Edmund the third: he notes that Nathaniel Spencer, the great grandson of the poet, had three sons, the eldest of whom (our Edmund the third) married Anne Freeman, and that one of the two brothers, whom he describes as 'the last of the Spensers',[168] was murdered by his housekeeper; but he then adds, rather confusingly, 'there was a later than he, "Edmund Spenser of Mallow," probably the nephew of the murdered man, and the son of Edmund Spenser who married Anne Freeman. He died in Mallow in 1790'.[169]

There is, however, no documentary evidence that Edmund and Anne Spencer had a son, nor is there a single mention of one in the surviving correspondence (and we would surely expect at least one mention in 117 letters if the Spencers had a son, especially given that their daughters are mentioned). Gibson, however, then states that 'Doctor Todd speaks of a daughter of this Edmund Spenser of Mallow, as having married a Wm. Burns, who held some office in the English custom-house',[170] and in doing so reveals that he is thoroughly muddled about this generation of Spencers, since the woman spoken of here was Rosamond, daughter of Edmund and Anne.[171]

Gibson adds, moreover, two further intriguing details about his 'Edmund Spenser of Mallow': first, that he had sought for the stone bearing the 'sad epitaph' in the graveyard at Mallow without success, but was 'informed by two or three persons

166 Charles Gibson, *The History of the County and City of Cork*, 2 vols (London: Thomas C. Newby, 1861), I, p. 313.

167 Welply, 'The Family and Descendants of Edmund Spenser', p. 58. We might also note that people at this period were not necessarily as precise about relationships as we might expect them to be: Spencer describes himself as the 'Great Grandson' of the poet in the *Proposals* he had printed for the collected works he intended to publish.

168 Unfortunately he does not say which one.

169 Gibson, *History of the County and City of Cork*, I, p. 313.

170 Ibid., I, p. 314.

171 According to Welply's 'Pedigree of Spenser' ('The Family and Descendants of Edmund Spenser', p. 60) the husband's name was James, not William; but he also notes that Rosamond Spencer's husband 'seems to have been a government official' ('The Family and Descendants of Edmund Spenser', p. 58), so we can be fairly certain that this is the woman meant by Doctor Todd.

that they had seen the name of Spenser on one of the stones';[172] and second, that he suspects this to be the Spencer mentioned in a letter of 2 March 1793 in which the writer says, 'I have lately heard that within a few years, a lineal descendant and namesake of the celebrated poet Spenser was resident at Mallow: that he was in possession of an original portrait of the poet [...] with many curious papers and records concerning his venerable ancestor'.[173] The first of those details may be regarded with some suspicion as possibly a case of kindly natives doing their best to be helpful and so saying anything that they think will aid a stranger in his pursuit of local knowledge; the second, though, chimes with Spencer's *Proposals for Printing by Subscription the Works of Mr Edmund Spencer* in which he promises 'a more Exact Account of his Life', one possibly based on hitherto unpublished documents in his possession.

Gibson's argument is confused and much of it is based on hearsay, but it looks as though we should at least consider the date he gives for the death of his Edmund the fourth as possibly the year of Edmund the third's death. We should be cautious about accepting it without question, though, since if Spenser did die in 1790 he would by then have been eighty, a considerable age in the eighteenth century. Life expectancy of men who reached thirty was about sixty in the second half of the eighteenth century in England, so would have been slightly lower in Ireland given its relative impoverishment (life expectancy in Scotland was lower than in England).[174]

The final question might be whether, if we accept the date for his death as possible, we also give some credence to that epitaph with its reductively negative summary of Spencer's life. Certainly on achieving his majority he suffered financial distress as a result of his father's mismanagement of the estates, his guardian Busteed's palpable dishonesty, his father-in-law's apparent duplicity, and possibly his own extravagance; he also endured a long period of dreadful uncertainty up to 1752, when he eventually found employment in the revenue.[175] But from then to the point at which we lose sight of him he held a post in the Irish administration and was, at the same time, an agent for three substantial property-owners. He may have been working long hours for not a great deal of money, but, if the absence of complaints in his letters about a lack of income is anything to go by, he was financially secure. He may even have become the owner of rentable property himself if Welply is right in saying that in the early 1750s 'he seems to have been the owner of tenements in Castle Street' in the centre of Dublin — an investment that may have enabled him to retire in later life and make that move back to Mallow.[176]

It is possible, therefore, that Spencer spent his final years living once more the life of a gentleman in the country where he grew up, comfortably restored to the social position which this correspondence shows him struggling so hard to maintain. It

172 Gibson, *History of the County and City of Cork*, I, p. 314.

173 Ibid.; his reference for the letter is *Anthologia Hibernica*, 1793, pp. 189–90.

174 E. A. Wrigley and R. S. Schofield, *The Population History of England, 1541–1871* (Cambridge: Cambridge University Press, 1981), p. 250; R. A. Houston, *The Population History of Britain and Ireland 1500–1750* (Cambridge: Cambridge University Press, 1995), p. 40.

175 See Barnard, *Irish Protestant Ascents and Descents*, p. 293.

176 Welply, 'The Family and Descendants of Edmund Spenser', p. 57.

is equally possible, however, that in his later years he was oppressed again by that sense of low self-esteem that can be seen in some of his letters to Francis Price and looked back upon the past with a sense of gloomy regret.

But we are allowing ourselves here to be manœuvred into dubious speculation. In the end, disappointing though it may be having learnt so much through his correspondence about the detailed instances of the world Edmund Spencer inhabited, it is perhaps safer simply to accept that we do not know when, where, or how he departed from that world.

The Archive

Francis Price took care to store his considerable correspondence, and his widow and their son continued that habit, though with perhaps less consistency than Francis had. The son, Richard Parry Price, married twice, his first wife, Dorothea Byrne, dying in childbirth but leaving him a son, Francis Parry Price, who in time inherited the Overton and Birkenhead estates. Richard then married Anne Puleston with whom he had a son they named, rather confusingly, Richard Parry Price who inherited the estates his mother brought to the marriage and who consequently assumed the name Puleston.

It is this later son of Richard Price and grandson of Francis Price who, we can confidently assume, took charge of the considerable family archives and who possibly arranged for them to be properly bound in hard-cover volumes of approximately folio size numbering twenty seven altogether (of which thirteen contain the correspondence) and which became known as the Puleston Manuscripts. They were deposited in the National Library of Wales in 1921 by Crawshay Wellington Puleston.

The letters are bound into the volumes in such a way that, where the original paper is in good condition, they are glued into the spine of the volume along the folded edge or the left hand side of the sheet and so that the first side of the sheet on which the letter is written becomes the recto side of the page thus formed.[177] Where a sheet is damaged or in delicate condition it has been glued to a supporting sheet of paper on the address side of the sheet, holes having been made in the supporting paper to reveal any writing on that side of the sheet. The edges of the holes in the supporting paper have then been chamfered to obtain a smooth transition from the

177 Spencer mostly forms his letters in the standard way: for longer letters a whole sheet of paper is folded once in half to create four pages or sides; the letter is written with the middle fold to the left and starting on the first side; once the letter is finished, with the first side uppermost, the folded sheet is folded twice again, horizontally, into equal thirds, and then twice vertically but this time unequally, so that the left-hand edge of second folded portion falls short of the right-hand side of the packet thus formed leaving an edge across which wax can be applied to seal the packet; on the opposite side from the seal is a blank panel in which the address is written. Shorter letters are formed in a similar way, except that the folded sheet is cut in half along the spine to create a two-sided sheet of paper; the letter is written on one side, then the sheet turned anti-clockwise through ninety degrees; the right-hand side is folded over, but so as not to meet the left-hand edge; the top half of this folded sheet is then folded down but again so as not to meet the bottom edge; the uncovered bottom portion is then folded upwards to create an edge which can be sealed, and the address is written on the panel on the opposite side from the seal.

supporting paper to the original paper. This has had an adverse effect on legibility in only one case, and that is the letter of 1 September 1760: folio 117 which is a uniquely shaped sheet.[178]

Each sheet or folio has a number written in pencil in a circle in the top right-hand corner of whichever side the letter starts on, this being effectively an archivist's accession number. Though these numbers are not, strictly speaking, part of the transcription they provide a useful way to identify letters and other sheets and so have been retained, being enclosed in square brackets in the top right-hand corner of the page preceded by the word 'folio'. There is other archival numbering on some of the sheets but these have been ignored as they are of no help in identifying the folios on which they appear and have nothing to do with the original purpose of the letters.

Four of the letters in the volume containing the Spencer letters are not by him: the first two, folios 1 and 2, are to Alice Price from a tenant in Dublin and they post-date the earliest of the Spencer letters by some years. They have no apparent connection with the Spencer letters and there is no obvious reason for their being in this volume in terms of date, addressee, sender, or subject. They do explain, however, why the Spencer letters start at folio 3. The final two are from a Mr Williams to Francis Price and as they do have a bearing on his correspondence with Edmund Spencer they have been transcribed and are placed in Appendix I of this edition.

The Transcription

This edition aims to provide a fully diplomatic transcription of the contents of Puleston 20: NLW MS 3580E; that is to say, it aims to transfer as much as possible from the original manuscript into print. Transcription, though, is a process of approximation, and hence of loss. As Temma Berg puts it: 'no matter how obsessively you try, a printed letter will never look like the manuscript letter in your hand [...] [p]rinting inevitably and forever changes a written letter'.[179] However determinedly one tries to retain the characteristics and quirks of the autograph, one will always fail, if for none other than the simple reason that 'autographs are individual, print is uniform'[180] and that individuality varies not only from hand to hand — it varies within each hand: almost every instance of a given letter's inscription by a given writer will vary from all the other instances of that letter across the writer's life, and this is something that print can never hope to capture. Transcription helps modern readers by paring away the obfuscating aspects of unfamiliar handwriting, outdated orthographical conventions, and the deleterious effects of time on paper. However, simply by regularizing the almost infinite variation that characterizes handwriting, it cuts the reader off from the material substantiality of the original manuscript and our sense of the writer as an active, creatively thoughtful presence flowing across the page. A transcriber has to negotiate between what can be transferred

178 See the first note to this letter for further explanation.

179 Temma Berg, 'Truly Yours: Arranging a Letter Collection', *Eighteenth-Century Life*, 35, 1 (2011), 29–50 (p. 38).

180 Brant, *Eighteenth-Century Letters and British Culture*, p. 4.

from manuscript to print and what is recognized to be unique in the particular manuscript being transcribed.

For us the straightforwardly transferable seems to consist of Spencer's spelling, abbreviations, lineation, inter-line interpolation, and the positioning of any material outside the main body of the letter such as salutations, valedictions, postscripts, and afterthoughts, the placing of which have been retained because they are deliberately conscious acts on the part of the writer that might indicate, amongst other things, the social relationship between him and his correspondents and late or hurried revision.[181] The key word in that sentence, of course, is 'seems'. In general Spencer's hand is regular and clear, and his orthography, as has been observed, is very close to modern conventions; however, it soon became apparent to us that even in this apparently uncomplicated area, compromises would have to be made. The first was in the transference of his use of /u/ and /v/ in the middle of words since those letters are almost impossible to distinguish; their occurrences were therefore silently regularized to conform with modern orthographic convention.

Capital letters present a similar difficulty in that they are not always clearly upper case, especially /A/s /N/s and /M/s, all of which are formed in the same way as the lower case letters and so differ only in their relative size. Moreover, sentences are not always started with a capital and nouns are sometimes capitalized but by no means regularly, so that determining a specific usage through the writer's habits was not possible. This is not a simple matter as capitals might be an indication that Spencer regards a noun to be of particular significance (though it might also be simply a quirky decision, or an error): in the letter of 19 August 1744: folio 25, for example, he initially writes /the french/, as though he starts off thinking of the people of that nation as somehow below his notice, but then later relents and allows them the recognition of a capital.

Spencer's occasional use of obsolete marks is also problematic, especially in abbreviations such as in the word /pann/ in l.17 of the first letter (folio 3). These marks are no longer readily available, and here we have had to resort to what are in effect symbolic substitutes. One frequent mark that Spencer uses to signify abbreviation is a kind of superscript Greek /E/, as in the date on letter of 14 February 1743: folio 18; this mark is represented in the transcript by /∂/ though that is a very approximate rendering of his mark, and does not by any means cover all the varying ways in which Spencer makes or uses it. It is not always easy to tell, for instance, whether he is using this mark to indicate a superscript modern /y/ or a form of the obsolete letter thorn (the much misunderstood, not to mention misused, /y/ that appears in the self-consciously antiquated /ye/ of /ye olde tea shoppe/ and which actually represents, and was pronounced, /th/).

The other major aspect of the manuscript where we accepted that we would have to employ symbolic equivalents is where words or passages are irretrievably uncertain, illegible, deleted, or missing. In those cases we have had recourse to conventional transcription code, sometimes supported with explanatory footnotes.[182]

181 See, for example the valediction and side note to 19 November 1745: folio 37.

182 A key to the code is provided at the end of this Introduction.

Probably the most complicated area is punctuation. Spencer's punctuation has been retained as much as possible but with the acknowledgement that decisions are not always clear-cut. Commas, full-stops, colons, and semi-colons are all difficult: dots are not always easily distinguishable from small downward strokes, and the problem is compounded by spots of ink which might be random or accidental marks, or seepage of ink from the other side of the sheet. Again, because Spencer's punctuation does not follow modern rules it not easily predictable: commas, full-stops, and semi-colons seem interchangeable, and he will often use a colon where we would have a full-stop. When he does use a full-stop he frequently starts the next sentence with a lower case letter. He is prone to the grocer's apostrophe, especially in /its/ as a possessive.[183]

He also uses dashes very flexibly, both orthographically and semiotically. Sometimes they are straight and short (the length, say, of three or four of his letters); sometimes they are long (as much as half a line) with highly flourished upward and downward curls at their extremities.[184] They are almost always set low on the line which suggests strongly that they are being used as full stops, a theory that is reinforced by the fact that there is no other punctuation mark used with them; more specifically, perhaps they indicate full stops with an extra pause.[185] It is, furthermore, quite possible, given that there is usually a distinct change of subject after a dash, that they could also be acting as paragraph markers. If that is the case they might be designed to save space on the page, an important consideration for someone in Spencer's financial situation given the high price of paper.[186]

All these considerations render the punctuation more liable than the spelling to necessary editorial intervention, and rather than burden the footnotes with too much detail this intervention is mostly done silently.

The spacing between words is perhaps more contentious. In some situations, such as in formulaic valedictory expressions like /DearSir/, or in his signature, Spencer clearly runs words together. In those cases the lack of spacing is observed in the transcript. There are also longer breaks in some lines which seem to act as quasi-paragraph breaks, and these too have been observed, being given approximately the same length as they are in the manuscripts. However, handwriting does not regularize spacing between words in the way that print necessarily does, so where

183 See 27 November 1749: folio 88, ll.24 & 28 for examples.

184 This makes them very hard to render adequately in print, and we have compromised here by representing them only as straight lines.

185 Alexandra Harris, in *Weatherland: Writers and Artists Under English Skies* (London: Thames & Hudson, 2015), suggests that Keats used this punctuation mark in much same way, but in his case because 'he had to write furiously to keep up, preferring dashes to full stops because they were quicker' (p. 260).

186 For an interesting discussion of the use of dashes in eighteenth-century correspondence see Betty Rizzo, 'Banter and Testimony, Supplication and Praise, in the Letters of Christopher Smart', in *Sent as a Gift: Eight Correspondences from the Eighteenth Century*, ed. by Alan McKenzie (Athens & London: University of Georgia Press, 1993), pp. 68–89; it is interesting that Rizzo's observations on Smart's dashes correspond closely to Spencer's deployment of the mark: 'Dashes employed nowadays must be 1 to 3 ems. Smart's dashes, however, defy such standardization. Some of them are laid in low, like underlining, while others rise to the midletter position. They vary in length' (p. 85).

Spencer is, for instance, crowding words through lack of space the transcript acknowledges that he obviously intends to leave gaps between these words but can do so only by leaving the same space as it does between uncrowded words.

One other, very minor, variation from the manuscript is that placing superscript letters directly over the full stop marking an abbreviation cannot be achieved in the technology used for the print transcription, so the full stop precedes the superscript in the transcripts.

The question of ordering the transcription was a different matter. The order of the folios in the archive is generally chronological but there are instances where this is not the case; as these exceptions have no apparent rationale, are possibly the result of accidents that occurred in the archiving process, and disrupt the narrative quite severely the individual documents have been ordered as far as is possible chronologically.[187]

This means that the letter archived at the very end of the collection as folio 121, written in Chester when Spencer was on his way home from a visit to the Prices in Wales and thus datable to December 1741, is placed after folio 5 in the transcript. Similarly, the single letter from Spencer's daughter, Rosamond, to Alice Price is archived as folio 128 but is dated by Rosamond as 18 September 1758; that letter is therefore placed between two of her father's letters dated 12 May 1758: folio 110 and 8 December 1758: folio 111.

The three sheets written by Francis Price (folios 124, 125 & 126) are also archived together at the end, but as they can confidently be shown to be connected to particular letters from Spencer, they too have been placed in their chronological position so that these examples of Price's responding to letters from Spencer can be read in their proper place in the narrative formed by the collection as a whole. Their ordering in the transcript has not been determined by their dates (which are beyond conjecture) but by their relation to Spencer's letters and to one another.

There is one final category of material that is contained in the archive, and that is a number of sheets with accounts, expenses, and other tabulated information relevant to Spencer's work as the Prices' agent in Ireland. These cannot all be dated with certainty, and though they provide a fascinating sidelight on the narrative of his relationship with the Price family, they have been left where they are in the archive at the very end of the collection; this decision was made, it has to be said, without any great reluctance given that what they tell us about that relationship does not depend greatly on when they were produced.

The decision to adopt a chronological order for the transcription determined, in turn, the formula adopted for referencing the letters and other sheets. Though the archival numbers (written in circles and usually in the top right-hand corner of the sheet) provide an easy way of finding any given sheet in the archive, once we had arranged the collection chronologically these numbers no longer acted as a simple primary reference tool. We have therefore referenced letters by date first, and then by folio number, and other sheets simply by folio number. It is hoped that,

187 Most of the letters are clearly dated; where they are not it is possible to assign them a date with a very high degree of certainty. Conjectural dates are given in square brackets.

in combination, the date and folio number will make letters easy to find. Since only six of the sheets are out of order as determined by the folio number, generally speaking, that number will remain the easiest way to locate a letter. For the few remaining sheets which have no date further information will be given, wherever possible, about adjacent sheets that will enable readers to find them with reasonable ease.

Key to Transcription Conventions

<*> / <****> / <*** ** ****> = illegible letter / word / phrase, the approximate length of the word or phrase being indicated by the number of asterisks; explanations for the illegibility are given in footnotes when thought necessary or helpful.

[*example*] = unclear letters or words that can be deciphered with reasonable certainty.

~~example~~ = legible deletions.

[*~~example~~*] = unclear deletions that can be deciphered with reasonable certainty.

<~~xxxx~~> = illegible deletions.

{*blot*} = editorial explanation or information (such as missing material, or the nature of damage that removes or obliterates letters, words, or phrases).

italics = letters, words, phrases, or passages in a different hand from that of the main body of a letter or document.

—————————— = end of a page in original letter

Addresses are given at the head of each letter in roman type and enclosed in square brackets; additional material written around the address and in a hand other than Spencer's is italicized and also enclosed in the square brackets.

Please note that the folio numbers (in square brackets in the top right-hand corner of the page), having been added at a later date for archival purposes, are not strictly part of the transcription of the letter or sheet to which they apply and so are not covered by these conventions.

Chronological Listing of the Folios

Spenser uses Old Style when dating letters up to 1752; in order to clarify the chronological sequence the New Style year is indicated here in square brackets when he gives a date in Old Style — e.g, 10 January 1743[4].

Where a date, place of origin or addressee is not given in the letter it can be conjectured, nearly always with a high degree of certainty; where this is the case the conjecture is enclosed in square brackets (see the letter in question for an explanation of the conjecture).

Date	*Folio*	*Addressee*	*Place of Origin*
6 February 1732 [3?]	3	Francis Price	Ballinguile, near Charleville
2 August 1741	4	Francis Price	Castlelyons
21 November 1741	5	Francis Price	Dublin
[December 1741]	121	Francis Price	Chester
[January 1742]	6	Francis Price	[Dublin]
4 October 1743	7	Francis Price	near Charleville
8 November 1743	8	Francis Price	near Charleville
22 November 1743	9	Francis Price	near Charleville
6 December 1743	10	Francis Price	near Charleville
13 December 1743	11	Francis Price	near Charleville
27 December 1743	12	Francis Price	near Charleville
10 January 1743[4]	13	Francis Price	near Charleville
21 January 1743[4]	14	Francis Price	Dublin
31 January 1743[4]	15	Francis Price	Dublin
	[The intervening sheets are not letters.]		
14 February 1743[4]	18	Francis Price	Dublin
25 February 1743[4]	19	Francis Price	Dublin
26 March 1744	20	Francis Price	near Charleville
15 May 1744	21	Francis Price	Renny, near Castlelyons
29 May 1744	22	Francis Price	Renny
29 June 1744	23	Francis Price	Renny, near Castlelyons
24 July 1744	24	Francis Price	Renny
19 August 1744	25	Francis Price	Renny
29 September 1744	26	Francis Price	Renny
5 November 1744	27	Francis Price	Renny
18 January 1744/5	28	Francis Price	Renny
4 March 1744[5]	29	Francis Price	Renny
10 April [1745]	30	Francis Price	near Castlelyons
23 May 1745	31	Francis Price	Renny
1 July 1745	32	Francis Price	Renny
26 July 1745	33	Francis Price	Renny
20 August 1745	34	Francis Price	Renny
10 September 1745	35	Francis Price	Renny
10 October 1745	36	Francis Price	Renny
19 November 1745	37	Francis Price	Dublin
30 November 1745	38	Francis Price	Dublin [College Green]
[Conjectural dating]	124	[Draft written by Francis Price]	
7 December 1745	39	Francis Price	Dublin
[?] December [1745]	40	Francis Price	Dublin
[21 January 1746]	41	Francis Price	Dublin
4 February [1746]	42	Francis Price	Dublin
24 February 1745[6]	43	Francis Price	Dublin

15 March 1745[6]	44	Francis Price	Dublin [Fishamble Street]
5 April 1746	45	Francis Price	Dublin [Fishamble Street]
19 April 1746	46	Francis Price	Dublin [Fishamble Street]
15 May 1746	47	Francis Price	Dublin
27 May 1746	48	Francis Price	[Bennet's Bridge, Kilkenny]
24 June 1746	49	Francis Price	Renny
16 July 1746	50	Francis Price	Renny
26 August 1746	51	Francis Price	Renny
3 October 1746	52	Francis Price	Renny
10 November 1746	53	Francis Price	Renny
16 December 1746	54	Francis Price	Renny
26 January 1746[7]	55	Francis Price	Renny
26 February 1746[7]	56	Francis Price	Renny, near Castlelyons
28 March 1747	57	Francis Price	Renny
25 May 1747	58	Francis Price	[Renny]
16 June 1747	59	Francis Price	Renny, near Castlelyons
9 October 1747	60	Francis Price	Renny, near Castlelyons
16 October 1747	61	Francis Price	Renny
17 November 1747	62	Francis Price	Dublin [Dick's Coffee House]
5 December 1747	63	Francis Price	Dublin
15 December 1747	64	Francis Price	Dublin
5 January 1747[8]	65	Francis Price	Dublin
[1]6 January 1747[8]	66	Francis Price	Dublin
2 February 1747[8]	67	Francis Price	Dublin [Dick's Coffee House]
4 February 1747[8]	68	Francis Price	Dublin
16 February 1747[8]	69	Francis Price	Dublin
1 March 1747[8]	70	Francis Price	Renny, near Castlelyons
25 March 1748	71	Francis Price	Renny, near Castlelyons
25 April 1748	72	Francis Price	Renny
13 May 1748	73	Francis Price	Renny
3 July 1748	74	Francis Price	near Castlelyons
5 August 1748	75	Francis Price	[Renny]
13 September 1748	76	Francis Price	Renny
25 October 1748	77	Francis Price	[Renny]
8 November 1748	78	Francis Price	Dublin [Fishamble Street]
1 December 1748	79	Francis Price	Dublin [Fishamble Street]
10 December 1748	80	Francis Price	Dublin
20 [January] 1748[9]	81	Francis Price	[near Castlelyons]
[Conjectural dating]	127	[Draft of memorial]	[Not applicable]
[Conjectural dating]	125	[Draft written by Francis Price]	
[Conjectural dating]	126	[Draft written by Francis Price]	
21 February 1748[9]	82	Francis Price	near Castlelyons

28 February 1748[9]	83	Francis Price	near Castlelyons
2 June 1749	84	Francis Price	near Castlelyons
21 July 1749	85	Francis Price	near Castlelyons
25 September 1749	86	Alice Price	near Castlelyons
16 November 1749	87	Alice Price	Dublin [Dick's Coffee House]
27 November 1749	88	Alice Price	Dublin [Dick's Coffee House]
2 December 1749	89	Alice Price	Dublin [Dick's Coffee House]
28 July 1750	90	John Buchan	Dublin
30 August 1750	91	John Buchan	Charleville
31 December 1750	92	John Buchan	Charleville
19 April 1751	93	John Buchan	[Charleville]
14 January 1752	94	Alice Price	Dublin
26 June 1755	95	Alice Price	Dublin
19 July 1755	96	Alice Price	Dublin
18 November 1755	97	Alice Price	Dublin
24 February 1756	98	Alice Price	Dublin
8 April 1756	99	Alice Price	Wicklow
8 April 1756	100	Richard Price	Wicklow
9 July 1756	101	Alice Price	Wicklow
29 August 1756	102	Alice Price	Wicklow
26 September 1756	103	Alice Price	Wicklow
10 October 1756	104	Alice Price	Wicklow
11 November 1756	105	Alice Price	Dublin
22 December 1756	106	Alice Price	Wicklow
21 February 1757	107	Alice Price	Dublin [Mary Street]
[Conjectural dating]	123	[Summary of legal expenses]	
23 March 1757	108	Alice Price	Wicklow
7 August 1757	109	Alice Price	Wicklow
12 May 1758	110	Alice Price	Dublin
18 September 1758	128	Alice Price	Waterford [from R. Spencer]
8 December 1758	111	Alice Price	Waterford
15 February 1759	112	Alice Price	Dublin
27 October 1759	113	Alice Price	Waterford
8 December 1759	114	Alice Price	Dublin [Mary Street]
31 December 1759	115	Alice Price	Waterford
12 March 1760	116	Alice Price	Waterford
1 September 1760	117	Alice Price	Waterford
27 February 1761	118	Richard Price	Waterford
21 October 1761	119	Richard Price	Waterford
28 June 1762	120	Richard Price	Waterford
[28 November 1774]	122	[Accounts sheet]	

THE LETTERS

[folio 3]

[To Mr Fra[*nc*]is Price.
at Overton near Wrexham
<*> Chester [*Post*]]

Feb: 6: 1732

Dr Couz

I am extreamly obliged to you for your kind Epistle and more so for your good Advice. I should have troubled you long e'er this with a Letter but feard it may not be taken as [*well as I*] hoped, but now to my great Satisfaction, am now convinced of the contrary. As to my matrimonial Affairs I hope I have taken Such [*Care of them as*] it will please all my friends; being to gett a Thousand pounds & three years [*Diet &*] Lodging

This first letter is severely faded on the recto side, and many areas of the page are also damaged by staining; this deterioration is possibly the result of the sheet's having been exposed on the top of the collection before it was bound into the collection Puleston 20: NLW MS 3580E; the inside of the sheet (on which are the last two lines of the letter, the valediction, and address of origin) is much less faded, and that would support such a theory. The letters have been numbered in pencil (usually in the top right-hand corner) starting at 3, numbers 1 and 2 being letters from two other correspondents which have been bound into the same volume as the Spencer letters. This letter is interesting in that it uses /-ed/ forms of the past tense, a spelling that Spencer had mostly abandoned by the time of the next letter in the collection for /-d/, some eight and a half years later; as he is at most twenty-one years old when he wrote this it may not be considered surprising that he changes his habits in that period.

Address] Overton is some ten miles south-east of Wrexham in Wales; that might not seem 'near' given eighteenth-century transport, but Spencer does, at the end of this letter, describe Ballinguile as being 'near Charleville' where the distance is eight miles, and Renny he gives as being near Castlelyons, where the distance is nearly twelve miles, though he will be using the Irish mile which was about a third longer than the British mile (see also note to l.24 below). /Overton/ is very faint. The remaining letters to Francis Price have only his name as an address: this is because Price obtains franks from friends which he then sends Spencer (see note to l.21 of 16 June 1747: folio 59).

Date] given that Spencer often uses Old Style when giving dates it is possible that this letter was written in February 1733.

Salutation] /Dr/ is an abbreviation of 'Dear' and /couz/ of 'cousin'; however, the precise relationship between Spencer and Price — if, indeed, there was any — is unknown: 'couz' could mean 'cousin' in the currently predominant sense of 'son of an uncle or aunt', but it could also refer to any number of familial relationships outside the immediate circle of parents and siblings as well as simply indicating a strong friendship (*OED*, n. 5.b). It is interesting that Spencer never again uses this form of address to Price in the salutation of his letters.

1–4 I am [...] the contrary] this first sentence implies that there was some correspondence before this — at least one letter to which Francis Price replied and to which this one is the response — and also that there has been some sort of hiatus in the friendship between Spencer and Price (or that Spencer thought there had been); however, as we have not got

for my self Serv^{ts} & Horses, besides near four years that I have [*been*] already here for which I am to pay Nothing, I should be in far better circumstances tha[*n I am at pre*]sent were I used as a Guardian‸$^{\text{ought to}}$ ~~and~~ behave to a Minor, for Upon <***> to the [*Case*], Coun: Busteed entirely left [*me*] to my self, [*without*] takeing <********> [*to*] place me any where to [*keep me*] out of [*bad*] Company, which <**********> pleased to afford [*me*] Caution [*enough to avoid*], and thereupon <*****> [*Mr Freeman for*] my Guardian who upon Enquiry into my Affairs discovered, that not [*One*] penny Intrest was paid to S^{r}Richd Mead since the Death of my Father, which you may [*readily judge*] <*> augment a very great load on my embarrased Fortunes, [*These four years the Rent of*] Killcoleman has been paid to S^{r}Richard, being <**> hundred pounds pann

the earlier letters, and there is a nine-year gap between this and the next one, we have no idea what happened to cause Spencer's worry.

10 Coun:] i.e., a counsellor, a member of the legal profession who gave advice to clients and conducted their cases in court.

10 Busteed] this was one of the two trustees of Spencer's father's will; it is interesting that Spencer does not mention the other one, Arthur Hyde (see Barnard, *Irish Protestant Ascents and Descents*, p. 293), who is possibly the Col. Hyde, referred to in the letter of 28 March 1747: folio 57, l.5, and who became MP for Cork in that year, or possibly, as Welply suggests in 'The Family and Descendants of Edmund Spenser (contd)', p. 55, his father, who was also called Arthur Hyde; however, since the elder Hyde died in in 1720 or 1721 he would have been a guardian for only about a year; the son was only twenty two or twenty three years old when Nathaniel Spencer died in 1719 so may seem too young to take on such a responsibility, but he was elected MP for Youghal in 1721 (holding it until 1727) and was a married man; whichever Hyde it was, he may not be mentioned here because, contrary to Barnard's belief that he was as dishonest as Busteed, Hyde possibly did behave 'as a Guardian ought to' towards Spencer by arranging for him to attend school (see the Introduction). See also, however, 2 June 1749: folio 84, where Spencer suggests that Hyde believes 'getting and keeping Money to be the main Pleasure of Life' (ll.14–15). Sometime before 1720, the year of Nathaniel Spencer's death, Hyde married an Ann Price from Co. Tipperary; as that county is adjacent to Co. Cork it is remotely possible that he thus had a family connection with Francis Price, and hence also with the Spencers.

13 *Mr Freeman*] the woman Spencer has just married was named Freeman so this could be his father-in-law; Welply states that Spencer's father-in-law 'asserted in 1734, that Edmund "had been greatly wronged by his guardians, and that he is a great sufferer by their ill-conduct"' ('The Family and Descendants of Edmund Spenser', p. 55). However, Spencer also refers in l.24 to an uncle who speaks to Lord Barrymore about his affairs, so it could be a brother of the father-in-law. He mentions elsewhere a William Freeman (29 September 1744: folio 26, l.2; 23 May 1745: folio 31, l.40; 26 August 1746: folio 51, l.3; 28 February 1748: folio 83, l.18) describing him in the last of those letters as a cousin, and given that familial relationships could be quite loosely defined it is possible that this is the same person, especially as in folio 31 he calls Freeman his 'one friend left in Ireland' (l.40) and in folio 83 says that he fixed the price of Renny when it was sold in 1748, suggesting that Spencer considered him trustworthy, especially concerning financial affairs. That is more than could be said for the father-in-law, whose dubious behaviour with regard to Spencer's financial affairs is described by Francis Price in the narrative of Spencer's troubles given in folios 124 & 125 — though that duplicity had at this stage yet to be revealed.

Notwithstanding all this palpable Fraud committed by the good Counsellor he still proffesses a Sincere Friendship & Affection [*for me & out*] of his exceeding Liberality acknowledges himself 500$^{£}$ in my [*debt but*] to [*his*] <*> disatisfaction will prove three times the [*Sume*], tho I [*am unsure*] whether ever I ∧^{shall} gett a Shilꝺ from him –– . By the Advice of my Lord Barrymore / who was so kind to speak to my Uncle on my affairs / and the rest [*of*] my friends I design to dispose of Renny & the Wood, which together [*with*] my wife's Fortune will make me entirely easy & stock <**************> I have taken into my own Hands, where I [*design to build*] <*********> managed so that I shall this year make above two hundred <**>

———————————

14 S^{r}Richd Mead] possibly the great-grandson of Sarah Travers, the sister of the Elizabethan Spenser; in 1738 Mead had mortgages amounting to £2,000 on estates left by the poet to his descendants — see Hadfield, *Edmund Spenser*, p. 412, and also folio 124, where Price notes that Spencer's father sold off three parts of his estates and mortgaged 'the remains [...] for 2000' (ll.12–13); the implication here may be that Busteed passed on the rents of Kilcolman to Mead rather than paying the interest due on the mortgages, thereby building up a debt for Spencer to repay later while simultaneously depriving him of the rents to Kilcolman. Price's accounts of Spencer's early life in folios 124 and 125 (see note to 124, l.17 and 125, ll.36–38) may indicate that Kilcolman had to be given up by Spencer to pay off some of those debts, perhaps also redeeming the mortgage by passing it on to Mead, who later had a legal dispute with a Captain Web which involved Kilcolman and possibly related to the rents, see 29 May [1744]: folio 22, ll.14–17 and note.

17 Killcoleman] Kilcolman Castle was once the residence of Edmund Spenser. It was roughly thirty miles due north of Cork, ten miles north-west of Renny (where Spencer grew up and lived for several years during the period of this correspondence), and about three miles due west of Ballinguile where he is now writing.

17 pann] this should perhaps be transcribed as /p[er] ann/ as the /p/ has a stroke before it which doubles the descender so possibly making it the conventional abbreviation of /per/; however, since Spencer abbreviates, his abbreviation is kept here.

20 500$^{£}$] the superscript letter is not very clear here, though elsewhere these marks are more obviously a flourished /l/ and hence short for /livres/; they are therefore represented here as /$^{£}$/. In this instance the mark is actually placed above the number rather than after it.

22 Shilꝺ] most probably an abbreviation of /shilling/; the last letter of this word, which looks very like an /l/, ends with an upward flourish often used by Spencer (and often in a superscript form) to indicate abbreviation.

22 Lord Barrymore] James Barry, 4th Earl of Barrymore (1667–1748) was descended from an Anglo-Norman dynasty settled in Ireland since the twelfth century and was heir to one of the oldest baronies in Ireland. He owned substantial estates in Co. Cork but seems to have spent most of his life in England; between 1724 and 1727 he appears to have been 'firmly installed at Rock Savage in Cheshire as heir both to the extensive Rivers estates in that and the neighbouring counties and to the influence that these exerted over the political life of north-west England', but in 1727 he returned to Cork and to Irish political life, whilst keeping a house in London and remaining an MP for Wigan. He served in William II's army in the late 1680s, later converted to Jacobism and in the 1740s was accused of conspiring to support a French invasion to restore the Young Pretender, though after the

It gives me great pleasure that you Design to be with us next Summer and shall expect your arrival with Impatience because I am

D[r] Couz

Your Affectionate Kinsman
& very humble Servant
Edm Spencer

If you please to favour me
with a Letter Direct for me
at Ballinguile near Charleville

collapse of the 1745 uprising he was not prosecuted (*DIB* & *ODNB*). (See also 26 March 1744: folio 20, ll.6–9.)

24 Renny] according to the address given in 15 May 1744: folio 21, Renny is 'near Castlelyons' but it is in fact some twelve miles north-west of that village and is much closer to Castletownroche. It lies on what is now the N72, just above the River Blackwater and some twenty miles due north of Cork. In 8 November 1743: folio 8, Spencer tells his cousin that 'The bad Price for all our Commoditys has obliged my Tennant to surrender Renny, so that I must take it into my own hands the first of May next'. In 15 May 1744: folio 21, he writes that 'I have at last settled Renny for this year', but 'coud not undertake to occupy the Land', and so, 'in Order further to assist the Tenant am come to board with him'. Whether this is the same tenant as the one who occupied Renny in 1743 is impossible to say. Nothing is left of the buildings Spencer would have known.

Postscript] Ballinguile is just north of Buttevant, eight miles north of Mallow and some seven miles south of Charleville, which is roughly forty miles north of Cork on the road to Limerick and, according to Lewis, Ireland, 'is of comparatively recent origin, having been founded [...] in the year 1661'. Spencer's wife came from Ballinguile. Contrary to his later usual practice Spencer gives no address at the head of this letter, but this may be where he is writing from now as he expects to be there when he receives a reply from Price.

[folio 4]

[To Francis Price Esqr]

Dear Sir /

The great Dependance I have on your friendship, on Account of the many Obligations received when you continued in this Kingdom, makes me trouble you with this, to give you an account of the Disapointment I received by the Death of Baron Wainwright, by whom I was promised a pair of Colours, w.^{ch}, had he lived, I should certainly have obtain'd; on his promise, I set my Land & sold my Stock, & have been these two years at great Expence at Lodgings, which makes the Disapointment the more considerable. I have been frequently advised by my friends, that if I coud by any Means be made known to the Duke of Marlbourough, his Grace woud certainly procure some Employment for me either civil or military, on Account of my Family, and in consideration of my being descended from the famous Poet of his Name. what I therefore earnestly beg of you, is, that you woud please to speak to the Lord Barrymore, to apply to the Duke in my Favour / if he is intimate with him / or some other of your Acquaintance, that may be known to him; and I am certain that by that Means I shall obtain something to help to main = tain my growing Charge; what little I have left being so shatterd that without some Help / which by your Assistance I expect / I cannot possibly subsist. I hope you will pardon this Trouble; & comply with this Request of Dear Sir

Your affect.^{te} Kinsman & most
obliged humble Servant
Edm Spencer

CastleLyons
August the 2.^{d} 1741

2–3 when you [...] Kingdom] this is the first indication that Price originally lived in Ireland and subsequently moved to Wales; for further information about Price's familial connection with Ireland see 19 July 1755: folio 96, and the Introduction.

5 a pair of colours] the two flags (one royal the other the regimental) belonging to a regiment and hence, by metonymy, an Ensign, the lowest rank of commissioned officer, and the soldier responsible for these flags, particularly in battle.

6 set] probably 'let on a lease', the usual sense in which Spencer uses this word (*OED*, *set*, v.57.a).

9 Duke of Marlbourough] Charles Spencer, 3rd Duke of Marlborough (1706–1758), best known for his service in the Seven Years War (1756–1763), was at this point a colonel in the 38th Foot. He was the grandson of the famous first duke, John Churchill (1650–1722), and inherited the title after the Duchess of Marlborough, his aunt, the daughter of the first duke, died (*ODNB*). Though the surname was shared, a family relationship between Spencer and the Duke, if any existed at all, would have been extremely remote.

17 shatterd] 'damaged or destroyed' (*OED*, v.2.c); the word is slightly uncertain in the manuscript.

Address CastleLyons] a village approximately eight miles south of Fermoy and fifteen miles north of Cork, 'chiefly in the barony of Barrymore' (Lewis, Ireland). The castle (which burned down in 1771) was the main Irish residence of Lord Barrymore and and the place of his burial.

[folio 5]

[To Fran.^{s} Price Esqr]

Dear Sir

I am now using the Interest of the late Baron Wainwright's Friends to procure for me the Comission which the Lord Lieutenant promised that Gentleman for me, & as 'twill be an Affair that will take up some time I believe I must continue in Town the whole Winter. I therefore propose doing my self the Pleasure of waiting on you at Christmas / if you continue at home at that Season, / & stay for the fort = night at Wales, that this Court will be in the Country. for besides the pleasure I shall receive in seeing you twill be far less Fatigue to go to Chester than to the County of Cork & back again. if I may flatter my self with the Hopes of a Letter please to direct at the Custom house Coffee House. I am Dear Sir

Your affect.^{te} Kinsman
& most humble Servant
Edm Spencer

Dublin
Novr the 21.st 1741

6–7 I therefore [...] at Christmas] as the following two letters demonstrate this pleasure Spencer duly gives himself, but as is revealed by the letter from William Pearde to Price (printed in Appendix I) that pleasure was somewhat delayed by his arrest for debt in Dublin on Christmas Eve of this year

9 Country.] the stop is not absolutely certain here, but Spencer frequently does not capitalize the first letter of a sentence (as in l.12).

14 the Custom house Coffee House] one of the many coffee houses in the vicinity of the old Dublin Custom House which was situated at the southern end of Essex Bridge on Essex Quay (and hence on the opposite side of the Liffey from the present Custom House which was not built until the 1780s); coffee houses were commonly used as places to conduct business in this period, so presumably their use by people from outside the city as informal *poste restante* addresses would have followed on from that practice (see Máirtín Mac Con Iomaire, 'Coffee Culture in Dublin: A Brief History', Dublin Institute of Technology, <http://arrow.dit.ie/cgi/viewcontent.cgi?article=1139&context=tfschafart> [accessed 12 August 2014].

[folio 121]

Chester Saturday Evening

Dear Sir

As soon as I dispatchd Francis, I strolld to the bowling green; where I heard a piece of news that I could not forbear informing you of, Mr Dickens y^{e} Doctors nephew has privately married one of the miss Houghton's, & her father is so angry at it, that he will not see her, tho' tis thought she made a better match than if she had let him choose for her. I saw your friend Hurt who tells me, that I shall have the honour of Mr Coppinger's his Lady's & son's Company aboard the Yacht, which is ex=pected at Parkgate to morrow. my Lord Barrymore came home last night. I beg you will present my best Respects to Mrs Price and my dear Mr Richard: & believe that I am Dear Sir

Y^{r} sincerely affec^{te} Kinsman
& obliged humble Servant
EdmSpencer

Service to all inquiring friends

Address of origin and date] as the folio number shows, this letter was placed out of order before those numbers were added and, lacking a date, was presumably just put in at the back of the sheaf of papers. It has been placed here to maintain the chronology of the narrative. As the valediction refers to 'Mrs Price and my dear Mr Richard' the letter was clearly written to Price; it most likely follows 21 November 1741: folio 5 (in which Spencer proposes to visit Price in Wales for Christmas) and precedes [January 1742]: folio 6, from which the date is also missing, but which refers to landing at Dunlary near Dublin after a rough sea voyage (which would have been from Chester). The letter from William Pearde to Price (referred to in the note to ll.6–7 of the previous letter) which describes Spencer's arrest in Dublin on Christmas Eve 1741 when he was about to 'sett Sail for England' (l.5) corroborates this date. Such spelling habits as would be consistent with the date also correspond, and folio 6 has a similar postscript: 'Pray give my Service to All enquiring friends'. The letter was written in pencil on an A5-sized piece of thick paper, possibly in haste in his inn.

Addressee] there is neither an addressee nor address for the letter so how this reached Price is a mystery; it is possible that the letter was not actually sent from Chester but was enclosed with the next letter which was written in Dublin.

1 Francis] the rather peremptory 'dispatchd' and use of the first name suggest that Francis was a servant, quite possibly one sent to Chester with Spencer to bring back a horse lent to him for the journey by Price.

4 Mr Dickens [...] nephew] most likely the son of Dr George Dickins, a Liverpool acquaintance and regular correspondent of Price.

9 Mr Coppinger's] Jack Coppinger was a friend and tenant of Lord Barrymore who leased Barryscourt, Carrigtwohill, about thirty miles from Spencer's home at Renny. Thomas Kingsbury writing to Francis Price notes that the Coppingers visited the Barrymores in December 1746 (letter dated 15 December 1746, Puleston 24: NLW MS 3584E).

11 Parkgate] a village on the Wirral Peninsula north of Chester; in the eighteenth century it was on the River Dee and an embarkation point for Ireland.

11–12 my Lord [...] last night] given the speed of the contemporary postal service Spencer could not have received news of Barrymore's return to a house in Ireland or London so this must be Rock Savage, a house in Runcorn, Cheshire, which was at one point Barrymore's main residence; as it was only a few miles from Chester Spencer has presumably picked up some gossip, possibly from servants or employees of Barrymore in Chester on the Lord's business.

13 Respects to [...] Mr Richard] Francis Price's wife and son respectively; this is the first time Spencer sends his respects to them, and from now on every letter to Price ends with the same phrase (or something very similar); as the adoption of this valedictory formula follows immediately after his Christmas visit to Overton, it perhaps suggests that Spencer met them for the first time on that occasion.

[folio 6]

[To Francis Price Esqr]

not make Port till two o'clock in the afternoon of Wednesday & then forced to land at Dunlary, where I found it difficult to get a convenience to bring me here wch after two hours delay to procure, cost me double what it ought to have done. The Lord & Lady Meath were of the Passengers, of wch there were a great many, my Lady is a very agreeable good humourd person & the only one aboard / except me / who was not sick: So that I had the sole pleasure of her company, which was very entertaining, & diverted her at times at Cards. I have troubled $_{\wedge}$^{you} the more with this tedious acc.^{t} of my passage as I have not heard anything since I arrived worth acquainting you of. I intend to wait on the Doctor to morrow — morning & leave town on Munday or Thursday next; but that must be as I can procure a place in the Stage — I entreat you will make my best Respects acceptable to Coz.^{n} Price & my dear Mr Richard: that God may bless her & you with the continuance of health & life to him I hope you will believe are the sincere wishes of D^{E}Sir

Your most affect.^{te} Kinsman
& obliged humble Servant
Edm Spencer

Pray give my Service to
All enquiring friends

The date, address, salutation, and some of the first lines are missing from this letter which has been cut quite substantially across the top. It would appear to follow the Christmas visit to Wales proposed in the letter of 21 November 1741: folio 5 as it describes arriving in Ireland after a voyage from Chester (see the preceding letter, folio 121, written in Chester) which would date this letter January 1742. The intention to stay in 'town' for some days (l.14) suggests that it was written in Dublin (but see next note).

2 Dunlary] probably Dún Laoghaire, 'a Sea-port, situate on the South side of Dublin Bay' (Carlisle, Ireland) and approximately seven miles from the centre of Dublin, rather than Dunleary near Cove in Co. Cork (the latter being some fifty miles west of Cork and so well out of the way for a ship plying between North Wales and Ireland, unless the ship was heading for Cork but the storm forced it further along the coast). However, (a) the reference to 'town' suggests the capital, and (b) if he had landed in Dunleary one would expect Spencer to go straight from there to his house near Charleville (about a thirty-five mile journey further on from Cork) rather than stop off in Cork for several days.

3 convenience] some form of conveyance such as a coach (*OED*, n.7.d).

5 Lord and Lady Meath] Chaworth Brabazon (1686–1763) became 6th Earl of Meath in 1715; he was MP for Dublin 1713–1714; he first married his aunt's chambermaid but never lived with her; in 1731, he married Juliana Prendergast with whom he had been in love for several years, though she had 'little or no fortune and [was] far from handsome' (*HIP*).

13 the Doctor] possibly the unnamed Doctor referred to in folio 121; this may or may not be Doctor Kingsbury, who handled some of Price's Irish business affairs (see 25 May 1747: folio 58) and who, it would appear from 25 February 1745: folio 19, lived in Dublin.

[folio 7]

[To Francis Price Esqr]

near Charleville October the 4.th 1743

Dear Sir

I have the Favour of yours, which gives me great Pleasure as by it I am informed of your & Family's being well: I return my sincere Thanks for the Trouble you give your self in soliciting for me, & do not doubt but thro' your interest I may yet be provided for; be it so or not your many Favours bestowed on me, shall be always most gratefully ~~ac~~= knowleged --- I congratulate you on the fine Weather which has attended your husbandry; Muck / no doubt / will soon retrieve Ast[*er*]y ground: since my landing there has been the finest Weath.^{r} that was ever ~~since~~ seen at the season, I have cut & reekd hay since the beginning of the last Month — I returned last night from Roches Country where I have been these ten days, & where I had the Favour of seeing Mr Welsh, who is in very bad plight having lost his House; he wishes himself in Wales again, from whence I believe he woud not be in any Hurry to return. They are poor Farmers in that Country, for half their Corn still remains in the Fields, but to my great surprize Capt Stannard has not one old stack in his yard. The Acc^{t} of Mr Stradwick is like the rest of his Memoirs, very miraculous, & his Fathers Benediction, I think, worthy the giver & receiver. I fear the Jamaica Expedition will produce little more than the Savoy mines; but with my whole Soul I pitty his poor Wife sure the party that

brought her into this Misfortune, will take Care of her in her Husband's absence, if they have a scruple of Honour Honesty or Conscience left. This Country is so baren of any affair worth mentioning that I have nothing to inform you that coud any ways entertain; the Complaints of the Farmers ab^{t} the lowness of <~~x~~> Commoditys is all that's to be heard, & Landlords dunning their Ten.^{ts}, which happens pritty much to be my Case, for where I expected to have reced a little money upon Demand, I was obliged to be content with a putt off, & coud not in conscience press too home as marketts go -------
My wife joins me in our best Respects to you Mrs Price & my Dear Mr Richard. believe that I am D^{E}Sir

Your sincerely affec^{te} Kinsman
& obliged humble Servant
EdmSpencer

Pray present my Service to Mr Smith & all friends

7 Weather] Spencer mentions the weather in 16 letters altogether, mostly, as here, in relation to agricultural activities but sometimes for its own sake, as in 1 March 1747: folio 70, where he describes a journey home from Dublin during which the weather changed from an intense frost to snow, then to rain, and finally to 'very pleasant Weather: so that in this one Journey, I have it to say I experienced most Sorts of Weather' (ll. 6–7). Commenting on the weather in this way was a comparatively new development: Harris (*Weatherland*) notes of the seventeenth-century diarist John Evelyn that 'weather was not part of the daily texture of his recorded life until the 1680s. From that time [...] there begin to be comments about warm days, groans about rain, a sense of how weather affects one's clothing, work, and spirits. By the 1710s Jonathan Swift would be keeping up a running commentary [on the weather] in his letters' (p. 124); by the middle of the eighteenth century it was becoming fashionable to take note of and discuss the weather as a sign that one was interested in the scientific principles of the Enlightenment, see Jan Golinski, *British Weather and the Climate of Enlightenment* (Chicago: Chicago University Press, 2012).

9 Ast[*er*]y ground] obscure; the reference to 'your husbandry' and the tentative 'no doubt' suggest that Spencer is responding to something Price mentioned in his last letter; for *astre* ('a hearth or home') *OED* gives an example from 1882 illustrating a specifically Welsh usage, '[In] Montgomeryshire [...] Auster-land is that which had a house upon it in ancient times' so this could be a piece of ground owned by Price on which a house once stood (perhaps an earlier building which Bryn y Pys replaced) and where the soil is therefore particularly poor; whatever the explanation the comment is interesting in that it reveals Spencer's close, practical interest in agricultural matters such as soil cultivation.

10 Reekd] 'piled up to form ricks' (*OED*, *reek*, v^{3}).

12 Roches Country] as it is suggested in 2 February 1747: folio 67, ll.2–3, that Welsh lived in Ballyhooly, a village on the Blackwater River near Renny, this is presumably the area around Castletown-Roche which lay very close to Renny, midway between Mallow and Fermoy.

18–19 The Acc^{t} [...] Memoirs] Mr Stradwick is probably Henry Strudwick, a mutual acquaintance; Puleston 18: NLW MS 3578E contains two letters (folios 80 and 82) from Henry Strudwick, both being dated 1740 and from Dieppe in France; in the second of these letters he says that he has visited his father in France; the word 'Acc^{t}' may refer to a conversation between that Mr Strudwick and Price which Price reported in his last letter to Spencer; no memoirs by an author named Stradwick or Strudwick come up when the name is entered in Eighteenth Century Collections Online (ECCO) so 'Memoirs' may be a mildly sarcastic observation on this gentleman's tendency to reminisce at length — and perhaps somewhat pompously — when in company. Whether the references to the Jamaica expedition and the Savoy mines that follow are also connected to him is not obvious from the grammar or the syntax of the passage, though the colon might indicate some such connection, and the mention of 'his wife' in l.22 might also refer us back to him and his 'memoirs'.

20–21 the Jamaica Expedition] probably a reference to the unsuccessful naval operations undertaken during the early 1740s to wrest control from the Spanish of the major sea routes through the West Indies and thence to their colonies in Central and South America; Admiral Vernon, the naval commander, had made Port Royal in Jamaica his centre of operations. Factional squabbling at home, dissension between Vernon and Wentworth (the military commander), and severe depletion of their forces through disease all contributed to the failure of the campaign and the two commanders were recalled to England in early 1743. Spencer possibly makes a comparison between those events and the Savoy mines because the lack of military success in the former case might have undermined confidence in the financial viability of the English colonies in the West Indies and the poor returns in the latter case might have shaken confidence in European ventures, thereby temporarily discouraging other investment.

21 Savoy mines] the island of Sardinia, famous since antiquity for its lead and silver mines, was granted to the House of Savoy by the Treaty of the Hague in 1720; the mines were reopened in 1740 by a consortium of English and European backers but their management of the operation made no real economic impact (Geoffrey Symcox, *Victor Amadeus II: Absolutism in the Savoyard State 1675–1730* (Berkeley: University of California Press, 1983), p. 29).

28 dunning] 'making persistent and importunate demands for money that is owed' (*OED*, v^{3},1).

[folio 8]

[To Francis Price Esqr]

near Charleville Nov'^{r} the 8.th 1743 –

Dear Sir

I have the Favour of yours & thank you for the Entertaining Acc^{t}. you give of your Neighbourhood: I can't say I'm concern'd for the Difference between the Rector & his Patron, as I believe twill be a Means to continue the Tyth in your hands; but for the Benefitt of the Parish in general, I wish 'twoud please God to call

On the side of the letter where it was sealed someone has written at right-angles to the name: 'Cutting underwood | John Rogers [*S*]i<*>erman'; [*S*]i<*>erman could be part of the man's name or his occupation; the first letter is fairly clearly an /S/ but the third looks smudged; it could be either /l/ or /v/, and if the former would make /siler/, a type of osier (*OED*, 2) making /Silerman/ a man who cut or harvested osiers; however, *OED* has no entry for such a word, or for /osierman/.

3 the Rector] until 1867 St Mary's Church, Overton, was a chapelry in the parish of Bangor Monacorum (later known as Bangor Is y Coed) so strictly speaking the rector

of Price's parish was the priest at Bangor-on-Dee (some two and a half miles north of Overton); in 1743 that was William Philips (Parish Records for Bangor Is y Coed, St Dunawd). St Mary's, Overton, was looked after by a curate; rather confusingly the term 'rector' was also used of a 'perpetual curate' (i.e. a priest who was appointed by a patron and licenced by the Bishop but who could not be dismissed by his patron) and so could have been applied to the curate of St Mary's if that benefice was a perpetual curacy; the curate of Overton at this point was Samuel Roe (Parish Records for Overton, St Mary). It is quite possible, however, that Spencer was unaware of these subtleties of nomenclature, and may simply be alluding here to Price's local priest, i.e. the curate of St Mary's; in support of that is a comment in his letter of December [1745]: folio 40, ll.17–20, which suggests ill-feeling between Mr Roe and his patron (Thomas Lloyd/Trigger, see note to l.6 below): 'I believe Mr Rowe [*must*] have been [*in his*] <***> he spoke disrespectfully of the old [*Trigger*] for tho I am [*cons*]<**> coud not say any Thing too bad of him, yet <**********> but [*Hopes of*] continuing in the Parish after [*such a Declaration*]'; the Parish Records for Overton tell us that on 25 December 1745 'Joshua Adams succeeded ye Rev[eren]d Sam[ue]l Roe in the Curacy of Overton', and Mr Roe left Overton to take up a benefice in Wednesbury, near Birmingham, some fifty miles away.

3 his Patron] a patron was a person, usually a local landowner, who held the gift of an ecclesiastical living (*OED*, n.4); according to Lewis, Wales, the Lloyd family of 'Gwern-hailod and Overton' held the patronage of the living of Bangor Monachorum from 1680–1830; a letter of 1683 drafted by or on behalf of the Bishop of Chester tells us that 'Tho= lloyd Esq [is] the true & undoubted Patron of Bangor' (Puleston 15: NLW MS 3575E, folio 1, ll.16–17; a catalogue note to this volume gives the date of the letter; for the letter itself see Appendix I); according to Derrick Pratt ('A Description of Bangor Parish 1699', <http://bangor-on-dee.co.uk/bangor_parish_1699/> [accessed 21 May 2016]) this position was held in 1743 by a Thomas Lloyd; for the possibility that he is the same Thomas Lloyd as the one the Bishop's letter refers to, see note to l.6 below.

4 continue [...] your hands] after the dissolution of the monasteries some of the lands that passed into secular ownership also brought with them the rights to their tithes; as the arrangements were not always clear they were often the cause of dissension and dispute, and even as late as the mid-eighteenth century law cases relating to tithes could be extremely complex. The 1741 schedule of tithes for Hawarden and Bangor lists 'Mr Francis Price for Maes Gwalody at 30$^{£}$ to Acc^{t} for and Settle to pay y^{e} Curate' (Flintshire Record Office, D/BJ/A40, Schedule of Hawarden Tyths and Bangor Tyths, 1741); which curate is not specified but Maes Gwalody (just to the west of Price's house, Bryn y Pys) lay about a mile from Overton so was presumably, like Bryn y Pys, part of the curacy of Overton; interestingly, there is no amount credited against Price's name in any of the adjacent 'sums paid' columns for the years 1739, 1740 & 1741, the three years covered by this schedule (unfortunately this is the only schedule for tithe payments in Bangor that has survived for this period); it is possible, therefore, that the phrase 'twill be a Means to continue the Tyth in your hands' indicates not that Price felt that he was due the tithes, but that he believed he should not pay them, thus keeping the money 'in his own hands', whilst Lloyd believed that Price should pay those dues (as Lloyd himself did); the Bishop of Chester's letter referred to in the note to l.3 above, and which Thomas Lloyd, the patron of Bangor, countersigns, concludes with a statement that seems to connect the revenues of Bangor parish with the payment of the curate of Overton's stipend; if that is the payment which the schedule of tithes for Hawarden and Bangor records as the responsibility of Francis Price, the Bishop of Chester's letter may therefore also have some bearing on the triangulated dispute Price has described in the 'Entertaining Acc^{t}' which Spencer is responding to here.

the honest Trigger to some other Country. I hope you finishd the drawing out your Muck before the Weather broke / if you have the same sort of ours / for since the 10th of last Month, we have continued Storms and Rain. This Country is now very dull; all our Members of Parliament & their Familys being in Dublin, & so are numbers of our Gentlemen who have money to Spend or who have any Hopes of Preferment. Your friend Col Barry has made a pritty Penny of his Borough, he got 600 guineas of Berthridge Badham & 700£ of Mr Leeson son of Leeson the Brewer on Stephens Green, besides what there

6 Trigger] the general sense of ll.2–6 ('I can't say [...] Country') suggests that the antecedent of 'Trigger' is either the rector or the patron; apart from the fact that he seems generally detested (in all six letters where he is mentioned Spencer speaks of this man only in the most disparaging terms) the only thing we know about Trigger is that he died shortly before August 1748, as Spencer responds to news of his decease in his letter of 5 August 1748: folio 75. That would rule out both the rector of Bangor, William Philips, who was buried at Bangor in June 1762 (Parish Records for Bangor Is y Coed, St Dunawd) and the curate of Overton, Samuel Roe, who left Overton in December 1745 for a new benefice in Wednesbury, and so could not have continued being a thorn in the side of the good people of Overton until mid-1748; Thomas Lloyd, however, the patron of Bangor, was buried in St Mary's Church, Overton, on 10 June 1748 (Parish Records for Overton, St Mary); it seems reasonable to conclude, therefore, that he is 'Trigger'. Given that Alice Price was the widow of another Thomas Lloyd (not the same person, as he died before 1735), it is quite possible that Francis Price was related by marriage to Thomas Lloyd/Trigger, which in turn would explain Spencer's comment in 5 August 1748: folio 75: 'if I mistake not you have a Right to something considerable upon his Death' (ll.3–4). Whether this is the same person as the Thomas Lloyd mentioned in the Bishop of Chester's letter (see second note to l.3 above) is questionable, given that if they are one and the same he would have been well in his eighties on his death in 1748, but it is by no means impossible that they are as in every other reference to Trigger in this correspondence Spencer attaches the epithet 'old' to the nickname and is almost certainly referring to him in the phrase 'the old Gentleman of Overton' (16 December 1746: folio 54, l.1); that said, though, we must allow here for the fact that both 'Thomas' and 'Lloyd' were common Welsh names. The meaning of the nickname is not obvious but it is reasonable to assume, given Spenser and Price's dislike of the man, that it was not complimentary; if a noun, it possibly derives from the trigger of a gun, suggesting a short-tempered and bellicose man (Sir Lucius O'Trigger in Sheridan's *The Rivals* (1775), the only Irish character in the play, is hot-headed and aggressive); the reputation of the late eighteenth-century Irish politician Richard Martin (1754–1834) for duelling earned him the nickname 'hair-trigger Dick' (Marianne Elliot, *Wolfe Tone* (Liverpool: Liverpool University Press, 2012), p. 30); alternatively this could be a reference to the mechanism that springs a trap (*OED*, *trigger*^{I}, 1) thus suggesting a person who enjoyed leading people into situations which put them at his mercy; as the word was also pronounced 'tricker' in this period there could be a pun that reinforced such a meaning. Less likely derivations could be someone who 'walks briskly' (*OED*, *trig*, v^3), 'dresses neatly, a dandy or coxcomb' (*OED*, *trig*, a^{I}.B and v^4.I.1), or 'eats greedily, who stuffs himself' (*OED*, *trig*, v^4.II.2).

12 Col Barry] a member of the extensive Barry family of which the head was Lord Barrymore (see 6 February 1732: folio 3); Spencer suggests Col. Barry will make an equal sum from this parliamentary seat when Badham dies (see next note and 24 July 1744: folio 24, l.9).

might have been settled with Loyd the new Rector, so that this has been a fortunate Year to him: he was so concernd for the Death of the Major that he intended to have removed to Cork & quitted improving his estate, but that Design is now laid aside. young Counc.r Harwood is returned for Doneraile in the Room of Col Waller, what might have been the Purchase of ‸ it of the worthy Lord is not known — Your old Acquaintance Hodder Roberts has married the widdow of one Addis a Grocer in Cork ~~by~~ with whom he has got 40£ a year & some silver, & is fixd in Cork, he has given up Bridgetown to his eldest Son, who will not

13 Berthridge Badham] Brettridge Badham (c.1678–1743/4) was a prominent politician in Co. Cork (*HIP*); Collector of Customs and Excise for Youghal and Dungarvon, and briefly MP for Charleville (1713–1714) he was elected MP for Rathcormac, Co. Cork, in 1743 following the death of William Fitzherbert in April 1742 but died himself soon after, being succeeded by Leeson (see next note; see also Barnard, *A New Anatomy of Ireland*, pp. 165–66; for Badham's death see 24 July 1744: folio 24, l.9).

14 Leeson son of Leeson] the elder Leeson was a brewer on Stephens Green, Dublin, and a successful property speculator; the son was left a considerable fortune, enabling him to become an art collector and connissseur; he was elected MP for Rathcormac in 1743, holding the seat until 1756; in that year he became Baron Russborough, then Viscount Russborough in 1760, and Earl of Milltown in 1763; Primate Stone wrote of him in June 1748 (possibly with considered disingenuity) that 'His merits are, a great fortune and constant attachment to the King and his government. His demerits are a common failing of a Bourgeois Gentilhomme, and I think those only — excepting what may arise from his having made pecuniary application, of which I have no knowledge'. He died in 1783, 'extremely rich: an old debauchee' (*HIP*).

15 Loyd [...] Rector] Col. Barry, as the patron of the parish, has clearly just appointed (or agreed the sale of) the living of Rathmacormac to a new priest but that he is called Loyd is presumably a pure coincidence (see note to line 6).

18 Counc.r Harwood] William Harward (1694–1770), MP for Doneraile 1743–1760 and Lanesborough in 1761, 1768 & 1770; as a counsellor he represented James Annesley, who lost his case in the 1743 trial Spencer refers to in 6 December 1743: folio 10, and, more successfully, Lord Netterville in his trial for murder, mentioned 21 January 1743: folio 14 (*HIP*).

19 Doneraile] a town between Charleville and Cork, some ten miles south of the former and twenty five miles north of the latter; the parish contained Kilcolman (see 6 February 1732: folio 3).

19 Col Waller] John Waller (1690–1742) was MP for Doneraile 1727–1742 (*HIP*).

21 Hodder Roberts] he lived in Britsfieldtown on Carrigaline Bay, near Cobh (see James Fraser, *Guide Through Ireland* (Dublin: William Curry, Jun. and Company, 1838), p. 159); his death is reported in 25 March 1748: folio 71.

23 Bridgetown] one mile from Castletown-Roche on the River Blackwater; Bridgetown Priory, opposite Renny Castle on the Blackwater, was the thirteenth-century Augustinian foundation that the castle was built to protect. It was owned by Sir Henry Sidney and, later, Edmund Spenser's friend, Lodowick Bryskett.

be as well liked as the Father. Mr Row I suppose is every day swetting after Woodcocks, we have as great Plenty of them here as we had before the great Frost — The bad Price for all our Commoditys has obliged my Tennant to surrender Renny, so that I must take it into my own hands the first of May next, but how I

———————————

shall be able to stock it I have not yet found out; at present I board at my brother in Law Crofter's at Churchtown, to whom I am to pay 36$^{£}$ pann^{d}; I lead a sober indolent Life, now & then a hunt, for which I am now very well mounted, but still tis a Way I don't like as I woud chuse to be employd in some Business that might help to maintain my little Family — By this I am sure I have tired you, & am sorry this Country does not afford anything with which I might entertain you — I believe [~~*by th*~~] the Stocah has sett out to pay you a visit — My Wife joins me in h our best Respects to You, Coz^{n} Price and Dear Mr Richard. I am Dear Sir Your sincerely affect^{te} Kinsman

& most obliged hble Servt

Edm Spencer

My Service to Mr Smith &
the rest of my Sober Acquaintance

24 Mr Row] i.e., Samuel Roe, the curate in charge of St Mary's Church, Overton (see note to l.6 above).

30 my brother in Law Crofter's] Spencer married Ann Freeman, and his sister Barbara married Edmond Conolly, so, if Crofter is the surname of his brother-in-law he would be the husband of his wife's sister, an extended but acceptable usage of the term (*OED*).

30 Churchtown] probably the hamlet of that name some four miles south of Charleville.

36 Stocah] an obselete term for 'an attendant on an Irish foot soldier' (*OED*, *stokaghe*; in Johnson and later dictionaries *stocah*; *OED* gives only two illustrations, both from Spenser's *A View of the Present State of Ireland*); given the addition of the definite article, this is most likely a nickname for a mutual acquaintance. (See also 29 June 1744: folio 23.)

[folio 9]

[To Francis Price Esqr]

near Charleville Novr the 22^{d} 1743

Dear Sir

The Election for Knight for the County of Kerry has been so extraordinary, that I coud not forbear giving you an Account of it; the Candidates were Mr FitzMaurice brother to the Earl of Kerry & Mr Hassett son of Colonel Hassett, tho there are but three hundred Voters yet the Election lasted a fortnight & was at last carryd by FitzMaurice by forty odd Majority, I send you a list of what Mr Hassett prepared for his Voters, vizt 4 tuns of Wine, 2 D.^{o} Ale 2 D.^{o} Cyder 2 D.^{o} Beer, 40 Sheeps, 20 Bullocks, 60 Hams, 40 Pigs, a hogshead of Shrub, 600 fowls, Venison, Veil, &c. this Acc^{t} I reced of one of his Voters who was at Tralee during the whole Election, never were such rare doings seen in Kerry before; The worthy Col Danny was the busiest person there, who by overholding the Sovreignty of Dingle coud not return himself for that Borough, & had not Interest enough to sett up for the County, he therefore gave all his to Mr FitzMaurice / who did not ask it, / against his own brother in Law Hassett. & by his Behaviour lost himself on both sides. Thus I have given you a long Detail of a great Nothing & am sorry this Place does not afford somewhat with which I might entertain you better — My Wife joins in our sincere Respects to you Mrs Price & my Dear Mr Richard, / whom God Preserve / I am Dear Sir Your sincerely affect^{te} Kinsman

& obliged humble Servant

Edm Spencer

1 Knight] more fully, 'Knight of the Shire', the member of parliament for a constituency (*OED*, n.4.c).

3 Mr FitzMaurice] being brother to the Earl of Kerry he was part of a family which 'dominated co. Kerry for generations' (*ODNB*).

4 Mr Hassett] Mr Hassett never succeeded in becoming an MP.

8 vizt] an early form of 'viz' or 'videlicit', Latin for 'that is to say'.

8 D.^{o}] probably an abbreviation of 'ditto', i.e. tuns (casks of 252 gallons or 1,150 litres capacity).

10 Shrub] a kind of punch made with oranges, lemons, sugar, and rum (*OED*, n^{I}.1).

10 Veil] veal; *OED* gives the spelling for sixteenth-century Scotland only.

10 Reced] an abbreviation of 'received'.

11 Tralee] the county town of Kerry, and situated in the south-east of Ireland on the Atlantic coast, some sixty miles from Cork.

13 overholding the Sovreignty] 'sovreignty' was a term used of certain governmental bodies in Ireland, in this case the Corporation of Dingle, the head of which was known as the sovreign; to 'overhold' was to continue for a further year in office as sovereign.

14 Dingle] a town on the western coast of Co. Kerry, twenty five miles further along the promontory that runs west from Tralee.

[folio 10]

[To Francis Price Esqr]

near Charleville December the 6.th 1743

Dear Sir

I have the Pleasure of yours of the 19th ult. which I woud have answerd before, but that I was in Roches Country till this Day, since the middle of last Month; I heartily thank you for the many pleasing Acc.^{ts} you give me, but had the Satisfaction of hearing of Sir Watkin's Success before yours arrived, I am only concerned that the Penalty laid on Middleton is too small, & wish the whole Tribe was to accompany him to Christmas with Sir George. I sincerely wish Doctor Apperley as good a Verdict at Westminster Mr Annesley had at our four Courts, you / no doubt / have heard that he has cast his unjust Uncle --- There is so little Business at

2–3 Roches Country] see 4 October 1743: folio 7, l.12.

5 Sir Watkin's] Sir Watkin Williams-Wynn, 3rd Baronet (1692–1749), from Llanforda, near Oswestry, was MP for Denbighshire from 1716–1749, Mayor of Oswestry in 1728 and of Chester in 1732; he was a leading Jacobite politician and the head of the Jacobite club, the Cycle of the White Rose (see l.23 below); in the 1741 election for Denbighshire he lost the seat to John Myddelton of Chirk Castle (l.6) because the sheriff, interestingly named William Myddleton, illegally discounted some of his votes; the result was successfully challenged in the new parliament and in July 1742 Sir Watkin was returned for the seat; William Myddleton was committed to Newgate and dismissed from his offices (<http://history ofparliamentonline.org/volume/1715–1754> [accessed 8 March 2016]). The reference to Christmas and Sir George in ll.7–8 cannot be explained.

8–10 Doctor Apperley [...] unjust Uncle] Dr Apperley told Price in a letter dated October 1743 that he was involved in a court case over his wife and that he 'has not as much money as is assumed' (Puleston 21: NLW MS 3581E); the matrimonial nature of the case seems to link it, in Spencer's mind, with the recent and sensational trial, held in Dublin in November 1743, in which James Annesley successfully sued his 'unjust Uncle', Richard Annesley, over the question of which of them should inherit the estate of Lord Altham, James Annesley's father and Richard's brother; the case hinged on the identity of James Annesley's mother, his uncle insisting that she was a maidservant and not the legitimate wife of Lord Altham; Richard Annesley apparently tried several times to kidnap his nephew in order to prevent him from pursuing his claims, and hence, perhaps, Spencer's more violent description of the man in ll.31–32 of this letter (*DIB*). Whether Doctor Apperley's verdict was good or not we do not know, but he certainly did not get it soon as the case was still going on a year later in November 1744.

our Parliament House, that a great many Members have alterd their Resolution of attending, as they do not expect a Call of the House, at soonest , till after Christmas --- A Pamphlet of Poultneys intitled faction detected by the Evidence of Facts, is what engages most of our Gentry here & is universally approved of, I have not yet seen it; but wish if it is answered / as I hope it is / & that you have the answer, you will please to send it to me, for I believe they dare not print it in this Kingdom --- As one old Maiden in your neighbourhood has broke the Ice, who knows but the Ladys at the Hall may make Conquests, I suppose the eldest will insist upon being some years younger than Miss Eyton, I wish with all my Soul she was marryed to Shylock. pray inform me how you have settled about the Tyths for the next Year: I congratulate you on the Addition of so many ∧worthy new Members to your Cycle, we have our own Clubs here too, / but such Clubs! / I have not the Honour of being a Member to any one of them, / unfortunate [*!*] — the grandest is our

9 our four Courts] the main Irish court buildings which were situated in Dublin and were the location of the Supreme Court, the High Court, the Central Criminal Court, and the Dublin Circuit Court.

10 cast] 'defeated in an action at law' (*OED*, v.14).

13 a Pamphlet of Poultneys] *Faction Detected by the Evidence of Facts, Containing an Impartial View of Parties at Home, and Affairs Abroad* was published anonymously in 1743, when it went through three editions. It was thought to have been written by William Pulteney, Earl of Bath (as Spencer believes) but is now ascribed to John Perceval, Earl of Egremont.

21 Shylock] perhaps the nickname of a mutual acquaintance of Spencer and Price notorious for his miserliness, or the character from Shakespeare's *The Merchant of Venice* used to define the type of marriage partner suitable for this lady.

22 inform [...] Tythes] see 8 November 1743: folio 8, l.4 and note.

23 your Cycle] a Jacobite club; when formed in 1710, 'every significant landowner within a ten mile radius of Wrexham was a member' (<http://www.bbc.co.uk/blogs/wales/posts/jacobites_in_wales> [accessed 18 February 2015]); evidently Price's political sympathies appear to have been with the Stuart cause: his correspondence with James Barry, 4th Earl of Barrymore (Puleston 22: NLW MS 3582D) reveals an extremely close relationship and he was one of Lord Barrymore's executors (see 2 February 1747: folio 67, ll.31–34) which also suggests he was part of the inner circle of a man seen as the leader of the Jacobite cause in England (see 26 March 1744: folio 20, ll.6–9). If Spencer shared those sympathies that might explain why he saw Lord Barrymore as a likely patron; but see note to l.26 below on the Dettingen Club.

25 unfortunate [*!*] —] the marks after /unfortunate/ are not clear; it is just possible that the word should read /unfortunately/ as the end of the /e/ continues to ascend and would connect with the vertical stroke to make a looped /l/ (which is how Spencer forms an /l/); however, the /y/ is entirely absent, unless the marks that form the dot beneath the exclamation mark and the dash are part of a letter mostly missing because the pen lifted off the paper whilst it was being formed; even then, though, these marks would not fit the configuration of his normal /y/, and if Spencer intended to form a /y/ the pen would have to have lifted off the paper for almost the entire time he was forming that letter, and that would be uncharacteristic of his penmanship.

Dettingen Club, which has a great many Members as it is the newest, & by their Excess in Drinking will, I believe, be of short Duration. As I was going to conclude I reced a letter from Dublin, which informs me that the Estate Mr Annesley sued for is £400 pan$^{\partial}$ in the County

———————————

of Meath, & that he will be allowd his Seat in our House of Peers as Lord Altham, as soon as he will demand it, the Uncle has so vile a Charact.^{r} that he's univerally unpitied. Our Commons have laid an additional Duty upon Clarets of £3 p Tun: & = £1:13:0 p Tun upon Port, & a Duty of Six pence a hyde upon all hydes exported raw ___ A Nephew of Col Massey's has carried off Miss Ingoldsby a Lady of £1200 — pan$^{\partial}$ & is gone with her to France, a Reward of three hund.^{d} pounds apiece for taking of him and his Associates is offerd by the Governt. She is a Lady not very happy in her Charact.^{r} -- My Wife joins in our best Respects to you Coz.^{n} Price & Dear Mr Richard I am Dear Sir

Your sincerely affec.^{te} Kinsman
& obliged humble Servant
Edm Spencer

My humble Service to
Mr Smith & all friends

26 Dettingen Club] named, presumably, in honour of the defeat of the French by an allied force under George II, at Dettingen (now Karlstein am Main in Bavaria) on 27 June 1743. Spencer's attitude to it is not clear: does the 'unfortunate [*!*]' suggest that he would like to join but that, being, like Price, a Jacobite sympathizer, he considers it 'unfortunate' that the biggest new club in his area is one with Hanoverian leanings or does it simply indicate that, as Barnard suggests (*Irish Protestant Ascents and Descents*, p. 296) his 'meagre resources excluded [him] from the swells gathered in the Dettingen Club'. In either case, the suggestion that it will not last long may carry a hint of *Schadenfreude*. (For further discussion of Spencer's political views see the Introduction.)

28 reced] see 22 November 1743: folio 9, note to l.10.

35–36 A Nephew [...] of £1200] the *DIB*'s description of this episode as an 'abduction and rape' (entry for *Massey, Charles*) suggests that Spencer's account is possibly suffering from eighteenth-century gender myopia, and that the person whose character is 'not very happy' (l.38) might be the gentleman rather than the lady.

36 pan$^{\partial}$] the final flourish here is much more pronounced, see 6 February 1732: folio 3, l.17 and note.

[folio 11]

[To Francis Price Esqr]

near Charleville December the 13.th 1743

Dear Sir

Since my last I have settled a Scheme, by which / if it hits / I expect to procure some pence, it's this: I have consulted with sev.^{ll} acquaintance about reprinting Spencers Works, by whose Means I have got acquainted & agreed with Grierson the Kings Printer who has advised me to publish by Subscription, & if I can procure 500 Subscribers 'twill be very well worth my while to undertake it. the Price must be one Guinea for every subscriber half to ^{be} paid in hand & the remainder at the Delivery of the books which are to be Six Volumes & which shall be put to the Press as soon as the Subscription is full. As you have a numerous Acquaintance I believe upon your solicitation a Number of Subscribers may be procured among them, & therefore beg you will be so kind to inform me how many I may expect from that Quarter. If my Lord Barrymore & Sir Watkin were applyd to, I believe they could procure a good many especially as they are now in London. I set out to Morrow to try my interest among the Gentlemen in the Country & shall give myself no Rest 'till I try to compleat the Subscription, or at lest 'till I know if 'twill be worth while to sett about it in earnest; which as soon as I can fix I will publish Proposals. I entreat the Favour of your Animadversions on this Scheme, as soon as your Leisure will admit. My Wife joins in our best Respects to you, Coz.^{n} Price & Dear Mr Richard, Dear Sir

Your most affectionate Kinsman
& obliged hbleServt

Edm Spencer

P.S.
I fear you have not seen Mr Trevor
since you mentioned him to me
my service to Mr Smith & all friends

4 Grierson] George Grierson (1680–1753), King's Printer in Dublin, 1732–1753. Born in Scotland he moved to Dublin *c.*1703 where he set up as a bookseller in Essex Street; he succeeded to the office of King's Printer in 1732. He had an excellent reputation as a printer largely as a result of his wife Constantia's scholarship and proof-reading skills. Members of the Grierson family held the position of King's Printer throughout the eighteenth century (*DIB*; see also Mary Pollard, *A Dictionary of Members of the Dublin Book Trade* (London: Bibliographical Society, 2000), pp. 254–56).

9 Subscription] this method of publication, by which a list of subscribers was built up for a forthcoming volume, and who would pay part of its cost upfront to persuade a printer that he would see a return on his investment, became one of the standard ways of publishing in the eighteenth century.

13 Sir Watkin] see 6 December 1743: folio 10, l.5 and note.

PS Mr Trevor] in the letter of 30 November 1745: folio 38, Spencer requests Price to ask Mr Trevor to intervene on his behalf with a person in the Dublin administration who might be able to find him a job; Price appears to do this in the letter of recommendation that he then drafts (folio 124); this postscript may be a gentle reminder to Price that he has suggested doing this.

[folio 12]

[To Francis Price Esqr]

near Charleville December the 27.th 1743

Dear Sir

I have the Pleasure of yours, & am sorry to find the good Lord Gower has lost his Place, which is now filld by a Person fit for the dirty Work which he had refused to be concernd in, our papers likewise inform us that the worthy M.^{r} S{*blot*}s is created a peer; fit Company for those who have gone before him – I am concernd for the poor Alderman's bad state of Health & by the Acc^{t} you give, fear is soon to follow his Sons. I congratulate Mr Smith upon his Stock of Health, which I realy believe is in a great Measure owing to his so frequent use of your Elixir Salutis ----- I lately writ to you about a Scheme I had form'd of printing by Subscription Spencer's Works, in which I have been so encouraged by the Gentlemen of Fortune & Interest in this Country, that / by their Advice / I intend to go to Dublin as soon as the Parliament meets, to solicite personally the filling the Subscription. a Letter from you to Doctor Kingsbury upon that Head, woud be of singular Service to me, as he has a numerous acquaintance, & no doubt

2 the good Lord Gower] John Leveson-Gower, 1st Earl Gower (1694–1754) and leader of the Tory party in the Lords; in 1742 he became Lord Privy Seal but resigned in December 1743, that presumably being the place he has lost (*ODNB*).

4 M.^{r} S{*blot*}s] this name is either deliberately or accidentally blotted out; it begins with an /S/ and ends /s/, and may well be /Sandys/; if so it would be Samuel Sandys (1695–1770), MP for Worcester until December 1743, when he was elevated to the peerage as Baron Sandys of Ombersley (*ODNB*).

6 poor Alderman's] another of the correspondents' nicknames (in this case an affectionate one) for a mutual acquaintance; the letter of 29 May: folio 22, makes it clear that he is a neighbour of Price; the word could mark the friend referred to simply as a senior and dignified person, or, specifically in Ireland, as a magistrate (*OED*, 3).

9 Elixir Salutis] a famous proprietrary medicinal cordial invented in 1647 by Thomas Daffy, a clergyman of Leicestershire; basically a purgative, it claimed to cure more or less anything and despite the fact that it probably cured nothing remained popular throughout the eighteenth century (<http://en.wikipedia.org/wiki/Daffy's_Elixir> [accessed 10 March 2015]).

14 Doctor Kingsbury] two men of this name are referred to in this correspondence, this one and a 'Mr Kingsbury'; both acted for Price as his representative in Ireland, the Mr Kingsbury succeeding the Doctor some time after that gentleman's death in May 1747 (see 25 May 1747: folio 58); Mr Kingsbury was definitely a lawyer as we are told in 8 April 1756: folio 100 that he ceased to act for the Prices on his 'removal to the Temple'; Dr Kingsbury's profession is less certain: he may have been a physician given his title, but that could equally indicate a lawyer with a doctorate; it is possible that they were related but the letters contain no evidence of that; Mr Kingsbury would certainly appear not to be Dr Kingsbury's son as that young man was still at college when his father died (see 13 May 1748: folio 73).

coud get a great many of them to subscribe. I beg your Advice whether I should advertize it in the London Papers, & if you think that many there woud subscribe: Mr Oliver thinks there woud, & has writ to Lord Talbot to promote it. Nothing new has happened here lately worth mentioning. My Wife joins in the Compliments of the Season to you Mrs Price & Dear Mr Richard I am D Sir

Your sincerely affct^{te} Kinsman
& obliged humbleServ^{t}
Edm Spencer

Pray let me know if I shall trouble you with any Proposals & rec.^{ts} --

18 Mr Oliver] this is possibly the same person as the Col. Oliver mentioned in 23 May 1745: folio 31 (where he is described as 'my Dear Worthy Friend', ll.30–31) and 15 May 1746: folio 47 (where it is said he would have provided for Spencer had he lived); certainly the behaviour here of Mr Oliver is that of a good friend.

18–19 Lord Talbot] Possibly Richard Francis Talbot (1710–1752), Earl of Tyrconnell, a soldier and diplomat, son of Richard Talbot (who styled himself 'Lord Talbot'); Carlisle described him as 'a Jacobite Irishman, of blustrous qualities, though with plenty of sagacity' (*DIB*). He was campaigning in Bavaria and Upper Alsace in 1743 but may well have been back in Ireland by December when this letter was written.

[folio 13]

[To Francis Price Esqr]

near Charlevil^{le} Jan$^{\partial}$y the 10.th 1743

Dear Sir

I have the Pleasure of yours, which ∧^{gave} me great Concern as by it I find the Small Pox is so near Brynypiece, God preserve my dear Mr Richard from that loathsome dangerous Distemper: for when such a Disorder gets into a Neighbourhood tis difficult to keep a person free enough from any Communication with it. I shall be under great uneasiness for my dear Lad, while I think it continues in Overton. This Week I intend for Dublin to try my Fortune among the Members of Parliament in regard to the Publication of Spenser's Work; if I may judge by the Promises I have already received, I am not to doubt of Success: I must beg a letter of yours to Doctor Kinsbury & any other Persons you think you can influence to forward my Subscription. The Post is just going out so am forced to conclude. my Wife joins in our best respects to you Mrs Price & Dear Mr Richd_ Dr Sir

Your sincerely affec^{te}

Kinsman & obliged hbleServt

Edm Spencer

Addressee] written in pencil and ink around the name on the address side of the sheet, and at right angles to the address, are three sets of figures which are additions of sums of money; a fourth single sum is a repetition of the total of one of those pairs.

Date] Spencer uses here what is presumably a tilde to abbreviate /January/; it looks something like an upper case /E/ and is between the /n/ and the /y/; there is also a supralineal line across the top of the word and through the tilde; this is very similar to the mark used to abbreviate /per annum/. The year is given Old Style here and on the next four letters.

2 Brynypiece] the name of Francis Price's house in Overton. It was situated off Argoed Lane about a mile outside and north-west of Overton; the original house no longer exists.

12 Kinsbury] spelled /Kingsbury/ elsewhere.

[folio 14]

[To Francis Price Esqr]

Dublin Jan$^{\partial}$y the 21.st 1743

Dear Sir

I have been in Town these three Days, & have just sett my Proposals to the Press. I have great Dependance on the Favour of your Interest in this Undertaking of mine, & beg you'll please to send me enclosed a Letter to Doct.^{r} Kingsbury who has great Acquaintance in Town. I am convinced at your Desire my Lord Barrymore & Sir Watkin ~~they~~ woud speak of me to the Spencer family which I am advised woud be of singular Service to me, as I intend dedicating this Edition to the Duke of Marlbourough —— The Lord Nettervill's tryal is put off on acc^{t} of a Flaw in the Commission, tis not known what Day 'twill come on, but generally thought he will escape — The call of our Commons will be on Munday next to hear the Petition of a Member who wants to resign, but tis thought he will not be allowd to do so, as twould afford a bad President & may hereafter be often done in a jobbing way —— Pray present my best Respects to Mrs Price & my Dear Mr Richard I am Dsir

Direct to me at the Scales & sugar Loaf fishamble Street

y^{r} most affec^{te} Kinsman
& obliged humble Servant
Edm Spencer

2 sett] Spencer consistently spells /set/ thus, but this is possibly a mistake for /sent/ as although what he sent to the press (that is, his *Proposals for Printing by Subscription the Works of Mr. Edmund Spencer*) would have been 'set' (i.e. in type) the expression 'to set to press' with that sense is not noted by *OED*; it is possible, however, that his lack of familiarity with printing may have led him to use this bit of technical vocabulary wrongly.

11 Lord Nettervill's tryal] Nicholas Netterville, 5th Viscount Netterville (1708–1750), was tried for the murder of Michael Walsh from Meath in 1742; Netterville insisted on being tried by his peers in the Irish House of Lords where he was acquitted in 1743 for want of evidence, the two principal witnesses having died so that their evidence could not be given in court; the trial was a cause célèbre (*DIB*).

18–19 a jobbing way] possibly, given the parliamentary context, in the sense 'using public office for private or party advantage' (*OED*, vbl.n^{2}. 3) but if so this use would pre-date *OED*'s first example by some forty years; that sense, however, could be seen as little more than a minor variation of sense 2: 'buying and then selling in order to profit'.

PS fishamble Street] this street, south of the river, ran between Wood Quay/Lower Exchange at its northern end to Skinner Row/Castle Street at its southern end; being thus in the centre of Dublin it was a conveniently short walk to the Exchange and the Parliament House, both places where Spencer might expect to find potential subscribers to his proposed publication.

[folio 15]

[To Francis Price Esqr]

Dublin Jan$^{\partial}$y the 31.st 1743

Dear Sir

I reced yours of the 11th ins.^{t} yesterday & according to your Order send inclosed 12 rect.^{s} & under another Cover 12 more, they are all signd therefore you must receive half a guinea from every Subscriber upon giving one of them. your Aquaintance Mr Ellis at Oxford could get some off: I have pritty good Encouragement here & am in Expectation / with your Assistance / to be able soon to put the Work ~~soon~~ to the Press, but it will not be requisite to publish proposals in the London Papers. Lord Nettervills tryal is to come on next Friday & some do not scruple to say that he will be found guilty – Our famous Eagle Tavern is shut up to the surprize of every body, for the Owner was thought to have been in top Circumstances. My best Respects to Mrs Price & Dear Mr Richard concludes Dear Sir

Your affec^{te} Kinsman
& obliged hble Servt
Edm Spencer

My Service to Mr Smith & all friends — I congratulate the Alderman upon Peggy's Pregnancy

10 Lord Nettervills tryal] see previous letter, note to l.12.

12–13 Our famous [...] shut up] the Eagle Tavern was located on Cork Hill, which ran northwards from the eastern end of Castle Street, only a few yards from Fishamble Street where Spencer was lodging; 'Richard Parsons, Earl of Rosse and first recorded Grand Master of the Irish Freemasons, is stated to have established a Hell-Fire Club in the tavern about 1735' (Sean Murphy, *A Short History of Dublin's Temple Bar*, <http://homepage.eircom.net/~seanjmurphy/dublin/templebar.htm> [accessed 30 July 2015]). Rosse died in 1741, some three years before this letter was written, but whether that, or the activities of the club he established, had anything to do with the 'shutting up' of the tavern Murphy does not say.

At this point in the archive are two copies of the *Proposals for Printing by Subscription the Works of Mr. Edmund Spencer* [sic] numbered in pencil as folios 16 and 17. Each folio is a formed of a sheet folded in half to form four pages. On the first page is the announcement with, in the top right corner, 'Dublin, Jan. 23, 1744'. The second page sets out the 'Conditions', below which is the statement of receipt for half a guinea (that being the first instalment of the subscription fee) signed in ink by Spencer; the number /174/ is printed between the statement and signature, this being the first three digits of the year, leaving the day, month, and final digit of the year to be filled in by hand. On the third page is a sample of *The First Book of the Fairy Queen*, which consists of the first two verses of that book. The fourth page is blank. These two documents are presumably two which Price was unable to place succesfully with subscribers and hence were left over from the consignment of *Proposals* sent to him by Spencer (see previous letter).

16 *Dublin, Jan.* 23, 1744.

PROPOSALS

For PRINTING by

SUBSCRIPTION.

THE

WORKS

OF

Mr. *Edmund Spencer.*

In SIX VOLUMES.

WITH

A New Glossary Explaining the Old and Obſcure Words.

AND

A more Exact Account of his LIFE, by his Great Grandſon

EDMUND SPENCER,

Who has undertaken this Work at the Deſire of ſeveral Perſons of Diſtinction who are Admirers of that Celebrated Poet, and willing to ſhew a Mark of Favour to his Deſcendant.

CONDITIONS.

I. THIS Work ſhall be put to the Preſs as ſoon as poſſible, and printed in Six neat Pocket Volumes, on the ſame Paper and Letter with the Propoſal and Specimen annexed.

II. The Price to Subſcribers will be one Guinea; Half of which to be paid at Subſcribing, and the Remainder on Delivery of a compleat Sett well Bound and Letter'd.

III. The Subſcribers Names ſhall be printed.

SUBSCRIPTIONS are taken in by the Editor, and by GEORGE and ALEXANDER EWING, Bookſellers in *Dame-ſtreet*.

RECEIVED from
Half a Guinea, being the Firſt Subſcription Payment for Mr. *SPENCER*'s WORKS. 174

Edm Spencer

THE

FIRST BOOK

OF THE

FAIRY-QUEEN:

CONTAINING

TheLengend of the Knight of the Red-Crofs, or of Holinefs.

I.

LO, I the Man, whofe Mufe whilom did mafk,
As time her taught, in lowly Shepherds weeds,
Am now enforc'd a far unfitter Tafk,
For Trumpets ftern to change mine Oaten Reeds
And fing of Knights, and Ladies gentle Deeds;
Whofe Praifes having flept in Silence long,
Me, all too mean, the facred Mufe areeds
To blazon 'broad, amongft her learned Throng:
Fierce Warres, and faithful Loves, fhall moralize my fong.

II.

Help then, O holy Virgin, chief of nine,
Thy weaker Novice to perform thy Will,
Lay forth out of thine everlafting Scrine
The antique Rolls, which there lie hidden ftill,
Of Fairy Knights, and faireft *Tanaquill*,
Whom that moft noble *Briton* Prince fo long
Sought through the World, and fuffer'd fo much Ill,
That I muft rue his undeferved Wrong:
O! help thou my weak Wit, and fharpen my dull Tongue.

III.

[folio 18]

[To Francis Price Esqr]

Dublin Feb$^{\partial}$y the 14.th 1743

Dear Sir

I have the Pleasure of yours with One enclosed to the Doct^{r} which I will deliver in a day or two: the books I publish shall be delivered to the Subscribers at your side the water Duty free / at Chester: & if I can procure Subscriptions in London, to those that chuse it, they shall receive theirs there. I shall be greatly obliged to you if you can prevail on some of your numerous Acquaintance to inform the Duke of Marlbourough of my Design of Dedicating this Edition to him, I am advised twoud be of great Service to me. the 13.th of March begins Corke Assize where I must attend & expect a great many Subscribers, I have already reced for 50 —— We are in great Hurry here on Acc^{t} of the Brest Squadron, our *{erased}* Soldiers have been aboard the Transports these ten Days, & tho the Wind has often since offerd fair, yet they must not sail till further Orders; the Lord Lieut.^{t} had broke up House three Weeks since, but upon the Arrival of the last Packett has opend again, & tis not known when he is to sett off for England. Nothing to be met with now but most Solemn & Important Countenances among your woudbe Politicians, to construe which I cannot undertake; but nothing

———————

less than an Invasion is apprehended; nor ~~do~~ as I think was ever less Occasion to be suspected: but those affairs I always leave to deeper Politicians & am not a bit uneasy for any Consequences, as let what will happen. I have nothing to lose — My best Respects to Mrs Price and Dear Mr Richard concludes Dear Sir

Your most affec^{te} Kinsman
& obliged humble Servt

Edm Spencer

The Latter End of last month I sent you enclosed under two Covers 24 proposals with the rece.^{ts} sign'd for 10.£ you will be so kind to receive half a guinea for every one you dispose off

1–2 One enclosed [...] day or two] the Doctor is Kingsbury, and the enclosed letter is sent in response to Spencer's request in 21 January 1743: folio 14, ll.4–6, that Price should write to Kingsbury asking him to promote the proposed *Works of Mr Edmund Spencer.*

12 Brest Squadron] a large French fleet observed by British naval intelligence which caused considerable alarm: see Sir Herbert William Richmond, *The Navy in the War of 1739–48* (Cambridge: Cambridge University Press, 1920), p. 6.

14–15 Lord Lieut.^{t}] at this point William Cavendish, 4th Duke of Devonshire (1698–1755).

16 Packett] either a parcel of letters (*OED*, n.1), or, more likely here, the 'packet boat' (*OED*, n.2) that plied weekly between Holyhead in Wales and Dublin carrying mail and passengers; the service had been instituted by John Manley who took over the franchise of the Post Office under Cromwell in 1653 (see How, *Epistolary Spaces*, p. 24); the plural form of the word in 15 December 1747: folio 64 and 16 January 1747: folio 65 would suggest that Spencer uses it there in the former sense.

[folio 19]

[To Francis Price Esqr]

Dublin ffeb'^{y} the 25th 1743

Dear Sir

The Letter you was so kind to send to Doctor Kingsbury in my Behalf, I delivered & he promised me all the Assistance in his Power; I intend next Week to sett out for Munster where I hope to procure a great many Subscribers: & am advised by a great many, to sett out next Spring for Oxford & London where tis thought if I am properly recommended A great many Subscribers will be got: I beg your Advice herein. We are here in a great Fluster since the first appearance of the Brest Squadron, several~~ly~~ Priests have been secured & two French Officers & / as tis supposed / two of their Recruits are in close Durance: A proclamation is issued promising a Reward of One thousand pounds to any person who shall discover any Officer enlisting men for forreign Service. a general embargo is laid on all Shipping & tis not known how long the Duke must stay at this Side the Water. so you see we are here in great Confusion. Please to direct your next to me at Charleville I present my best Respects to Mrs Price & my dear Mr Richard I am DSir y.^{r} most affectionate Kinsman & obliged humbleServant Edm Spencer

3–4 I intend [...] for Munster] Munster is one of the provinces of Ireland; Spencer consistently uses it synecdochally to refer to his home in the same way as someone who lives in York might say, 'I'm going back to Yorkshire tomorrow', rather than specifying the precise place.

10 secured] 'arrested and imprisoned' (*OED*, v.4).

12 in close Durance] 'in strict confinement' (*OED*, *close*, adj.11.a; *durance*, 5).

16 the Duke] i.e. the Lord Lieutenant, the Duke of Devonshire (see ll.14–15 of previous letter).

[folio 20]

[To Francis Price Esqr]

near Charleville March the 26.th 1744

Dear Sir

Yesterday I returnd from Cork assyzes where were great Rejoicings for Admiral Matthews's Success against the Spaniards & French tho' the Particulars of the Fight are not yet arrived: the Priests in this Country are all fled or hid, one who was taken near Bandon is to be transported: The Account that came of Lord Barrymore's being under ∧^{arrest} gave me great Concern, since then there have been guards on his House at CastleLyons, & all places where any Papers were kept are seald up & Centinels on the Chambers. poor Capt David John Barry died last Week & was carried thro' Cork to CastleLyons to be interrd; there were but very few at his Burial ---- My Subscription goes on but very slowly the badness of the Times & dread of a French War are pleaded as Excuses by a great Many: if those were cleard up I expect better Success. my Wife joins in best Respects to you & Coz.^{n} Price & dear Mr Richard I am Dear Sir

Your very affec^{te} Kinsman
& obliged humbleServant
Edm Spencer

My service to Mr Smith
& all Friends

2–4 Admiral [...] arrived] when the particulars did arrive rejoicings were no doubt somewhat less enthusiastic since the Battle of Toulon, fought between 22 and 24 February 1744 in the Mediterranean, was hardly an English success: Mathews's command of the engagement was confused and inneffective; the enemy ships slipped past the English blocade with only one loss and achieved their objective of resupplying an Italian base; Mathews was subsequently court martialled and discharged from the navy in 1747 for his poor conduct of the battle (<http://en.wikipedia.org/wiki/Thomas_Mathews> [accessed 3 June 2015]).

5 Bandon] this village, approximately twenty miles south-west of Cork, was a noted Protestant planter town, developed by Richard Boyle, the Great Earl of Cork (1566–1643). Edmund Spenser's daughter, Katherine, lived there after her marriage to William Wiseman in the early 1600s (Hadfield, *Edmund Spenser*, pp. 407–08).

6–9 The Account [...] Chambers] Late in his life Barrymore became an active Jacobite intriguer, and he was seen by many Jacobites as their leader in England; he was placed under house arrest at his residence in Cavendish Square, London, (in 1743/4?) on the evidence of a French agent who named him as being a participant in a plot to aid a French invasion of England; he was eventually released on bail of £60,000 (*DIB*).

10 Capt David John Barry] a son of Richard Barry, 2nd Earl of Barrymore; he lived at Barry Hall, Co. Cork; he was MP for Belfast in 1727 and the High Sheriff of Cork for 1728 (<http://www.thepeerage.com> [accessed 15 April 2016]).

[folio 21]

[To Francis Price Esqr]

Renny near Castleyons May the 15.th 1744

Dear Sir

I have at last settled Renny for this year, as Cattle are very dear & no price for Butter & I had but little Mony, I coud not undertake to occupy the Land, & have therefore made an Abatem^{t} in the Rent & likewise in Order further to assist the Tenant am come to board with him; as I have now the Opportunity of angling frequently I beg the favour of you to send me a few of the smallest sort of Indian Grass, for none of the kind are to be met with in Cork —

I am in this Country but two Days, so have not as yet learnd any News worth sending: young Causabon died last Week at his Seat at Carrick, he was a very honest young Fellow & was lately married to one of Sir John Rogerson's Daughter's, another of them was married to Col Jephson's eldest Son who she buried within the year, dangerous Women to attack! The worthy Col S^{t}Leger is very ill & tis to be hoped will not recover, for sure a Country will not suffer by losing such a Tyrant. I hope Mrs Price & Dr Mr Richard are very well, my wife joins me in our best Respects to you & them. My Service to Mr Smith & all friends I am D^{r}Sir your sincerely Affec.^{te} Kinsman & obliged humbleServ.^{t}

Pray have you the Tyth this Year Edm Spencer

1 Renny] see 6 February 1732: folio 3, n. to l.7.

2 Cattle [...] Butter] Irish cattle were bred to produce higher milk yields in the late seventeenth and early eighteenth centuries: William Petty estimated that Irish cattle at pasture would yield 384 gallons of milk annually, higher than many cows in England (Nicholas Russell, *Like Engend'ring Like: Heredity and Animal Breeding in Early Modern England* (Cambridge: Cambridge University Press, 1986), p. 129).

4 Abatem^{t}] 'reduction' (*OED*, 2).

7–8 Indian Grass] 'an old name of silkworm gut used by anglers' (*OED*, *indian*, adj.4.a).

10 Young Causabon] William Causabon (c.1688–1744) was MP for Doneraile 1715–1727 though probably, according to *HIP*, 'not a very active MP'; he was also high sheriff of Co. Cork in 1723 and a lieutenant colonel in the Cork Militia. He was, through his mother, a grandson of Arthur Hyde. The 'young' could be ironic, affectionate, or intended to distinguish him from his father.

11 Carrick] Lewis, Ireland, gives a Carrig, two miles east of Mallow on the road to Fermoy, but there are several 'Carricks' in Ireland and it is not possible to identify this one with any certainty.

12 Sir John Rogerson] a prominent Irish lawyer (1676–1741).

13 Col Jephson's] for Colonel Anthony see 23 May 1745: folio 31, note to l.3.

15 Col. S^{t}Leger] the St. Leger family were a powerful Anglo-Norman dynasty in Kent and south-west Ireland, who had been immediate neighbours of the Spencers. In 1703 the head of the family became Viscount Doneraile, living at Doneraile House, next to the Kilcolman estate.

PS the Tyth] see 8 November 1743: folio 8, l.14, and 6 December 1743: folio 10, l.22.

[folio 22]

[To Francis Price Esqr]

Renny May the 29.th 1744

Dear Sir

I have the Pleasure by your last to find that you and y.^{r} family are well, God continue it: I did not think my afternoon Companion the Lawyer was a man of that Gallantry that by y.^{r} Acct. of the Bastards, I find he was. I hope his brother in Intrigue the Alderman has his Peggy with him to comfort him, since by his Confinem.^{t} / which I am sorry for / he cannot take the Pleasure of fishing at the Dee. Assure my Dear friend M.r ^^{Richard} that I did not forget my Promise of the Eagle: for last ffeb^{r}y I writ to the County of Clare to my brother Kane to set folks to search for a Nest, but by my not hearing from him lately, I fear he has mist, if so, I will next Season apply in two or three other places, & tis hard if I shall be dissapointed every where. Nothing New but that Capt Web has cast Sir Richard Mead in the Appeal about Kilcoleman which so nearly touchd the Knight that he gave up the Ghost a few Days after the Acc.^{t} came, he left a Son about a Month old, who if he lives will have a vast Fortune. I find my Lord Barrymore has orderd the plate of CastleLyons to be carryed over, which inclines me to believe he never intends another trip hither: I thought that woud be left as an Heir Lome. My Wife joins in our best Respects to you Mrs Price & Mr Rich^{d} I am D^{r}Sir y.^{r} very aff.^{te} kinsman & obliged hbleServ^{t}

EdmSpencer

5 the Alderman] see 27 December 1743: folio 12, l.6 and note.

7 the Dee] the River Dee runs just west of Overton.

8–9 Assure [...] Eagle] Spencer finally finds Richard Price an eagle some two years later, see 26 January 1746: folio 55; this interest in exotic birds shown by the nine-year old boy continued into his adult life; by 1773 (when Richard Price was thirty seven years old) he had put together a collection of sufficient interest to attract the attention of the naturalist Thomas Pennant who visited Overton and was particularly impressed by a pair of rare

Angola vultures which Pennant says was an 'undescribed species' (*Tours in Wales*, 2 vols (Caernarvon: H. Humphreys, 1883), II, p. 292). It is worth noting that Pennant discovered the Kinnoull portrait of Edmund Spenser, the poet, when he visited Dupplin Castle, near Perth, in 1776 (see Hadfield, *Edmund Spenser*, pp. 414–17).

9 County of Clare] Co. Clare lies on the mid-eastern side of Ireland, between Limerick to the south and Galway to the north.

10 brother Kane] Welply ('Edmund Spenser: Being an Account of Some Recent Researches into his Life and Lineage', pp. 257–60) gives no such name (forename or surname) for either a brother or brother-in-law of Spencer in his pedigree of the Spenser family.

14 cast] see 6 December 1743: folio 10, l.10 and note.

16 Acc.^{t}] possibly the legal term for a writ requiring a person to render an account; since Mead was at one point in receipt of the rent of Kilcolman (see 6 February 1732: folio 3, ll.14–17 and note); the case may have involved his accounting for those rents.

19 carryed over] i.e. to England.

[folio 23]

Renny near Castelyons J[~~xxx~~]^{une} the 29.th 1744

Dear Sir

The topick of most Conversation now is about two Prizes lately brought into Kinsale which are very considerable: & tis said two Men of War will be stationed there which gives the Neighbouring Gentlemen great Satisfaction, for they were obliged to remove themselves & Effects to town for fear of the Privateers which are constantly plying about those Coasts. ~~Gen~~ Counc.^{r} Stowell / a gentleman of very good fortune / has declared himself Candidate for Kinsale, with Mr Southwells Interest; & is opposed by Gen.^{ll} Parker. I suppose the Papers give you an Acc.^{t} of the military madness of the Citizens of Dublin, who almost every day are reviewing marching &c in this part of the Country, farming is minded more than Militia affairs — The races of Carrigtohill were last Week at which there was a great Appearance of Gentlemen of Rank. the great Plate was won by a Horse that Mr Deane bought at last Chester Races; his Lady has miscarryd a Second time, so the Councell.^{r} stands a good Chance for that Estate. Our Harvest here will be very late; Barley which formerly usd to be reap'd the first Week in July is not yet on the turn; but most Corn fields greatly damaged by the constant Storms & rains we have had this fortnight passd, which by the price

---

it bears is no great Loss --- The poor Stokah is every day fishing, with very little Success; for Lismore Wears is in such good Repair that few Salmon can come up. My Wife joins in best Respects to you Mrs Price & dear Mr Richard I am DearSir your most affectionate Kinsman and

obliged humbleServ

Edm Spencer

2 Kinsale] approximately fifteen miles south of Cork on the estuary of the River Bandon.

8 Mr Southwells] possibly Edward Southwell, MP for Downpatrick, 1727–1755, son of Edward Southwell, chief secretary for Ireland and MP for Kinsale from 1692 until his death. Kinsale was part of his family's extensive Munster estates (*DIB*).

9 Gen.^{ll} Parker] General Gervais Parker (1695–1750), a British soldier from a Jacobite family who was governor of Cork and then Kinsale, becoming commander-in-chief of the Irish army from 1740–1750.

13 Carrigtohill] a village some ten miles east of Cork, now spelled /Carrigtwohill/; horse racing still takes place there.

15–16 the great Plate [...] Chester Races] Derek Jarrett (*England in the Age of Hogarth*, rev. ed. (New Haven, CT: Yale University Press, 1986, pp. 154–55) points out that as roads improved there was an increased interest in speed and horse racing between 1750 and 1780, and English horses were favoured as they were universally admired for their strength and endurance. After the Restoration there was a quantum jump in the development of 'professional' horse racing, with the establishment of trophies and organized gambling (ibid., p. 94). Nicholas Russell, in *Like Engend'ring Like* (p. 60), notes that the thoroughbred for racing was a late seventeenth- and early eighteenth-century phenomenon.

22 Stokah] see 8 November 1743: folio 8, note to l.36.

23 Lismore Wears] Lismore is a town some thirty five miles north-east of Cork and on the Blackwater, a river favoured for salmon fishing; /Wear/ was a common eighteenth-century spelling of /weir/ and such a structure might have prevented salmon from getting to the upper reaches of the river; alternatively it could mean an enclosure of stakes placed in a river for trapping fish and, again, that would explain why few salmon were in the river by the time it reached Lismore. The pluralization is slightly odd, but Spencer may well simply be referring to a number of these structures.

[folio 24]

[To Francis Price Esqr]

Renny July the 24.th 1744

Dear Sir

I have the Pleasure of yours of the 11.th ins^{t} & am concernd I applyd for the Indian grass, since it has given you so much Trouble to procure it, I woud rather have been without it than have occasiond you such fretting as I am convinced the hunting for it did. I am greatly obliged to you for the Acc.^{ts} you so kindly give of what passes in your Neighbourhood, & wish 'twas in my Power to find out anything here to entertain you with: the only thing new is that Mr Badham died last Week, by which Colonel Barry has another opportunity of returning a Member for Rathcormuck & consequently of receiving Six or Seven hundreds more: the Lord Kingston is dangerously ill, which happens well for young Thornhill / who married Badham's Daughter /. he it seems was to have been attackd by the Lord & Parson Rider who I believe you know: for Badham in his life loved Law so well, that he woud do nothing to ∧^{hinder} his daughter's being involved in it during hers. he was a Man endued with all the cunning &c of the old Trigger except his Hippocrisy for I never coud hear that ∧^{he} attempted to pass for an honest man: & therefore I think a less dangerous person to be dealt with than your worthy neighbour. I send you inclosed a receipt to make Gooseberry Vinegar, which I hope will come time

———————

enough to you to have some made. if you approve of it 'tis recommended by the Dublin Society, & is said to be as good for pickling &c as any white wine vinegar & you will see by the rec.^{t} vastly cheaper. you give me a poor Acct. of your success in procuring Subscribers, mine I thank God has been better: I intend to be in Dublin next October to put the Work to the Press, but fear I shall hardly clear my Expences _____ My Wife joins in our best respects to you Coz.^{n} Price & Dear Mr Richard. I am Dear sir

your most affec^{te} Kinsman
& obliged humble Servant
Edm Spencer

9 Mr Badham] Brettridge Badham, MP for Rathcormac 1743–1745. See 8 November 1743: folio 8, l.13 and note.

11 Rathcormuck] Rathcormac in Co. Cork, twenty miles north of Cork on the Dublin to Fermoy road. Spencer's spelling is possibly slightly phoneticized: Lewis, Ireland, spells it /Rathcormac/ though Carlisle, Ireland, spells it as Spencer does.

12 Lord Kingston] possibly James, 4th Baron Kingston, of Michelstown, Co. Cork; if so, no doubt to the disappointment of 'young Thornhill', he survived the illness, dying in 1761. A Lord Kingston is also mentioned in the letter of 10 November 1746: folio 53, ll.15–16.

22 Gooseberry Vinegar] valuable in the eighteenth century for both culinary and medicinal purposes, vinegar served to preserve food and disguise smells; many varieties were available, often created like this one through infusions.

[folio 25]

[To Francis Price Esqr]

Renny Aug.st the 19th 1744

Dear Sir

I am just returnd from Cork Assyzes, where I continued two days extraordinary to attend the Tryal of the Lieut.^{t} of the Old Noll Privateer for killing one of the Crew of the Thurloe Privateer; the Affair happened thus; The Thurloe saild from Cove on a Cruise & met & took a french ship bound to Martinico, but was imediately attacked by a french pri=vateer of considerable force who took the Thurloe & her Prize & put 40 french aboard her & left but 16 English, & did intend with both those Ships to have stolen from Cove harbour what Merchantmen lay there, but was luckily prevented by the Old Noll who met them not far off Land, & after a few Shot the French sheerd off & left her in possession of the Thurloe & her Prize: both which as 'tis thought will be deemd good Prize to the old Noll, whose Capt. imediately put his Lieuten.^{t} aboard the Thurloe to command there, but the 16 English that were left aboard refused to obey him as they disputed the Le=gality of the Prize, & upon his ordering one of the Mutineers into Irons the rest were rushing on him to secure him, which obliged him to run the foremost thro' the Body which so intimidated the rest that they submitted to his orders; he gave himself up imediately & was tried by a Jury of the top Gentlemen of this County & was honourably acquitted: tho' / as there happened upon this Acc.^{t} a Dispute between the County and Citty, in which Jurisdiction that part of the River is / the Citty has obliged him to enter into Bonds to stand his Tryal before them the next Assyzes, but the Merch.^{ts} having so great a Regard for the Officers of the Old Noll

3–4 Old Noll [...] Thurloe] *Old Noll* and *The Thurloe* were privateers that worked together (consorts) with particular success against the French (see Gomer Williams, *History of the Liverpool Privateers and Letters of Marque: With an Account of the Liverpool Slave Trade* (London: Routledge, 2013), p. 39). Both ships were named in honour of notable English Protestants, the former taking the nickname of Oliver Cromwell, and the latter the name of one of his secretaries of state, John Thurloe, who was, between 1653 and 1660, successively head of Cromwell's intelligence service and postmaster general, in which capacity he vigorously pursued the postal service's habit of covertly opening letters as a means of state surveillance of the population; his state papers, including his vast correspondence, were published in seven volumes in 1742 (*ODNB*). See also l.39 of this letter and note.

5 Cove] a village to the south-west of Cork on the northern side of the stretch of water that connects Cork with the Celtic Sea and part of Cork Harbour (now spelled /Cobh/).

6 Martinico] Martinique, a French island in the eastern Caribbean Sea; it is still a French territory.

did not oblige him to find any Bail, but only pass his own Recognizance of fifty pounds & enlarged him there upon, so that he is again aboard. I have been the more particular in the Acc.^{t} of these two Ships as they both belong to Liverpoole & of consequence you are acquainted with the Owners, it seems both Ships belong to the Same Gen=tlemen. I was aboard the Old Noll & think no Cost has been spared to equip her for the Purpose. The Terrible another Liverpoole Privateer has sent ~~in~~ a prize into Waterford. At last they have fitted out a privateer from Dublin which is call'd the Boyne but she has not yet Saild — My Wife joins in our best respects to you & all Friends, I am Dear Sir

Your most affect.^{te} Kinsman
& obliged humble Servant
Edm Spencer

P.S.
There is a son of unfortunate Dick Chinnery's aboard the old Noll / I believe you knew Dick in Mallow / who is allowed by his Officers to be a Lad of Courage & to have behaved gallantly in all their

28 pass] 'pledge' (*OED*, v.48.a).

29 Recognizance] 'a sum of money pledged as a surety for performance of a future act and rendered forfeit by the neglect of that performance' (*OED*, n.1).

29 enlarged] 'set free' (*OED*, v.6.a).

35 the Terrible] *The Terrible* was later to become well known when she was captured by the French in 1756, the first year of the Seven Years War. Her famous captain, William Death, was killed in the encounter.

37 Waterford] a substantial port on the estuary of the River Suir, some seventy miles east of Cork.

38 the Boyne] an 80-gun Royal Navy ship, launched in 1692 and scrapped in 1763. Another ship with a designation that reinforces the Hanoverian Protestant ascendancy, it was one of a number named after the victory of William III over James II at the battle of the Boyne, west of Drogheda, on 1 July 1690, which secured the future of the British monarchy as Protestant. (See also 19 August 1744: folio 25, note to ll.3–4.)

PS Dick Chinnery's] a Mr Chinnery ran a school in Charleville near Renny, and it is possible that Spencer was sent there for his education (see the Introduction).

PS knew] first written as /know/ but corrected by over-writing the /o/ with an /e/.

PS Mallow] on the River Blackwater, some seventeen miles north of Cork and about eight east of Castletownroche; Price had an interest in some property there which is the subject of some of the later correspondence (see 23 May 1745: folio 31 to 10 September 1745: folio 35) and that fact, taken with what is said here, suggests that he spent some time here when he lived in Ireland.

Engagem.^{ts} a Word or Line from you to any of the owners woud procure him some little Command aboard the Thurloe when they Man her again, & by it you will greatly oblige a good Many of your Friends on this Side the Water, his father having left not a groat to any of his poor Children obliged this Lad to try his Fortune at Sea ___________

[folio 26]

[To Francis Price Esqr

When you open this Letter turn over]

Renny Sepr the 29.th 1744

Dear Sir

Since my last I have till yesterday been a perfect truant, I have spent all that Time at Mr Freeman's & Mr Oliver's, buck hunting, the latter is now come to his Villa at Kilcummer to spend this winter in Foxhunting: I am advised by all my Friends here to postpone the Publication of Spencer's Works to next Parliam.^{t} winter, by that time 'tis thought I shall have a pritty full Subscription; This month has proved so very stormy and wet, that the harvest is not yet got in; & the corn & hay so damaged, that a dear Spring is to be dreaded with the loss of Cattle if that shoud prove bad, I hope you've had better weather at your side the Water. Just this ins^{t} arived yours of the 12.th I am greatly obliged to you for your Correspondance especially as I know how little you Care for the Trouble of writing, An Advertizem.^{t} has been in the papers sometime to man the Dublin Privateer, in my Opinion she has over mettle for her Burthen, the Terrible Privateer of Liverpoole has brought into Cove last week a Martinico Man & a French Privateer, which she will carry from thence to Bristol, as she is obliged to perform Quarentine if she stays here on Acc.^{t} of her having taken Some of the Martinico Crew aboard: the reason of the Quarentine I can't find out, but this is the Acc.^{t} I yesternight reced from Corke — My Wife joins in our best Respects to you Mrs Price & dear Mr Richard I am Dear sir

Y. sincerely affec^{t} Kinsman & obliged
hmb: Serv: Edm Spencer

My service to Mr Smith & all Friends

Turn over

After I had seald this Letter I opend it to acquaint you with the disagreeable Account I have just received that the [Old Noll] is taken the Occasion this, a stout Merchant Man 600 tuns [victuald] at [Cove], pritty well gund & Mand after a stout [Resistance] was taken by ∧^{a} French Privateeer who put 100 of her hands aboard & then sheerd off; the poor old Noll met the Privateer & gave her Chase till she decoyd her to the Latitude where she expected her Prize to meet her & then gave the old Noll Battle which lasted two hours, at which time the Prize came up to the assistance of the Frenchman & shatterd the poor Noll to that Degree that she was forced after the Loss of two of her Masts & hulld in several Places to strike, she was ransomd by the Capt who left his Lieut.t to pledge for the payment for l500 as I am informed. She is now at Passage near Cove in a miserable Plight.

Addressee] the instruction: 'When you open this Letter turn over' is upside down in relation to the addressee's name when the letter is unfolded.

2 Mr Freeman's] see note to 6 February 1732: folio 3, l.14.

3 Mr Oliver] possibly the same as the Colonel Oliver whose death in 1745 is reported in 23 May 1745: folio 31, though the omission of the military title here would be odd.

4 Kilcummer] a village less than a mile north of Renny, one and a half miles south-east of Castletownroche, and some twenty miles due north of Cork.

15–16 over mettle [...] Burthen] i.e. more ordnance than she was able to carry safely; 'mettle' was a variant spelling of 'metal' which could refer to either the total mass or the effective power of the guns on a ship; the 'burthen' was the carrying capacity of a ship, now expressed in tons (*OED*, n.3).

17 Man] i.e. a man-of-war (*OED*, n^{I}.14).

26–43] This side of the page is written with a much lighter inking with the result that see-through from the other side so substantially interferes with the legibility that the writing is all but invisible. The two instructions, 'When you open this Letter turn over' and 'Turn over' are both in the same light inking, so we can see that they were added after the verso side was written: clearly Spencer realized that Price may well not see that anything was written on that side of the sheet.

32 sheerd] 'changed course' (*OED*, v^{2}.1.c).

33 she] i.e. the French privateer.

34 Latitude] perhaps in the precise sense, but possibly more in the wider sense 'general locality, area' (*OED*, 4.c).

39 hulld] 'struck in the hull by cannon shot' (*OED*, v^{2}.2).

40 strike] 'to lower a sail as a sign of surrender' (*OED*, v.17.c).

41 l500] i.e. £500, the /l/ standing for 'libra' (Latin for 'a pound').

42 Passage] Passage West, a town on the north-east side of the River Lee as it passes from Lough Mahon into the sea near Cove.

[folio 27]

[To Francis Price Esqr]

Renny Novr the 5.th 1744

D[^{r}] Sir

Since my last we have a Continuation of the terrible Weather I then gave you an Account of so that a Scarcity is with Reason expected this Spring; most of the Corn of this Country is still in the Fields, & the hay almost entirely rotted, tho the Price of Grain is not yet advanced, except Oats, & beef of five hun.^{d} p Carkass is but five [*shill*] & nine pence p Ct, a less price than the Graziers gave for them poor, & as in y^{e} County of Limerick they are almost under Water & entirely lost their hay, 'tis thought this Season will demolish a great many $^{\text{in that county}}$∧ who if Cattle bore a tolerable Price woud be in very good Circumstances. Thus have I given a Detail of our Misfortunes on this Side the Water, tho I can see but little of it, for I have been these three Weeks confined to my Chamber by a Sprain in my back I rece'd in a fall leaping a Ditch, and find my self but slowly mending tho I am at the Expence of Doctor & at the trouble of taking all his nauseous pres=criptions. We have the dismal Acc.^{t} of the Loss of Victory Man of Warr with the Exaggeration of her ^{having} been lost by her being badly built & tis said Admiral Vernon discovered the Ignorance of the Master-builders a good while ago, tho no notice was taken of him. As soon as I shall be able to stir abroad I intend to try to procure as much as will buy 40 heifers which I expect will be very cheap on Acc.^{t} of the Scarcity of hay

———————————

& I shall keep them in my young Wood, where there has not been a Beast these eight years; they can now do no harm there, as the trees are grown out of their reach and it will maintain that number this Winter & till Aprill next without a bit of Hay, & I may expect to be very well paid for their Keep. My Wife joins in our best Respects to you Coz.^{n} Price & dear Mr Richard, my Service to Mr Smith & all acquaintance. I am Dear Sir

Your Sincerely aff.^{te} Kinsman
and obliged humble Servant
Edm Spencer

Salutation] the unusual contraction of the salutation may be simply /D/, the superscript letter being no more than a flourish on the /S/.

6 five hun.[d] p] i.e. five hundredweight per carcass.

7 shill] the word is not entirely clear but this is most likely, as in 6 February 1732: folio 3, l.22, an abbreviation of /shillings/.

7 Ct] i.e. a hundredweight, often abbreviated to just /C/.

8 poor] 'in their lean condition, before feeding up for market' (*OED*, adj.3.a).

16–17 Expence of Doctor] a doctor who requires payment suggests a fairly high status medical professional; if that is the case, Spencer was probably fortunate to have access to such a skilled person (though his comment on the treatment suggests that he failed to appreciate this); Laurence Brockliss ('Religion and Social Mobility in Eighteenth- and Early Nineteenth-Century Ireland', in *Ireland and Medicine in the Seventeenth and Eighteenth Centuries*, ed. by James Kelly and Fiona Clark (Farnham: Ashgate, 2010) pp. 73–10 (p. 73)) suggests that, on the basis of the 1851 census and other reasonable assumptions, trained physicians would have been thin on the ground in Ireland in the mid-ninetenth century so it seems highly likely that the same situation prevailed in the preceding century, especially in the country districts. As to the 'Expence' see note to ll.2–3 of the next letter.

19 Victory Man of Warr] the flagship of the British fleet, launched in 1737, lost with all hands in a violent storm off the Channel Islands, possibly due to rotten timbers or being top heavy, or bad seamanship.

20–21 Admiral Vernon] Edward Vernon (1684–1757), a prominent naval commander noted for his victories in the War of Jenkins' Ear; he was responsible for many naval innovations. (See also 4 October 1743: folio 7, note to ll.20–21.)

[folio 28]

[To Francis Price Esqr]

Renny Jan$^{\partial}$y the 18.th 174^{4}5

Dear Sir

Since my last to you <~~xx~~> / wherein I gave an Acc.^{t} of a Fall I received / till Tuesday last, I have been in Cork under the Physicians hands; being in a very dangerous State & very near a confirmd Consumption, the Nocturnal Sweats & irregular Hecticks continued for above a Month which had almost tript me off, & have so emaciated my little carcass that were you to see me now you woud scarce know me, & what is as bad have reduced my purse to a much lower Ebb. the Weather is so very uncertain that I cannot mend as fast as I shoud if I coud take the benefit of Air if the Season was milder.

I have the Pleasure of your two Letters & will write to Doct^{r} Kingsbury as soon as priviledge comes in, but am advised by all Friends not to publish till next Winter when our Parliament meet: as our present Lord Lieuten.^{t} is of the Country Party & So many others of that Side are now in play, I flatter my Self, you will not forget me, a proper recommendation from some of your Friends to those in power, woud, I am certain, do my Business with Ld Chesterfield, & a very small place woud content me as I fear I shall not be able to hold out long without some such pro= vision. there is no trouble <~~xx~~>^{or} / almost / Slavery that I woud not try to go through to procure honest bread for my little Family I hope I shoud behave so as not to disoblige any friend that woud apply for me by my conduct therein. My Wife joins in our sincere Wishes for many happy Years to you Mrs Price

———————

& Dear Mr Richard I am Dear Sir

Your very affec.^{te} Kinsman
& obliged humble Servt
Edm Spencer

Date] it looks very much as though Spencer could not make up his mind whether to date this letter 1744 or 1745 as both the /4/ and the /5/ are quite clear, and though the former is superscribed and the latter slightly subscribed, the /4/ is not an insertion: there is no caret, both numbers are well spaced, and they are much the same size as the /1/ and the /7/. The reference to the 'Acc.^{t} of a Fall' in l.2 makes it clear that this letter follows the previous one (5 November 1744: folio 27, ll.13–15) and the naming of Lord Chesterfield as the new lord lieutenant (ll.14–18) confirms the date as January 1745 so the letter is definitely not out of chronological order; however, Spencer is in the habit of dating Old Style — and indeed dates the next letter thus — so to date this letter 1745, even as an afterthought, would be very unusual for him; it is tempting to speculate that being still unwell he is simply confused, but that does not really satisfactorily account for this anomaly.

2–3 in Cork [...] hands] a mere two months after his back injury (see previous letter) Spencer is suffering a serious illness, but this time he is being treated in Cork, presumably at the house of his physician (as people often were in the early modern period before hospitals were widespread). It is possible that Spencer's use of the term 'physician' and the fact that he has had to go to Cork for treatment suggest that this man is of a slightly higher status than the 'doctor' who treated him in Renny; however, Spencer often uses the title 'doctor' for lawyers so that term may simply indicate the level of education attained by a professional person (see also 18 November 1755: folio 97, note to ll.9–10). Possibly because of the physician's higher status, but possibly because of the length of the treatment, this spell of medical care was more expensive than the treatment two months earlier because Spencer tells Price in the letter of 23 May 1745: folio 31, ll.38–40, that it was only the generosity of his friend Col. Oliver that 'enabled me to pay off a Debt my late Illness obliged me to contract in Cork, & which my own slender Circumstances he knew could ill afford me to pay'.

3 dangerous State] Spencer was nursed through this illness by his daughter, Rosamond (James Kelly, 'Domestic Medication and Medical Care in Late Early Modern Ireland', in *Ireland and Medicine*, ed. by Kelly and Clark, pp. 109–35 (p. 117)).

4 Consumption] i.e. tuberculosis, which reached epidemic proportions in the eighteenth century, replacing leprosy as the most common disease as more people migrated to the cities. The airborne bacteriological nature of tuberculosis was only properly understood in the early twentieth century and 'consumption' was often used to describe any chronic lung disease, although Spencer is correct to associate night sweats and weight loss with the disease.

5 Hecticks] 'consumptive or wasting fevers' (*OED*, n.1.a).

6 tript me off] 'finished me off', 'sent me into the next world' with perhaps a hint of being 'turned off' the gallows.

12 as soon as priviledge comes in] i.e. as soon as he has been granted the right to print this book (*OED*, *privilege*, n.6.a).

14 our present Lord Lieuten.^{t}] i.e. Philip Stanhope, 4th Earl of Chesterfield (1694–1773); appointed on 8 January 1745, he did not arrive in Dublin until 31 August of that year, and remained in post for just under two years. A noted wit, intellectual, and astute holder of the office, his main achievement was dissuading Irish Jacobites from joining the '45 rebellion.

14 the Country Party] a group of English politicians (rather than a formal party) of those opposing the dominant Court Party; Spencer, too, allies himself with the group in Ireland (later the Patriot Party) that opposed the established political interest (also known in Ireland as the Court Party — see 19 July 1755: folio 96) and he recognizes here that he has more hope of finding work in the Dublin administration under this new Lord Lieutenant.

18 Ld Chesterfield] see first note to l.14.

[folio 29]

[To Francis Price Esqr]

Renny March the 4.th 1744

Dear Sir

Since my last which gave an Acc.^{t} of my ill State of Health, I am so greatly recoverd, that by consent of my Physicicans I venture out hunting & have recoverd that Appetite which I had so long lost. I trouble you with these Acc.^{ts} as I am certain everything that conduces to my benefit gives you Pleasure ----- Since this Day Sennight we have two feet thick Snow on the Ground & no likelyhood of a thaw, as the Season is so far advanced & Hay very scarce, numbers of black Cattle are falling off & the lambs die as soon as dropt in the County of Limerick they are in a deplorable Condition through the Loss of their Potatoes & as their chief dependance now lies on Roch's Country for Corn which is ~~now~~ raised to a very dear Price, we shall have a very late Harvest as the Season for sowing Winter Grain was so wet that the farmers coud not sow Wheat or Beerbarley till December & the present Weather / besides the dearness / hinders the sowing Spring Corn. We expect the War to be continued whatever the Politicians urge to the contrary for the Hulk is arrived at Kinsale which is never sent but when a tedious War is expected. French Prizes are brought thither daily, & there are at present about 1100 prisoners there which with about forty families of the ~~persons~~ Shipwrights, Victualers etc belonging to the Hulk has made Kinsale so flourishing that House rent is so raised

———————————

as to yield twenty Pounds p ann$^{\partial}$ for one that a few Months ago woud have produced but Six or Seven pounds. An Embargo is laid on the Harbours of Corke & Kinsale Harbours only, which is to be continued for Six Weeks, the reason as is supposed, this some time ago there saild from Cork Seventeen Ships laden with Beef and butter, fourteen of which were taken by the French, so that tis very justly suspected that they were designedly carried to France as the French are $\wedge^{in}$ great want of Provisions & $\wedge^{the}$ Merchants of Cork not unacquainted with the Methods of supplying them at a very dear Rate, which no doubt they are to get for those Ships which have been taken besides the Insurance _____ My Wife joins in our best Respects to you Coz.^{n} Price & dear Master Richard I am Dear Sir your sincerely affec.^{te} Kinsman & obliged

humb: Servt Edm Spencer

My humble Service to
Colonel & all Friends

Date] Spencer returns to giving the year unquivocally in Old Style.

6 Sennight] i.e. seven nights, and thus a week back.

12 Roche's Country] see 4 October 1743: folio 7, l.12 and note.

18 the Hulk] 'a ship, no longer seaworthy, used as a prison' (*OED*, n^{2}.3.b), in this case for prisoners-of-war.

[folio 30]

[To Francis Price Esqr]

near CastleLyons April the 10

Dear Sir

Since my last nothing worthwhile has happend in [*these*] Parts to acquaint you of, but the vast Losses of Cattle which has been all over the Kingdom but especially in the North, where very few remain alive: in and about Newcastle in the County of Limerick Hay sold for Eight Shillings p hund.^{d} Provisions of all kinds are at a very dear rate 7 shil p kinderkin for Oats 8 shill 6^{d} for English & 7[/]6 for Beer barley, very few Potatoes to be had & those as dear as they were the Year after the great Frost, Wheat is the cheapest Article as several Vessells have brought large Cargo's of it from England, Beef & Mutton at three pence the pound & very little good of that. I hope you find the Season more reasonable on your Side the Water. I must trouble you again in Favour of Mr Chinnery who is just returnd from France where he remaind some Time Hostage for the Old Noll, a letter from you ∧^{to} Mr Sam: Seel woud be of singular Service to him as it woud make his Owners take him for more than a Common Hand. I have now my Books ready for the Press but do not intend to print them till Winter as I expect to procure a good Number of Subscribers when our Parliament m[*eet*] Pray will you have the Five Setts / you wish for / in your own Name? My Wife joins in our best Respects to you Mrs Price & Dear Mr Rich^{d} with my Service to all Friends I am Dear Sir

Your Sincerely affec^{te} Kinsman
& obliged humble Servant
Edm Spencer

Date] after the /10/ (which is itself uncertain) there is probably a year but it is now completely faded out; however, the references in the first few lines of the letter to losses of cattle and high food prices almost certainly follow on from the previous letter of March 1745, so the year of this can confidently be assumed as also 1745.

1 these] this word looks very like /those/ but it is on the badly faded edge of the sheet and it may be that only the loop of the /e/ is left; the more likely word /these/ has therefore been suggested here.

4 Newcastle] i.e. Newcastle West, twenty five miles south-west of Limerick.

5 hund.^{d}] i.e. hundredweight.

6 kinderkin] usually 'kilderkin', a cask the size of half a barrel (or the quantity that could be contained in such a cask).

6 7[/]6] i.e. seven shillings and sixpence (37.5 pence in decimal money); the forward slash looks like a /p/ which might be thought to indicate /£7/, but if oats are selling at 7 or 8 shillings £7 would be an implausible price for beer barley, so the slash has been represented here as the conventional mark between shillings and pence in pre-decimal money.

8 the great Frost] this would be the frost that occurred in Ireland in January 1740, rather than the one that Spencer describes in his previous letter. It was one of the most extreme events in the Little Ice Age that afflicted Europe between (according to the widest estimate) the beginning of the fourteenth and the middle of the nineteenth centuries; the effects of that frost and the following bitter winter of 1740/41 caused a famine that reduced the population of Ireland by about 40%. We have no contemporaneous mention of it in any of Spencer's letters because of the gap in the correspondence between 6 February 1732: folio 3 and 2 August 1741: folio 4.

11–15 I must [...] Common Hand.] someone has pencilled square brackets around this passage, possibly Price to remind himself to act upon the request which was originally made in the postscript to the letter of 19 August 1744: folio 25.

[folio 31]

[To Francis Price Esqr]

Renny May the 23^{d} 1745

Dear Sir

Yours of the 3^{d} of April did not come to hand till a Month after the Date, since which Time I have been thrice at Mallow, the two first Times I coud meet with little Intelligence but now find that, The Checkleys had but One Holding in Mallow which lyes opposite the End of Killmallock Lane / now called Fair Lane / & joins Saverys Holdings / now Dobbs's /. Checkley's Holding was taken by Thos

3 Mallow] see 19 August 1744: folio 25, note to postscript.

3 I coud [...] Intelligence] the enquiry that Spencer here undertakes, and which he describes in l.2 of 26 July 1745: folio 33 as 'the Mallow Affair', is to occupy him for the next fifteen weeks and cause him considerable vexation. For the modern reader any attempt to understand this 'affair' is hindered by two aspects. First, we have only one side of the conversation between Spencer and Price, so we do not know precisely what Price has asked him to establish. Second, Irish land tenure arrangements could be appallingly complicated as a result of a practice by which properties were let to one person, then sub-let by that lessee, and then sub-let yet again, sometimes several times over; furthermore, quite separate people could take out mortgages on leased properties, as Alderman Hoar appears to have done on this one (see ll.15–18 of this letter). All that is partly at the root of the difficulties Spencer encounters, but he has two further problems. One is that not only does he have difficulty identifying who owns the property in question, he even seems to find it hard to identify the actual building itself (see 20 August 1745: folio 34, ll.14–16), presumably because the documentation of all these various transactions and the processes leading to them is so complicated. The other aspect is that Col. Anthony Jephson is involved in this complex chain of ownership and leasing (see ll.5 & 6). He is clearly someone Spencer dislikes intensely: note his comment in l.5 of the letter of 20 August 1745: folio 34 that 'twoud be easier to find out the Longitude than Jephsons Matters', and the warning he gives Price in ll.27–29 of this letter, to 'be very cautious how you correspond with Anthony

Checkley from one of the Jephsons, & was on the Marriage of his Son Phillip to one Joans settled on their Issue. It was a long Time disputed amongst the Checkleys but at last came into the Hands of one Charles Checkley Grandson to Philip, who about the year 40 or 41 sold the Interest to Henry Wrixon Esqr who paid off all the Debts and Arrears & got a new Lease from Anth: Jephson in his own Name, & has built two Hansome Houses on the Premisses: I cant hear of any Conveyances to or from Bulkeley, Price or Roberts at any Time, but hear that Ald.^{n} Hoar of Corke had in Philip Checkley's Time a Mort= gage on the Holding & on that Acc.^{t} did for some Time receive the Profit Rent, but cannot find out what Time or by whom the Mort= gage was redeemd: By all Acc.^{ts} I find the Lease was for Years & not for Lives, so the Time of the Decease of the Persons you mention can signify nothing, nor can I think by what Pretence Jephson can make a Demand to you for any Arrear, especially as he has

& keep Coppys of all the Letters you may write to him'. As well as serving as an officer in the army, Jephson was MP at various times between 1713 and 1755 for Mallow, which his family more or less ran (*HIP*). The result is that when Spencer makes enquiries in the town he finds himself up against a local *omertà*, and when he does find someone who will give him the information he needs his informant insists that it is given on the strict understanding that his name will be revealed to nobody, as 'did the worthy Colonel find out that he made this Discovery he would certainly ruin him as 'tis in his Power to do so' (20 August 1745: folio 34, ll.36–37).

4 Holding] this could mean 'tenure' in the sense of the right to occupy a property, or 'the property itself '(*OED*, vbl.n.1.c and 3.a); Spencer seems to be using it throughout this discussion in the latter sense.

14 Conveyances] 'transferences of property by any legal act' or 'the written documents by which such transfer is effected' (*OED*, 7.a and b).

14 Price] this is possibly a relation of Francis Price, and possibly the same person as the Capt. Price who is mentioned as receiving the rents from this property in 20 August 1745: folio 34, ll.18–19; that person is more than likely Francis Price's father, he being named on Price's memorial tablet in St Mary's Church, Overton, as 'Captain Richard Price'; he would therefore be the link Price has to this property; if it seems odd that in neither case does Spencer describe the person as Price's father, we should remember that there would be no need for him to be reminded of the relationship.

17 Profit Rent] 'a rent of which the amount is due to a tenant's improvements' (*OED*, *profit*, n.7.b).

18–19 for Years [...] for Lives] a lease could be granted for a number of years stated in the lease, but their duration was sometimes linked to the length of life of a number of specified persons, the termination being determined when the last of these persons dies; these named persons were known as 'lives' (*OED*, *life*, n.8.b).

24 Mr Wrixon] presumably the Henry Wrixon mentioned in l.11. (We might note here that Col. Jephson complained in 1748 that a Nicholas Wrixon, attorney, had insulted him when travelling between Cork and Dublin, suggesting that bad blood existed between the two families, possibly as a result of the wrangling over this Mallow property, see *HIP*, IV, 477–78.)

granted a new Lease of the Premisses, which were of value enough to satisfy any demand to them; if the above account be not sufficient, as soon as you Order I will wait on Mr Wrixon / who is Coz.^{n} German to my Wife / & know from him the Bargain he

——————————

has made with the Colonel; but am confident that a new Lease is a Receipt in full for all Rent & Arrears: be very cautious how you corres= pond with Anthony & keep Coppys of all the Letters you may write to him -----------

I must now give you an Account of the Death of my Dear Worthy Friend Colonel Oliver who was taken off by a spotted Fever to the Regrett & Loss of the Country in General, but in Particular to no one so much as to me, to whom he was a real Friend & whose Loss I shall severely feel, especially the ensuing Session of Parliam.^{t} at which Time he was resolved to have made a vigorous Push in my Favour. His having livd as long as he did however was happy for me, for very lately his generosity enabled me to pay off a Debt my late Illness obliged me to contract in Cork, & which my own slender Circumstances he knew coud ill afford me to pay. I have now but one Friend left in Ireland & that's Wm Freeman who lives so fast, that God knows, he cant long remain, but while he does I shall be a gainer: no news here but our Overthrow at Tournay & sending off from Corke Forces to recruit. My Wife joins in our best Respects to you Mrs Price &dear Mr Rich.^{d}. Dear Sir

Your Sincerely aff^{te} Kinsman
and obliged humb Servt
Edm Spencer

My humble Service to
Mr Smyth & all Friends

25 Coz.^{n} German] a cousin in the stricter modern sense: a child of one's aunt or uncle.

31 Colonel Oliver] possibly the same as the Mr Oliver with whom Spencer goes hunting in September 1744; the omission of the military title in that letter (29 September 1744: folio 26) would be odd but not unusual for Spencer.

31 spotted Fever] usually typhus or meningitis.

35 a vigorous Push] presumably to sign up subscribers for the proposed *Works of Mr. Edmund Spencer.*

39 Wm Freeman] see note to 6 February 1732: folio 3, l.14.

41 Overthrow at Tournay] no doubt referring to the Battle of Fontenoy which took place on 11 May 1745 near Tournai, a Dutch held city which was being besieged by French forces; the English army had been sent, along with their Hanoverian, Austrian, and Dutch allies, to relieve Tournai, but were met by the French at Fontenoy; in the ensuing battle the English Foot were defeated, their final retreat being caused, ironically, by the charge of an Irish regiment in French service.

[folio 32]

[To Francis Price Esqr]

Renny July the 1.st 1745

Dear Sir

I've reced yours with an Abstract of the Lease of the Mallow & went yesterday to Mallow, but coud not meet / upon the closest Enquiry / with any Person that coud give me a satisfactory Acc.^{t} ab.^{t} it or the Lives; Philip Checkley died about ten years ago, End & Noble died in Corke, of which I shall make Enquiry about there; if you think it necssary to do so imediately, upon rece.^{t} of your next orders I will go to Corke, but think 'twill do at our Assyzes which will be in the next Month. I shall there see the Gentleman who at present has the holdings & know from him the tenure of his Lease. Never was seen such unseasonable Weather as we have from the beginning of April, which still continues so, not a Day or night without Rain, & so cold that Fires are still kept, & not an hour of summer has yet been seen. Our worthy Colonel Jephson is at present in the Dumps, for being the eldest Capt in the Regiment he was orderd to Flanders with the Draughts, but as he does not care to venture his sweet person on the Water when he had marchd the Men to Cove & shipd them, he there pretended to have been taken violently ill & had himself bled & blisterd, but as soon as the Transports sail'd he returnd to Mallow in as good a Condition as he left it: how twill be taken to send off the Men without an Officer, a little Time will discover. My Wife joins in our best Respects to you Mrs Price & dear Mr Rich.^{d} I am Dear Sir Y.^{r} sincerely aff^{te} Kinsman

& most humble Servant

My Service to Mr Smyth & all Friends Edm Spencer

5 End & Noble] see the next letter, ll.3–5.

6 Necssary] Spencer has left out a letter here, though whether it is the first or the second /e/ is not obvious.

16 Draughts] 'groups of soldiers selected for a specific duty' (*OED*, n.XI.34).

20 blisterd] like bleeding, a common medical treatment of the period; it was believed to drain the body of fluids that were thought to be causing the illness and involved deliberately raising and then puncturing blisters on the patient's skin.

[folio 33]

[To Francis Price Esqr]

Renny July the 26.th 1745

Dear Sir

Since my last I have made several Enquirys about the Mallow Affair, to very little Purpose, but hope to receive Some Information at our Assyzes which begin the Eight of August. I find there lives one Mich: End a young Quaker in Corke & one John Noble, I will find those out & perhaps learn something ab.^{t} it especially if their fathers were the Lives in the Lease, I shall find the certain Time of their Deaths. But I expect the most satisfactory Acc.^{t} from Mr Wrixon who is in possession of the Holding & lives in Corke. For some Time past we have had fine Weather wch still continues & gives Hopes of a good Harvest tho a late one, not a field of Barley in this Part of the Country yet fit to cut, tho of other Seasons our Bear Barley harvest began the first Week in July. By this Time poor Welsh has reachd Brynypiece, he can give you a dismal acc.^{t} of the scarcity that reigns here, & a more dismal one of himself for realy the poor Fellow deserves to be pittyd, as he labourd under a tedious Fit of Sickness in those dear Times: when he returns please to send me some Riga Cabbage Seed & some white Strawberry Plants, for I meet none of that Sort in this Kingdom. I cant but be concernd for your putting out my friend Mr Richard to School, as I know very well the great Grief twill give his good Mamma to have him removed from her own Eye. Pray can't you get a sober discreet Tutor for him in the House? sure some of your Friends in Oxford coud send a proper person from one of the Colleges, which may afford him Learning enough & save his Mamma

———————————

a great Deal of Anxiety and Trouble: I hope for her Ease & Satisfaction you have alterd your Resolution. My Wife joins me in our best Compliments to Coz.^{n} Price & you & dear Mr Dick I am Dear Sir

Your Sincerely aff^{te} Kinsman
& obliged humble Servt
Edm Spencer

My Service to Mr Smith
& all Friends

6 their fathers [...] the Lease] i.e. the persons whose length of life determined the duration of the lease.

12 Bear] i.e. 'Beer'.

16 those dear Times] i.e. in the last winter, /dear/ most likely having here the sense of 'hard, severe, grievous' (*OED*, *dear*, a^{2}.2).

17 Riga Cabbage [...] Strawberry Plants] there was a variety of cabbage called Russian in the eighteenth century (*OED*, *Russian*, n. and a., 2.b) and in 28 March 1747: folio 57 Spencer asks Price to send him some 'Russia Cabbage Seed & a few Plants of the white

Strawberrys'; as Riga was part of the Russian empire at this period the varietal name used here, even if by mistake, would no doubt be perfectly understandable to Price. Strawberries had been grown in gardens since the early middle ages in Europe, the great reputation of the fruits produced in the Bishop of Ely's garden at his London residence in Holborn during the fifteenth century being recorded in Shakespeare's *Richard III* when Gloucester says to the bishop, 'My Lord of Ely, when I was last in Holborn, | I saw good strawberries in your garden there' (III iv 31–32); however, interest in them increased in the eighteenth century due to the availability of new strains. The eighteenth-century passion for exchanging new and exotic plants is exhibited also in Sir Horace Walpole's correspondence; on 12 March 1743 Sir Horace Mann wrote to him from Florence asking on behalf of an Italian friend for some tea seed from the Botanic Gardens at Chelsea, and for 'any other curious exotics' (*Horace Walpole's Correspondence, Yale Edition*, ed. by W. S. Lewis, 48 vols (New Haven, CT: Yale University Press, 1937–1983), XVIII, 183–84, <http://images.library.yale.edu/hwcorrespondence> [accessed 10 February 2016]), while Walpole himself responded to a request from George Montagu in November 1755 for some exotic tree plants by sending no less than 139 from his own 'small nursery' (ibid., IX, 176–77).

26 Mr Dick] i.e. Richard Price, this is the only time Spencer refers to him by this diminutive.

[folio 34]

[To Francis Price Esqr]

Renny August the 20.th 1745

Dear Sir

It's so long since I had the Pleasure of a Letter from you that I conclude you are from home, perhaps putting the finishing Strokes towards the building the Square. I assure you I have not been idle in making Enquiries about the Mallow Affair twoud be easier to find out the Longitude than Jephsons Matters: the People of Mallow are so cautious of even saying any ∧^{thing} about him that I almost despaird of getting any Intelligence tho' I applyd to none but

3 the finishing [...] Square] this is probably Cleveland Square in Liverpool. Price's wife, Alice, was the daughter of John Cleiveland who owned the Birkenhead Priory estate (which Alice inherited on his death); in January 1713, three years before he died, Cleiveland took a lease on some land on the other side of the Mersey between Toxteth Park to the south-east and Dale Road to the north-west and in 1740 this lease passed to Francis Price (Liverpool Record Office, Lease Register for Liverpool Corporation, 352 CLE/Con 3/2, 1672–1767); this comment suggests that Price has embarked on developing the land, building Price Street off the eastern end of Hanover Street and (at the other end of Price Street) Cleveland Square, unless he was simply finishing off what his father-in-law had started earlier in the century. Both the street and the square are unassuming contributions to the city's architecture, but they have served the purpose of memorializing the family names.

5 twoud [...] Longitude] finding an accurate method of establishing the longitude was seen in the early eighteenth century as so vital to Britain's maritime interests that the Longitude Act of 1714 offered a prize of £20,000 to the inventor of the first practicable method of determining a ship's longitude at sea; some ten years before Spencer wrote this letter John Harrison, a Yorkshire carpenter and self-taught clock-maker, had actually solved the problem, building a clock that kept time so accurately, even on a storm-tossed ship, that it could be used to establish the measurement to half a degree; however, the scientific

those that I was certain ought not to regard him. The holding of Checklys that I mentiond was sett to Wrixon happens not to be that in Dispute as appeard to me by the abstract of the Lease, by which it mentions one on the other side of the Street which has been so long out of Checkleys Possession that it lost that Name & consequently was the more difficult for me to find out, however I made a shift to procure the following Acc.^{t} vizt Checkly's holding bounded by Maretts holding on the West & by Daniel's on the East, is now calld Sullivan's Holding. Cornelius Sullivan a great While ago ∧$^{\text{took it}}$ from John Chinnery or one Dennis I am told for forty Shillings pan.$^{\partial}$ Anthony Callaghan who for a long Time after reced Rents for Capt Price always received Rents for the Capt from said Sullivan / as Sullivan's Widdows says / Sullivan about Eighteen Years ago takes a Lease from Anth: Jephson at forty shillings pan$^{\partial}$ renewable for ever. whether his Lease commenced from that Time or was to comence at the Death of the Lives in Checkly's Lease I cannot find out. but this is certain, That, Sullivan mortgaged

———————————

this Lease to one of the Newman's & built a good Slate-House on the premisses where he ∧$^{\text{/ Sullivan /}}$ always dwelt till he died which was about the year 1734; on his Decease Newman possesses himself of the Holding: Jephson & Newman soon after came to an Agreement he pays off Newman, takes up Sullivan's Lease & setts the Holding to James Sullivan by the year at Five pounds who now holds it under Jephson. N: B: said James is Son to said Cornelius. As to the Lives all I can learn is that ~~they~~ $^{\text{two of them}}$ have been dead a long Time, ~~except~~ one William End son of Willm End that lived in Mallow if he was a Life ~~he~~ is still in being∧.$^{\text{\& now in Cork}}$ The greatest Part of the above Acc.^{t} I have from a person now in Mallow to whom I am under a Strict Engagement that his Name shall never be made use off on this Acc.^{t} for did the worthy Colonel find out that he made this Discovery he woud certainly ruin him as 'tis in his Power to do so. I suppose when the Colonel finds that you know Affairs he will be glad to drop his Claim but if you can have any Demand to him I wish you woud work him, be cautious how you write to him & keep Copys of y^{r} Letters. My Wife joins in our best Respects to you Mrs Price & Dr Mr Richard

I am Dear Sir

Your Sincerely aff^{te} Kinsman
& obliged humble Servant
Edm Spencer

P.S.
My Service to M.r Smyth
& all Friends

establishment could not bring itself to recognize the achievement of this humble 'mechanic' who had outclassed the country's elite astronomers and mathematicians, and it was not until 1773 that he was publicly acknowledged and awarded the prize money: see Dava Sobel, *Longitude* (London: Fourth Estate, 1995).

9 sett] i.e. 'let to, given over to by means of a lease' (OED, *set*, v^{I}.57.a).

14 vizt] an alternative representaton of /viz/, i.e. 'videlicet' (Latin for 'that is to say', or 'namely').

18 Capt Price] see note to l.14 of 23 May 1745: folio 31.

40 work him] there is possibly a hint of the sporting sense of this phrase in Spencer's usage of it here: 'to pursue an animal with care and determination' (*OED*, v.12.g); alternatively, in the light of the following 'be cautious', he may mean, 'make your way slowly and gradually' (33.b).

[folio 35]

[To Francis Price Esqr]

Renny September the 10.th 1745

Dear Sir

I am greatly surprized at your long Silence as tis near three Months since I had the Pleasure of a Letter from you, tho in that Time I have written four or five most of them about the Mallow affair particularly my last gave a full Account how that holding lies, & that End is still alive in Cork & well. for a considerable Time I thought you were at Liverpool & expected to hear from you when you came home, but as I know you never stay very long there, it gives me the greater Concern that I shoud be so long without receiving even a Line to inform me how you & your Family are, sure you must think me very ungratefull if I am not anxious about knowing how you are, which I have no Opportunity of but by a Letter from you. Perhaps my Letters miscarry as they are under a Cover, for which Reason / if I do not hear shortly / my next shall be directly to you. As I never did any Thing / even in Thought / to deserve your Slighting me, I cannot lay any Thing to my own Charge that shoud Occasion this Neglect of me, & therefore must impute it to some other Cause as yet unknown to me. My Wife joins in our best Respects to you Mrs Price and Dear Mr Richard I am Dear Sir

Your Sincerely aff.^{te} Kinsman & obliged
hbleServ.^{t} Edm Spencer

6 at Liverpool] see l.3 of the previous letter, and note.

12–13 under a Cover [...] to you] a 'cover' was the envelope or outer wrapping of a package of letters to different people who lived in a single locality; the cover bore the address of a chosen destination from which the individual letters were then distributed to the people named on them, thereby saving money on the postage; fearing that some accident or mistake has led to his letters being mislaid, lost, or perhaps even sent to the wrong person, Spencer considers addressing the next letter specifically to Price (as he had the very first letter in this collection, which is addressed to 'Overton near Wrexham Chester'); as it happens, he gets a reply from Price in the next ten days (see next letter, l.1) and so reverts to his normal practice. This comment does suggest, though, that Spencer's letters to Price were sent with letters to another person (or other people) who lived near Overton, and that person could be Sir Watkin Williams-Wynn, a close neighbour and friend of Price: Spencer says to Price in his letter of 9 October 1747: folio 60: 'I suspect you did not receive either of mine in answer to your last Favour, tho directed as usual under cover to Sir Watkin' (ll.2–4, and note to l.2); why he should be corresponding with Sir Watkin cannot be explained as there is not the slightest hint in these letters that he is doing so; it may simply be, though, that Spencer is using Sir Watkin's franks (see 19 December 1745: folio 37, note to address) and that it would arouse the suspicion of the postal service's surveillance agents if franked letters from Sir Watkin were seen to be passing from Ireland to any address other than his own (see also 16 June 1747: folio 59, l.21).

[folio 36]

[To Francis Price Esqr]

Renny October the 10.th 1745

Dear Sir

I have the Pleasure of yours of the 20th ult which gives the greater Satisfaction as tis so long since I heard before. I am greatly pleas'd that Mr Richard is fixed at school & that to his liking, tho' I cannot but pitty from my Soul his poor Mamma, who no Doubt is very lonesome without him, Pray how far is Wem from Brynypiece? --

I intend for Dublin the latter End of this Month to put my Books to the press, of which I shall make but a bad Hand, as I have not received as many Subscriptions as bore my Expences & the Troubles now in Scotland will be a great Damp as People must think of other things than Books, however I must go on, coud I be properly spoken of to the Lord Lieutenant I woud not doubt having something done for me, which I shall very soon have the greatest Occasion for, as Renny will certainly in a short time be sold by Order of Court, & then God only knows which way I must turn my Self to gett Bread ——————

We have had a fine latter Harvest to save our Corn and Hay but the Weather is now so bad & has been so these ten days past that few of our husbandmen have been able to draw home their Corn, our butter still keeps up to One or two & Thirty shillings the hundred but Beef is very low to great Disadvantage of the County of Limerick ———

I congratulate the Colonel on his Recovery, & shoud be very sorry for any Mischance that might happen him, I find Punch is still the never failing Remedy, I wish he may long make Use of it Pray my Compliments to him & all other Friends. My Wife joins in our best Respects to you and Coz.^{n} Price & dear Mr Rich^{d} I am Dear Sir

Your Sincerely aff.te Kinsman
& most humble Servant
Edm Spencer

5 Wem] a small market town in Shropshire some twenty miles from Wrexham; the school there was founded in 1650 by Sir Thomas Adams, Lord Mayor of London in 1645.

8 Troubles now in Scotland] Charles Stuart's forces occupied Edinburgh on 15 September 1745, greeted by cheering crowds. On 18 September James was declared King of Scotland. This news had clearly reached Renny.

[folio 37]

[To Francis Price Esqr

Free

Barrymore]

Dublin November the 19.th 1745

Direct to me at the Widdow Thornton's on College Green

Dear Sir

Since my last nothing occurd worth troubling you about, I have been three Days in Town upon a view of being recommended to the Lord Lieutenant but as yet cannot meet with a Friend who has Intimacy enough with any of the Persons about Court to ask such a Favour, though many Comissions have been already given yet there are more to dispose of, this is my Dernier Resort & if I do not procure something very shortly I know not what may become of me. sure you must have some Acquaintance ~~with~~ who are intimate with the Earl of Chesterfield or some of his Favourites by whom you may have me recommended to him, which if properly applyd for woud without the lest Doubt get me into some way of bread, which if not speedily done I shall be shortly in the most melancholy Circumstances of any body living. I am truly sencibly of your good Nature & beg you will now exert it by applying to a few of your many Friends in my favour , w;^{ch} / as we have now a generous Lord Lieuten.^{t} justly & universally esteemd the most generous Man in the World, / by a proper Application in my Behalf, may do something <~~xxx~~> for me to remove those dreadful views of Beggary & Want to which I dread I shall too shortly be reduced. the many Obligations I already lye under to you makes me flatter my self that you will not be indolent in this particular on which my future Welfare so much depends. My best Respects to Mrs Price & dear Master Richard conclude D.^{r}SirY.^{r} sincerely aff.^{te} Kinsman & hble Ser.^{t}

[*Edm Spencer*]

Address *Free Barrymore*] this is a postal frank, i.e. the signature of a person, such as an MP, who was entitled to send letters free of charge; as a member of the House of Lords Barrymore would have been entitled to this privilege and he is obviously passing some on as a favour to his friend Price who in turn encloses some when he writes to Spencer (which the letter of 9 October 1747: folio 60 suggests was their practice) who can then use them for his replies; until 1840 postage on letters was paid by the recipient and the charge was based on the distance the letter had travelled; the postage account which Spencer later sends to Richard Price (see obverse of folio 122) gives some idea of how expensive receiving letters could be, so having access to franks was a useful perk, not only for someone on a low income such as Spencer but also for a wealthy man like Price, given that he maintained such a substantial correspondence. In the present instance the frank would appear to have been wasted, though, because Price's address is not on this letter, suggesting that this one has been included, as is Spencer's usual practice, in a package sent 'under cover', quite possibly using another frank (see 10 September 1745: folio 35, ll.12–13 and note). See also

16 June 1747: folio 59, ll.20–21, where Spencer asks Price to send him 'a few franks' so that he can write to a brother-in-law in Scotland; we might assume that these would have been franked by Lord Barrymore (who was still alive at that point) since, as his house in Ireland was near to where Spencer lived, franked letters signed by him leaving Ireland would not attract attention in the way that letters from Ireland bearing Sir Watkin's frank might have done (see note to 10 September 1745: folio 35, ll.12–13).

7 Dernier Resort] 'last resort' (French), originally the last court to which an appeal could be made (*OED, dernier,* a.1.b).

9 Earl of Chesterfield] see 18 January 1744/5: folio 28, l.14.

Side note] College Green is the square opposite Trinity College, Dublin. The Parliament House is also located in this square.

Signature] the bottom right-hand corner of this letter is both faint and crowded, making the signature unclear.

[folio 38]

[To Francis Price Esqr]
at the Widdow Thornton's on College Green Dublin November
the 30.th 1745

Dear Sir

I return you my unfeigned Thanks for both your Letters the former in which was inclosed one for Mr Hill shoud have been answered by the last Packett but that I waited to give you an Acc^{t} of Mr Hill's Reception, which I cannot now do as I have not yet met any Person intimate enough with him to introduce me, but expect in few Days to have an Opportunity of delivering your Letter to him, coud a Line or two in my Favour be obtaind from Mr Trevor either to Mr Hill or Lady Middleton, I shoud be certain of Success. I find likewise by your Second kind Letter that you have me in your Thoughts & shall for ever gratefully acknowlege all your kindnesses and do assure you I never contracted a Debt since I left Wales but w.^{h} was occasiond by my long Illness and which I have already dischargd but as I have a Suit at Law which requires Mony constantly and as I cannot venture to sett a Lease of my Land but from year to year which hinders my getting near the Value of it, are the reasons why I cannot be in better Circumstances than I am, which I hope will clear up your kind Enquiry in that particular. I am very glad that my good friend Mr Richard is pleased with his school & hope by all op= portunitys you will present my compliments to him. My best Respects to Mrs Price concludes, Dear Sir

Your Sincerely affectionate Kinsman
& obliged humble Servant
Edm Spencer

My Service to Mr Smyth & all Friends

Address] alongside Price's name and at right angles to it someone has added up three sums of money.

11 I never [...] left Wales] as the letters of 21 November 1741: folio 5, [December 1741]: folio 121 and [January 1742]: folio 6 show, Spencer was in Wales over the Christmas holiday of 1741.

13 a Suit at Law] this is the long-running legal wrangle with the Power family over Renny, concerning which see 17 November 1747: folio 62, note to l.5, and which, as he says in l.14, prevents him from being able to lease it for more than a short period at a time.

19 compliments] it looks as though Spencer originally wrote /complimints/ but it may be that he simply put a dot above the /e/ (having perhaps mistaken his poorly formed /e/ for an /i/) and then tried to scrub it out.

[folio 124]

The case of Mr Edmond Spencer who Arthur Trevor Esqr is requested to recommend to ∧$^{\text{the Honble}}$ Arthur Hill Esqr for his intrest with y^{e} Commissioners of Ireland to procure him a harth money collection or some other place in their gifts ——————————

The unfortunate circumstances of this young gentleman have been many: he was born to a plentifull estate ∧$^{\text{three parts of}}$ which his father sold [*privatly*] not for half the worth the remains he mortgaged for 2000, ∧$^{\text{dyed \&}}$ left him ∧$^{\text{an infant}}$ under y^{e} gaurdian ship of one Busted a Lawyer who instead of paying y^{e} intrest yearly, Sunk it him self, and when y^{e} minor came [*of*] age he found the whole mortgaged [*estate*]

124] this is a draft (it is written in pencil) of either the letter sent to Arthur Trevor in response to Spencer's request in his last letter, or of the 'narrative' Price tells his correspondent he has enclosed with that letter; it gives a fairly detailed history of Spencer's financial troubles following his coming of age and marriage and in that respect is very similar to folio 125 (placed in this transcription after the 'memorial' Spencer sends Price with 20 [January] 1748: folio 81). It is possible that both this sheet and 125 were written at the same time, one being a second drafting of the other, but there are very good reasons for believing that 125 was written in response to the later letter from Spencer, hence its position in the transcription; placing folio 124 here is tentative, but Price clearly sent something very like this at this point.

1 Spencer] it looks very much as though there is an /s/ on the end of the name, but Price is given to flourishes on final letters and this is probably such a flourish; there is a similar one on the final letter of the name /Trevor/ in the next line.

5 harth money] i.e. hearth-money, a tax on hearths or fireplaces; it was abolished in England in 1689 but remained in force in Ireland until the nineteenth century.

17–19 the whole [...] chancery] this seems to suggest that the whole of Spencer's inherited

eaten up with principall & intrest, and
was Sold in chancery for that end,
the Guardian dyed insolvent so that no
= thing could be expected from thence
after ye misfortune of selling
in order better him self he had a mind
to save y^e little remains that was not in
the above mortgage, but subject to a
debt of, 500, and accordingly married
was to have a thousand pound in three
months, and free quarters for him his
wife servants & horses three years, which
would have don tollerably well, but in
= sted of receiving his wifes fortune, his
father in law coaxed him to be bound for
him for four hundred pounds, which he
was forced to pay in less than [*a year*]
———————————
the father was broken and y^e young
couple turned agrazing : Baron Wainwright
knowing y^e [*hardships and*] [*sufferings*] of
as Judge of ye Exchequer
this Spencer promised him his intrest
for a pair of colours [*ashad*] did [Mr Justice]
Lindsay and accordingly [*represented*]
his case to the Duke of Devonshire, [*who*]
promised him a comission immed[*iately*]
but like a true courtier when the two
advocates dyed (unhappy for ye poor man)

estate had to be sold on his coming of age though in fact only part of it was and that part was most likely Kilcolman (see folio 125, ll.36–38 and note); it may be that Price means 'only that part of the estate that was mortgaged', i.e. again, Kilcolman, though it could just possibly refer to property in Connaught in the mid-west of Ireland which Welply says was granted to Spencer's grandfather, William, in 1657 ('The Family and Descendants of Edmund Spenser', p. 50) and which 'would seem' to have been 'sold or mortgaged' in 1733 (ibid., p. 57); however, Welply, who clearly did not know about these letters, appears to have confused the Connaught estate with Renny, and that confusion, plus his uncertainty, make it most unlikely that the Connaught property is meant here. It is true that Renny was also subject to a mortgage (see 17 November 1747: folio 62, note to l.5, and 6 February 1732: folio 3, note to l.14) but Price may not have been so familiar with that aspect of Spencer's financial affairs, or may simply have forgotten about it.

35 turned agrazing] 'turned out, sent packing' (*OED*, v^I, 2.b).

38 ashad] if this is /as had/ the two words seem to have been written partly over one another here in haste, the writer then correcting the /had/ to /did/ but failing to strike out the /had/.

he forgot all and so ye application provd abortive — The Scheme that ye Judges went upon in their application to the Lord Leutenant was grounded, on the great Service that Spencers grandfather did to King William & his army at the battle of Achrim by shewing them the difficulties, defiles & passes, which saved the protestant army from beeing destroyed they beeing not acquainted ~~wi~~ in the country, as the Irish army was, ^{as} the Grandfather was, having married his wife from that country, and the constant adherence of him & his son to the revolution & ye protestant line in the illustrious house of Hanover, the first part of this case, is, only to move pitty the last to seccond pettitions in a publick way he has a wife, two Children, and a trifle to subsist them

50 battle of Achrim] i.e. the Battle of Aughrim, Co. Wicklow, 12 July 1691; the defeat of the Jacobite forces resulted in the effective end of Jacobite resistance to William in Ireland (only Limerick held out for a few more months). See ll.14–22 of folio 125 for a slightly fuller account of the grandfather's heroic actions. (On William Spencer, see Welply, 'The Family and Descendants of Edmund Spenser'.)

[folio 39]

[To Francis Price Esqr]

Dublin Decr the 7.th 1745

Dear Sir

I at last met an Acquaintance of Mr Hill's so kind as to introduce me & was kindly received when he read your Letter, but gave me but little Hopes of getting any Thing by his Means as he said his interest is not very considerable; but if I coud procure any person in Power to recommend me he woud concur with them in any Thing in his Way, which I hope in some Time to be able to do, & am preparing a Petition which if I can procure to be deliverd properly ∧ to the Lord Lieutenant shall shortly know my Fate: I am certain that if Mr Hill pleas'd he coud do a great Deal but great People must be treated tenderly. Tho the generall Complaint here is the Want of Money, yet our Gentlemen & ladies drive away in Dress and Expences as if they knew no want, but Numbers appeard the last Ball Night at the Castle in Irish Poplins the Precedent being shewen by Lady Chesterfield, & indeed they are come to vast Perfection in that Manufacture, for a white or plain yellow Poplin with colourd sprigs at a little Distance looks equal to a rich Silk & sure comes much cheaper. This Day our Irish Bar= risters in their proper Habits waited on the Lord Lieutenant with an Address to be transmitted to his Majesty —

My best Respects to Mrs Price & to my good Friend Mr Richard concludes Dear Sir Y^{r} very aff.^{te} Kinsman & obliged hble Servant

Edm Spencer

12 drive away] an unusual intransitive use of the word with the sense of something like 'go at it like there's no tomorrow'.

13 Irish Poplins] a fabric woven of silk warp and worsted weft which was made particularly in Ireland; the term also often referred to the fashionable dresses made of the material.

[folio 40]

[To Francis Price Esqr]

Dublin Decr th<******>

Dear Sir

Yester[*day*] came in the [*five*] Par<*********> expected by the Politicians which [*brought*] <***************> glad that my good Friend Mr Richard has [*got the better of*] <***> [*I*] think twas very lucky that he was at home when <********> [*M*]amma's Care must be of [*great Help to his*] <*********> always got the better of any [*Disorder*] <xxx> <**********>

[*The Suit*] you mention is [*still with the*] <**********> [*an order*] for Sale of the Lands which I am [*at great*] <***> [*and*] shall [*continue*] to do so as long as [*pos*]<***> [*better*] <**> sure this woud be a bad [*time*] to sell land, [*& very diff*]<**> a purchaser few People <***> have Money [*in*] <*** *****> & of consequence half the [*Worth*] of the Place woud [*not be*] <***> [*The only*] chance I have of getting anything is if any [*new*] <**> [*be raisd*] which is talkd of, but I fear the [*majority*] of [*th*]<*> be against it, tis to be debated the thirt[*eenth of*] next Mo[*nth*] [*take*] place, I have been assured of a Pair of <***> but [*look*] <**> sorry Chance. I believe Mr Rowe [*must*] have been <***> he spoke disrespectfully of the old [*Trigger*] for tho I am [*cons*]<**> coud not say any Thing too bad of him, yet <**********> [*but*] [*Hopes of*] continuing in the Parish after [*such a Declaration*] Respects to Mrs Price [*&*] Mr Richard [*wishing them &*] you happy Years concludes Dear Sir

Your very affectio[*nate*]
[*&*] obliged humble <***>
EdmSp[*encer*]

My Service to Mr Smyth & all Friends ——

This letter is very badly damaged with stains; it also looks as though the right-hand edge has been torn off. The year can confidently be taken to be 1745: there is no reason to question the position of the letter in the archive, the / Dec.^{r}/ is perfectly clear and it fits with the months of the preceding and following letters, whilst the discussion of the sale of Renny (ll.8–12) reflects the stage Spencer has reached in that affair.

3–6 glad that [...] any [*Disorder*]] Richard Price seems to have been a sickly child which may explain the unease Spencer expresses in 26 July 1745: folio 33, ll.18–25, at the idea of his being sent away to boarding school. In May 1749 he is sent to stay with the family physician, Dr Buchan, in Liverpool and Buchan writes to Price four times within eleven days (including two letters on the same day) to assure him that Richard (then thirteen years old) is getting better and able to return home (Puleston 18: NLW MS 3578E, letters of 7, 11 & 17 May 1749).

[folio 41]

[To Francis Price Esqr]

[*Dublin Jan'y the 21st 1746*]

Dear Sir

By this Time I suppose all your Christmas Entertainments are pritty well over, our Parliament had but a short Recess for they broke up on Christmas Eve & met on the 18th Ins.^{t}, Twas thought that four new Regiments woud have ∧^{been} raisd, but as the Rebels have retreated, I believe twill not be done. I ∧^{can} give no Acc.^{t} of what is doing in the House, for by a late Resolution no Person is admitted but a Member, not even to the Gallery. Last Night being the Prince of Wales's Birthnight there was a grand Ball at the Castle, where every Person was dressd in the Manu facture of Ireland, the Ladys all in sprigd Poplin, & yet we have our Street crouded with poor Weavers, for Money was never known to be more scarce & the Cloathiers will not venture to make more Cloaths that they expect a ready Sale for. Your old Acquaintance Sir Matthew Deane is now in Town, & looks as well as he has done since I remember, tho' I shoud think the fatigue of so long a Journey might have discomposed one of his Years. My best Respects to Mrs Price & my dear Friend Mr Richard & Service to Mr Smyth & all Friends conclude Dear Sir

Your most aff^{te} Kinsman
& obliged humble Servant —
Edm Spencer

Place and date] This information is badly faded; the first three letters of the place name may well be /Dub/, and as the preceding and the following letters were written from Dublin it is likely that this letter was also written there. The formation of the word for the month looks very similar to the formation of /January/ in the letters of 10 January 1743: folio 13 (see note to Date) and 18 January 1744/5: folio 28; the number /21/ is comparatively clear; moreover, given the information in ll.2 & 3 the date must be after 18 January. Someone has pencilled in /1745/ below the address and date line and as 1745 Old Style fits with the information about the movements of Charles Stuart's army in l.4, 1746 has been adopted as the year — though, it has to be admitted, on the basis of deduction rather than legibility.

4 the Rebels have retreated] in early December 1745 the Jacobite forces retreated from Derby (the furthest point south that they reached, and roughly seventy five miles due east of Overton) and were back in Scotland by late December of that year; they gained a victory at Falkirk on 17 January 1746 but news of that may well not have reached Ireland when Spencer wrote this letter; however, Charles Stuart's army was by now no longer considered a threat, being ill-equipped and exhausted, and it was finally defeated at Culloden on 16 April. Spencer's use of the term 'rebels' is interesting given Price's apparent Jacobite sympathies (see 6 December 1743: folio 10, note to l.23): is he perhaps taking precautions against his letters being opened and read? Or is it that Price disapproved of armed insurrection, preferring rather a political and constitutional solution to the question? Alternatively, like his Jacobite friends Lord Barrymore and Sir Watkin Williams-Wynn, Price's support of Charles Stuart was possibly conditional on a successful military campaign, they being 'acutely aware that a domestic rising of artisans and tenant farmers would be tantamount

to suicide' and so, along with other Welsh Jacobites, 'continued to procrastinate' (*ODNB*, entry for *James Barry, 4th Earl of Barrymore*).

7 Prince of Wales] Frederick, estranged son of George II and Caroline of Brandenburg-Anspach (1707–1751), a cricket enthusiast who may have died as a result of a cricketing accident.

7 Birthnight] 'the evening of a royal birthday and the festival held thereon' (*OED*, n. 3.a)

8 grand [...] Castle] Irish balls, especially in Dublin, were often noted as spectacular social events: see Anon., 'The Lord Mayor's Ball', in *Verse in English from Eighteenth-century Ireland*, ed. by Andrew Carpenter (Cork: Cork University Press, 1998), pp. 412–13.

[folio 42]

[To Francis Price Esqr]

Dublin February the 4th

Dear Sir

I troubled you with two Letters since I had the Pleasure of your last, which induces me to believe that you have been from Home: in my last I gave you an Account that your old Friend Sir Mathew Deane was in Town, he this Day sett out for Munster; I supd last night with him when he desired me to present his Compliments, & is in as good Spirits ∧^{as} I have known him for some years past. An Embargo is laid on all Commoditys, to continue for three Months; but tis hoped that Butter will be allowd to be exported, as 'tis a perishable Commdity & what is now made woud not be worth a Shilling the hundred in April next; the Merchants of Corke / I am informed / are preparing a Petition for that Purpose, which 'tis to ∧^{be} wish'd will have the desired effect. I have nothing more to communicate so conclude with my best Respects to Mrs Price & dear Mr Rich^{d}

Dear Sir Your very affec^{te} Kinsman

& obliged humble Servant

Edm Spencer

My Service to Mr Smyth
& all Friends

Date] there is a mark after the day number but it is now indecipherable; either the year was abbreviated and has faded, or was not included at all; however, Spencer's reference to his mentioning Mr Deane in his last letter makes it clear that this follows the previous one.

[folio 43]

[To Francis Price Esqr]

Dublin Feb'y the 24th 1745

Dear Sir

According to your Order, I made close enquiry on the Quays these three Days past, but coud receive no Acc.^{t} of Capt Shaw, the Yatch is now on this Side, but cannot be particularly informed of her Sailing as that must be entirely governd by the Warrant, without which she cannot stir. Poplins are from three to four shillings a yard the hair Colours & browns are pritty but the white and straw colours I think beautyfull, as the Sprigs make greater Show on them, they are the dearest. If you have any particular Reason to know of Captain Shaw's being on this Side, let me have proper Order & your Commission shall be executed. There is now a Recess of the Parliament & the Town is very thin, but what Time the Lord Lieuten^{t} intends for England is not known: we were here greatly surprizd at the late change in the ministry & as much at the sudden rechange, which no doubt has put every Thing in the former Posture. My best Respects to Mrs Price & my good friend Mr Richard

My Service to Mr Smyth & all friends

I am D^{r}Sir Y.^{r} very aff^{t} Kinsman
& obliged humble Servt
Edm Spencer

Date] as in the abbreviation of /January/ in the letter of 10 January 1743: folio 13, the superscript mark between the /b/ and the /y/ of 'Feb^{y}' is not at all clear, so the apostrophe is an approximation. Spencer has given the year Old Style.

14–15 what Time [...] not known] Chesterfield left Ireland in April of this year.

16 rechange] 'changing or altering again' (*OED*, n.3); Spencer may be referring to the mass resignation of government ministers that had recently taken place in protest against George II who in turn tried to engineer a new government led by the opposing party.

[folio 44]

at Mr Lumbards in Fishamble Street Dublin March 15th 1745

Dear Sir

I am glad that the Stuff for Cozin Price was sent by one of the Crew of the Yatcht, for I think there is not the least Danger but she'll get it safe, for those Fellows have an excellent hand ~~for~~ ∧^{at} conveying a Bundle ashore without the knowlege of the Officers, who except properly fee'd woud convert it to their own Use ----- I am glad to find that my good Friend Mr Richard is well God keep him so. I suppose the Old Colonel received his Fit of the Gout / which you mention / by drinking a little too much acid in his Punch: as you have an excellent hand in making & a proper Method in applying that Elixir, I believe by this all Thoughts of the Disorder are vanishd, pray my Compliments to him. The Town is now very thin, & barren of anything entertaining; it is not known what Time the Parliament will be prorogued nor when the Lord Lieuten^{t} intends for your Side the Water, he is so well liked here, that we wish he was to continue always with us. Colonel Witched died two Days ago by which a Regiment of Dragoons is ready for some Favourite, & a Seat in Parliament for the Borough of Wicklow is vacant. My best Respects to Mrs Price & Love to dear Mr Rich^{d} I am Dear Sir

Your very aff^{ec} Kinsman
& most humble Servnt
Edm Spencer

Address] the address for this letter is missing.

Date] Spencer is using Old Style here; as on the letter of 21 January 1746: folio 41, someone has written /1745/ in pencil underneath the date at the top right-hand corner of the sheet.

7 Gout] caused by an excessive production of uric acid, often through the excessive consumption of rich food and alcohol, gout was seen as the result of a privileged, often male, lifestyle, as it spread rapidly in the eighteenth century: George Nuki and Peter A. Simkin, 'A Concise History of Gout and Hyperuricemia and their Treatment', *Arthritis Research & Therapy* 2006, 8 (Suppl 1).

12–13 nor when [...] the Water] see note to ll.14–15 in previous letter; the approving comment on Chesterfield's Lieutenancy that follows was possibly motivated by Chesterfield's surprisingly tolerant attitude towards Ireland and his recognition that harsh repression was more likely to encourage rebellion than prevent it (*ODNB*), the latter attitude a marked contrast to the one expressed by the writer's great-great-grandfather in his *A View of the Present State of Ireland*.

14 Colonel Witched] Col. Samuel Warter Whitshed (born 1685), MP for Wicklow Borough 1715–1746, was, at his death, a brigadier-general with a colonelcy of the 12th Dragoons (*HIP*); see also next letter, ll.14–15 and note.

16 Wicklow] the county town of Co. Wicklow, a port and parliamentary borough, some thirty miles south of Dublin.

[folio 45]

[To Francis Price Esqr]

at Mr Lumbards in Fishamble Street Dublin
April the 5th 1746

Dear Sir

Since my last nothing has happened here worth relating, the Town is now pritty thin & the more so as all the Lawyers are gone the Circuit. The Quarter Master General & several other Officers are sett out to mark out Ground for a Camp at Bennets bridge within three miles of Kilkenny, where ten Companys of every Regiment of Foot in this Kingdom are to be encampd this Summer, the remaining four Companies to be sent to Garrison: 'twill afford a hansome sight & no doubt but People from all Parts of the Kingdom will go to see it, by which Kilkenny will be greatly enrichd. I still expect something will be done for me; in the mean Time the old Proverb / while the Grass grows &c / is veryfied in me, as I've been obliged to continue so long in this expensive Place. One Colonel Bligh on your Side the Water has obtaind the Regiment of Dragoons late Brigad.^{r} Whitcheads. My best Respects to Mrs Price & my dear friend Mr Richard with service to Mr Smyth conclude Dear Sir

Your very aff^{te} Kinsman
& obliged humble Servant
Edm Spencer

3 the Circuit] the passage of law courts around the countryside.

5 Bennets bridge] a village five miles south of Kilkenny on the River Nore.

11–12 while the [...] &c] 'while the grass grows, the horse starves' (Tilley, G423), that is, the horse is likely to die if it waits for the grass to be turned into hay; Spencer's abrupt abbreviation of the proverb suggests he feels about it much as Hamlet did: 'Ay, sir, but "While the grass grows" — the proverb is something musty' (*Hamlet*, III ii 343–44).

13 Colonel Bligh] Thomas Bligh (1685–1775), army officer and politician, second son of Thomas Bligh of Rathmore, Co. Meath, Ireland. In 1746 he was transferred from the 20th Foot to the 12th Dragoons and a year later was transferred to the colonelcy of his old regiment, the 5th Dragoon Guards, which had then become the 2nd Irish Horse. In 1754 he became lieutenant-general (*ODNB*).

14–15 Brigad.^{r} Whitcheads] Samuel Whitshed again (see previous letter, note to l.14); it looks as though Spencer originally wrote /Whiteheads/ but then overwrote the first /e/ heavily to convert it to a /c/. He is here referred to more correctly by his final rank as brigadier-general.

[folio 46]

[To Francis Price Esqr]

at Mr Lumbards Fishamble Street Dublin April 19th 1746

Dear Sir

To the universal Regret of all Sorts and Conditions of Men our good Lord Lieutenant, is preparing for England, & will sail with the first fair Wind, & it is doubted he will return to us any more. our Camp is still talkd of but not for a Certainty, for ∧^{as} by all the Accounts we receive the Rebells are in a very sinking Condition, if they shoud be entirely demolishd, no Camp will be form'd, to the no small Satisfaction of all Subaltern Officers, whose pay woud not subsist them on so expensive an Affair: but to the very great Regret of all People in & about Kilkenny & the adjacent Parts, who will be enrichd if such a Thing shoud happen. As the Parliament is now prorogued the Members are hurrying out of Town. I suppose many of them with very light Purses, tho the Lord Lieutenant did all in his Power to encourage Parsimony, & to his immortal Honour / tho fond of Play / he discontinued the Groomporters that bane to youth, & to make amends to the Keeper, instead of the Profitts which might arise by the Table has settled forty pounds a year on him during Life. My best Respects to Mrs Price & my good friend Mr Richard, Service to Mr Smyth conclude DearSir

Your very aff^{te} Kinsman &
obliged humble Servt
Edm Spencer

5 the Rebells [...] sinking Condition] they had, in fact, quite sunk, the Battle of Culloden having taken place three days before Spencer wrote this letter.

7 Subaltern Officers] junior officers below the rank of captain.

14 Groomporters] the Groom Porter was an officer of the royal household in Dublin Castle who had, amongst other duties, oversight of the gaming tables, deriving some of his income from the fees from those tables; it may be that Spencer is here using the word to refer to the office itself, rather than the holder (whom he refers to as 'the Keeper'), or even as a term for the activities the holder oversaw; as a plural the word could also mean 'loaded dice' (*OED*, 2).

[folio 47]

[To Francis Price Esqr]

Dublin May the 15.th 1746

Dear Sir

We have nothing new here, to give you an Account of but Rejoicings all over the Kingdom for the Defeat of the Rebells, which has already had that Effect in this Kingdom that the Price of Wool is considerably augmented — I am so much tired of attending Levees that I intend shortly for Munster & have still some Promises, but how or when they may be performd I cannot determine; however, the Expence has been a Certainty, the Death of poor Mr Oliver has been a real Loss to me, had he lived I shoud have been provided for some Way or other this last Parliament Winter: If any Body coud be prevaild on to hint about me to the Lord Chesterfield on your Side the Water, to back those who have already spoken of me / as I am told some have / it woud without Doubt be of vast Service to me. my best Respects to Mrs Price & Mr Richard with service to M^{r}Smyth & all Friends conclude Dear Sir

Your very aff^{te} Kinsman and
obed.^{t} hble Servt
Edm Spencer

5 Levees] 'assemblies held in the early afternoon by the Lord Lieutenant as the sovereign's representative' (*OED*, n^{2}.2.b); only men were allowed to attend them.

8 the Death [...] Oliver] the Col. Oliver whose death is reported in 23 May 1745: folio 31, and the same Mr Oliver who helped Spencer promote his proposed *Works of Mr Edmund Spenser* (27 December 1743: folio 12, ll.18–19); they also hunted together (29 September 1744: folio 26, ll.2–4).

[folio 48]

[To Francis Price Esqr]

May the 27.th 1746

Dear Sir

The 24.th Ins.^{t} carryed off your old Friend Mallaky Kelly after a few days Illness, as you may have some Business in his hands, that will make it necessary for you to employ another speedily, makes me give you this timely Notice of his Death, that you may give order accordingly, & at the same Time give me Leave to recommend one to you of undeniable Character, the Gentleman I mean is Mr John Wallis of Bride Street who is employd for many of the top Gentlemen in our Country: he has been my Attorney for many years, & by his dealing with me I can take upon me to averr that he is an honest Man, which you[']ll allow to be a sufficient Tryal & a bold Word. You'll oblige me vastly if you'll try him & if he deals contrary to the Character I give of him, I shall with Concern bear being told that I have deceived you, which I hope you are convinced is contrary to my Inclination. if you have not present Occasion for him, at any Time hereafter that 'twoud be necessary I intreat you'll employ Wallis. in the Mean Time enquire into his Character which I will be bold to say he need not be ashamd of. I am now at the Camp in my Way to Munster & beg your next Favour may be to Renny my best Respects to Coz.^{n} Price & Mr Rich^{d} I am DSir your very affectionate Kinsman & most hbleServ.^{t} Edm Spencer

8 John Wallis] another lawyer named Henry Wallis is also mentioned in these letters but only once (see 28 June 1762: folio 120) and whether these two men were related is never indicated. Spencer's letters to Francis Price contain no suggestion that Price employs John Wallis, but as his widow later makes use of Henry Wallis (two letters from Henry Wallis concerned with her legal affairs in Ireland are archived in Puleston 25: NLW MS 3585C, folios 15 & 16, see Appendix I) it is possible that he does, and that also suggests that the two men are related and share a practice. The letters from Henry Wallis are actually to Spencer and they suggest that the two men were on intimate terms with one another; we might also note that a Wallis later buys Renny from Spencer (see 28 February 1748: folio 83, ll.15–17) but which one is not specified.

8 Bride Street] this ran northwards along the eastern side of St Patrick's Cathedral.

19–20 I am [...] Camp] this is presumably the proposed military camp at Bennet's Bridge, Kilkenny mentioned in 5 April 1746: folio 45, l.5, and 19 April 1746: folio 46, ll.6–10; the second of those letters states that the construction of the camp is still uncertain but it would appear from this one that it was established after all, and if so, since Spencer is on his way home from Dublin to Renny (where the next letter is written) it would make sense for him to stop there overnight; this also suggests that he is following the standard route from Dublin to Cork as given in *Taylor and Skinner's Maps of the Roads of Ireland* (London & Dublin, 1778, pp. 116–22) which goes through Bennet's Bridge; at Fermoy he could have turned west to take the diversion from the Dublin-Cork road to Mallow which Taylor and Skinner show running along the northern side of the Blackwater through Ballyhooly and Castletownroche (p. 123); alternatively he could have taken the route from Killworth to Mallow, dropping down to Renny just before Castletownroche; Taylor and Skinner say this road is shorter than the Fermoy-Mallow road though with the rather ominous warning that 'it is not kept in proper Repair' (p. 123). The lack of address on this letter might be because Spencer's location is temporary.

[folio 49]

[To Francis Price Esqr]

Renny June the 24.th 1746

Dear Sir

Last Week was the Race time at Mallow where was a vast Appearance of Ladys and Gentlemen of Fortune three Plates of Thirty pounds each & three of Twenty each were run for & at the long Room were Assemblys every night. a sort of Riot happend one Day at the Course begun by one Massey / the same who carryd off Miss Ingoldsby / by whom one of the Jockeys was so beaten that his life is despaird of, a Private Sessions will be held at Mallow to Morrow on this Account where the Gentleman will be very well tickled, as he has the Misfortune of not being liked or regarded by any person of Figure or Character in this Country. Our Circuits begin very early this Vacation the Judges go into Cork <~~xx~~> three Weeks hence. I have nothing more thats new to acquaint you with at present — my Wife joins in our best Respects to you & Mrs Price & Love to Mr Richard my Service to Mr Smyth & all friends I am Dear Sir

Y^{r} sincerely affec^{te} Kinsman
& obliged humble Servant
Edm Spencer

1 Race [...] Mallow] Mallow was already well-established as a venue for horse racing on the flat by this date; the first steeplechase was run in 1752.

6 Massey [...] Ingoldsby] for Massey's abduction of Miss Ingoldsby see 6 December 1743: folio 10, ll.35–36.

[folio 50]

[To Francis Price Esqr]

Renny July the 16.th 1746

Dear Sir

I have been here a few Days & had the Honour of a Visit from Dick Welsh, who surprizes me with an Account that some Person is setting up a Title & disputing your Right to Part of your Estate in this Kingdom, who it is he cannot tell me nor can I conjecture; & hope there is nothing in the Report for I shoud be very ungratefull if any thing that gave you Concern or Trouble woud be indifferent to me, & therefore entreat to know whether there is any Thing in the Rumour. The Death of Mr Lyddele the Earl of Chesterfields Secretary I fear will be of bad Consequence to me, as he had promised to be my Friend & put that Nobleman in Mind of me when any Thing woud happen in the Way for my advantage, but I am so used to Dissapointments that to meet with them is become almost indifferent: however I have procured some sort of Bread for my Brother who is a Coast Officer at Ringsend with a Promise of being advanced. My Wife joins in our best Respects to you Mrs Price & my good Friend Mr Rich^{d} I am Dear Sir

Y.^{r} sincerely aff.^{te} Kinsman
& obliged humble Servant
Edm Spencer

My Service to Mr Smyth
& all Friends -------

Address] there are a number of additions of sums of money on the address side of this letter around Price's name, some of the amounts being very considerable; the larger sums — the total of which is £370 — have names against them and so may be payments made or owed to Price by these people, or made or owed by him to them.

14 my Brother] Spencer had two younger brothers, Nathaniel and John; the latter had died by 1748, so this could refer to either of them; however, about twelve weeks later in his letter of 3 October 1747: folio 52 Spencer recounts how his brother Natt (Nathaniel) has been given a job in the excise by the Recorder of Dublin with a promise of advancement; the account is more detailed than this one but is so similar in many particulars that one suspects he simply forgot that he had already told Price about this and repeated the story in the later letter.

14 Ringsend] an area of Dublin where the River Dodder joins the southern side of the estuary of the River Liffey.

[folio 51]

[To Francis Price Esqr]

Renny Aug.st the 26.th 1746

Dear Sir

Since my last I have met with nothing worth giving you an Account of, as I have spent most of that Time in Duhallow at Mr Freeman's, & anything relating to that Part of the Country must be quite forreign to you who, I believe, are not ac= quainted with that Barony. A few posts ago I read an Account in one of our Papers, that one Mr Kent a Gentleman of a small Estate in Cheshire was taken up for uttering treasonable Words, pray is this our Acquaintance from Boston? Dick Welsh sett out Yesterday for Brynypiece to make a setting Dog & take Partridge for Mr Richard, I am surprized how that old Fellow can still bear the Fatigue of trotting backwards & forwards every Year, which he does to a Miracle. We had last Month as great a Flood in Blackwater as ever I remember to have seen in the Depth of Winter, occasiond only by one night's Rain, it carryd off all the hay that was on the Inches & spoild the Corn & grass that were uncut, but since we have blessed Weather for our Harvest, which promisses a plentifull Winter & Spring & never was known better Crops of Potatoes. My Wife joins in our respects to you Mrs Price & my good Friend Mr Richard I am Dear Sir

Your very aff^{te} Kinsman
and most humble Servant
Edm Spencer

my Service to Mr Smyth
& all Friends ——

3 Duhallow] A barony in the northern part of Co. Cork; for Freeman see note to 6 February 1732: folio 3, l.14.

8 Boston] neither Carlisle, Wales nor Lewis, Wales mentions a Boston in Cheshire, but Bartholomew's *Gazetteer of the British Isles, Statistical and Topographical* (Edinburgh: John Bartholomew and Co., 1893) does list a Bostock near Middlewich in Cheshire, some twenty five miles from Overton; Spencer may have misheard or misremembered that name.

9 make a setting Dog] 'train a dog to indicate fallen birds by running to them and pointing at them with its muzzle' (*OED*, set, v^{I}.123.a).

11 to a Miracle] 'in such a way that it seems miraculous' (*OED*, *miracle*, n.2.b), but regarding Welsh's energy, see 26 February 1746: folio 56, note to ll.5–6.

12 Blackwater] the river that runs near Renny.

14 Inches] 'meadows by a river' (*OED*, n^{2}.b, where it is given as a Scottish usage only).

[folio 52]

[To Francis Price Esqr]

Renny October the 3.^{d} 1746

Dear Sir

I am concerned to find you have such an able Antagonist as Serjeant Marshall, as tis in his Power to make it an expensive Suit to you without being much out of Pockett himself; for being an Amicus Curiæ Lawyers & Attorneys will appear for him gratis, while yours will expect large Fees & furnish you with swingeing bills of Cost, I sincerely wish you a good Riddance of him, but fear you'll find it a tedious Job to shake him off —— My Brother Natt has at last got into Bread by Means of the Recorder of Dublin, & Colonel Brown in whose Regiment he was for some Time a Troper but was discharged after a fatiguing Winter's Duty in Dublin for being half an Inch under Size: upon a Petition to the Colonel he sayd he shoud be better provided for & accordingly with the Recorder, they recommended him to Com.^{r} Grey who has made him a supernumery of Excise with a promise of being full Gauger the first that happens & the Recorder has faithfully promised that he will not stop till he has made him a Surveyor of Excise. so that at last he is ∧^{in} a good Way & likely to continue so, if he does but behave well. Woud to God I was even so provided for, but that I do not know when to Expect. ——— The Mayor of Cork has received Orders to provide Quarters for 6000 Men, which tis supposed are to be embarkd on some Secret Expedition; but whether they are our Forces or some from your Side the Water I have not heard. There is an embargo on Beef and Pork which has lowerd the Price of those Commoditys, but Butter still holds at a good. ∧^{rate} we've had very good Harvest Weather & a plenty full Crop of Corn & Potatoes, but these three or four Days have been very stormy and Wet My Wife joins in Respects to you Mrs Price & my good Friend Mr Richard I am Dear Sir

Your very aff.^{te} Kinsman
& faithfull hbleServ^{t}
Edm Spencer

my Service to Mr Smyth
& all Friends ———

2 Serjeant Marshall] a 'serjeant' was a senior attorney (*OED*, 6); Robert Marshall, 1697–1774, was a rich and successful lawyer, at this time second serjeant-at-law; he acted as chief counsel in the Annesley case (*DIB*). (For the Annesley case see 6 December 1743: folio 10, l.9 and note.)

3 Amicus Curiæ] a disinterested legal advisor, lit. 'friend of the court' (Latin) (*OED*).

7 Recorder] a magistrate or judge (*OED*, *recorder*^{I}.1.a).

8 Troper] probably a mistake for /Trooper/, 'a cavalry soldier' (*OED*,1.a).

11 Com.^{r}] abbreviation of 'Commissioner', the title of the head of the Dublin Excise.

12–13 supernumery [...] Gauger] the word 'supernumery' suggests 'not belonging to the regular staff' (*OED*, *supernumerary*, adj.1.b) but 'supernumerary gauger' seems to have been the title of a regular position in the Irish Excise at this time (see *A Detailed Account of the Establishment for the Collection of Excise at the Port of Dublin*, House of Commons, 1823, <http://www.dippam.ac.uk/eppi/documents/9650/> [accessed 25 June 2014]). A 'gauger' was a customs officer who measured the contents of casks, etc. (*OED*, n.1). Robert Burns described himself as one in 1789.

14 Surveyor of Excise] a superior position, possibly still in the gauging section of the Excise.

[folio 53]

[To Francis Price Esqr]

Renny November the 10.th 1746

Dear Sir

The Week before last arrived at Cove a Part of Admiral Lestocks Squadron, consisting of Six Men of War and Thirty Five Transports; which landed Six Thousand Forces, who are quarterd in & about Corke but tis not known how long they are to continue there, some small Matter of poor Plunder is brought with them taken ~~at~~ on the French Coasts. however they are wellcome to Corke as the Marketts will rise a little which were so low that Beef of four hundred & a half W.^{t} was but at 8^{s} pC^{t} to the great Loss of the County of Limerick Farmers———

In my last I gave an Account of my Brother Natts Success. he is now Gauger at Strabane in the North of Ireland, & is promised to be advanced to a surveyor the first Vagancy. however if that shoud be forgot, he may be content, as he has forty pounds ayear present Sallary —

We have nothing new in the Neighbourhood, but that the Lord Kingston & his Family are sett out for your Side of the Water. but how long he is to continue from home is not known. never was seen finer <~~xxx~~> Weather than has been these five or Six Weeks past. My Wife joins in our best Respects to you Coz.^{n} Price & my Dear Friend Mr Richard I am D^{r}Sir

Y.^{r} very aff.^{te} Kinsman
& most obed^{t}Servt
Edm Spencer

my Service to Mr Smyth
Friends ———

1 Cove] see 19 August 1744: folio 25, l.5 and note.

2 Admiral Lestocks] 1679–1746, a controversial naval officer whose career was dogged by accusations of inefficiency; he had only recently been appointed admiral when Spencer was writing, and died in December of this same year (*ODNB*).

8 Beef [...] at 8^{s} pC^{t}] i.e. beef carcasses weighing 450 pounds are selling at only eight shillings per hundredweight; cf. 5 November 1744: folio 27, ll.6–8, where Spencer complains that 'beef of five hun.^{d} p Carkass is but five shils & nine pence p Ct, a less price than the Graziers gave for them poor'.

11 Strabane] A town in Co. Tyrone, 100 miles north of Dublin.

12 Vagancy] a slip of the pen, presumably, for 'vacancy'; but Spencer seems to have had some difficulty with the word, as in the letter of 16 June 1747: folio 59, ll.15 & 17, he twice, within three lines, scratches out the third letter in the word (though in neither case does the erased word look like a /g/).

15–16 Lord Kingston] see letter 24 July 1744: folio 24, l.12.

PS] the bottom left-hand corner of the letter has been torn off, removing the usual 'and all'.

[folio 54]

[To Francis Price Esqr]

Renny December the 16.th 1746

Dear Sir

The Account you give of the old Gentleman of Overton does not in the least surprize me, as I always was of Opinion that his roguish Designs woud not end but with his Life, which happen when it will, I believe will be with the general Consent of the whole Neighbourhood. I am sorry for the Loss of your Tenants as I believe 'twill be difficult to procure other, since the Times are so bad at your Side of the Water as you describe them: we are in a far different Situation here, for since the gen.^{ll} Embargo was taken off, / which happend the middle of last Month / Beef got such a Rise that most of it is sold off already, the poor old Dairy Cows which are hardly able to drive to Corke, & which you must remember, goe under the Denomination of French Beef, are sold at Eight shils pC^{t} while good Beef is at 12 or 13 shils pC.^{t} so that Landlords will have their Rents well paid & Tenants grow rich, but so little is the Current Specie of the Kingdom at present that only Dublin Bills are the Payment of any middling Sum at Corke. & this is entirely attributed to the late Reduction of the Coin, which has brought it so near Par, that all the Portugal Coin is carryd for England. The Forces under the Command of Gen^{ll} Sinclair that landed at Corke some Time ago are marched to Limerick and Gallway, but as I am informed are speedily to march back again & reimbark for Flanders: they have occasiond this Country to be unhealthy at present, having introduced an ugly Fever of which many have died. The highland Regiment cut a fine Figure, they realy are a Corpse of very clever Fellows & their odd Dress contributes not a little to sett them off. My Wife joins in our best Respects to you Coz.^{n} Price & Mr Richard wishing a merry Christmas & many happy Years I am DearSir

Y.^{r} very affectionate Kinsman
& Sincere humble Servant
Edm Spencer

my Service to Mr Smyth
& all Friends ————

1 the old [...] Overton] Spencer's rather caustic observation in ll.2–3 that 'his roguish Designs woud not end but with his Life' suggests that this old Gentleman is seriously ill and

if we put that together with the observation only a month later (5 January 174[8]: folio 65, ll.12–13) that 'old Trigger holds out surprizingly, had he been good for any thing he woud have gone off before this' it would seem very likely that the Prices' neighbour, Thomas Lloyd, is being referred to here.

6 other] the singular form was common at this period (*OED*, pron. or n.B.5.b).

10 drive] 'move', an unusual intransitive usage which seems to have died out in the nineteenth century (*OED*, VII).

13 Specie] money in its physical form of coins (*OED*, 3,b).

16 Par] equality between market value and face value (possibly meaning that nothing is to be gained by trading currency on the local foreign exchange).

16 Portugal Coin] large sums of Portuguese money came into Ireland because of the considerable trade between the two countries, and at this period, as David Lammey notes, 'Irish merchants particularly regarded Lisbon as a lucrative market because of the favourable terms of the Methuen treaty of 1703' ('The Irish-Portuguese Trade Dispute, 1770–90', *Irish Historical Studies*, 25, 97 (1986), 29–45 (p.30)); however, unfavourable exchange rates are leading Irish merchants to change the money in England thereby taking its value out of Ireland.

17–18 Gen[ll] Sinclair] James Sinclair (or St Clair), 1687/8–1762, second son of the 10th Lord Sinclair. A career soldier, he was at this point a lieutenant general in the Royal Scots; in 1746 he was appointed to command an expedition to Canada; however, bad weather caused the fleet to be delayed in the channel, the operation was called off, and St Clair was diverted to a raid on Brittany; it is quite possible that he was therefore in Ireland with the Royal Scots at the very beginning of 1746, and the seemingly uncertain movements of his troops described by Spencer would be consistent with there being delays later in the year in relation to the Canadian expedition (*ODNB*).

[folio 55]

[To Francis Price Esqr]

Renny Jan'^{y} the 26.th 1746

Dear Sir

Tho I have been trying constantly every Season since I left Wales for an Eagle for my good Friend Mr Richard according to my Promise to him, yet I coud not get one, till last Week by Accident I met one in the County of Limerick that is very tame having been a Pet these ten Months: with some Difficulty I prevaild on the owner to part with him & have him here & will send him over the next Trip Mr Welsh takes to you. I believe Mr Richard will be greatly pleased with him as he is very gentle & has been reared among fowl but never annoys them. The Forces under Sinclair that arrived at Corke some time since & marchd off to Limerick & have returnd back to Corke where they are to reimbark, but for what part I have not heard 500 Highlanders have been quarterd at Mallow this fortnight with their Officers, waiting for their Transports to be victuald: & are greatly liked, as they behave themselves so well that not the least Complaint can be made of one of them. By this I suppose all your Christmas Junkettings are over, we had a dull one here, tho never had Opportunity for a merry making with greater Reason as every Commodity in the Country bears a very top Price, but I think the People seem to grow duller every Year ——— My Wife joins in our best Respects to you Mrs Price & Mr Richard I am with Service to Colonel Smyth & all friends Dear Sir

Y.^{r} truly aff^{te} Kinsman
& most obed^{t} Servant
Edm Spencer

Date] the year is again given in Old Style.

2–3 an Eagle [...] Richard] this is the promise originally mentioned in 29 May 1744: folio 22, ll.8–13.

5/9 very tame/very gentle] eagles did not have a particularly good reputation amongst early modern falconers, John Ray, in *The Ornithology of Francis Willughby* (London: printed by A. C. for John Martyn, 1678), saying that the eagle 'is indocile and uncapable of Discipline, and not to be tamed by any humane endeavour' (p. 57); George Turbervile in *The Booke of Faulconrie or Hauking, for the only Delight and Pleasure of all Noblemen and Gentlemen* (London: by Henry Bynemann for Christopher Barker, 1575) suggests that 'by reason she is so huge and ventrous, [the eagle] might happily offer force and violence to the eyes and face of hir keper, if at any time she should conceiue displeasure against him' (sig. A5^{r}); John Ray does, however, qualify his opinion, saying that 'we have heard of Eagles that have been reclaimed and trained up for fowling. Though it be rarely done' (*The Ornithology of Francis Willughby*, p. 57); Spencer would appear to be fortunate in finding Richard Price such a rare example of the bird.

10 Sinclair] see previous letter, ll.17–18 and note.

[folio 56]

[To Francis Price Esqr]

Renny near CastleLyons Feb'^{y} 26.th 1746

Dear Sir

I had not the Pleasure of knowing of Mr Welch's Arrival until I reced yours, when I found that a Hurt he had got in his Heel on Shipboard which obliged him to stay at Home, hinderd me of the Favour of a Visit from him — As soon as he is able to travel I will send him off with Donnohoh; tho I believe I shall find it difficult to prevail on him to quit his Lady till she is deliverd, who it seems is in her last Month — The best Place to keep the Eagle is your Court Yard, where you may let him loose, as he cant fly: nor will he attack any one without being hunted or provoked. I have him now among the Poultry which he never offends, but is content with a Crow a Day / being his Allowance / which he nicely picks & dissects, care must be taken not to give him any salt Meat, but he'll eat any offall, I am told that Eagles do grow till they are three years old, if so, this will be a large one as he is not one year old yet. I intend to have an Affair made something like a Cage which Welch may carry as a Pedlar does his Box which I think will be safer for the Bird & easier for him than any other Method I can think of & will furnish him with what will make them both welcome at their Stages — My Wife joins in our best Respects to you Coz.^{n} Price & my Dr Friend Mr. Rich^{d}

I am Dear Sir

Your very aff^{te} Kinsman
& most humble Servant
Edm Spencer

Date] Old Style.

5 Donnohoh] the name of the eagle (see previous letter); it was also an Irish surname.

5–6 I shall [...] deliverd] given that Spencer says of Welsh that he is 'surprized how that old Fellow can still bear the Fatigue of trotting backwards & forwards [i.e., between Ireland and Wales] every Year, which he does to a Miracle' (26 August 1746: folio 51, ll.10–11) one might be surprised that he still has the energy to beget children; however, see also 2 February 1747: folio 67, ll.1–2.

10–11 a Crow a Day] assuming that the crow is dead (one wonders how else it could be persuaded to go anywhere near the eagle) Donnohoh seems to be on iron rations: John Ray states that the bird's reputation is that it 'takes not Carrion or dead Carcasses; feeding only upon the flesh of such animals as she kills herself' (*The Ornithology of Francis Willughby* p. 56); however, he does later say of a Crested Eagle he himself once had: 'if you cast a bird to it, whether alive or dead, it catches it in its Talons, and with its Bill handsomly plumes [i.e. plucks] it, and then tearing it in pieces swallows down both flesh and bones' (ibid., p. 63); Donnohoh, though, appears to be a more delicate feeder.

14 not one year old] if he is not yet a year old and his previous owner had him for ten

months (see 26 January 1746: folio 55, l.5) Donnohoh must have been captured very young; this may be a clue as to why Spencer could give him such a good character reference in his last letter, as Turbervile states that 'He that will haue the Egle to be good and tractable, muste deuise to take her an Eyesse in the Eyrie' (*The Booke of Faulconrie or Hauking*, sig. A 5^{r}).

17–18 will furnish [...] their Stages] i.e. the cage, the implication, presumably, being that a man accompanied by a loose eagle would not be entirely welcomed by the hosts of the inns he will need to stay at.

[folio 57]

[To ———
Francis Price Esqr
at Brynypiece near
Wrexham]

Renny March the 28.th 1747

Dear Sir

Mr Welch carrys the Eagle which I hope will get Safe to Brynypiece & please my good friend Mr Richard, he went in this Country by the Name of Donnohoh. Your old Friend Sir Matthew Deane is at last deceased, I hear of Colonel Hyde only who has Sett up for this County in his Room —— You are to compliment Welch on the Birth of his Daughter, when he returns I beg you'll please to Send by him to me some Russia Cabbage Seed & a few Plants of the white Strawberrys. My Wife joins in our best Respects to Mrs Price&Mr Richard I am Dr Sir

Y.^{r} very aff.^{te} Kinsman
& most humbleServ.^{t}
EdmSpencer

My Service to Col Smyth & all Friends. I furnishd the bear.^{r} with the needfull.

4 Sir Matthew Deane] Tory MP for Charleville (1713–1714) and Co. Cork (1728–1747) (*HIP*).

5 Colonel Hyde] i.e. Arthur Hyde, the man Barnard identifies as one of Spencer's trustees during his minority (see 6 February 1732: folio 3, note to l.11); he did, as Spencer seems to expect he would, succeed Deane as MP for Co. Cork in 1747 which office he held until 1760; previously he had been MP for Youghal, 1721–1727 (*HIP*).

6 his Room] i.e. his position as the MP for Cork (*OED*, n^{1}.13.b; cf 13.a, 'an office or post, especially one belonging to a particular person').

9–10 Russia [...] Strawberrys] see also 26 July 1745: folio 33, l.17 and note, where Spencer asks for 'Riga Cabbage Seed & some white Strawberry Plants'.

PS I furnishd [...] needfull.] this could mean either that Spencer has made sure that Welsh has been provided with all the money he will need for his journey, or that Spencer has given him the money to pay for the seeds and plants requested; it also implies that this letter was carried by Welsh rather than being posted, which might explain the unusual form of the address.

[folio 58]

[To Francis Price Esqr]

May the 25.th 1747

D^{r}Sir

I am very glad to find the Eagle arrived safe & greatly pleasd that my good friend Mr Richard is not dissapointed in his Expectations of him, as you inform me he approves of him. My uncle Peard sent me a guinea by your Order which is five & six pence more than I gave Welsh for his Journey; shall I give that to his Wife or keep it for him 'till his Return? I hope this Month has answerd your Lands better than by your last I find you expected, for then it threatened to be very dry & so it did with us, but these three Weeks past we have had very wet Weather, by which we flatter our selves with a plentifull Harvest — The only thing new among us, is, that Lord Barrymore is landed in Dublin & soon expected at Castlelyons, I intend paying my Complim^{ts} as soon as I hear he arrives there. One of our late News papers gave an Acc.^{t} of the Death of Doctor Kingsbury wch gave me Concern lest it may be of Detriment to you in your Affairs in this Kingdom __ My Wife joins in our best Respects to you Coz.^{n} Price & Mr Richard I am D^{r}Sir

Your very Affec.^{te} Kinsman
& most obed.^{t} Servt
EdmSpencer

My Service to Mr Smyth &
all enquiring Friends ——

4 my uncle Peard] Barnard identifies this person as a half-brother to Spencer (*Irish Protestant Ascents and Descents*, p. 296); no such name, though, appears in Welply's 'Pedigree of Spenser' ('The Family and Descendants of Edmund Spenser', p. 60); a William Pearde was a frequent correspondent of Francis Price and reports to Price in a letter of 26 February 1742 (Puleston 19: NLW MS 3579D) that Spencer was arrested for debt on Christmas Eve, 1741 (see Appendix I); he also writes to Price urging him to help Spencer by speaking to Lord Barrymore and the Duke of Marlborough (7 August 1741, Puleston 19: NLW MS 3579D). The name Pearde occurs later in relation to a dispute about the payment of rents for the Mohire estate in Castlelyons which was owned by the Price family (28 July 1750: folio 90 and ff.) but it is extremely unlikely that he is the same person as is referred to here: nowhere in the many references to him is that Mr Pearde identified as a relative of either Spencer or Alice Price; on the contrary, possibly indicative of a lack of family relationship is that in 29 August 1756: folio 102, ll.3–4, Spencer tells Alice Price that 'he says that, he is very much obliged to you & Mr Price for y.^{r} Friendship to him'; he is never named other than as 'Mr Pearde' so we have no forename to help us with this question.

13–14 Lord Barrymore [...] at Castlelyons] this bit of news, the discussion of agricultural matters and the fact that the previous and following letters were written from Renny (which is often described as being 'near Castlelyons') all suggest strongly that this letter was also written from Renny.

16 Doctor Kingsbury] see 27 December 1743: folio 12, note to l.14.

[folio 59]

[To Francis Price Esqr]

Renny near Castlelyons June the 16.th 1747

Dear Sir

I am greatly obliged to you for having me in your Thoughts & by your asking what Employment I woud chuse, gives me great Encouragement to think that yourare pretty certain of your Application being of Effect in my Favour, far be it from me to attempt begging any Thing very considerable I assure you I shall be content <~~xx~~> tand very thankful for any Employ, the Custom house is the easiest, the military the genteelest, but thank God I am able & willing to undertake any place even that requires the closest Application & am convinced that if I was once put in, I shoud at some time or other rise, which induces me to intreat being put early on the List for that is the mean thing as a Lord Lieutenant always provides first & better for those recommended to him on your Side the Water than on this Side. 'Twill be time enough for me to enquire for Va<~~x~~>cancys when I hear next from you by wch time you can let me know of your certainty of Success, for Va<~~x~~>cncys there is no Danger they happen dayly. Not the best news here but the politicians all employed to no Effect about the Dissolution of the Parliament. I shall be vastly obliged to you for a few franks as I want to write to a brother in law in Scotland — and beg the Favour of Mrs Price to send a little of the Jesuits Drops / if any to spare / when Welsh comes home. I have performd great Cures with what she gave me —— My wife joins in our best Respects to you Mrs Price & my good friend Mr Richard I am

My Service to Mr Smyth D^{r}Sir Your very affec^{te} Kinsman
& all Friends ________ & sincere hbleServ.^{t}
EdmSpencer

7 tand] it looks as though Spencer started writing /to/ but changed his mind and overwrote the /o/ with the /a/ without deleting the /t/.

12 mean thing] perhaps a mistake for /main thing/, but possibly in the same sense as in 'the mean way' — 'a course adopted to achieve a certain end' (*OED*, mean. a^{2}, 4). It is also just possible that this is an uncharacteristic phonetic spelling.

15 & 17 Va<~~x~~>cancys] see 10 November 1746: folio 53, note to l.12.

21 franks] envelopes bearing the signature of a person (such as an MP) entitled to send letters free through the state postal service (*OED*, n^{5}.1 and 2). Price, as has been seen, was able to obtain franks from his friend the Earl of Barrymore (see the address to 19 November 1745: folio 37 and note) and these are likely to be the ones he sends Spencer in response to this request, but a comment in the next letter shows that they also regularly used those of Sir Watkin Williams-Wynn, MP for Denbighshire and an old Jacobite friend (see note to 9 October 1747: folio 60, l.4).

22–23 Jesuits Drops] i.e., Walker's Jesuit Drops, 'the most certain, cheap, pleasant, safe, effectual, and immediate cure ever discovered for gleets and seminal weaknesses both sexes are subject to, though ever so obstinate, of ever so long continuance, and by whatever means occasioned, and also for the venereal disease, from its slightest to its most malignant symptoms. Likewise, for the gravel, stone in the bladder, and all scorbutic cases of ever so long a standing; [...] likewise, all nervous disorders, the gout, rheumatism, and all disorders in the stomach' (from an advertisement in *The Edinburgh Advertiser*, February 1772, <http://thequackdoctor.com/index.php/walkers-jesuits-drops> [accessed 10 August 2014]). Spencer's advice shows how medical advice circulated among local and family networks (Kelly, 'Domestic Medication', p. 128).

[folio 60]

[To Francis Price Esqr
at Brynypiece near Wrexham
Chester]

Renny near Castlelyons October the 9.th 1747

Dear Sir

Tis so long since I had the Pleasure of a Letter from you, that I suspect you did not receive either of mine in answer to your last Favour, tho directed as usual under cover to Sir Watkin: I therefore enclose this to a Friend in Dublin to put into the Office there, by which Means 'twill arrive with the less Expence to you. I entreat you will inform me if you received my Letters that if they missd I may ~~aqain~~ aquaint you with the Contents. I am informd that Lady Ann Barry is in so bad a state of health that 'tis thought she cannot recover. My Lord has such a Run of grand Company that I have not been to wait on him, as I do not know ^how one in my Way may be liked among so many of the best Fortunes, but as I suppose he will have more Time to himself when most of our Members are gone up to Parliament: I will then take the Opportunity of waiting on him. I woud not trouble you with this Stuff but that I have~~ng~~ nothing new to tell you My Wife joins in our best Respects to you Coz.^{n} Price & Dr Mr Richard

D^{r}Sir

Your very aff.^{te} Kinsman &
most obed.^{t} Servt
EdmSpencer

4 under cover] see note to 10 September 1745: folio 35, ll.12–13. Sir Watkin's house at Llanforda, Oswestry, was about twelve miles from Bryn y Pys, a comfortable distance for Spencer's letters to be carried on the final leg of their journey by a servant.

4–5 I therefore [...] Office there] there is a Dublin postmark on the address panel which includes the date /[OC] 13/, i.e. 13 October.

6 less Expence] by sending it under cover to his friend in Dublin to be forwarded from there to Overton, Spencer has almost halved the distance the letter would have had to travel, and so saved a few pence on the postage Price would have had to pay; Price was a wealthy man, but Spencer's behaviour here is dictated, no doubt, by that aspect of the etiquette of eighteenth-century correspondence which required that the expense imposed by the sender on the receiver should be kept as low as possible. See also Spencer's further apologetic explanation in the first ten lines of the following letter.

[folio 61]

[To Francis Price Esqr]

Renny October the 16.th 1747

D^{r}Sir

Your last Favour did not come to hand till last Tuesday / too late to answer then / tho dated the 30.th ult. & ought to have arrived before, but that I suppose 'twas missd in the Post Office Dublin: had it come according to the Date, it woud have saved you the Expence of a Letter from me, which I lately writ, on a surmise that my former had not reachd you, & for which I beg your Pardon, & which I shoud not have written unless under Cover, had I been certain that Sir Watkin had been at the Time returnd. I fancy you rem$^{\partial}$ber Tom Burgess, a hearty honest Farmer who lived at Lab a colly near the River Funcion. he was noted for keeping a good House & drinking a vast quantity of Spirits. but about ten Days ago after a nights hard drinking, the next Day took a Fancy to milk & water of which he took but one Draught / & the only one he had ever taken of that Sort of Liquor / <~~xx~~> wch proved his Destruction, for it threw him into a Disorder that carried him off in four Days to the great Regret of his Neighbourhood, as he was a good natured honest old Batchelour $^{in\ the}$ <~~xx~~> 61.st year of his Age. I heartily recommend his End to be a warning to the Colonel not to make use of too cooling Liquor at his Age————

My Wife joins in our Compliments to you Mrs Price & my good friend Mr Rich.^{d} I am D^{r}Sir Your truly aff.^{te} Kinsman & Ser.^{t} EdmSpencer

1–10 Your last [...] returnd.] see note to l.6 of the previous letter.

8–10 & which [...] returnd.] the syntax is awkward, suggesting at first sight the opposite of what Spencer clearly intends; 'unless' is equivalent to 'except' or 'other than' (*OED*, prep.2.d) and the insertion of 'and' after 'Cover' would make more obvious the parallelism of the two conditional clauses on either side of it: 'I would have written only under cover, and only then if I had known that Sir Watkin was at home'.

10 rem$^{\partial}$ber] Spencer uses the same tilde as he does for abbreviating the months in 10 January 1743: folio 13, 21 January 1743: folio 14, 31 January 1743: folio 15, 14 February 1743: folio 18, and 18 January 1744/5: folio 28; here, however, the top flourish moves to the right rather than the left; as in the earlier instances there is a supralineal line above the word and under the tilde which here extends from the /r/ to the /b/ of /rem$^{\partial}$ber/.

11 Lab a colly [...] River Funcion] Labacally, a hamlet near Glanworth, Co. Cork, is situated approximately three miles north-west of Fermoy and six miles due east of Castletownroche; there is also a cairn there, now known as Labbacallee Wedge Tomb, so Spencer may be referring here to the general area rather than specifically to the village. The Funshion runs about half a mile north of Labacally; it is a tributary of the Blackwater which it joins some two and a half miles west of Fermoy (Bartholomew, *Gazetteer of the British Isles*, entries for *Labacally* and *Funshion*).

[folio 62]

[To Francis Price Esqr]
Dick's Coffee house Dublin Novr 17.th
1747

DearSir

Last Sunday I arrived here with one Mr Bowen a Gentleman of Fortune who has settled in our Country for the Benefit of Sporting, & was pleased to let me ride up a horse of his: as the Account between the Powers and me is to be settled this Term, 'twas necessary that I shoud be here; Renny will soon be sold, I wish you woud purchase it, as I am convinced twill go for less that tis worth, & if, for an easy purchase, you woud lay out any Money on this Side the Water, you coud easily know the value of it, & your bidding may be of Consequence to me & yet get you a great Bargain. As the British Parliam.^{t} are now met, your Friend will have it in his Power to perform his Promise to you which is my only Hope every thing else having faild. My best Respects to Mrs Price & my good Friend Mr Richard —— I am DearSir

Your truly aff.^{te} Kinsman
& most humble Servant
EdmSpencer

Address Dick's Coffee house] Dick's was the oldest coffee house in Dublin occupying rooms in Carberry House in Skinner Row, which ran into the eastern end of Castle Street; it was established in the late seventeenth century by the bookseller Richard Pue above his shop, a location which resulted in its being patronized mainly by literary people; it was demolished in 1780 (Mac Con Iomaire, 'Coffee Culture in Dublin'). See also 13 May 1748: folio 73, ll.12–13.

5 the Powers] this family was linked by marriage to the second branch of Edmund Spenser's family: Hugolin, the grandson of Spenser and Elizabeth Boyle, inherited part of his grandfather's Irish estate (including Renny), but had it confiscated after the Civil War due to his having been a Catholic; it was subsequently reinstated, much impoverished, and in 1673, Hugolin mortgaged Renny to his daughter Dorothy's husband, Pierce Power. After the Williamite Wars (1689–1691) Hugolin, who fought on the Jacobite side, was declared an outlaw with the result that his lands were again forfeited but this time, in 1697, transferred

to his step-cousin William (the grandfather of Spencer) who had fought on William's side — see the Memorial, folio 127: 'William the Third [...] granted certain other Land in this Kingdom unto William Spencer the Mem$^{\underline{list's}}$ Grandfather for his Ser[vices] to the Crown [...] particularly for his Services at the memorable Battle of Aghrim' (ll.5–9; the Memorial is located after the letter of 20 January 1748: folio 81); William almost immediately passed them on to his son, Nathaniel (Spencer's father) and in the same year the two of them mortgaged Renny (along with the Kilcolman estate). Pierce Power sought to have Renny returned to him, and it was determined that Nathaniel was now liable for the estate and that he had to pay Power for them. Nathaniel was later forced to sell off much of his land to repay his inherited debts but it looks as though the debt to Power was not one of them as the opening sentence of 3 July 1748: folio 74 implies that his descendants (presumably his son and grandson, both also called Pierce) were putting pressure on Spencer to sell Renny in order to get their money (see Hadfield, *Edmund Spenser,* pp. 407–12, and 'A Mortgage Agreement of Hugolin Spenser, Edmund Spenser's Grandson', pp. 329–35).

[folio 63]

[To Francis Price Esqr]

Dublin December the 5.th 1747

DearSir

I received your Favour by the last Packett, & pursuant to your Direction, return the enclosed; as to enquiring about a Vacancy, twill be of no use, as they are generally filld as fast as they happen. the best Way to succeed, is first to obtain the Promise, & as it must be done by some of the Secretarys here, if they are inclined to make it good, there will be Opportunitys enough for it. if tis by one of the Lord Lieut.$^{t's}$ Secretarys the Gentleman intends to provide for me tis constantly in their Power. however hit or miss you shall always have my sincere acknowlegements for this and all your Favours —— That Part of the Lands of Renny which lye on the North Side of the River were set during my minority for £100 pan$^{\partial}$ & if they are not worth more I am sure they cannot be less as I turnd out on them three lar<★★> Lime Kilns, the Lands on the South Side were never sett as there was wood on the most Part of them, wch I cut down, & have taken great Care of since & is as fine growing wood as any in the Kingdom. Since my last to you the Officer's Report in my Cause was £1170:- so that my Intention is to Mortgage the whole for £{*blot*}1200 — & let the Mortgagee join in a Lease of the Premisses wch will secure him a good Tenant & I think good Security for his Money which I expect to procure at five p C.^{t} there is no Chief Rent payd out of it but a Quit rent of Six p.^{ds} p an$^{\partial}$. I am obliged to you for your intention of writing to Lord Barrymore about it, but as he has the Powers greatly at heart / who have used me basely / & as he is a very great man: I woud not choose to deal with him; for shoud he at any Time take it into his head he ~~woud~~ may crush me to Atoms.

I took the Opportunity of my being from home to have my little Girl

inoculated for the small Pox / wch I never had / & she has recoverd them finely
& had but 25 spots, I wish with all my Soul my Dear Mr Richard was
passd them as well. my best Respects to Mrs Price & Mr Rich^{d} —
I am Dear Sir y$^{\partial}$ very aff.^{te} Kinsman
My Service to Mr Smyth & all Friends & most humble Servt
EdmSpencer

4 happen] first apparently written as /happyn/, the /y/ then being over-written with the /e/.

8 their] possibly written as /thier/ originally; there are two dots above the third and fourth letters/ and the fourth is over-written.

11 set] 'let on a lease' (*OED*, v^{I}.57.a).

12 lar<★★>] most likely /large/, but the last letters of the word are completely lost through fading at the edge of the sheet.

13 Lime Kilns] lime, produced by calcining limestone or shells in kilns, was used to improve the quality of soils.

16 Cause] i.e. the court case which Spencer believed was likely to take place as far back as 10 October 1745 (see letter of that date, folio 36, ll.12–13).

20 Chief Rent] 'annual rent paid under a tenure held directly from the owner' (*OED*, *chief*, n.13).

20 Quit rent] 'a rent paid in lieu of services' (*OED*).

22 the Powers] see note to l.5 of the previous letter.

26 my little Girl] this would be his second daughter, Rosamond as his first, Ann, died in 1743 (a fact not mentioned in any of the surviving letters to Price); Rosamond's year of birth is unknown, but Ann was born in 1734 so the younger girl would have been at most 13 years old at this point.

27 inoculated [...] small Pox] inoculation for small-pox was introduced to England from Turkey by Lady Wortley Montagu in the early 1720s; the publication in London of the American physician Zabdiel Boylston's *Historical Account of the Small-Pox Inoculated in New England* in 1726 and Boylston's subsequent election to the Royal Society would have increased awareness and acceptance of the procedure (<https://en.wikipedia.org/wiki/Inoculation> [accessed 1 February 2016]).

[folio 64]

Dublin December the 15.th 1747

DearSir

I return my most gratefull Acknowlegements for y.^{r} last Favour, which I received by Yesterdays Packetts. & return the inclosed because you mentiond it in y$^{\partial}$ former Letter that I shoud do so. as to my enquiring for a Vacancy, 'twoud be to no purpose, as there are always Candidates ready, one of which woud certainly be appointed before I coud receive an Answer to my Notice. The Way to succeed is by being well recommended to the Commissioners of the Revenue ∧$^{\text{or one of them}}$ who if he had a Mind to comply with such Request, woud imediately order me a Letter for Instructions & when I produce a Certificate of being qualified, may have Opportunitys enough to provide for me. Mr John Ponsonby son of Lord Besbourough who is married to one of the Duke of Devonshires Daughters, is the First Commissioner & by his Rank & Interest is of the greatest Weight at the Board: if I shoud get a Place that woud require Bail, I am confident I can procure such for some Thousands, as I thank God I have always been honestly inclind, & am considerd in my Neighbourhood as an honest Man. Whether I succeed or not I shall during my Life with the greatest Gratitude acknowlege all your Favours & am with my best respects to Mrs Price & Mr Richard Dear Sir

Your sincerely affec.^{te} Kinsman
& most humble Servant
EdmSpencer

If I get a Letter to a Comiss.$^{\partial}$
I can be introduced by the Collector
of Corke———

2 Packetts] the plural here (and in the next letter) indicates that Spencer is using the word to mean 'packages of letters' rather than 'packet boat' (see 14 February 1743: folio 18, note to l.16).

11 John Ponsonby] the second son of Brabazon Ponsonby, 1st Earl of Bessborough; he married, in 1743, Elizabeth Cavendish, daughter of William Cavendish, 4th Duke of Devonshire (who was then Lord Lieutenant of Ireland), and in 1744 inherited his father's position as First Commissioner of the Revenue (*DIB*).

14 Bail] here in the sense simply of security (presumably for good behaviour in office) rather than in a criminal or penal context.

[folio 65]

[To Francis Price Esqr]

Dublin Jan∂y the 5.th 1747

DearSir

Yours dated Christmas day did not come to Hand till Yesterday as we had three Packetts due. I shall take Care to follow your Directions in answering Mr Williams's Letter / when I receive it / & letting you know of it. I have no notion of leaving Town for some Time as there is nothing like being on the Spot if I am recommended at all, however I will wait in Expectation of [*it*]

The Town is very thin of Company as most of the Nobility & Gentry are returnd to the Country for the Holydays, where it must be very pleasant as the Weather is extreamly mild. Our House of Commons met Yesterday but have Nothing to do but pass a few private Bills & some relating to the Turnpike Roads.

Your old Trigger holds out surprizingly, had he been good for any thing he woud have gone off before this, but he is left for a Scourge to your Parish. I realy believe that was even his Speech taken from him, he woud make a Shift by Signs to shew his good Qualitys —

I sincerely wish you & yours many happy Years & am D$^{\partial}$Sir

Your Sincerely aff.^{te} Kinsman
& most obed.^{t} Servant
EdmSpencer

Date] Spencer is using Old Style again for the date here (and for the next five letters).

3 Mr Williams's] the identity of this person is uncertain; two letters from an H. Williams to Price dated 24 November 1747 and 3 December 1747 discuss this matter (see Appendix I); the later one was sent under his own frank, thereby suggesting that he might have been a member of parliament and the address, Grosvenor Street, would lend support to that idea; the one MP whose name fits is Charles Hanbury-Williams (1708–1759); however, he lost his seat (Monmouthshire) during 1747, becoming then Envoy to Dresden (<http://www.historyofparliamentonline.org> [accessed 18 February 2016]), where one might therefore have expected him to be during that year. He did have an interest in Ireland, though, and could easily have been in England at the time these letters were written. See also the following letter, [*1*]6 January1747: folio 66, l.1.

15 Shift] 'a piece of sophistry, an evasion, subterfuge' (*OED*, n.4.a).

[folio 66]

[To Francis Price Esqr]

Dublin Jan∂y the [*1*]6.th 1747

DearSir

I have not yet received a Letter from Mr Williams tho' by your last Favour you seemd to expect that it woud soon have been sent, when I do receive one I shall follow your Directions & return a Letter of Thanks, in as good a Stile as I possibly can, & which, I believe you'll advise, to be, as concise as possible. The only news here is the Death of Lord Barrymore; of which no doubt you've had an Account from Castlelyons before this, as I'm informd he has <~~xxx~~> ^{named} you one of his Executors: a few Hours before he dyed / I'm told / Dominick Roch was arrested at his Suit for a vast Sum of Money & sent to Gaol ---

Our Parliament have now a Recess to the 25.th of Feb∂y, & will then have little to do, except to try the Merits of the Election which is now carrying on with great Vigour between Mr Fitzpatrick / a late convert / & Mr Eyre, w.^{ch}ever happens to be returnd, tis thought the other will petition.

Pray how long woud you have me continue in Town in Expectation of Mr Williams's Favour? if it shoud arrive & I at the time in the Country some Places may be disposed of before I could get up to solicite for one: so I think I had better make Shift to stay some time longer here. I forgot to mention above that Ld Barrymore was buried very privately ——
My best Respects to Mrs Price & Mr Rich^{d} I am Dsir Y∂ very affte
Kinsman & most hbleServ^{t} EdmSpencer

Date] the mark before the /6/ may be a deletion or the number /1/ rather heavily drawn to cover what was originally written. The year is given Old Style.

1–3 I have [...] been sent] in Williams's last letter to Price, sent on 3 December 1747 (see Appendix I), he asks for Spencer's address, so if we allow for another exchange of letters between him and Price the delay is not unreasonable; Spencer, of course, does not know this so we might forgive him his impatience.

[folio 67]

[To Francis Price Esqr]

Dick's Coffee house Dublin Feb∂y the 2.^{d} 1747

Dear Sir

I received y∂ Favour by Welsh, who has slipd his Skin / like the Serpent / & seems young again; I fear the Food of Ballyhooly will so ill agree with his Constitution after Brynypiece that the poor fellow will be reduced in a few Weeks to his pristine Appearance ———
Just as I had wrote thus far the Packett arrived wch brought me y∂ Favour of the 29.th ult I fear 'tis too late for me this night to know w.^{t} sorts of Stuffs were most admired at the Castle the last Birth night, tho I have sent to a Lady who was there & if she be at home I shall be able to inform, ∧^{you} if not, you shall have an Acc^{t} by the next Packett. my being ignorant in those Matters was occasiond by being confined to my room this fortnight past by a violent Cold, wch is very rife in Town, & which I have had to a severe Degree, I am still afflicted with a hard Cough——
I return my sincere Thanks for y∂ many Favours, & shall for ever most gratefully acknowlege them. I gave a rec.^{t} for y∂ last Bill as I shall do for this, but in Acc^{t} take Notice that I receive from Mr Kingsbury Irish Pounds. As for giving you An Acc.^{t} of AVacancy twill be impossible for me, as they are generally promised long before they happen, nor do I expect even after I am recommended to be put in bread in a considerable Time, wch makes it the more necessary to have speedy Application made—
A terrible Accident happened at Kinsale last Week in the House where the French & Spanish Prisoners <~~xxx~~>∧^{were} confined, a Party of whom at Cards having a Quarrell, in the Scuffle threw a Candle on their bed wch being of Straw imediately flamed out & sett all the beds in the Place on Fire & before Assistance coud be procured, burned to Death a great Number of those unhappy Wretches, as the Smoke of the Straw

———————

15–17 I gave [...] Irish Pounds] the receipt of a bill of exchange from Price along with Spenser's note that he is registering this in an account that carefully records that he takes the money in Irish pounds both suggest that he is borrowing money from Price. In 3 July 1748: folio 74, l.12, he acknowledges that he is in debt.

16 Mr Kingsbury] he appears to have taken over from Dr Kingsbury as one of of Price's legal agents in Ireland (see 27 December 1743: folio 12, note to l.14).

19 put in bread] i.e. provided with a living, as in the expression 'in good bread' meaning 'to have a good position or living' (*OED*, *bread*, n^{1}.5.b).

19–20 in [...] Time] i.e. for a considerable time.

21–28 A terrible [...] broke out] the fire was in Desmond Castle, used to keep French prisoners in the period and known as the 'French House'; fifty four prisoners died in the incident and the castle was badly damaged.

hinderd them of finding the Way out: & Numbers of them were asleep in the Garretts when the Fire broke out——
Lady Dowager and Lady Barrymore are expected in Town next Week. I suppose in their way to England. Ld Barrymore is not yet arrived here tho dayly expected. I hope y∂ Executorship will be easy to you tho if it be true / as I am told / that the worthy Colonel Jephson is another of the Exec.$^{∂s}$ you may not find it so very easy to have to deal in any affair that he is concerned in. if it be true that he is one, I shoud suspect that the Lord was failing in his Senses when he appointed him — My best Respects to Mrs Price & Mr Richard ————

I am Dear Sir
y∂ sincerely aff.^{te} kinsman
& most hble Servant
EdmSpencer

P.Sc——
I've just received an Acc^{t} that several Sorts of Poplins were worn the birth night — plain, sprigd, & striped, & <~~xxxx~~> flowerd & striped, of all Coulours both in the Ground & the Flowers — I think the prittiest Sorts are white or straw colourd Ground with blue Stripes & Flowers between, but by w.^{t} I can learn there is little Variations from w.^{t} they were last parliam.^{t} Winter———
I will tomorrow search the Shops & let you know more particularly by the next Packet, but tis now too late —

29 Lady Dowager] the widow of the previous Lord Barrymore, father to the recently deceased Lord Barrymore.

30 Ld Barrymore] i.e. the 5th Earl, heir to the recently deceased Lord Barrymore.

[folio 68]

[To Francis Price Esqr]

Dublin Feb$^{∂}$y the 4.th 1747

DearSir

I send enclosed some Patterns of Poplins which are those that are most worn now, ∧ by ladys of fashion as the spriggd are old Fashiond & worn by the lower kind of People I send none of them, there are other sorts of which I cannot send a Pattern as they are flowerd all over, but those are [*r*]ekond paltry & are very little worn: the lowest Price of those I send are two & two pence & the highest Price three & Six pence p yard. The two Lady Barrymores and Mr Barry are arrived in Town. if you have Business with any of them it { *hole* } <*> { *hole* } you to know that they are here. Lord Barrymore is not yet arri{ *hole* } <~~x~~> hourly / it seems expected/ some Attorney is gone down to Castlelyons to tak{*hole*}ssesion for him. My best Respects to Mrs Price & M.^{r}Rich^{d} I am

D.Sir y∂ sincerely aff.^{te} kinsm^{n}

& most obed.^{t} Servt

EdmSpencer

This sheet is badly damaged with substantial holes in it.

[folio 69]

[To Francis Price Esqr]

Dublin Feb$^{∂}$y the 16.th 1747

DearSir

By the Directions you are pleasd to give in your last Favour I intend to leave Town the End of this or beginning of the next Week, but fear your Friend may be dissapointed in the promises made to him in my Favour as he only expects that when Vacancys happen that I shall be provided for, had I received the Letters I expected to a Comissioner it then woud have been in my own Power to have solicited for an Employment by giving him no rest till he had sent me out of the Way, but as the Case is now, I fear I shall be obliged to wait in Expectation of something without obtaining it: however with the most Sincere Acknowlegements of your Kindness, I shall for ever have a gratefull Sense of your many Obligations conferd on me; the person who best Solicits is the soonest provided for, & for giving an Acc.^{t} of a vacancy 'twoud be of little Effect, as 'twoud be filld up before my Letter coud reach you, allowing for the Time twoud take for me to find out Such Vacancys——— I not only sent out Patterns of Poplins, but also pinnd Notes to them of the Shops were I got them, & to the best of my recollection the Prices which are from 2/2 to 3/6 p yard. Please to direct your next Favour to me at Renny near Castlelyons. My best Respects to M.^{rs}

Price & M.r Richard with Service to the Colonel I am Dr Sir
Y∂ truly aff.te
& most obed'
[*E*]

Address] the address side of this sheet contains, to the right of Price's name, two columns of figures that are added up, and, to the left, two other figures (also added up) against words that might be /acres/ and /in Royston/. The writing is not Spencer's. There is a Royston in Ireland that would then have been just outside Dublin and Price may have had some property interest there.

Signature] only half of the /E/ is visible; the rest of the signature is missing because of a tear across the bottom right-hand corner of the sheet.

[folio 70]

[To Francis Price Esqr]

Renny near Castlelyons March the 1.st 1747

DearSir

According to your last Directions I set out from our Metropolis, as soon after I received your Letter as I coud get a Conveniency w.ch happened last Wednesday & was the coldest Day I think I ever felt, being an intense Frost, the next Day was mostly Snow, the Day after that rain, but Saturday, / being the last day of my Journey / <~~x~~> very pleasant Weather: so that in this one Journey, I have it to say I experienced most Sorts of Weather I have not been long enough at home to hear anything new worth troubling you with: poor Cap.t Stannard a few Weeks since was nabbd by our Sheriff & carryd to Gaol for £500 for which he had been bound for one M.r Colclogh, but the week before the last was redeemd by his brother / the Recorder of Dublin / who paid the Mony — the Cap.t was brought home in Triumph, having been met by all the Crew of Ballyhooly with Mummers, Pipers &c & the night concluded with Bonefires, Illuminations / where there appeard a pain of Glass / & other Demonstrations of Joy — My Wife joins in our best Respects to you M.rs Price & M.r Richd I am DearSir

Y∂ Sincerely aff.te Kinsman
& most humble Servt
EdmSpencer

3 Conveniency] i.e. a coach, probably public, to take him home (*OED*, *convenience*, n.7.d).

14 Mummers] performers of folk, or mummers, plays. These were unscripted, so presumably improvised for specific events.

15–16 a pain of Glass] ? — perhaps a kind of firework or some other type of pyrotechnic illumination.

[folio 71]

[To Francis Price Esqr]

Renny near Castlelyons March the 25.th 1748

DearSir

Since my last nothing new has happened in this Country, except the Death of your old Acquaintance Hodder Roberts who after a Weeks indisposition with an inflammation on the Lungs, died to the regrett of most of the Neighbourhood —— I was last Week at Corke, where I saw the True blue Privateer <~~x~~> being a Vessell of about Sixty Tuns, four Carriage Guns four Pounders, ten Swivels & Seventy Men the famous Capt Chip / who in an open boat saild from Dantzick to Kinsale / Comander; she has brought in a Prize, vizt a Ship of 170 tuns bound to Martinico, which is reckond to be worth a good Deal of Mony. The Privateer was fitted out by some Merchants ^$^{of\ Corke}$ who having formd a sort of independent Company & appointed Commissioner Cavendish their Capt calld themselves the True blues & are allowd to be more expert at the Exercise of the Firelock than most of the Standing Army —— My Wife joins in our best Respects to you Mrs Price & Mr Rich^{d}

I am D$^{∂}$Sir

Y∂ most aff^{te} Kinsman

& most humble Servant

EdmSpencer

2–3 Hodder Roberts] see 8 November 1743: folio 8.

5 True Blue Privateer] this ship was noted in *The Gentleman's Magazine* 18 (1748), p. 127. The term 'true blue' was applied to Scottish Presbyterians, especially those who were politically Whig, from the seventeenth century on, but it also meant 'staunchly faithful to one's principles' (*OED*, *blue*, 6.b and 1.e).

7 Swivels] guns mounted on a swivelling bracket.

7 Capt Chip] this is presumably the Captain Chip whose death was reported in *Pue's Occurrences* on 15 July 1755, though there he is said to have sailed from Hamburg to Cork, not Danzig to Kinsale; if it is the same man he was, when he took command of *The True Blue*, seventy eight years old, since he died 'in the 85th year of his age', the report noting that he had 'of late [...] lost his understanding' (website of the Immigrant Ships Transcribers' Guild, posted by Nick Reddan, <http://immigrantships.net/newsarticles/ireland1700_1819.html> [accessed 7 August 2015]).

12 Commissioner Cavendish] Sir Henry Cavendish (1707–1776), who became commissioner of the Irish revenue in 1747 and teller of the exchequer in 1756; he left over £67,000 of public money unaccounted for on his death.

14 Exercise [...] Firelock] the 'firelock' was the mechanism in which a piece of flint struck metal to produce a spark which ignited the gunpowder in the gun's barrel, but it was also generally used (as it is here) to mean a musket furnished with a such a device. By 'exercise' Spencer may simply be commending the True Blues for their successful use and application of the weapon in action (*OED*, n.1.b, though illustrated only up to 1685); he

may be referring, however, to the military training exercise known as the 'manual exercise' as set out in the *New Manual Exercise as Performed by His Majesty's Dragoons, Foot-guards, Foot, Artillery, Marines, and by the Militia*, 2nd edn (London: printed for J. Millan, 1758) and if so his commendation would seem to be well-deserved as no less than fourteen pages are given over to the description of the procedure.

14 Standing Army] the permanent professional army established in England during the Interregnum.

[folio 72]

[To Francis Price Esqr]

Renny April the 25.th 1748 ---

DearSir

Never was seen so bad a Season as this Spring has been & still continues, the Farmers losing great Numbers of Cattle thro' Weakness for want of Hay, as not a Blade of Grass can peep by reason of the cold Winds which have made this Month appear more like March than April. — Capt Barry & his Brother Arthur left Castlelyons last Week, they were there for some Time but did not reside at the Castle but at Killsaintan, wch looks as if there was not a right Harmony between my Lord and them. The Tenants of the Barrymore Estate were all drove last Week for the March Rents, a bad Prospect of what they must expect for the future.

No Alterations in this Neighbourhood since my last, but that for some time to come the people of any Fashion here will be very low in Cash, as most of the Women are gone or have sent to Kinsale to get great Bargains of <~~xxx~~> China & other fine Neednots aboard two Indiamen wch are to continue there 'till a Leak in one of them is stopd. So many of those Ships have been at Kinsale Galway & Limerick since the commemcem^{t} of the War that most of the running Cash of the Country has been carryd off by them & a house is not thought to be furnishd that has not a parcell of Jarrs & Images of China in it. — I had not the pleasure of a Line from you since I came to Munster. My Wife joins in our best Respects to you Mrs Price & my good Friend Mr Richard

My Compliments to Mr Smyth & all Friends ——

I am D^{r}Sir y.$^{\partial}$ sincerely aff^{te} Kinsman & most obed.^{t} Servt

EdmSpencer

6–9 Capt Barry [...] and them.] Capt. Richard Barry and Arthur Barry were two of the sons of the 4th Earl of Barrymore; Capt. Barry later secretly marries, forming an alliance of which 'my Lord', his brother, the 5th Earl, clearly disapproved (see 2 June 1749: folio 84); in a letter from Arthur Barry to Francis Price, dated February 1748, we are told that his brother 'goes on still in his scandalous course of life I have reason to suspect, he will give as much trouble as Possible' (Puleston 17: NLW MS 3577C).

8 Killsaintan] i.e., Kill Saint Anne, an area just to the west of Castlelyons.

10 drove [...] Rents] 'driving for rent' was the practice of seizing a tenant's cattle and impounding it to collect unpaid rents (*OED*, *drive*, v.3.c).

15 China] the taste for chinoiserie reached its height in the middle of the eighteenth century.

15 Neednots] 'unnecessary things' (*OED*), the more candid eighteenth-century equivalent of our 'must-haves'.

[folio 73]

[To Francis Price Esqr]

Renny May the 15.th 1748 ---

DearSir

Your Favour of the 4.th Ins.^{t} I received this Day; I am very confident of your Sincere Endeavours to procure me an Employment, which shall for ever be gratefully acknowleged by me. I shoud not think it so very difficult for a Person of Interest, on your Side the Water, to procure a small Employment, as I every Day observe that even upon Irish Interest Numbers get considerable Places who have not been in Employ before: but this I believe must be done by Persons who know where to apply. Our Newspapers have killd Lady Williams a Month ago, but that is very common with them. I was suprizd with an Advertisement in the last Paper, that all the Furniture & Household Goods of the late Doctor Kingsbury were to be sold by Auction, his Books were sold at Dick's Coffee house while I was in Dublin, as he was in great Business & as I thought in good Circumstances I shoud have thought they might have been kept for his Son who is / I think / in the College. Not the lest News in this Country, but the Farmers in top Spirits for the Peace as they expect great Prices for Beef Butter & all other Comoditys held up very well during the War. Poor Major Welstead who I believe you knew, is just going off in a Dropsy, he married a young Girl a few years since by whom he has five Children, & has not as much as will bury him his Estate being Settled on his first Wife's Children — My Wife joins in our best Respects to you Mrs Price & my good friend Mr Rich.^{d} I am Dear Sir

y∂ sincerely aff^{te} Kinsman
& most humble Servant

My Service to Mr Smyth & all friends —— EdmSpencer

9 Lady Williams] i.e. Ann Vaughan, the wife of Sir Watkin Williams-Wynn, see 5 August 1748: folio 75, l.6.

12–13 Dick's [...] Dublin] this is where Spencer stayed when in Dublin the previous year, see 17 November 1747: folio 62.

19 Dropsy] swelling caused by a build-up of fluid, often related to kidney and heart problems. William Withering (1741–1799) realised that foxgloves could alleviate the symptoms. Samuel Johnson died of dropsy in 1784.

[folio 74]

[To Francis Price Esqr]

near Castlelyons July the 3^{d} 1748——

DearSir

This Fortnight passd I have had a weary time of it, upon a Notice I receivd that my very good Friends the Powers had playd me a slippery Trick, & pushd for the sale of Renny this Term, which I did not in the lest expect: & tho I had two Lawyers / of the Top / two Days pleaded to put of a Sale till the next Term, yet it was orderd to be posted, but by a Flaw in the Advertizem.^{t} I have gaind Time till the next Week which has enabled me to procure a Friend who has promisd to bid highest upon the Sale & if need be will deposite a fourth part of the Purchase Mony, & hold over till Michaelmas Term; this has cost me a great many Miles riding, & had I not a very faithful Attorney I must have been ruind, as my land
& of Consequence I must have been still in Debt
woud have gone for a Trifle for Want of Bidders; ^ but as I hope to have the long Vacation, I shall hunt for a good Purchaser; & by November next I may say adieu every Foot: but what I must do then God only knows; I shall not trouble you with my Soliloquys as I know you are in Pain enough for me without encreasing y∂ trouble with my own irksome Thoughts on this Occasion -- Therefore conclude with my Wife's and my best Wishes for Peace and Happyness to you and yours DearSir

Y∂ truly aff.^{te} Kinsman &
assured humble Servant
EdmSpencer

2 the Powers] see 17 November 1747: folio 62, note to l.5.

3–4 this Term] i.e. Trinity Term, which ran from June to July and was followed by Michaelmas Term (l.10) which ran from October to December; in between was the long vacation (l.13).

9 hold over] 'in law, to remain in a property beyond an agreed termination of the occupation' (*OED*, *hold*, v.42.a); it reads as though it is the friend who will 'hold over' but the clause in which the term occurs is connected to the earlier clause 'which has enabled me to', and thus relates to Spencer.

12 still in Debt] see 2 February 1747: folio 67, ll.15–17 and note.

14 every Foot] i.e. every foot of his land.

[folio 75]

[To Francis Price Esqr]

August the 5.th 1748 —

DearSir

I congratulate you & your Parish on the Decease of the Old Trigger, as I know it must be a great Ease to all, for I dare say he continued troublesome to the last: if I mistake not you have a Right to something considerable upon his Death. Our Newspapers gave an Account of the Marriage of Sir Watkin with this Addition that his Lady just before her Decease entreated him to marry Miss Shakerly; this must be a great Dissapointm^{t} to his Brother Richard who expected that his son woud be the Heir; but yet twoud be a greater Dissapointment to Sir Watkin if his present Lady shoud happen not to breed. Nothing new in this Country but that Mr Taaf is at Castlelyons setting all the Demesnes, even the Park, ^{for} wch purpose he is killing the Deer very fast & if I am rightly informd they will shortly be entirely disposed of – Old Stannard of Ballyhooly dyed last Week __ My Wife joins in our best Respects to you Mrs Price & my good Friend Mr Richard I am D^{r}Sir

Your most aff.^{te} Kinsman
& obed.^{t} humb$^{\partial}$ Servt
EdmSpencer

4 you have [...] his Death] for a possible explanation of this comment see 8 November 1743: folio 8, l.6.

6 his Lady] i.e. the Lady Williams whose death was prematurely reported in the newspapers before 13 May (see 13 May 1748: folio 73, ll.8–10).

7 Miss Shakerly] Frances Shakerly (1717–1803); a portrait of her with her son was painted by Sir Joshua Reynolds in 1768, it hangs in the Tate Gallery, London.

11 Mr Taaf] a member of an aristocratic family that owned lands in Sligo and other parts of Ireland and who appears to have — or believes he has — some claim on the Barrymore estate in Castlelyons; on 14 May 1748 Arthur Barry wrote to Francis Price: 'We find that Taafe, and Company are committing great depredations at Castle Lyons, and that the goods in the Castle are apportioned, & if a speedy stop is not put to these Illegal proceedings, we fear they will soon be disposed'; in July of the same year he told Price: 'Mr. Taafe (the hopefull Lord Governor) tries to get our estate from us in Ireland', and in August, 'Mr. Taafe wants to break the settlement' (all letters in Puleston 17: NLW MS 3577C); however, what claim Mr Taaf had on Castlelyons is, unfortunately, not explained. The Taaffe family had recently been involved in bitter internal litigation over an inheritance (*ODNB* entry for *Taaffe, Nicholas, sixth Viscount Taaffe*). Spencer's observation on this business would suggest that this letter was written, like the next one, at Renny.

12 setting [...] Demesnes] 'setting' probably means here 'planting with young trees' (*OED*, *set*, v^{I}.119) which would explain why the deer are being killed as they eat the bark and so destroy the trees; given the presence of deer and the reference to a park, 'demesnes' most likely refers to land attached to the mansion and used for pleasure (*OED*, 3.c).

[folio 76]

[To Francis Price Esqr]

Renny September the 13.th 1748

DearSir

Since my last I have been at our Assyzes & constantly since riding from Place to Place, to obtain bidders for Renny, 'twill be sold the tenth of November next, & I am in Hopes will sell for the full Value as I expect a good many will bid for it.

Our Farmers are in top Spirits on the ensuing Peace, for Beef is on the rise, Butter a high price the whole Season, Wool a good Price & Corn is expected to be very dear. our harvest is very late, & in a great many places they are still mowing Hay tho' the Weather is very changeable.

There has not happened anything new in this Neighbourhood since my last. but at Cashell races Mr Perry a young Gentleman heir to twelve hundred a year was basely murderd by one Shannahan, they had a quarrell at a Tavern after Supper from whence they sent their Seconds for Pistols to decide the Dispute by a Shot, Shannahan's Second came first, & as soon as he enterd the room Shannahan took a pistol from him & imediately shot Perry thro the head. both he and his Second were secured & are now in Gaol, well guarded by a Company of Militia of which Perry was Captain, & tis expected that a Comission of Oyez will be granted for their immediate Tryal.

My Wife joins in our best Respects to you Mrs Price & Mr Rich^{d}

I am DearSir Y.$^{\partial}$ most aff.^{te} Kinsman

My Service to Mr Smyth & all friends & ob.^{t} hble Servt

EdmSpencer

On both sides of the outer sheet, on either side of the address to Price and reading the opposite way round to that address are some additions of sums of money against various items of expenditure such as 'Dinner [...] Supper [...] Breakfast [...] wine [...] trinkit for my wife'. This is not Spencer's hand (nor would it be at all likely that he would have made these notes on a letter before sending it) but is very similar to the hand in the three drafts (folios 124, 125 & 126) written by Price; it looks as though Price had the letter with him when he was travelling and used it to make notes of his spending. We might observe that he spends as much on wine on one occasion, 2/6d or 12.5 pence, as he does on the 'trinkit' for his wife.

6 ensuing Peace] the Treaty of Aix-la-Chapelle was signed on 24 April 1748, after the Conference of Breda, concluding the War of the Austrian Succession, but this did little to stem the colonial conflict between Britain and France (although the treaty did counter the Jacobite threat to Hanoverian rule: see Riding, *Jacobites*, p. 498).

12 Cashel races] Cashel is in Co. Tipperary, about fifty miles north-east of Mallow. Horse racing emerged as a popular sport in Ireland in the later seventeenth century.

12–14 Perry... Shanahan] Shanahan and his second, Mr. Long, were found guilty of murder in Dublin in early September 1748, the trial being briefly reported in the country news section of *The Dublin Courant*, 3–6 September 1748, which Spencer may well have been reading.

[folio 77]

[To Francis Price Esqr]

DearSir

There is not the least thing new in this Country that I coud entertain you with. I must set out for Dublin the first of next Month as my Land will be sold the tenth, & what I am to do after God only knows. I find by the papers that Lord Fitzwilliams is returnd to England without remembering his promise about me, but I am so used to Dissapointments that the Shock is not half so great me as it woud be to another, however I shall soon be in a way that 'twill be impossible for me to subsist without some Employment. I shoud be mighty glad to hear from you as 'tis a great while since I had the Pleasure of a Letter from you — My Wife joins in our best Compliments to you Mrs Price & my good friend Mr Richard I am Dear Sir

Y.$^{∂}$truely aff.^{te} Kinsman
& most humble Servant
EdmSpencer

October the 25.th 1748 --

2–3 I must [...] next Month] this presumably situates Spencer in Renny, his last address, when he wrote this letter (but see 28 February 1748: folio 83, note to l.12). In fact he does not set out until about a week later than this as he says in the next letter, written from Dublin on 8 November, that he arrived in the capital the day before.

4–5 Lord Fitzwilliams] William Fitzwilliam (1719–1756) was a member of the Irish Privy Council; it sounds as though Price had written to him on Spencer's behalf.

7 great me] a /to/ has been omitted between these words.

[folio 78]

[To Francis Price Esqr]

Dear Sir

I came to Town yesterday & tho 'tis said our Munster roads are infested by highwaymen yet I had the happyness not to meet any of them; tho if I had they woud have got but slender booty. one Freny who h[*as*] a gang in the County of Waterford & sometimes visits <**> Corke road is greatly dreaded as he is very desperate, but about ten Days since Eight or nine of his gang & harbo[*urers*] were taken & are lodged in Kilkenny Gaol, & tis expected he w[*ill*] also soon be secured as Seventy pounds are offerd for him dead or alive ———

Next Thursday the Sale of my Land will come on, but will not be closed 'till eight days after, I have not a cert[*ain*]<*> whether 'twill sell well or not, you shall hear of it as so[*on*] as'tis over. My best respects to Mrs Price & M^{r} [*Ricd*]

I am DearSir Y.$^{\partial}$ most aff.^{te} Kinsman

& obed.^{t} humble Servt

EdmSpencer

at Mr Lumbard's apoth$^{\partial y}$

fishambleStreet Dublin

Novem.^{r} the 8.th 1748 —

4 Freny] James Freney, born 1719, came from a respectable Kilkenny family; following financial difficulties he took to the road and was proclaimed an outlaw in 1748; he surrendered in April 1749 but managed to do a deal with the law which allowed him to emigrate; most of the rest of the gang were hanged. At some point he returned to Ireland and became a customs officer at New Ross, near Waterford. In 1754 he published an autobiography, *The Life and Adventures of Mr James Freney*, which was a huge success; he died in 1788 (<http://en.wikipedia.org/wiki/James_Freney> [accessed 12 March 2015]). On the popularity of Freney see also Connolly, *Religion, Law and Power*, p. 210.

[folio 79]

[To Francis Price Esqr]
at Mr Lombard's apoth$^{\partial y}$ fishambleStreet
Dublin Decr the 1.st 1748 --

Dear Sir

I have at last closed the Sale of Renny and after paying off all Incumbrances, expect to have between four & five hund$^{\partial}$ pounds to my Self but how to dispose of the mony I am not yet fixed, for to expect to be able to live only on the Iterest I can't think of & must therefore turn it to some Way that will bring in more than Six percent — There are Six Packetts due which I believe will bring me a Letter from you — I must acquaint you with a thing that will greatly surprize you. Harry Harrison who has lived like a Hermit for many y$^{\partial}$ & still continues to do so, has last Week remitted to the Society for promoting Protestant Schools, one thousand pounds in a Lump, by wch Charity I believe he expects to pave the way to wipe off his Extortions &— with wch he might be hereafter chargd My best respects to Mrs Price & Mr Rich^{d} I am D^{r}Sir Your very aff.^{te} Kinsman & most hble Servt EdmSpencer

I hope to be able to leave Town in a fortnight —|

10–11 Harry Harrison] the letter of 21 February 1748: folio 82 tells us that he was the vicar of Castlelyons; The Incorporated Society in Dublin for Promoting English Protestant Schools in Ireland (to give it its full name) was founded by a charter granted by George II in 1733, and hence they were also known as charter schools (see 21 February 1748: folio 82, note to l.11); their aim, according to their programme, was to rescue Catholic children 'from the dangers of Popish superstition and idolatry, and their bodies from the miseries of idleness and beggary' (<https://en.wikipedia.org/wiki/Irish_Charter_Schools> [accessed 10 August 2015]). The sum of money that Harrison left is equivalent to the annual sum granted by the king in the original charter, and Spencer's sly suggestion that this ostentatious performance of charity has the appearance of someone using good works to bargain with the Almighty for a reciprocal gift of grace gives Harrison's behaviour a neatly ironic 'Popish' inflection.

[folio 80]

[To Francis Price Esq$^{\partial}$]
Dublin Dec.$^{\partial}$ the 10.th 1748 —

Dear Sir

Next Munday I intend to begin my Journey to Munster & beg your next Favour may be directed to me near Castlelyons: in my last I gave you an Acc^{t} of what I intend to do to get bread, namely to buy some Employment but it may happen to be some Time before I can meet with a person who will sell. a pretty tolerable one is now vacant in the Customs by the Death of one Mr Percivall, but as my Scheme is not to venture any of my little fund upon any Chance, I shall make no Enquiry about it —

I am advised by Numbers of my Friends to make Application to the Duke of Marlborough, but in what Manner is the Question, I think a Memorial from me if properly handed to him may meet with Success; & perhaps he woud take Some Notice of me, tho I do not intend to put my Self to the Expence of a Journey about it 'till I find what Succes may attend the Memorial: Sure among your numerous friends or Acquaintance Some person may be found who will be kind enough to perform this small Favour & I flatter my self / & by all your kindnesses to me have reason to dare / that you will make Enquiry after such an [*one*] <****> will make Application to have it do[*ne, the*]<****> shall be short

——————————

& therefore not tiresome — There are now ten packetts due wch has kept from me the pleasure of any Letters from you Since I came to Town. My best Respects to Mrs Price & my D.^{r} friend Mr Rich^{d} I am Dear Sir

Y.$^{\partial}$truely aff.^{te} Kinsman
& obed.^{t} hble Serv.$^{\partial}$
EdmSpencer

My Service to Mr Smyth & all friends ———

12 a Memorial] see folio 127 (situated after the next letter, 20 [January] 174[*8*]: folio 81) for the draft of this Memorial, which Spencer duly sends with the next letter. Spencer's phrase in l.4 of that next letter, 'I send [*en*]closed the mem.^{l} you directed', indicates that this is actually Price's idea, and Spencer is here simply concurring with the suggestion rather than making it.

[folio 81]

{*hole*} 20.th 1748--

DearSir

Your Favour of the 27.th of Nov.$^{\partial}$ di[*d*] not arrive [*till the*] 6th [*ins.*$^{\partial}$] at [*w*^{ch}] time the [*t*] [*p*]acketts [*recd*] came together, & my being from h[*o*]me til tw[*o*] Days ago hinderd my answering y$^{\partial}$ [*kind* corres$^{d\partial}$] sooner -- I send [*en*]closed the mem.^{1} you directed but fear tis but indifferently done as [*I*] {*tear*} no one in this Country to [*draw*] one but my self——

I writt to you from Dublin to inform you that I was advised by [*Numbers*] of my Acquaintance to apply to the Duke of Marlborough & to beg of you to try to procure some [*person*] of his Acquaintance ~~tha~~ to hand a Mem.^{1} to him; if such a one can be prevaild on to do so, the Mem.^{1} must / I think / differ from the inclosed; as a prayer must be added ~~sigfyn~~ signifying that I throw my self on his generosity to relieve for my Grandsire's or name's sake or something to that Effect — but as soon as advised by you about the getting it done, I will apply to a Lawyer to have it nicely drawn ——

I have but a melancholy Prospect before me except Something can be speedily done, as I fear for present Maintainance I must break in upon my poor principle. I was obliged to give my brother & Sister £150 to join me in a fine or otherwise I coud not make a good Title. I do not value what trouble I shoud be at to get tolerable [su]bsistance & thank God I am able & willing to continue in any Office to write from Morning till Night -- Im sure I have reasons sufficient to rely on your good Nature in trying for a Place for me, wch whether it be procured or not shall be always gratefully acknowledged by me —— My Wife joins in our be{ *hole* }ects to you Mrs Price & Mr Richard

I am DearSir

Your most aff.^{te} Kinsman &
obed.^{t} humble Servant
EdmSpencer

My Service to Mr Smyth &
all inquiring Friends

Addressee] this is missing, the address side of the sheet showing only two additions of sums of money against the words /Hide/, /Beef/ and possibly /Tobaco/; as Spencer was enclosing another sheet with this letter it is possible he wrapped both in a separate sheet of paper which carried Price's name.

Address and date] there is a hole where the place name and month should be. The address and month are almost certainly Castlelyons and January 1748: the next letter is dated 21 February and starts: 'I had the Favour of yours of the 14.th ins.^{t} last Post' so this must predate 14 February. Also Spencer was in Dublin between 1 December (1 December 1748: folio 79) and 10 December (10 December 1748: folio 80), and he says in that last letter that he intends to leave Dublin on the next Monday to travel to Munster, i.e. home, as he tends to use Munster synecdocically for home; that is currently Castlelyons, which is where he asks Price in the letter of 10 December to direct any reply; 10 December was a Tuesday in 1748 so the next Monday was the 16th and Castlelyons was a good two or even three days travel from Dublin; he could not therefore have got there until around 18 or 19 December which would have been two days before he wrote this letter; unfortunately the vital number before the word 'Days' in l.3 is almost illegible but it could well be 'two', the /o/ having been removed by the tear in the letter that cuts across this word.

Lineation] the letter is badly damaged in the top section containing the first paragraph. Three vertical fractures run down the sheet (two through the first paragraph and the third to about halfway down the sheet) with the result that the lineation has been distorted; there is, further, bad fading and what appears to be see-through from the other side, though the letter is written on only one side of the sheet.

12 my Grandsire's] see folios 125 & 126 for the service done by his grandfather to the Crown.

12 name's sake] i.e. his great-great-grandfather the poet.

17 Sister] presumably his sister-in-law.

18 fine] possibly 'the compromise of a collusive suit for the possession of lands' (*OED*, n^{I}.6.b), but as we do not know what kind of title Spencer is referring to the specific meaning is uncertain (see also 28 February 1748: folio 83, l.21).

[folio 127]

The Mem[*orial of Edmund*] Spencer

Sheweth

That the Memorialist is Great Grandson of E{*paper torn*} Spencer the Poet, to whom her Majesty Queen Elizabeth {*paper torn*} graciously pleasd for his Writings and Service to the {*paper torn*} to grant certain Lands in this Kingdom of Ireland.

That his Majesty William the Third of glorious Memory also granted certain other Land in this Kingdom unto William Spencer the Mem$^{\underline{\text{list's}}}$ Grandfather for his Ser[vices] to the Crown during the late Wars in this Kingdom & particularly for his Services at the memorable Battle of Aghrim.

That all the said Lands descended to Nathaniel Spencer — the Mem$^{\underline{\text{list's}}}$ Father who mortgaged the same for several large Sums of Money, and soon after dyed, leaving the Memor$^{\underline{\text{st}}}$ then an Infant of very tender Years to the Care of a Guardian who neglected to apply the Income of said Lands to the Discharge of the said Nathaniel's Debts, but converted the same to his own use, and dyed insolvent in the Minority of the Mem$^{\underline{\text{list}}}$ whereby the Mem$^{\underline{\text{list}}}$ was deprived of any Redress for his sufferings which were so considerable that the Mem$^{\underline{\text{list's}}}$ said Estates were since sold for the Payment of his Father's Debts, and the Mem$^{\underline{\text{list}}}$ thereby reduced to very low Circumstances —

This is the draft of the memorial mentioned in the two previous letters and which was enclosed in the last one. It is written in a clear, bold italic script, presumably by Spencer himself as he tells Price that he fears it is 'but indifferently done as [*I*] <***> no one in this Country to [*draw*] one but my self', and that, once Price has reviewed it, he will 'will apply to a Lawyer to have it nicely drawn' (20 January 1748: folio 81, ll.4–5 & 13–14). Spencer's suggestion that the final version 'must / I think / differ from the inclosed; as a prayer must be added ~~sigfyn~~ signifying that I throw my self on his generosity' (20 January 1748: folio 81, ll.10–11) also indicates that this is a draft, which would explain the lack of a conclusion to the narrative of his impoverishment. The heading is badly faded in the middle of the line, but the contents are obvious; there is also a tear on the right-hand side which has removed the final letters of the first three lines. It would appear from the next letter (21 February 1748: folio 82, ll.18–22) that Price thought that the suggestion that he might send it to the Duke of Marlborough was after all either not possible or not advisable. As the folio number indicates, this item was archived at the end of the collection, but is better placed here as it was, as noted, enclosed with the previous letter.

1 Great Grandson] an odd mistake: he was, of course, the great-great-grandson of the poet.

[folio 125]

The case of Edmund Spencer Gentleman of The kingdom of Ireland
1st Edmund Spencer is great great Grand son of ye Poet Spencer that did write ye fairy Queen ——
2:^d: he was born to twelve hundred a year, but through the extravagance of his father it was above half sold before he dyed, ~~he left him in bad~~ the remaining part of y^e estate was incumbered and y^e poor Edmund Spence the

————————————

He is great grandson of y^e Poet Spencer His ~~was~~ grandfather ^ ^William Spencer^ was verry instru = mental in preserving King Williams army at y^e battle of Achrim, for he knew all y^e Defiles and narrow passes which y^e English army were ignorant of, & had it not been for the Said William Spencer King James's army would have don them more mis = chief & ~~destroyed~~ than they did —— He is verry well affected to the present establishment — & is about thirty four years old_ and writes an excellent hand & understands figures This unfortunate young man was born to above twelve hundred pounds a year three parts of which his father privatly sold for not half its worth (beeing under no settlement) dyed and left the remain der mortgaged and left him an infant under ye guardian ship

————————————

[*of*] a lawyer who instead of paying ~~y^e~~ yearly ye intrest sunk it & when ye minor came of age he fond that part of ye estate that was mortgaged eaten up in principal & intrest & was sold in chancery to pay both — ye Guardian dyed insolvent

[*& it*] was lost upon his death —
the remaining estate / sold last term /
was destroyed by [*y^{e}*] mortgage ~~upon~~
~~it~~ fixed upon it, irredeemable for
[*a vast*] number of years, by his grand
father at [*9 ßC^{t}*] —— there was a small
wood upon this estate, which he
was obliged to cut down, for the
following reason —
~~he had proposed matrimony to~~
~~young gentleman~~ he married
a gentlemans daughter in his neigh
bourhood & was to have a thousand ^{pounds}
with her, three years keep for y^{e} ^{young} couple
two servants & three horses but $^{ye\ father}$ instead
of paying y^{e} fortune <~~x~~> gott<~~x~~> his son
in law to be bound for him for 400£
which he was forced to pay in less than
a year_ & y^{e} father dyed a beggar_ so end<~~x~~>
ye prospect of   & their   y^{e} farther assistance
^ fortune, keeping, and ~~was [*succeeded*] by~~
~~a wife and two children — without any~~
of maintaining a wife & two children
~~thing to maintain them~~ _
~~The~~ His two friends in Ireland that
promised him their assistance are
dead, Baron Wainwright & Mr Justice
Lindsey —

Like folios 124 & 126 this would appear to be a draft (written in pencil) for a letter that Price intends to send to influential friends in a position to help Spencer in his search for paid work. It would be to some extent a response to Spencer's asking him in the letter of 20 [January] 174[*8*]: folio 81 'to try to procure some [*person*] of [the Duke of Marlborough's] Acquaintance to hand a Mem.[1] to him' (ll.8–9) and would also be what Spencer is referring to in the next letter when he says that he is 'concernd to think you have been obliged to stretch your Interest' (21 February 1748: folio 82, l.3). It has some verbal similarities to the draft in folio 124 (for example ll.27–40 of 125 with ll.10–20 of 124, and ll.53–59 of 125 with ll.26–33 of 124); both also start with very similar phrases: 'The case of Edmund Spencer Gentleman' (125) and 'The case of Mr Edmund Spencer' (124), so Price may have gone back to 124 to remind himself of certain details he wished to include here, or to a common source. What is more striking about this draft, though, is its similarity to the memorial that Spencer has sent to Price: both start with references to his great-great-grandfather, the poet Edmund Spenser (ll.3–5 of 125 and 2–4 of the memorial), secondly mention the services of his grandfather to William III at the battle of Achrim, and then cover the events that led to the loss of his estates (ll.27–46 of 125 and ll.10–20 of the memorial). That parallelism in the structure of the piece strongly suggests that it was written after Price had received the memorial and in response to it, and hence the decision to place it here. Another striking piece of evidence for this dating is l.42 which refers to 'the remaining estate / sold last term /'; if this was written in February (the month Price would have received the memorial) the last legal term would have been Michaelmas, which was the term in which Renny was sold (see 1 December 1748: folio 79). Possibly contradicting this date is the statement in ll.24–25 that Spencer 'is about thirty four years old' which was his age in 1746 when folio 124 was probably written (he was born in November 1711), but two years have passed since then so at this point he would be thirty six; 'about' leaves some room, perhaps, for Price to be two years out, but this could equally well be a consequence of his using an earlier source to write this one. The draft is clearly unfinished as it breaks off in the middle of the account of the promise of a commission in the army, and though that is the bottom of the page there is room for at least two more lines of writing; there is also an unfinished explanation of why Spencer had to cut down a wood in ll.46–49.

36 sunk] this word is very unclear, and may be /spent/, but /sunk/ is also used in folio 124, l.15, where it means much the same, i.e. 'appropriated for his own use' (*OED*, *sink*, 26).

36–39 when ye minor [...] chancery] we were told in 6 February 1732: folio 3 that the rents of Kilcolman were being paid to Sir Richard Mead leaving the interest on the mortgage on the property (possibly held by Mead) unpaid, and that this was part of Spencer's guardian's fraudulent mismanagement of the estates; it seems likely that the 'part of ye estate' that was 'eaten up' and then 'sold in chancery' in order to pay off the 'principal and intrest' was Kilcolman.

65–66 Mr Justice Lindsey] Robert Lindsay (1679–1743) was a Justice of the Court of Common Pleas in Ireland (Francis Elrington Ball, *The Judges in Ireland, 1221–1921*, 2 vols (London: John Murray, 1926), II, 203).

[folio 126]

D^{r} S^{r}
The unfortunate gentleman
in whose behalf I spoke [*to you*]
[*at Mr Har*] <**> [at] <***> is now
[*reduced to ye lowest ebb of fortune*]
[*beeing obliged last term in*]
Ireland to sell by order of court
[*his last stake,*] so that he and
his wife & children are in a fair
way of starving unless you
[*or*] some other compassionate
gentleman prevent ^{their} misfortune
by interceding with ye folks
in power above, to get some
place in ye revenue of Ireland
it makes my heart ake to
think of his sufferings a narrative
of which, you have enclosed
whatever part of it, you think
will be usefull in sollicitING for
him be so good to take out

———————————

make use of
and ~~give~~, to second y^{r} application
I need not give you any other
trouble; I am sure y^{r} good natur
will enforce y^{r} request & hope
ye desired effect of it —
I am Etc ——

This is almost certainly a draft of the letter (or letters) Price sends out to his acquaintances after receiving Spencer's Memorial, and acknowledged by Spencer in the first three lines of his next letter (21 February 1748: folio 82). It is dated by the phrase '[*beeing obliged last term in*] Ireland to sell by order of court [*his last stake,*]' which parallels 'the remaining estate / sold last term /' in folio 125, l.42 (see the opening note to folio 125) and so places it after the sale of Renny in December 1748. The precise order of this and folio 125 is debatable, but 125 looks like an immediate response to the Memorial and so is placed after it. Both this and 125 are very similar to the draft letter to Mr Trevor in folio 124, and all three may well derive to some extent from a common source now lost. This sheet, like 124 and 125, was placed at the very end of the archive, after Spencer's letters and the other documents he sent to the Price family and hence the folio number, but it is placed here in what is considered to be its proper chronological position in the correspondence.

16–17 a narrative [...] enclosed] this would have been very similar to what is contained in folio 125, and this reference is another suggestion that 125 was the earlier document.

[folio 82]

[To Francis Price Esq$^{\partial}$]

near Castlelyons Feb.$^{\partial y}$ the 21.st 1748

DearSir

I have the Favour of your last & shall for ever acknowledge most gratefully all your Kindnesses; tho' I am concernd to think you have been obliged to stretch your Interest, that on any other Account might have availd, but as I fear I am born still to meet with Misfortunes & Dissapointments, do expect / by the Contents of your last / that I must never hope to surmount them — I beg pardon for still harping on this unpleasing string but as I surely have so much experienced your Good Nature, flatter my self that you will pitty & excuse me —

The Vicar of Castlelyons died a few Weeks since, he sent to the Dublin Society £1000 last November for the Use of the Charter Schools, but how he has disposed of the rest of his Fortune I am ignorant, he was soon followd by his Brother John who deceased last Thursday; but I have not heard of any Charitable Disposition of his to pave the Way to wipe off any of his Scores — I fancy upon the Death of your old Trigger your Parish must [*be*] vastly quieter, tho you have not told me so ——

Tis a great Dissapointment to me that none of y[*our*] <******> acquainted with the Duke of Marlborough a[*s*] I <*********> might make him do something for a namesa[*ke*] <**********> them if a<******> may know some one that <**********> to him wch is [*all*] I woud require ____

My Wife <********> best Respects to you Co[*u*] <**>

{*part of sheet missing*}<***> _________ Your S<***>

& mos[*t*] <****>

The final paragraph of the letter is badly faded on the right-hand side, there is a stain towards the bottom left, and the bottom left-hand corner of the sheet has been torn off. The signature has been lost either by fading or possibly by the whole of the bottom edge having been torn or cut off.

Date] the year is given Old Style.

7 harping [...] string] to 'harp upon the same string' was proverbial (Tilley H638).

11 Charter Schools] these are the schools referred to in 1 December 1748: folio 79 (see note to ll.10–11) which were run by The Society for Promoting English Protestant Schools in Ireland. Spencer has presumably fogotten that he passed on the news about the death of this priest in the earlier letter.

[folio 83]

[To Francis Price Esq$^{\partial}$]
near Castlelyons Feb.$^{\partial y}$ the 28.th 1748

DearSir

I had the Favour of yours of the 14.th ins.^{t} last Post, with one from Mr Warburton to you, enclosed: wch was not necessary, to inform me that you are doing all inyour Power for me; for, sure, I must be a sad Wretch and undeserving your Favour, had I the lest Diffidence of any Thing you tell me who have already so greatly had Experience of your Regards for me, & which it shall be my constant Desire to deserve, by acting in whatever Sphere of Life I may be placed, to behave myself after such a manner as not to give you the lest Uneasiness / by my Behaviour / for having taken Notice of or professd a Friendship for me —

I have been removed from Renny these two years, & lodge with a Brother in Law near Castletown roch, to whom I pay £36 a year for me & my Family & find hay & Oats for my horses, I inform you of this as you desire to know who has bought Renny & where I am removed to; I sold it to Mr Wallis the Attorney, & the Sum∧^{he} is to pay for∧^{it} is to be fixd at the next Assyzes of Corke by my Coz.^{n} Will Freeman of Castlecorr, wch you must think ^{will}~~is to~~ be the utmost of it's Worth, I paid the Powers £1309 — my Brother & Sister for joining in a Fine of £150 a Debt of my Father to James

————————

Hennessy £100 & some others that must be cleard off as soon as I receive the purchase Mony, but wch I cannot yet ascertain
besides a deduction for the Quit rent
the amount of, & a large Bill of Cost ∧—— However what little may be left will be some provision for my Wife & Daughter in Case of Accidents, <~~xxx~~> but I am at a dead rent now as I cant put myself in any other Way till I know where I am to remove —

My Wife & I are sincerely concernd for Mrs Prices Indisposition & ardently wish her a speedy Amendment we join in our best respects to her Mr Rich^{d} & you

I am Dear Sir
Your truly aff.^{te} Kinsman
& most humbleServant
EdmSpencer

My Service to all friends, I congratulate the Col.^{l} on his Vigour ————

Date] the year is given Old Style.

5 Diffidence of] 'lack of confidence or faith in' (*OED*, 1).

12 I have [...] two years] this is odd as Spencer gave Renny as his address only five months ago in the letter of 13 September 1748: folio 76, and possibly wrote the next letter from there a month later. Renny is, however, hardly two miles from Castletownroche; could it be that Spencer has been living at Castletownroche for these two last years but by an elision of the short distance between the two places in his mind had enabled himself to hold on to the idea that he still owned and occupied Renny up to the very last minute before the sale?

13 Brother in Law] possibly this is the brother-in-law with whom Spencer and his family lodged in 1743 (see 8 November 1743: folio 8, l.30 and note) but if so he has moved from Churchtown to Castletownroche, a distance of some fifteen miles. (In the letter of 16 June 1747: folio 59, l.21, Spencer mentions a brother-in-law who lives in Scotland, but he is probably another person altogether.)

18 Coz.[n] Will Freeman] see note to 6 February 1732: folio 3, l.14.

19 Castlecorr] a village some thirty miles north of Cork.

20–23 I paid [...] ascertain] it is almost impossible to give meaningful equivalent monetary values for another specific date, but if one takes just the sums Spencer mentions, a total of £1,559, and converts them into their roughly equivalent value in the year this book went to press, the financial liabilites he has paid off amounted to a sum just short of a quarter of a million pounds.

21 Fine of £150] see note to 20 January 1748: folio 81, l.18.

26 dead rent] 'an unrelieved and unvarying fixed rent' (*OED*, *dead*, adj. 30).

[folio 84]

[To Francis Price Esqr]

near Castlelyons June the 2^{d} 1749

DearSir

Tis so long since I had the Pleasure of a Line from you, that I begin to dread that your Letters or mine have miscarryed in the Post; for I flatter myself that you woud not let four Months pass without giving me the Satisfaction ∧ of knowing how you & your Family were, therefore must suspect the carelessness of some of our Postmasters —

Nothing new in this Country but Mr Barry's Marriage which I make no Doubt you have heard of; & of the Privacy with which it was conducted; for the Ceremony was performd after Supper, unknown to most of the Servants, & is still carryd on in the same Manner for I do not hear of any Company haveing been at Castlehyde since the Nuptials. Tis supposed that the Colonel & Captain will agree very well, as tis thought they both esteem the getting and keeping Money to be the main Pleasure of Life ——

1 Tis so long] see ll.1–2 and note to l.2 of the next letter.

7 Mr Barry's Marriage] in 1749 Captain Richard Barry married Jane Hyde, the daughter of the man who was probably one of Spencer's trustees during his minority. Although Hyde was the MP for Cork and 'high in Co. Cork society' (Barnard, *Irish Protestant Ascents and Descents*, p. 293), the aristocratic Barry family possibly saw this as a poor match for one of theirs, and hence the 'privacy' felt necessary by the bride's family and the bridegroom, though Spencer slyy suggests that the groom and his new father-in-law (see note to l.13 below) will soon patch things up given their shared vice of avarice (a jibe probably prompted by Hyde's behaviour as a trustee when, Barnard suggests, he was equally responsible with Busteed for the embezzlement of the young Spencer's income from his estate). But see also 6 February 1732: folio 3, note to l.11.

12 Castlehyde] Castle Hyde was the main residence of the Hyde family; a castle of Norman origin about one and a half miles west of Fermoy, it gave its name to the village in which it was situated.

13 Colonel & Captain] Spencer refers to Arthur Hyde as a colonel in 28 March 1747: folio 57, l.5, though *HIP* makes no mention of any military career; the Captain is Richard Barry.

Valediction] missing, as the bottom of the sheet has been torn off.

[folio 85]

[To Francis Price Esqr]
near Castlelyons July the 21.st 1749

DearSir

Tis so long since I had the Satisfaction of a Letter from you, that I begin to despair of another, & dread that by Some / unforeseen at least undesignd / accident I might be unhappy enough to provoke your Slighting me, or else, sure, you wou'd before now have favourd me with a Line or two to inform me how you & yours are. Inured as I am to Misfortunes and in all appearance shall be more so, I assure you tis no small Addition to them that I shoud have the least room to think that I had any Way incurd your Displeasure / which your long Silence makes me fear / or that you shoud by any Means incline to suspect that all your Favours ~~were~~ have been heapd on one who had the least Tincture of Ingratitude. no Sir, it is, has been, & shall be my Joy to defy Mankind to impeach me that I have not / & for ever shall / ownd & gloryed in the Friendships I have / I must acknowlege <~~xxxx~~> undeserved / received from you; & all your kindnesses to me, I intreat you will relieve me from my Anxiety & believe that I am / with mine and my Wife's best Respects to you Mrs Price & Mr Richard /DearSir

Your truly aff.^{te} Kinsman
& obliged humble Servant
EdmSpencer

2 begin to despair of another] an unfortunately prophetic turn of phrase; Price was not offended, as Spencer fears he might be (ll.3–6), but is dying. He died on 22 July, the day after this letter was written.

13 impeach me] here in the more general sense 'accuse me' (*OED*, v.4.a).

Facing, left: Francis Price's monument in St Mary's Church, Overton.
The inscription reads:

Waiting the Summons of the last Trumpet
To rejoin their Immortal Partner
and rise togeather
Joint Conquerors of Death and Fellow Heirs of Eternity
Here rest the Mortal Remains of FRANCIS PRICE
late of BRYNYPIECE in the county of FLINT Esq. Who was Born at
BALLYHOOLY in the County of CORKE & Kingdom of IRELAND
June 4 1696
the son of Capn RICHARD PRICE of BRYNYPIECE and Mary His Wife
And having with Steady and sincere Aim plann'd the conduct of his life
By that Noble and Comprehensive Rule
To do Justice, love Mercy and walk humbly with his God
In the conscientious discharge of the several Duties of a Husband,
a Parent, a Magistrate, a Master, a Friend, and a Neighbour,
Lived Beloved and Died greatly Lamented
July 22 1749 Aged 53.

[folio 86]

Madam

As I always had the greatest Reasons to believe that my Affairs were not indifferent to you, by your Goodness in pittying my Misfortunes, & kind Solicitations to amend my Circumstances; I take the Liberty to inform you of what I / now / intend to do with the Remains of my shatterd Fortune. What little I have made a Shift to save from ravenous Creditors & rapacious Lawyers being too small to main= tain me & my Family by it's legal interest, & as I was unfortunately not educated in a Way of understanding Trade by which I might improve my Principle: I can think of no Method of procuring a Livelyhood but by going into the Army, & therefore intend as soon as possible to purchase a Pair of Colours; which tho' it will afford but poor Breads will nevertheless keep me above Want, & that is all I am now solicitous about —— I return my Dear Friend Mr Richard my sincere Thanks for his kind Letter, which I received Yesterday, & make n[*o dou*]bt but he will continue to bless you by his [*duty*] & Affect[*ion*] I propose going to Dublin in November next to purchase the Commission, & whilst it is making out, will do myself the Pleasure of waiting on you and him for a few Days, before I put my self [*und*]er the Command [*&*] staying wherever orderd by my Colonel; unless you think the sight of me may occasion you too many melancholy Ideas, which I sincerely wish were rather lessend than increased, & therefore shall be governd by your Instruction. Pray present my best Wishes & Respects to Master Price & believe that I am

Madam

Your most obliged & most obed^{t}

Servant

EdmSpencer

near Castlelyons

Septem.^{r} the 25.th 1749

Address] there is neither address nor addressee, but the address panel has written on it /E. Spencer | 1749 &c/ in what looks like pencil rather than ink and Alice Price's hand; the next letter, similarly, has no address or addressee, but the one after that (27 November 1749: folio 88) has the address written in full and a post-mark and this is the case for the next letter; after that, however, letters revert to having just the addressee and /Brynypiece/; for a while after Price's death, then, Spencer has been sending letters through the normal postal channels, suggesting perhaps that he has lost access to Sir Watkin's franks (see 16 June 1747: folio 59, l.21 and note), but then either regains that access, or is sending his letters to Alice Price in packets under a cover.

15–16 I propose [...] Commission] the next letter makes it clear that he fails to obtain this commission.

19–20 unless you [...] melancholy Ideas] it is only in this penultimate sentence that we get any suggestion in these letters that Price has died (that being the reason for the gap in his side of the correspondence that occasioned Spencer so much worry in the previous two letters). Given the two-month gap between this letter and the last we might assume that someone wrote to Ireland to inform Spencer of that fact, and that the letter responding to the news is missing, it being inconceivable that Spencer omitted to send his condolences to the widow and son.

[folio 87]

Madam

Pursuant to your Orders for that Purpose, I trouble you with this to acquaint you that I am arrived here; & hope for the Honour of your Commands in Relation to the Business you had designd for me to transact for you here. Nothing can give me more Satisfaction than the Hopes I have that I shall act in that or any other thing you will please to employ me in with such Care & Diligence as not to give you any Concern for placing any Confidence in me. I promise myself the Happyness of seeing you & my Dear Kinsman soon, whom God preserve & to whom present my best Respects. I am Madam

Dick's Coffee-House
Dublin Novr the 16.th 1749

Your most obliged & obed.^{t} Servant
EdmSpencer

Address] again, there is no address for this letter.

4–5 the Business [...] you here] Spencer has failed to get the army commission he was hoping to purchase in Dublin (see note to ll.15–16 of previous letter) but now appears to be working as an agent for Alice Price in Ireland which gives him some income until he eventually finds a post in the revenue some two and a half years later; his comment in ll.37–38 of the following letter, that his 'chiefest desire is that he coud be someway usefull', could be taken to imply that he is doing this work gratis and out of a sense of obligation to the Price family, but in 19 July 1755: folio 96, the reference to 'fees you was pleased to order me to deduct' (ll.8–9) makes it clear that he is being paid for this work. The 'Business you had designd for me to transact' (ll.4–5) is, as is apparent from the next letter, to look at one of the Price's houses in Dublin that has been reduced to a parlous state by its last tenant.

[folio 88]

[To
M.rs Alice Price
at Brynypiece near Wrexham
Chester]

Madam

I have the Mortification of telling you that I can give but a very sorry Account of Jessops House; for by what Information I coud procure from M.r Kingsbury he thought him so indifferent a Tenant that he was glad to take the House off his hands, but it really is in so ruinous a State that no other person will / I fear / become Tenant to it. M.r Kingsbury sent a Servant with me that I may view it, & I walked into every Room but I did not perceive one in any order or repair, the whole lower Floor is under Water, but as to any hopes of it's being carryed off by the main drain I look upon to be impracticable, for I do not suppose that for the sake of one house the Chapter of S.t Patricks will levy so great a Tax on the Inhabitants of that Quarter as may be necessary to search into their main Shoar, for I am informed that a hundred pounds woud not be sufficient for such a <~~x~~> Work; but perhaps another Method may be found out to divert this Inundation at a small expence, for which Purpose M.r Kingsbury has engaged a person to view the place & has promised to let me know the time, when I shall take Care to attend & have an Acquaintance with me who understands those Affairs that he might not be imposed on. The House is in a very bad part of the Town, such as a genteel person woud not reside in, but is very fit for a tolerable tradesman, for this bad Circumstance attends it, / tho it ~~is~~ has a good deal of room in it yet / the front is very small, & the value of ground here is according to it's front, there is a large Garden belonging to it which may turn to use to build on, but I am certain you will never

---

get the rent that Jessop paid for it, & I realy think you had better set it to some person that woud build than to think of repairing the house your self, for it is very old & ^the timbers^ almost decayd, & what has helped to it's ruin is that for three or four Years past Jessop had sett it in several different Lots to a pack of poor Tradesmen — I did not see the Lease but I think if Jessop had not a Clause of Surrender he ought to have returnd it in repair; I woud have askd for the Lease but that I feard your Agent might have taken it unkind, as he is but a young Gentleman, but I am resolved to enquire farther about it before I leave this ——
I return you my most grateful Acknowlegements for your kind present, you are still adding Obligations on one who is & will be for

Ever mindful of them & whose <****> chiefest desire is that he coud be someway usefull. My only return & that of my little Family's is that God may preserve you Comfort in the Life and Happyness of my Dear Kinsman, to whom present my best Wishes & regards & believe that I am

Madam / with the greatest Respect /
Your most obliged & obed.^{t} Servt
EdmSpencer

Dicks Coffee house
Dublin Novr the 27.th 1749

11–12 the Chapter [...] Tax] presumably the drain runs through land belonging to the cathedral in Dublin which therefore is responsible for maintaining it, and in turn has the right to levy a tax on nearby houses (or those served by the drain) for that purpose.

13 shoar] 'sewer' (*OED*, obs. form of *shore*, which is an obs. form of *shower*, which is an obs. variant of *sewer*).

25 turn] i.e. be turned; if this is not a mistake it is an unusual use of the word, perhaps deriving from the sense 'change so as to bring into a specified condition' which *OED* (v.41.a) illustrates only up to 1608.

26 set] 'rent'; Spencer usually spells the word /sett/, as he does just below in l.29.

31 Clause of Surrender] a clause in a lease setting out the terms on which the lease can be given up by the lessee before the agreed termination date; Spencer seems to think this may have included requirements concerning the condition of the house, as he says in the next letter: 'I can't but think that Mr Jessop ought to have been obliged to give up the house in some tolerable repair' (2 December 1749: folio 89, ll.17–19); it is also interesting to note that he says in a later letter about a dispute over repairs to another property leased to a tenant by the Prices that 'the general run of Leases in this Kingdom is, that the Ten.^{t} shall leave in Repair at the Expiration of his Term all Edifices & already erected or that shall be erected on the premises during his Lease' (31 December 1750: folio 92, ll.17–19).

34 leave this] either Spencer has left out a word such as 'city' here or we have to understand some such word as 'place' or 'business'.

[folio 89]

[To
Mrs Alice Price
at Brynypiece near Wrexham
Chester]

Madam

A Search has been made whether the Water that overflows the House / lately Jessop's / coud be carried off at any reasonable Expence, but Mr Kingsbury informs me that the fault appears to be in the main Drain, & therefore a Tenant can not be procured 'till that Annoyance be removed, wch might not happen for severall Months, but when that is effected he has a person ready to take in, but at a less rent than was paid by Jessop —

As I was informd that the Dean of St Patrick's & the Chapter had been already applied to about it, I thought it my Duty to attend them, but tho' I have ∧^{been} severall Times at the Deane's house I had not yet an Opportunity of conversing with him as he is out of Town; but he is positively expected next Munday, & then I shall expect to know peremptorily what may be depended upon & what not, as I shall take Care to be properly introduced to him.

I did intend myself the Honour of visiting Brynypiece the next Week, but I shall defer that Happyness 'till I know the utmost that can be done with the Deane; Yet I can't but think that Mr Jessop ought to have been obliged to give up the house in some tolerable repair, which I am sorry to say is not the Case, for it is almost in Ruins; of which I shall give you a fuller Acc.^{t} when I wait on you — Mr Kingsbury tells me that it is necessary for you to go through some forms in Law to intitle you to receive the Rents of the Parliament House, of wch he says he

———————————

has informed you, I believe it must be to procure a Probat of the Will in the Bishop's Court of the Diocese you dwell in, upon wch an order may be granted in their Prerogative Court. He tells me that he has some Leaves for me to carry over of which I shall be sure to take the utmost Care. I have had some Conversations with a person here about some Lands which / if what he says be true / are fraudulently detaind from you by the Heir of Doctor Hawksaw; I shall take proper Minutes of it for your Perusal & you may perhaps think it proper to advise with Council thereon, for I woud not by any means recommend a suit at Law without the best Advice & certainty of Success —— God bless & preserve you & my Dear Kinsman wch are the constant Wishes of Madam

/ with the greatest Respect /
Your obliged Kinsman & faithfull
humble Servant EdmSpencer

Dick's Coffee house
Dublin Decr the 2.^{d} 1749

13 peremptorily] 'definitely, conclusively' (*OED*, adv.1), without the currently predominant sense of 'dismissively, imperiously' (*OED*, adv.5).

24 Probat] most likely this refers to a copy of the verification of her husband's will rather than the process of verification itself (*OED*, n.2.a).

26 Prerogative Court] an ecclesiastical court which dealt with the probate of wills (*OED*, *prerogative*, n.6).

27 Leaves] sheets of paper, i.e. documents.

[folio 90]

[To M.rd John Buchan
Brynypiece]

Dublin July the 28$^{\underline{th}}$ 1750

Sir

As soon as I returned from the Country I wrote to you, & inclosed Copys of two Letters from M$^{\underline{r}}$ Price to Mr Pearde & some other particulars about Mohery; but not receiving any Account that the Letter came to hand, I conjecture that it might be mislaid in some of the Offices, where I know they are careless enough: if so please to acquaint me of it & I will send other Copys which I have by me. when I was with Mr Pearde he told me that he had a Sum ready to send to Corke when he coud find a bill coud be had for it which he dayly expected, I believe you have heard from him before now ———

I hope Mrs Price [*and*] Master continue very well, my best Wishes for their Happyness, &myRespects wait on them. My Complim.^{ts} to the rest of the Family & Mrs Buchan conclude

Sir

Your sincerely affec.^{te} Servant
EdmSpencer

When next you see Mr Mathews be so kind to tell him, that I sent a Bill for the balance due to him, Under Cover to Mr Breley ———

Addressee] John Buchan was a doctor on close terms with Francis Price who had looked after his sickly son in May 1749, frequently assuring his father that the boy was in good health (Puleston 18: NLW MS 3578E, letters from Buchan to Price dated 4 May 1749, 7 May 1749, 11 May 1749 & 17 May 1749). The care and concern for Richard Price expressed in Buchan's letters suggest more than a purely professional relationship, and that might explain why he is now acting in an almost legal capacity for Alice Price, at a time when she my well have been overburdened by legal and business matters following her husband's death.

3 Mr Pearde] this is the tenant of Mohire (see next note) who is to cause Spencer so much trouble for the next ten years. In the letter of 25 May 1747: folio 58 Spencer mentions an 'uncle Peard' whom Barnard (*Irish Protestant Ascents and Descents*, p. 296) identifies as his half-brother, but it is highly unlikely that he is the same person as the Pearde referred to here (see note to l.4 of the earlier letter).

3 Mohery] a house in Castlelyons that takes its name from the nearby area now called Mohera; Spencer's spelling varies but is most often /Mohire/. There is much discussion in the following letters about the Prices' title to the house and difficulties with its tenant.

[folio 91]

[To Mr John Buchan
Brynypiece]

Sir

Yours of the 5.th inst.^{t} came here last Post, but as I came from Corke but yesterday, I did not receive it till then. I am very much surprized that Mr Pearde did not make the remittance of £70 which / when I was at Castlelyons/ he assured me he had ready at that Time, & that for the Future he woud take care to be very punctual in his paym.^{ts} -- I should not think it a very difficult Matter to procure bills in Corke for larger Sums on any part of England; but own I may mistake as I never had any Occasion to buy for one, however shall direct him to ~~who~~ apply to a person who I believe will immediately furnish him with a bill — if the Money be ready —— As I am within 20 miles of Castlelyons, I will go there next Week to make a proper Inquiry who is fitt to recommend to Mrs Price for to undertake the settling about the Repairs of Mohery house; & tho' a Referrence will be attended with some Expence ∧ upon the meeting of the Referrees yet I woud by all Means recommend it before a Suit at Law which will cost a great deal & be attended likewise with many Disquiets & Uneasinesses & no one knows when it may be determined. If Mrs Price shoud have any Commands for me, please to direct as at bottom, & your Letter will be forwarded to me where ever I shall be — My Wife joins in our best Respects to her & Master Price. My Complim.^{ts} to Mrs Buchan & the Family of Brynypiece I am Sir with great Truth

Your Sincerely aff.^{te} humbServ.^{t}
EdmSpencer

I shall continue in this Country till Nov.$^{\partial}$ next ———

near Charleville Aug.st the 30.th 1750

10 within [...] Castlelyons] the distance between Castlelyons and Charleville is some thirty five modern British miles, but using the Irish mile, which at this period was roughly one quarter to a third as long again as the British mile, Spencer's estimate of the distance is accurate.

13 a Referrence] the process of submitting a dispute to a person of authority (usually through legal channels) for a decision or settlement (*OED*, n.1.a).

[folio 92]

[To
Mr John Buchan
Brynypiece]

Decr the 31.st 1750

Sir

I waited for several Weeks /since my last / in Expectation of a Letter from Mr Pearde according to his Promise, & wrote twice to him by Post, to no Effect; upon which I sent a Messenger on Purpose, thinking my Letters might have miscarryed, by him I received a verbal answer that I shoud soon hear from him; I waited three Weeks longer & being still dissapointed, I sett out a few Days since for Castlelyons, but on the Road my Horses were so violently seized with the present raging Disorder which renderd them incapable of pursuing the Journey, I was therefore obliged to lye by, & by much ado procured one for my Servant who I sent with a Letter to Mr Pearde desiring to know whether he had applyd to Mr Nason about the repairs of Mohery or not, he then wrote to Mr Nason & sent me his Letter which you have enclosed, but did not write to me. By Mr Nason's Letter I cant perceive that he had ever consented to leave the Matter in Dispute to Referrence, / though Mr Pearde told me he woud/ or that he had been applyed to about it, but I am certain that what he <~~xxx~~> says about leaving more buildings than he was obliged to, can be of no Signification for the general run of Leases in this Kingdom is, that the Ten.^{t} shall leave in Repair at the Expiration of his Term all Edifices & already erected or that shall be erected on the premises during his Lease, so that if a Ten.^{t} shoud build, he must also keep in repair. I wonder Mr Peard woud

7 my Horses [...] Disorder] there was a serious outbreak of equine influenza or equine catarrhal fever in the winter of 1750–1751 in Ireland (<https://en.wikisource.org/wiki/Equine_Influenza_Epidemic_of_1872> and <http://www.atsjournals.org/doi/abs/10.1164/arrd.1961.83.2P2.41?journalCode=arrd#.VrYZXekrzdk> [both accessed 6 February 2016]).

11 Mr Nason] Nason's position in this complex web of legal relationships is not clear: he might have been the Prices' lessee between Pearde and Harrison (see l.30), or he might have been a lessee who sub-leased to those two; on the other hand, the reference in l.27 to Alice Price's 'Landlord' could indicate that he is the owner of Mohire House from whom Mrs Price now leases, she having then sub-leased to Pearde; however, it is more likely that this 'landlord' is a purely hypothetical one, Spencer using it to point out that Alice Price, in Nason's position as a lessee, would not risk going to court over this matter, and that therefore it is unlikely that Nason would do that either. That Nason was ever the owner would seem to be contradicted, first, by what is said in the next letter about his having assured Mr Pearde (not Price) that 'upon giving up the premises [...] he woud put all the buildings in sufficient repair' (ll.6–8) and, second, by the fact that in 19 July 1755: folio 96 Spencer writes to Alice Price that he has found 'a Deed of Sale from Lord Buttevant to John Price of the said Lands [i.e. Mohire] in the year 1692' (ll.21–22) which strongly suggests that Price's grandfather (or some other relative) bought the property; however, that deed of sale also included a lease (granted to one Edward Denny) which is due to expire in 1765 so

trouble him about the Pew mentiond in Mr Nason's Letter, for I assured him that Mrs Price woud not insist upon that, nor did I think it worth her while. I am not a little surprized what shoud make Mr Pearde so very intent upon having the Repairs executed as he was some time ago, & at present so very indolent about them: if Mrs Price pleases I will go to Castlelyons & to Mr Nason, before ∧^{my}~~I~~ return to Dublin which will be about the latter End of February: If she thought that her Landlord woud not sue at the Expiration of her Lease for those Repairs, I think 'twoud not be worth her while to commence a Suit, nor at any rate without good advice, I believe she has a Counterpart of the Lease of Mohery to Harrison by which she will see whether he was not obliged to repair, tho Mr Peard assured me that on the back of Harrisons part there was a Covenant

———————

that he shoud, the Court woud oblige Nason to produce his part, but if possible to avoid it, I woud not recommend a Law Suit ——

There never was known in this Kingdom so general a Calamity as at present rages among Horses, there is scarce one in this Country fit to be rid a Mile, if it continues I know not how the Farmers will get their Spring Corn into Ground: our Newspapers give us the Same Melancholy Acc.^{t} of the Horses in England.

As I think 'twill be better not to leave the Country, I will wait on Mr Nason as soon as my horses are fit for Use or that I can gett others, perhaps upon proper application he may consent to an amicable Determination of the Affair ———

My best Respects wait on Mrs Price & Master wishing them many happy Years; my Compliments to Mrs Buchan Master Apperly & Mr Smyth I am Sir

Your Sincerely aff.^{te} humb:Servt

Direct, at Charleville EdmSpencer

that lease seems to have had a separate legal identity from the deed of sale. The lesson we can learn from all this, and the correspondence between Spencer and Francis Price about the property in Mallow (folios 31–34), is that property arrangements in eighteenth-century Ireland were extremely complicated.

14 Referrence] see previous letter, l.13 and note.

18 Edifices & [...] erected] the /&/ makes no sense here, perhaps Spencer lost concentration for a moment.

30 Counterpart] a copy of a legal document (such as a lease, contract, or a deed conveying property), particularly the copy kept by the grantor (*OED*, n.1).

30 Harrison] this is possibly Harry Harrison, the vicar of Castlelyons, whose death Spencer reported in the letter of 1 December 1748: folio 79; however, as one might expect a vicar to have a house provided with his benefice, it might have been his brother John (whose death was reported in the letter dated 21 February 1748: folio 82), though there is no indication in that report that he, like his brother the vicar, lived in Castlelyons.

45 Master Apperly] possibly the son of the Doctor Apperly mentioned in 6 December 1743: folio 10, but possibly the Doctor; Spencer is not always consistent with regard to titles.

[folio 93]

[To
Mr John Buchan
Brynypiece]

April the 19.th 1751

Sir

As soon as I received the Draft of the Deed from Co.^{r} Verling & had ingrossd it, I went to Castlelyons in order to have produced it to Mr Nason to be perfected; but calling on Mr Pearde he shewd me a Letter of Mr Nason's which he found among Mr Prices Letters wch he was looking over on another Occasion, & wch he did not recollect before, & farther said that he coud averr that Mr Nason upon giving up the premisses assured Mr Pearde that he woud put all the buildings in sufficient Repair as soon as he burnd some Lime, how far he has broke faith is evident by the Letter of his which I sent to Mrs Price some time since. I did not think it proper for me to apply to him to perfect the Deed till I had first acquainted Mrs Price with the Contents of his Letter & the Evidence that Mr Pearde says he can give, for perhaps she might <~~x~~> think it more adviseable to oblige him by Law to do justice than to deferr to a longer day as by the Deed woud be the Case, & Mr Pearde assured me that he is certain that Nason woud never retract from his first offer, but that he builds upon a belief that Mrs Price woud not commence a Suit at Law in this Kingdom. I send inclosed a Copy of the Deed & another of Nason's Letter for her perusal; if she will have the Deed executed, I shall leave it with my Wife to imploy a friend to see it properly filed & signd; if upon perusal of the Letter she will think it better to sue him, I shall as far as in my power take Care to have the Suit properly conducted, ^{yet}^<~~xx~~> I assure you I am not for her going to Law without good Advice / I mean Council / which I am sure she'll take on her side the Water before she will commence a Suit. I expect to be in Dublin the 25.th ins.^{t} please to let me have her Order directed as usual to me at Dick's Coffee house; <~~xxx~~> I am on a treaty

1 Co.^{r}] an abbreviation of 'counsellor-at-law', a legal functionary who gives advice and conducts a client's case in court.

2 ingrossd] 'had it written up formally' (*OED*, v.1).

3 perfected] i.e. enforced or made enforceable (by Nason's signing it, perhaps).

7–8 he woud [...] some Lime] lime was used not only for improving soil (as Spencer tells Price he does in the letter of 5 December 1747: folio 63, ll.12–13) but also for making both mortar and lime wash (which was used particularly in Ireland for painting buildings, see Brian Kaller, 'Burning the Bones of the Earth: Lime Kilns', <http://www.lowtechmagazine.com/2013/09/lime-kilns.html> [accessed 10 June 2016]); as Mr Nason has promised to 'put all the buildings in sufficient Repair' (ll.7–8) he presumably intends to use the burnt lime for one of those purposes.

27 on a treaty] 'discussing terms, negotiating' (*OED*, *treaty*, n.2).

with a Gentleman who wants me to go to London with him to see

———————

some Deeds executed & believe I shall conclude with him about it when in Dublin, if he will raise his Offer a little, therefore beg to hear from you before the 10.th of May as I think that's the time he appointed to sett out; if you think Mr Kingsbury has the lease of Mohery, I believe I shoud look for the Clause about repairs in it, My Wife joins in our best respects to Mrs Price & Master Price my Complim.^{ts} wait on Mrs Buchan & the family of Brynypiece I am Sir

Your Sincerely affect.^{te} humbServ^{t}
EdmSpencer

[folio 94]

[To Mrs Price
Brynypiece]
Dublin Jan. the 14.th 1752 ______

Madam

The Satisfaction you so kindly give in your Account of the Gayeties at Brynypiece during the Holydays, is greatly augmented, when I reflect on the Happyness it afforded to you, to see my dear Kinsman so well entertaind as I am sure he must have been all that time; many very many such Christmases may you see together: I assure you I am fully sensible of the Honour done me in your mention of them to me — I am not surprizd at any Persons being smitten with the Charms of either of the Ladies mentiond, especially one of an Age so susceptable of Love as the young Gentleman enamourd, but hope for the sake of the little Doctor, that it was not the younger

Date] 1752 was the year that the Calendar (New Style) Act 1750 came into force, making the legal year start on 1 January rather than 25 March; it is interesting to note that Spencer, who has hitherto dated letters written between 1 January and 24 March according to the Old Style now immediately adopts the New Style; this is evident from the references to the recent death of James Barry, 5th Earl of Barrymore (ll.40–41), and Orrery's *Pliny* (ll.22–33) which had been published in Ireland in 1751 and was being passed on to Alice Price as it had not yet been published in England (see relevant notes below).

7–19 I am not [...] to him.] the subject of this passage is a romantic interlude involving Richard Price which Spencer observed when at Overton, probably during the visit mentioned as having to be deferred in the letter of 2 December 1749: folio 89; the epithets 'my dear Kinsman' (l.3) and 'my Friend' (l.17) clearly refer to the young man, and 'the little Doctor' is quite possibly also a nickname for him, Spencer perhaps picking up on Lord Barrymore's way of addressing Richard's father as 'Doctor' (see Barrymore to Price, 22 February 1744, Puleston 22: NLW MS 3582D in Appendix I). As to the 'Glove [...] given in Challenge' (ll.11–13), perhaps a rival suitor was involved, but a glove was also conventionally a favour given by a lady to her knight and it might be that the younger sister (whom Spencer considers the one less preferred) gave the glove to Richard as a challenge

Sister prevaild, as I believe that woud give him great Uneasiness, if I may judge of Iclinations, by what I saw at Wrexham when a Glove was given in Challenge: Yet I am in pain for the Em= barassement it must Occasion to him, when ever the Queen of Hearts was present to which to give his Hand, but comfort my self with the Thoughts that one with so much Conduct as I know my Friend has, woud not be long at a Loss how to behave were ever two or three Ladies more by, who may think themselves not indifferent to him. I hope Miss Fleetwood's Partner was with her time enough ~~x~~ to partake of the Entertainmen.^{t}. Miss Carey told me he intended to see her before the Holydays —

Mr Kingsbury sent me Orrery's Pliny, $^{\text{in 2}}$‸$^{\text{vol.s}}$ & Remarks on Swift. I this day deliverd them / I hope / to a safe hand with the Poplin wch I hope will please you, & have directed them to Mr Mathews. I believe

———————————

when you read the Remarks you will think / with most of our People / that he is too severe upon the Deane, & under the borrowed Name of Friend exposes more than just, that celebrated Patriot. he is laughd, at not a little, for addressing those remarks to a Son who is grown up, & has been sometime at the University, & therefore might have been supposed to have read Swift before now, tho' the Peer, as you'll see by his Letters will not suppose it. I believe some things will be wrote on the Occasion, tho

to the elder one. Whether either of these young women was Dorothea Byrne, the person Richard Price eventually married, cannot be told from this letter, but, as this is eight years before his marriage in late 1759, if she is referred to here it would have been a long courtship — and understandably so if that was the case, given that Richard Price was only fifteen years old at Christmas 1751.

12 Iclinations] a mistake for /inclinations/.

22 Orrery's Pliny] the Earl of Orrey's translation of *The Letters of Pliny the Younger* (printed by George Faulkner) was published in Dublin in 1751, one year earlier than the London edition of 1752 (printed by James Bettenham for Paul Vaillant); his *Remarks on the Life and Writings of Dr Jonathan Swift* had been published in the preceding year.

27 just,] the comma here is decidedly odd, but the mark is very definite; the meaning, however, seems fairly clear — that the Earl exposes his own inadequacies more than he does those of Swift, a reading that would be in tune with Spencer's comments on the Earl in the rest of the paragraph.

27 that celebrated Patriot] the term 'patriot' is interesting here, chiming as it does with Spencer's use of the word in the letter of 19 July 1755: folio 96 (the next but one in this collection) where he refers to a town in which he has been canvassing as 'our Patriot Borough' (see note to l.6 of that letter).

33 on Acc.^{t} of Priviledge] possibly a reference to a law known as 'scandalum magnatum' which protected peers from defamation by a commoner; one of the privileges of the peerage, its use had more or less died out by the end of the eighteenth century (<https://en.wikipedia.org/wiki/Privilege_of_peerage> [accessed 11 August 2015]); the implication

on Acc.^{t} of Priviledge not made publick: I shall make it my Bussiness to inquire, & if procured will certainly send them to my Kinsman.

I shall make as strict an inquiry as possible, without naming Parties, about the Title of Mohire when the Councellors are in Town, wch will soon be as term begins the latter End of this Month, & I am so well assured of my friend Verling that I will prevail on him to get Opinions from others. the Lord Barry more is dead & has appointed his Mother ^{his} Lady & Lord Massareen Executors & Guardians to his Son ——

I was debarrd of the Satisfaction I flatterd my self with of seeing my little Family, these holydays, by a treaty I am on about the purchase of a small Employment, but wch is held at so high a rate that except some abatement is made in the Demand, I must not comply with it.

My best Wishes & Respects wait on you & Mr Price. with my Complim.^{ts} to the young Ladies, Mr Apperly & any Company at Brynypiece to whom I have the Honour of being known —

I am Madam / with great Deference / Your much obliged Kinsman

& most humble Servant

EdmSpencer

is clearly that Spencer looks forward to some of the things that 'will be wrote on the Occasion' being a good deal less complimentary to the peer than his own, rather restrained, comments.

40–41 Lord Barry [...] is dead] this was James, 5th Earl of Barrymore, who died 19 December 1751 (<http://www.cracroftspeerage.co.uk> [accessed 10 June 2016]).

41 Lord Massareen] Clotworthy Skeffington, 5th Viscount Massereene (1715–1757); he was created Earl of Massereene in 1756; the family had land in Co. Antrim as well as land and other titles in England (*ODNB*).

44–45 a treaty [...] small Employment] Spencer obtained a position in the Revenue Office in Dublin some time in 1752 (Barnard, *Irish Protestant Ascents and Descents*, p. 294) and that may well have been the one he was negotiating for here.

49 Mr Apperly] again, possibly the Doctor Apperly mentioned in 6 December 1743: folio 10, or his son.

[folio 95]

[To Mrs Alice Price
Brynypiece]
Dublin 26th June 1755 ——

Madam

Since your last Favour I wrote to you two letters, but had not an answer to either. I yesterday received bills from Mr Pearde for One hundred pounds payable twenty one days after Sight, as soon as they become due I will receive the Contents and remit ^^{it} you by bills on Chester — I intend to set out to Morrow for the County of Kilkenny, and return the Sixth of next Month at farthest — The best Wishes of me & my family wait on you & Mr Price I am Dear Madam

Y.r sincerely affec^{te} Kinsman
& most obed Servant
EdmSpencer

1 Since [...] letters] these two letters are missing from the collection; that, along with the gap of three and a half years since the previous letter, suggests that Alice Price has not been as careful (or as interested) as her husband had been in keeping track of and archiving her correspondence, either personally or in terms of over-seeing the employee whose job it was to do that. A different explanation for the gap could be that Spencer's employment in the Revenue Office has prevented him from doing any work for Alice Price, but this letter makes it clear that he has at least recently resumed doing some, and ll.36–40 of the last letter (14 January 1752: folio 94) state that he will pursue his enquiries into the Mohire affair which has been running since 28 July 1750: folio 90 and has been mentioned in every letter since, so one would expect some correspondence took place about that if about nothing else; Prof. Raymond Gillespie has suggested to us that letter collections of this period have sometimes been edited by contemporary or later owners to protect the reputation of the writer in some way. This is possible but there is no surviving external evidence to make this case, nor is there any indication in the surviving letters that any of the correspondents might have wanted to eliminate material that cast a critical light on members of their own family. The most likely explanation for the lacuna is that Spencer has continued to do work for Alice Price for the intervening three and a half years but that the letters he sent her have simply gone missing.

[folio 96]

[To Mrs Price]

Dublin 19th July 1755

Madam

Your favour of 23^{d} June arrived the middle of last Week, tho I was not at home to receive it till Tuesday last, having been detaind so much longer than I expected on Account of a disputed Election for Portrive in Mr Deanes Corporation, where the C--t party has seduced some of our Voters and tryd to force others on us who have no right to vote, however we have a legal Majority of right Voices and have returnd accordingly; they also have returnd for themselves, which will make it a Kings bench Affair where I make not the least Doubt of invalidating such a Number of their poll as will give us / what in truth we have / a large majority and preserve to us our Patriot Borough. this must plead excuse for your not hearing from me in due course. Above you have a bill for =87–11–2 English, Exchange at £8 ½ pCt for £95 Irish which with fees you was pleased to order me to deduct compleats £100 Irish being the contents of the bills remitted to me by Mr Pearde which became due this day ------- I do believe I did recommend your not executing a lease to Mr Pearde thinking it would have made him more carefull in his remittances to you, as I suppose he must have been, had he been pressd, and think so still except he has a mind to be litigious which in the End would turn to his own loss, besides twould be a dangerous plea for him to dispute as by it he would entirely be ejected tho' he should pay the rent pending such his Suit, but I believe he has no Such intention as he has remitted the above and promises to pay the remainder in October, and to my belief of the value of the Lands 'twill not be his Interest to loose them; as you can set but during the Minority of your son I believe twill be prudent not to offer a Lease, and if he pays his Arrear at the time he mentions twill also be needless --- If I don't forget I sent you a Copy of Mr Prices Letter to him which as it does not mention the payments to be english Money, I am of Opinion he is lyable to pay the Sum stipulated in the currency of this Kingdom only. I find in one of my pocket books the following Entrys -/ vizt / the Original lease of the [*Lan*]ds of Mohire granted to Edwd Denny Esqr for 99 years in the year 1666 -- and -- a Deed of Sale from Lord Buttevant to John Price of said Lands in the year 1692 <u>in which the above lease is recited</u>, one of the Witnesses, George Sympson Not^{r} pub.^{c}--- by the above there are ^^{almost} ten years unexpired, and by the recital of the lease in the deed of Sale I am assured that it is good and will be easily proved as a publick notary was a witness whose hand writing can also be readily proved, as there is so much of the lease to run, I [*c*]oncur in Opinion not to begin a Suit until Mr Price is of Age, and then a State may be drawn up for perusal of Some of the most Eminent Council for Advice. -- The mistake about the Ale I was since informd by Mr Fleetwoods Clerk was occasiond by his sending at the time he received yor kind Order, but two half barrells to make it therefore right he sent two more half barrells. --- I am a good deal Surprized at what you mention about Mr Chritchly who till now I always took to be a Man of Sense tho a little possitive; believe me Madam it gives me great concern to find you are treated thus indifferantly by Mr Prices relations on this side the Water, nor could I wonder or complain if you shook us all off. for my particular part I only entreat you'll please to continue the favourable Opinion you have been so good to show you have of me, until I give the least room to suppose I can deserve the contrary, for I must own that after the many and repeated favours I have received I should be the most ungratefull of Men were I ^^{to} shew the least remissness in any

---

Affair given in Charge to me by you. My Women join me in our best respects to you [*and*] Mr Price I am Madam

Your truely affectionate Kinsman
& most obedient Servant
EdmSpencer

This letter is noteworthy not only for the smaller and more cramped writing (which is imitated here by the smaller font) but because Spencer writes the word /and/ in full throughout rather than using /&/ and reverts from this point on to /could, would/ etc rather than /coud, woud/ etc as has been his consistent practice hitherto.

1 not [...] receive it] Spencer includes his wife and daughter in the valediction both here and in the previous letter; since this is something he does only when writing from home it suggests that he has moved, with his family, to Dublin where he has been working in the Revenue Office since 1752 (see 14 January 1752: folio 94, note to ll.44–45); this would confirm that the election 'in M.[r] Deanes Corporation' that 'detaind' him (and hence kept him from home) was in Co. Kilkenny where Deane had extensive property holdings (see 23 March 1757: folio 108, ll.20–26).

2 Portrive] now usually /portreeve/, a town official similar in status and function to a mayor.

3 M.[r] Deanes Corporation] this would be Innistiogue, Co. Kilkenny, fifteen miles equidistant between Kilkenny and Waterford, where the election of the new Portrive was being contested; the corporation is 'his' in the sense that Deane and his family control it (or at least have done hitherto) through their position as major land-owners; the parliamentary seat, which was usually in their hands, was wrested from the Patriot Deanes in this period by Sir William Fownes of the Court party.

3 C–t party] i.e., the Court Party, the party of the Anglo-Protestant Ascendancy.

4 right Voices] it is possible Spencer meant to write /eight Voices/ but still had the phrase /right to vote/ in his mind.

7 Patriot Borough] this indicates that Spencer aligns himself with that group of Irish people who desired greater independence for Ireland and reform of the Penal Laws and which later became identified as the Patriot Party.

8 =87–11–2 English] there is a mark above the /87/ which looks like /to/ but could be /le/ with a line through it (that being a feature of some of Spencer's superscript marks); if so it might mean /libra/ and would be the equivalent of, or another version of, the sign for a pound (which is in fact an elaborated /L/), see 29 September 1744: folio 26, l.41 and note.

14 such his Suit,] it would help if there were some punctuation before this phrase; it connects not with the previous clause but the following one so that the word 'such' parallels the following 'Such'.

22 John Price] Mohire was in Castlelyons, and Bernard Burke's statement that Francis Price was 'of Bryn-y-pys and of Castle Lyons' (Burke, *A Genealogical and Heraldic Dictionary of the Landed Gentry of Great Britain and Ireland for 1852*, II, 1070) could indicate a family link with that place; Price's father was named Richard so this might be his grandfather, but the connection could be more remote.

22 recited] 'rehearsed (specifically in a legal deed or document)' (*OED*, v.2.b).

23 Not[r] pub.[c]] i.e. notary public, 'a person authorised to draw up and attest legal documents' (*OED*, *notary*, 2.b).

26 State] either 'the right or title to a property' (*OED*, n.34.a) or 'a statement of a legal case' (*OED*, n.37.a).

30 M.[r] Chritchly] this is possibly the Harry Critchley who wrote to William Pearde to give him 'an acc.[t] of M:[r] Spencer, who was taken xmass Eve by two Baliffs as he was paying his way in Order to sett Sail for England' (Pearde to Price, 26 February 1741/2, ll.2–5, Puleston 19: NLW MS 3579D; see Appendix I).

31 possitive] 'assured, opinionated, cocksure, dogmatic, dictatorial' (*OED*, adj.I.1.3).

32 Mr Prices [...] Water] this, and the information about the seventeenth-century legal documents, indicate that Price is the direct relative of Spencer rather than Alice Price; the term 'cousin' used by Spencer to refer to her in the earlier correspondence is thus used in its looser sense.

Valediction] see note to l.1.

[folio 97]

[To M$^{\underline{rs}}$ Price
Brynypiece]

Madam

I continued for a Month before Term at Wicklow a Town twenty three miles from this where I am appointed Land Waiter, the Employment I hinted to you in a former Letter I intended to purchase, and expected to have received from Mr Wallis the Money Mr Pearde promised to remit, but he was so ill when Mr Wallis left that Country that he could not write, I therefore on coming to Town wrote a very pressing Letter to him & waited for his Answer to inform you of, I yesterday received one from his Son informing ∧^{me} that his father has been some months under Doctors & Surgeons hands & continues very ill which was the reason why a remittance was not made according to promise, and assures me that a bill shall very speedily be sent for as much as he can raise. if this be done and a tolerable paym^{t} made I believe you'll think it adviseable not to commence a Law suit, & the rent may be got by degrees, for my letter was not only pressing but also threatning, & I shall continue such until the rent is cleard off. I intend to remove my Family to Wicklow ∧$^{this\ week}$ but shall return the beginning of the next to attend some Suits of Mr Deane's, and shall be here once a fortnight at least as £1200 a year of [*H*]is estate is in & near this city. please therefore to direct any Commands you honour me with, to Wicklow, for if I should happen to be here when your letter come I have a friend in the post Office who will detain them

——————

for me, & if I am there I shall receive them without Delays my Wife & Daughter join me in our best Respects to you and Cousin Price I am Madam

Your sincerely affec^{te} Kinsman
& most humble Servant
EdmSpencer

Dublin
18th Novr 1755

2 a Town [...] from this] Wicklow is on the coast, some twenty three Irish miles due south of Dublin (approximately thirty English miles).

2–3 Land Waiter] a customs officer whose duty was to superintend the landing of goods and to examine them (*OED*, *landing*, vbl.n.8).

9–10 Doctors & Surgeons] 'doctors' are here distinguished from 'surgeons', recognizing the hierarchy of the medical profession, but again one wonders if the country medic is designated thus to indicate that he is of a lower status than the city-based 'physicians' (see 18 January 1744/5: folio 28, note to ll.2–3).

[folio 98]

[To Mrs Alice Price
Brynypiece]

Madam

I received your Favour the beginning of this Month, which I deferrd acknowledging at that Time having the Same day received a Letter from young Mr Pearde, acquainting me that his Father was much better and that he would shortly make a remittance, which however did not happen till yesterday, and as I am here I was determined to have executed a proper Power to Mr Wallis to have sued ∧^{him} this Circuit which he is to begin next Week, but very luckily / to save the Expence of a Suit / he by yesterdays Post remitted me a Dublin bill for one hundred pounds which will become due in twenty one days, at which time I will come to to[*wn*] <**>ceive it and send you a London bill; tho' [*by*] promise this w[*as*] to have been sent last Michaelmas or in October at farthest, yet I am glad it is come even now, as I was resolved punctually to have obeyd your Orders, and am certain Mr Wallis would have executed them most exactly, but believe you are better pleased to have a Suit defferd which this remittance has done. I am very glad to hear of your & Mr Price's being well, I shall return to Wicklow to Morrow and am Madam

/ with great Respect /
Your most obedient humble
Servant EdmSpencer

Dublin 24th Feb.^{ry} 1756

[folio 99]

[To Mrs Alice Price
Brynypiece]

Wicklow 8$^{\underline{th}}$ April 1756

Madam

I this day received your Favour of 29th of last ∧^{month} with Advice that you had received the bill, but can't possibly describe the Concern the greater part thereof gives me, on Acco.^{t} of the Letter therein mentioned to be received from one Mary Hely. I have the misfortune to find you take for granted that all containd therein are real facts, which I must beg leave to observe on the face of the thing can't possibly be, for, had she been the acquaintance of mine I am sorry to find you think her, I could better have informd her of the time Mr Price will be of Age, nor could I have sayd anything about the pretended Legacy, as I know nothing about the Will or had any occasion to enquire about it; but so far from being an Acquaintance, I do in the most solemn Manner averr that to the best of my Knowledge I never had the least Conversation with her in my Life, see her I often have as I did every person who lived in Castlelyons whilst I frequented that Town, but for several Years past I have not been there but twice that I went there by your Commands, particularly with Mr Nason which is a long time since, & for more than four years past I have not been nearer to it than Waterford, which is at least forty miles from that Country; I also most solemnly averr that I have not the least Connection with any person there, nor do I correspond with any other ∧^{there} than Mr Pearde and that only on your Business, I also appeal to Mr Price who is above telling an untruth on any Occasion, to declare upon his Honour to you if I ever poisond his Ears with recommendations to his Favour of the Author of the Odious Letter, or of any other person w'soever even of my self, or to act or do or attempt to do any thing but with y.^{r} Consent and approbation. No, Madam, I never did nor ever will, and I have∧^{not} the least dread but he will acquit me, as I expect your Goodness will oblige you also to do when you hear from him in answer to a letter I make bold to send enclosed for him, open, for your perusal. & when you are informd by him that I did not speak in any person's behalf

---

I think it must follow that I did not say he would, nor do I think she could have any Conversation with Mr Pearde thereon, by her not knowing but Mr Price was of Age, I therefore suppose she has got some body to write for her & made use of our Names in her Application to give it some sort of Sanction; mine I most solemnly declare she has traduced, and I make no doubt but she has Mr Peardes, for people in her low life will not stick at making use of any Means to gain what they desire. I very well remember your mention of the payment made by Mr Pearde, & also my answer, which then might have been a fit Opportunity if

I had it at heart, but realy I never once thought of since till now, and all I can say is that the rumour of the town is so ———— This Affair has quite disabled me from considering that part of your Letter about Mahiry with the exactness it requires, and as the post leaves this Town the same day it comes in, I beg leave to deferr saying any thing thereon 'till I can settle my self to consider it properly — I must further take the Liberty to congratulate you on having your Son so thoroughly sensible of his <~~xxxxxxx~~> duty as to make it cooperate with his Interest as it realy is, to advise with you on all Affairs in which he is interested, and hope & believe he always will, my family & I are sincerely glad of the Continuance of his health. with theirs & my best Respects to him & you, I still beg leave to subscribe myself Madam

Your much obliged & most obedient
Servant EdmSpencer

7–8 M.[r] Price [...] of Age] i.e. in just over a year's time, in May 1757.

26–27 a letter [...] for him] this is the next letter, 8 April 1756: folio 100.

31 but] this is an unusual use of the word; it is possibly related to the sense 'even' (*OED*, C.conj.6.b) and hence means 'even that' or 'even if', the overall implication being that Mary Hely could not have spoken to Mr Pearde because he knows when Richard Price is due to come of age and would have put her right.

36–39 I very well [...] is so --] it is not entirely clear whether this passage is a continuation of the discussion of the Mary Hely letter or whether Spencer has moved on to a new topic (the problems with the tenant of Mohire), though the mention of 'the rumour of the town' strongly suggests that it is the former; what is clear is that it relates to an earlier discussion in another letter which is not, unfortunately, in the archive. The long dash after 'so' does not indicate a deliberately unfinished and rhetorically hanging sentence but the end of the paragraph, and the word 'so' means 'thus, as described or indicated' (*OED*, adv.B.I.1).

41 Mahiry] *sic*, Spencer's spelling of /Mohire/ varies.

[folio 100]

[To Richard Parry Price Esqr]

Wicklow 8$^{\underline{th}}$ April 1756

Dear Sir

I was honourd yesterday with a Letter from your Mamma, which gives me the mortification of knowing that I lye under her heavy Displeasure, on Acco.^{t} of my name being traduced in a Letter you received from one Mary Hely of Castlelyons, where among other falsehoods it is <~~xxxxx~~> insinuated that I should say you would not forget her when you arrived at Age: as you know this is an untruth I entreat the favour of you to do me Justice & inform your Mamma if, at any time during the pleasure I had of being with you, I ever spoke one Word to you in her Recommendation, or even mentioned her to you, or if I ever recommended any other person to y.^{r} favour, or if I ever spoke to you about any business to you relating to your Affairs, or wrote to you thereon, /except on the <~~xxx~~> Request of y.^{r} Agency to be recommended to your Mamma on Mr Kingsburys removal to the Temple / as with Justice you can acquit me of these Articles or the least tendency thereto, I have some hopes I may recover the opinion I flatterd my self your Mamma had of me ——— I am proud to find your Inclination agrees with your Interest and earnestly recommend that it should always continue so, and that you may do or promise nothing but by the Advice and Direction of your good Parent, by which means you'll find yourself free & easy to enjoy with peace what Providence has blessd you with ---

With my best Wishes & those of my Family for your Welfare & Happiness I am Dear Sir

Your very affec^{te} Kinsman
& most humble Servant
EdmSpencer

12–14 Request of [...] the Temple] Spencer has presumably asked Richard Price to intercede on his behalf with Alice Price to appoint him as her main agent in Ireland — though given that he is now working full-time for the Revenue one wonders how he could have found the time to do this (see Barnard, *Irish Protestant Ascents and Descents*, p. 297); moreover, he is already acting as an agent for Mr Deane, a Dublin and Kilkenny property owner (see 19 July 1755: folio 96, ll.20–26, and 23 March 1757: folio 108, ll.21–26), and three years later takes on work for a Mrs Payne in Kilkenny (27 October 1759: folio 113, ll.28–29).

[folio 101]

[To Mrs Alice Price
Brynypiece]

Madam

Your last Favour came in due Course of Time, but I was from home, being obliged to go to the County of Kilkenny to sollicite Voters for an election of Magistrate for our Burrough, where we had the Happyness of a tolerable Majority, tho' at a very great Expence. By the enclosed Letter which I send for your Persusal, you'll find that Mr Pearde has been served with a Notice, and will also be served with Ejectments this Vacation, unless you please to give Orders for the Contrary. I answerd his Letter that 'twas not in my Power to do anything as tis put into Lawyers hands by your positive Order, but that I would acquaint you of the Contents and inform him of your Answer. Mr Hayman is certainly right that Copies are not sufficient, but that is only when a Cause comes to tryal, for if we are obliged to have a Suit Copies will be sufficient for Council to proceed upon. you need not send any Order for Money as Mr Wallis will not call 'till more Business be done, he will take down Ejectments with him next Week, when long Vacation comes on. My Wife & Daughter join me in our best Respects to you and Mr Price

I am Madam Y.^{r} most obed.^{t} humble Servant
EdmSpencer

Wicklow 9th July 1756

3 our Burrough] this is Innistiogue, see 19 July 1755: folio 96, note to l.3.

[folio 102]

[To M$^{\underline{rs}}$ Alice Price
Brynypiece]

Madam

As soon as I received your Favour I wrote to Mr Pearde, and yesterdays Post brought his Answer, wherein he says that, he is very much obliged to you & Mr Price for y.^{r} Friendship to him, he will do all in his Power to secure you after best Manner and thinks his Son joining him in a bond suff.^{t} Security for a larger Sum as what Patrimony he has is in his own Power, & does not by any Means intend to defraud you of a Penny. that as to part of Mr Barrys Estate being considerably advanced / which I mentioned to him / it was owing to Leases being taken when Lands were low, and therefore sen[*t*] an Acco.^{t} of the Manner he has applyed Mohire Lands, that he has lost above ninety pounds since his Commencem.^{t} by the Failure of Tennants, and that I shall receive from him a Remittance without much delay & he will be punctual for the Future.

I have wrote to Mr Wallis to delay serving Copies of Ejectment until I receive your further Orders, which will be of no hindrance to the Suit if you do not approve of the Security, as young Mr Pearde is of Age perhaps you may accept of their Bond on which when passd I will have Judgement enterd separate; but believe twill be advisable first that he should make the promised Remittance, by which we may calculate the Sum for which the Bond / if approved of by you / must be passd, and it will also be necessary for me to know what Time you will allow for Payment thereof, & whether you will grant it to be at one or more Payments. On the other Side I transcribe what he terms the Rent Role of Mohire Lands —

My Wife & Daughter join me in our best Respects to you and Mr Price. I am Madam

Y.^{r} most obedient humble Servant
EdmSpencer

Wicklow 29th August 1756

———————

40 Cows set to Philip Linchy at £1:19:– p Cow		£78:–:–
Farther Part of the Land set to Barry &c at		64:–:–
Daniel Callaghan's Part		17:10:–
a Labourer		2:–
John Denihy's part at		24:–:–
two fields we have for our horses		7:–:–
		192:10:–
	Rent	140:–:–
Renewing & Death of Cattle besides Repairs	Profit	52:10:–

6 what Patrimony [...] own Power] whether this refers to Mr Pearde's patrimony (i.e. inheritance) or his son's is unclear because of the vagueness of the pronouns; the latter would seem more likely as it would make the younger Pearde good security for the bond; the elder Pearde then returns to being the subject of the sentence after the /&/.

8 advanced] possibly 'raised, increased' (*OED*, ppl.a.5) The connection between leases on Mr Barry's land and that of Mr Pearde is not at all clear: it might be that Mr Pearde is trying to justify the poor returns on his sub-leasing of the Mohire lands by comparing his situation with that of Barry (the latter having taken his leases when land was producing less rent so that leases cost less, but now that rents have risen his profits on those cheaper leases have also risen); however, the rent roll states that part of the land was rented to the Barry family. It might be that 'advanced' has an entirely different meaning here, but one suspects that the real problem is that we are getting only a partial picture of another complex and contested legal arrangement about land (see note below).

10–11 he has [...] pounds] the rent roll shows a profit of £52.10.0 (£52.50 in decimal money), which hardly supports this assertion; perhaps that explains Spencer's somewhat derisive 'what he terms the Rent Role' (l.24).

rent roll] as noted for ll.10–11, this account throws no light at all on Mr Pearde's assertion that he has 'lost above ninety pounds' since taking on the lease of Mohire, and the second item, which states that part of the land is 'set to Barry' (i.e. rented to Barry) is extremely odd given that the Barrys claim they have a title to the Mohire lands (see 27 February 1761: folio 118, ll.8–13) and also appear to be charging Mr Pearde rent (see 21 February 1757: folio 107, ll.13–15), though that passage is not by any means clear; again, we have to acknowledge that we are here enmeshed in the complexities of eighteenth-century Irish land tenure arrangements.

5 John Denihy's] is this perhaps a descendant of the Edward Denny who took the ninety nine year lease on Mohire in 1666 which Spencer mentions in 19 July 1755: folio 96, ll.20–22, and which he implies there is still in force, even though John Price purchased the land twenty six years later?

[folio 103]

[To Mrs Price
Brynypiece]
Wicklow 26th Sepr 1756

Madam

As soon as I received your Favour of the Sixth Instant I wrote to Mr Pearde and also to Mr Wallis, from the latter I this day received a Letter which I send enclosed for your Perusal, if Mr Pearde is punctual to his Promise twill save you & himself a great deal of Trouble and Expence, which Expence would fall on him in the End. I think Mr Wallis's personal Application to him has had some Effect as it shewd him you had proceeded further than bare Threatening, especially as he lives within a few Miles of Castlelyons where his Father has a good Estate & consequently as much Power as another, which Consideration induced me to desire him to see Mr Pearde. By this Post I desire Mr Wallis to demand his Bill of Cost from him, & am sure he will serve the Ejectm.$^{[t]}$ ^{before} the first day of Term / 3^{d} Nov.^{r} / if the Agreem.t be not punctually observed for he is very exact in Business, the Acco.^{t} I send ^$^{to\ him\ is}$ as follows

1756
June 4..th Three Years Rent due for Mohire at £140 by the year. . £420:–:–
1755
June 26th A Remittance to me. £100:–:–
1756
Feb.^{ry} 23..^{d} A Remittance to me 100:–:–
200:–:–
Due 220:–:–

When this is paid, which I suppose will be by bills which will take some time before they become due, I shall take Care to remit at the lowest Exchange as I will attend the Course thereof for that Purpose; with our best Respects to you & Mr Price I am Madam

Y.^{r} most obedient humble Servant
EdmSpencer

25 the Course] Spencer possibly has in mind the term 'course of exchange' which was, strictly speaking, the price at which bills drawn on a foreign currency could be purchased, but it is more likely that he is using the word here metonymically to refer to the Exchange where such a transaction would take place.

[folio 104]

[To Mrs Price
Brynypiece]

Wicklow 10th October 1756

Madam

I have been these ten Days past in the County of Kilkenny collecting Rents, from whence I returnd last Night, & found the enclosed Letter from Mr Pearde, which being so different from what I expected by Mr Wallis's Letter / which I sent to you / that I also send it for your Persusal; I will not offer to hinder Mr Wallis from proceeding in the Law Way on this or any other Letter I may receive, until I have your Orders to do so, and am of Opinion the enclosed should be kept by you on Acco.^{t} of the Promise therein containd of giving ∧$^{\text{the Land}}$ ~~it~~ up to you[*r*] Order. perhaps I may receive some further Directions from you before Mr Wallis leaves that Country, which he will do about the First of November. With our best Respects to you & Mr Price

I am Madam

Y.^{r} most obedient humble Servant

EdmSpencer

Address] written in a hand other than Spencer's on the obverse side of the envelope and at right angles to the address is /May ye 1 — 1750 — 62 — 13/.

1–2 I have [...] collecting Rents] again, one wonders how he manages to keep his job in the Revenue if he takes this much time off to do work for his other employers.

[folio 105]

[From Mr Spencer with a bill on messrrs Barton & Smith merch^{ts} in London for one Hundred & thirty nine pound fourteen Shillings English value — of Irish 150
To Mrs Alice Price
Dated Dublin nov^{r} ye 11 — 1756
Brynypiece]

Madam

I received your Favour of 25th October at Wicklow last Friday, and forwarded yours to Mrs Pearde by that Post: On Monday I received a Letter from Mr Wallis that he had received from Mr Pearde £150, I therefore came here on Tuesday Evening & waited on Mr Wallis Yesterday who payd me the Money, for which you have above, Mes[*s^{rs}*] Carleton & Jeuers Bill on Messrs Barton & Smith in London at twenty one days Sight — – £139:14^{s} — at £7$^{1}/_{8}$ p cent Exch$^{\partial}$ for Irish £150 being the Sum sent by Mr Pearde —— Mr Wallis communicated a Letter he rece^{d} from Mr Pearde, to me, wherein is mentiond — that by ‘ his Order he paid £150 which with what he paid before makes £1022:18:8½ ‘ his rent to the 4.th June last / allowing £100 — for the first year wch was more ‘ than he made of the Land as the best part of the Season was over before his ‘ Commencement, / amounts to £1080 — so that he owes but £57:1:3½ next ‘ Christmas which he is not to pay till next June, as he is to be indulged till ‘ that time for Christmas rent, so that he hopes Mrs Price will think proper ‘ to have her Ejectment withdrawn —— Mr Wallis has desired by this Post that Mr Pearde will draw out his whole Acco^{t} & send it to him, as

———————

there is a very great Difference in the Account he received from me, an[*d*] what he says in his Letter, as soon as it arrives, I shall be sure to forward it to you with our Remarks. However in Order to keep your Ejectm.^{t} on, it was necessary to fyle the Service this Term and motion for Judgem.^{t} must be made thereon, then no further Proceedings shall be, till next Term / if then necessary, I mean if a dispute on the Acco.^{t} might happen / for if such motion was neglected now, a new Service must be the Case which would be expensive as there were above twenty Tenements served with Copies — I offerd to pay Mr Wallis but he declined it till the Suit was at an End, which he thinks may be in a short Time — With my best Respects to Mr Price I am Madam

Your most obedient humbleServant
EdmSpencer

P:S:
I intend to return to Wicklow
to Morrow

Dublin 11th Nov.r 1756

Address] the information about the bill and date is in a different hand from that of Spencer.

2 M.rs Pearde] i.e. 'Messers Pearde', the son is now included because of his acting as security.

10–16 ' his Order [...] withdrawn —] the inverted commas at the left-hand side of this and the next six lines presumably indicate a summary quotation of the contents of the letter from Mr Pearde as communicated to Spencer by Mr Wallis; though they are not closed the quotation continues to the word 'withdrawn' where the dash indicates a full stop or a paragraph break.

26 Tenements] either the buildings containing sub-tenants or by metonymy the sub-tenants themselves, who will also be subject to ejectment if the main tenant is ejected.

[folio 106]

[To Mrs Alice Price
Brynypiece]

Wicklow 22^{d} Decr 1756

Madam

I have been these three Weeks past confined to my bed till yesterday; I was taken ill of a Cold the middle of the last Month attended with a Cholick, which not being very violent I did not take proper care of till I grew so very ill that I was obliged to take to bed & employ a Physician who calld in a second, & neither had much hopes of my recovery till a few days ago, my Disorder a violent nervous Cholick which gave inexpressible torture, I should not trouble you with this tedious Acco.^{t} of my self but to shew that 'twas impossible for me before this / scarcely now / to acknowlege the Recc.^{t} of your favour which came when I was so ill that I could not read, my wife therefore enclosed it to Mr Wallis in Dublin, who answerd that he would write to Mr Pearde about the Contents, & this day I have received a letter from him that he is set out for the Country & will call on Mr Pearde & will bring the ballance of his Acco.^{t} if he can get it when he comes to term, that he has obtaind Judgem.^{t} upon the Ejectm.^{t} so that an habere / a term for an order for Possession / may issue at any time that he fails to pay his rent as it was brought upon the Title: I am therefore of Opinion that this will be better than any other kind of Security, for if he ^^{should} neglected paying rent you must be at the trouble of seeing his Security wch would be means of delay, now 'tis only to move the Court for this Order. I will write to them both by the next post but realy am not able now, <~~xx~~> I must observe to you that the whole bill of Cost can't be demanded of Mr Pearde tho I intend to ask it. I have considerd the difference in the Acco.^{ts} as to the first bill sent, in yours £62:13– in his £67:19: — and perhaps yours was English money and the Exchange might be the difference, but we shall soon know what he says to it. I am very glad to hear Mr Price is well, had I known he was at home I wo.^{d} have sent a bill on Chester instead of London, but I thought he was at Oxford. My family joins in wishing you & him many happy Years ——

I am Madam Y.^{r} most obedient humble Servant

EdmSpencer

I should inform you Madam that I had a letter from Mr Pearde before my illness, wherein he tells me that what he meant, by saying due at Christmas, was, that the ballance was not to be paid till then, as one half years rent is to be discharged when the other becomes due.

Address] on the address side of the sheet and at right angles to the address is, written in a hand other than Spencer's, what appears to be a shopping list, mostly for fish.

Side note 3 one half [...] due.] strictly speaking not 'when' but 'before', see 23 March 1757: folio 108, ll.16–17, which makes it clear that Pearde has promised to pay any outstanding instalment of rent before the next is due.

[folio 107]

[To Mrs Alice Price
Brynypiece]

Mr Conolly's Mary Street Dublin 21$^{\underline{st}}$ Feb.^{ry} 1757

Madam

In my last I gave you an account of a tedious fit of Sickness which hinderd me from being able to write to you for a considerable Time, since which I had a Relapse, which tho not so desperate as the former yet confined me a considerable Time, insomuch that I was not able to come to Town till three days ago, when I expected to have received from Mr Wallis the remittance promised by Mr Pearde, but find it neglected for Mr Wallis has not heard from him since he came to Town, he has wrote by the last Post to inform him that if he does not remit in a post or two, he has directions from me to issue the habere to the Sherrif, which I hope & expect may hasten it. I received a letter from him in Jan$^{\partial}$y which by the date should have come to hand sooner, but being put into a contrary bag delayd it for sev.^{le} days, & when I got it I was too much indisposed to answer it, I send it under this Cover for your Perusal, as to Ld Barry{*tear*} rent I believe he has a right to charge it, having received no order to the contrar[*y*] but Mr Wallis informs me he directed him not to pay it for the future. I send Mr Wallis's bill of Cost which he did not demand of Mr Pearde as he found he did not clear off the rent, & says it would have put an End to the Suit to have it paid by him which would hinder his taking out the Order of possession <~~xxxxx~~> except he went thro' fresh Services of Ejectm.^{t} & by which a great deal of time would be lost; this Order can be had at any time, in Vacation as well as in Term & as Mr Pearde by Mr Wallis's letter will find it so near I expect he will comply & remit the rent. I shall set out for Wicklow to Morrow, & return hither in a Week, you'll please to direct your Orders to me here. with my best Wishes to Mr Price

I am Madam / with great Respect /
Your most obedient humble Servt
EdmSpencer

Address] Mary Street was three streets north of the Liffey and ran parallel with Lower Ormond Quay on the northern riverbank.

9 habere] a legal order for possession of a property; see previous letter, l.14, where Spencer defines the term.

13–14 as to L^{d} [...] rent] the dispute with Lord Barrymore over what appears to be his claim that he has a right to charge rent on Mohire becomes another theme in the correspondence, which ends before the issue is finally settled; see also the note to the rent roll included in the letter of 29 August 1756: folio 102.

[folio 123]

Mr Edmond Spencer for Mrs Price . . . . Debtor

Trinity 1756 ——

		l	s	d
	Drawing a State of Mrs Price's Case with respect} to Mr Peard . . . . ____________	0.	6.	[0].
	To C. Wood therewith . . . . ___________	1.	9.	3
	attending him . . . . ____________	0.	6.	[0].
	Drawing and Serving a notice of over holding ___	0:	10˙	0
	Trinity 1756 ——			
Lessor Price against The Ejector —	Term fees . . . . ___________	0.	2.	6
	Drawing Summons in Ejectment	0.	5.	0
	24 Copies . . . . ______________	2.	19.	6
	Paid Serving . . . . ____________	1.	4.	0
	Drawing Swearing affidavit of the Service ______	0.	5	0
	Appearance for the Casual Ejector . . . . ________	0.	3.	0
	Drawing Declaration . . . . ___________	0.	3.	4
	Ingrosing . . . . ____________	0.	6.	0
	Signing and filing . . . . ___________	0.	4.	0
	Councill Signing . . . . ___________	0.	10.	0
	Michas 1756 ——			
	Term fee and Continuance . . . . __________	0.	4.	0
	Box Rule and motion to Receive Ejectment ____	0.	6.	0
	Rules to plead . . . . ___________	0.	2.	0
	Attorneys fees thereon . . . . ___________	0.	7:	6
	paid filing affidavit of the service . . . __________	0.	6.	0
	Certificate of no plea . . . . __________	0.	1.	6.
	Box Rule and motion for Judgement . . _______	0.	7.	0
	Councill . . . . ____________	0.	11.	4½
	To my Trouble and Expences going three times from my house in the County of Corke to — Castlelyons which is above ten Miles in order to Settle the accounts with Mr Peard ———	3.	[8].	3
		£14:	8:	0½

Mrs Price may Dispossess Mr Peard of his farm when she pleases . . . ____________________

This is a summary of Spencer's expenses for overseeing a legal procedure which does not in itself lead to Mr Pearde's ejectment from Mohire, but prepares for the final procedure which would see him ejected — that is, the issuing of a 'habere' or order for possession (see 22 December 1756: folio 106, ll.14–15). The latest that Spencer could have written this is December 1756 at the end of Michaelmas term that year (see l.20). When he sent it to Alice Price is less easily determined but the line in the previous letter, 'I send Mr Wallis's bill of Cost' (21 February 1757: folio 107, l.16) could well refer to this document, so it has been placed here.

8 over holding] keeping possession of a property beyond the agreed term (*OED*, *hold*, v.42.a).

15 Casual Ejector] the defendant in the fictitious action once allowed to determine a title to land (*OED*, *casual*, adj.10).

20 Michas] i.e., Michaelmas.

33 final total] the pence column is 10d short in the final total. A missing /1/ before one of the zeros in the pence column could account for it but Spencer makes an error in 27 February 1761: folio 118 so his addition is not faultless.

[folio 108]

[To Mrs Alice Price
Brynypiece]
Wicklow 23^{d} March 1757

Madam

I wrote to you fom Dublin the later End of last Term, & enclosed a Letter I had received from Mr Pearde some time before, and also Mr Wallis's Bill of Cost; in a few days after I received your kind Favour & return my best acknowlegements for the Concern you Express for my Indisposition, which has been very tedious, but thank God, I have got pritty well over it, & am gaining Strength daily, I defferd writing sooner as I expected your Answer to my last by the Packets which came in last Week, & expecting to hear from Mr Pearde by every Post as he had promised in a Letter to Mr Wallis before he left Town, however it being a considerable Time since I wrote my last and ∧^{not} receiving any Orders relative thereto, I fear it has miscarryed, & therefore judge it proper again to acquaint you that I have not yet received the promised Remittance from Mr Pearde, that he makes some Objections to the Account but nothing material, & therefore pray for further Directions, if you mean that the Habere should be issued; yet I have Expectations that as Mr Wallis is now in the Neighbourhood of CastleLyons he may make him the paym.^{t} or would you please that I should write that as he has broke his promise concerning the remittance of one half year's rent before the other became due, it is your Will that on every such Lapse he should imediately be calld to for the years rent together, perhaps this might make him more punctual, tis a method I pursue with Mr Deane's Tennants in the County of Dublin, & on my first being appointed his Agent I obliged one to pay a years rent the beginning of May which was due at Ladyday, by which I have them now so punctual that there is not this day a shilling due of last Michaelmas Gale in that County, tho' I cant say so much for the County of Kilkenny Tennants, as I must forbear with them being poor & a great Distance from Market; this cant be Mr Pearde's Case I hope. I trouble you with this to shew you our Method here. Our best Wishes attend you & Mr Price

I am Madam / with great Respect / Your most obedient humble
Servant EdmSpencer

24 Michaelmas Gale] Michaelmas (29 September) was one of the quarter days of the English business year and 'gale' is 'the amount of rent due at at a given time' (*OED*, n^{I}.1).

[folio 109]

[To Mrs Alice Price
Brynypiece]
Wicklow 7..th August 1757

Madam

I received you Favour, of the first Instant, this Day & think myself happy that I so far judged according to your Approbations, as not to have mentiond any Thing to Mr Pearde about the Quitrent which I judged the better Way until I had heard further about it, I write to Dublin this post to enquire who are Lord Barrymore's Guardians, and also to Mr Pearde about the Ten pounds you mention, acquainting him that you expect that Mr Price's Order will be produced or that Sum not allowed, this can still be done for I never gave him a Receipt in full & as they are only on Account of Rent, it therefore lyes open; I own I am a good deal surprized that it has been charged tho not payd; I also give Directions about Walsh according to your Order, & advise him to send a Remittance forthwith or he must expect to be calld to for a year's Rent or the Habere shall be issued against the Land before Term: I wrote a pressing & threatning Letter some time ago but have not received an Answer, I hope owing to a Miscarriage of the Letter. I am very much concerned for the Trouble you are still likely to combat in your Suit with Mr Lloyd, it shews evidently the Chicanery of the Law to be such, that honest People must be content to give up their Substance rather than hazzard the Chance of sueing, & will perhaps in the End oblige the Legislature to abridge our Statutes as in other Countrys, wch I fear will not happen unless an Act was first passd to disqullify Councellors or Attornies from sitting in the House. I am glad to find you are likely to get rid of Mr Walsh, and sorry that you are threatend with other Visitors, but that you orderd me to be silent on that Head, I should entreat the favour of having enquiry made of the Wretch / if she should go / whether I ever had any Conversation with her in my Life; but I beg pardon ∧^{for} even ~~for~~ saying this, Time I hope will shew that I am what I profess, an honest Man ——— I wish Mr Price a great deal of Pleasure on his Tour & a safe Return, & hope he has better Weather than we have, or twill a disagreeable Jaunt in the Welsh Mountains. my Wife and Daughter present their best Respects to you & him with those of Madam Your most obedient humble Servant

EdmSpencer

3 Quitrent] 'a rent paid in lieu of services' (*OED*).

19 abridge] 'curtail or diminish privileges, rights etc'. (*OED*, v.5).

20 disqullify] the /a/ has been omitted.

22 sorry [...] Visitors] clearly Mary Hely (see 8 April 1756: folio 99) is now threatening to turn up on the Prices' doorstep.

28 twill a disagreeable] /be/ has been omitted after /twill/.

[folio 110]

[Rec^{d} from E^{d} Spencer Esqr with a bill on Barton and Smith for £61–17–3 Englis dated Dublin may 12 — 1758

To Mrs Alice Price

Brynypiece]

Madam

The Bill I received from Mr Pearde being due this Day, I came here last Night and have negociated it at £7/½ p Cent and send you above Messrs Carlton & Jeuers on Messrs Barton & Smith Cateaton Street London Exch$^{∂}$ for 66:10 – Irish – – – – – 61:17:3
Rec.^{rs} fees of £70 – – – – – – 3:10
£70: ----

You'll please as soon as this comes to Hand to advise me of the Rec.^{t} thereof, and also what your Sentiments are relative to the Mohiry Affair, concerning which I sent you lately Coun.^{r} Woods Opinion. I shall return to Wicklow to Morrow Morning. my best Respects wait on you & Mr Price I am Madam

Your most obedient humble Servant

Dublin 12..th May 1758

EdmSpencer

4/5 66:10 / 3:10] the figure 10 represents 10 shillings in each case; when the two sums are added together the two 10s make 20 shillings, or one pound, making the total £70.

[folio 128]

[To Mrs Alice Price
at Brinnypeice]

Madam

We return our sincere Thanks for the kind share you and Mr Price take in our present Miss= =fortune; I shou'd have obey'd your Commands Sooner and acquainted you before now with the State my poor Papa was in, had he not been in so precarious a Way, that his Phy___ =sician cou'd not judge what to think about him. the tedious Confinements on his Back (forty four Days without being stir'd) affected his Nerves to that Degree that when he was taken up, in a short Time it threw him into a violent Fit of the Cholick, which lasted with vast Torture several Hours; and it was though^{t}∧ he cou'd not outlive it; However it pleas'd God to give him Relief when least expected; but he has been oblig'd to continue in his Bed till these two Days past, and as no ill Consquen= =ces attended his being taken up now, his Doctors make us hope they will remove him next Week into our own House. He directs me to acquaint you that the Papers now before Counc.^{lr} Wood are the last Paquet of Copies sent over by you,

———————————

And it was thought proper that he shou'd perusė them, as he might thereby enlarge or alter his former Opinion, which Mr Wallis thinks very necessary before he applys to other Council. Our best Respects wait on you and Mr Price I am Madam

your most obedient humble Servant

Rosam:^{d} Spencer

Waterford Sept$^{\underline{br}}$ y^{e} 18th: 1758 ---

As the folio number shows, this letter was placed out of order by one of the collection's archivists; it has been placed here to maintain the chronology of the narrative.

8 & 14 taken up] probably 'lifted from a prostate position' (*OED*, *take*, 93.a (a)), that being the position Spencer's illness has kept him in, we are told, for 'forty four days' (l.7); the implication is that when the physician first tried lifting him up the result was an immediate worsening of his condition, but on the second attempt it was recognized that he was recovering and so could be moved back home; the phrase, though, could also mean 'put into a carriage or on to a horse' (*OED*, *take*, 93.a (e)) which would suggest the experiment was to actually take him back home. In either case, it is interesting to note (a) that Spencer is being treated, again, at his physician's house, and (b) that Rosamond refers to those treating him as both 'doctors' and 'physicians' without any apparent distinction. (See also 18 January 1744/5: folio 28, ll.2–3.)

[folio 111]

[To Mrs Alice Price
Brinnypeice]

Madam

I expected before this Time to have been able to give you some further Acco^{t} concerning Mohire Affair, but such is my State of Health / owing to long Confinement / that I can't venture yet to undertake a Journey to Dublin, even in a Carriage, 'tho I had Business of Consequence to transact for Mr Deane this Term, wch I was obliged to postpone to the next: I have therefore wrote to Mr Wallis to send me Coun.^{r} Wood's further Opinion on the additional Copies before him, which shall be forwarded to you as soon as I receive it. I also expected to have been enabled by Mr Pearde to have sent you a Remittance, to which End I wrote to him as soon as I was able after my Illness, and received for Answer dated 3^{d} October last that I should very soon hear from him, & that for the future he would be more punctual in his Payments, being a considerable Gainer by the Death of his Cousin Meade; but not a word have I had since, and there will be three Gales due for Mohi[*re*] the [*L*]1..th Ins^{t} old Stile; I think it incumbent on me to aquaint you hereof to shew that even my tedious Indisposition did not hinder me from making Application for your Rent, & the Delay not owing to any of it remaining in my Hands, which might be thought the Payments from him being so very slow, notwithstanding repeated Promises of Punctuality. My Wife & Daughter join me in our best Respects to you & Mr Price with the good Wishes of the Season

I am Madam

Your most obedient humbleServ.^{t}

EdmSpencer

Waterford 8th Decr 1758

15 [*L*]1..th] the first mark is probably meant to be a /1/, making the number /11/ and that would be consistent with the superscript abbreviation /th/, but it looks quite definitely like an /L/ as in /Libra/ for /pound/; was Spencer possibly confused by the sound of /eleven/ as he wrote, and transmuted it to the /L/? Such a mistake would be consistent with his still feeling unwell.

Address of origin] in 1758 Spencer was transferred from the customs administration in Wicklow to supervise the Wexford hearth money district (see Barnard, *Irish Protestant Ascents and Descents*, p. 297); at that point he took up residence in Waterford, a seaport in south-eastern Ireland on the River Suir and the Waterford/Wexford border; this becomes his home address for the remainder of the correspondence.

[folio 112]

[*With a bill on Mr Folliot in Chester for £100 dated Dublin feb. 15–1759*
To Mrs Alice Price
Brynypiece]

Dublin 15$^{\underline{th}}$ Feb$^{\underline{ry}}$ 1759

Madam

Your Favour of 19th December came to Hand in due Course, on Receipt whereof I wrote to Mr Pearde as you orderd, and acquainted him that I intended for Dublin the beginning of Term & would certainly put the Habere in Force against him, unless prevented by a Remittance from him; the Consequence of which was, that on the 16.th Ult^{o} he sent to me to Waterford £115: –: — with an Assurance that he would soon remit more, & for the Future be more punctual in his Payments. I did not however arrive here till the 30.th being obliged to make easy Journeys as my Limb is very tender still; I attended Change constantly since my Arrival & found the Course of Exchange so high, that I delayd remitting in Hopes of it's lowering, but being informd that tis expected to rise I would not venture to delay any longer, and therefore you have above Messrs Carleton & Jeuers Bill at Twenty one days Sight on Mr James Folliot of Chester £100 Exch at £9¼ pc.^{t} for Irish £109: 5: –
Rec.^{rs} Fees of £115 by former Orders —— 5:15: –
£115: –: –

I take the Liberty to inclose the Letter of Advice, which you'll please to order to be delivered when the Bill is tender'd for Acceptance —

Counc.^{r} Wood having been dangerously ill at Corke last Vacation, has not ventured to come up this Term, & the Papers of Mohire Affair being all in his Hands, I did not pay the Bill of Cost to Mr Wallis till those are returned together with his further Opinion for which he was feed, but I took Care to inform Mr Wallis that he was not to proceed to take any Steps towards establishing the Title till further Orders; twill be Time enough to pay him out of M.r Pearde[*s*] next Remittance, for his Bill can't be considerable as there were no Proceedings in the Court in the Case. Counc.^{r} Kingsbury has given me the great Pleasure of knowing that both you & Mr Price are very well, & the additional Satisfaction of expecting to see Mr Price again, for he told me that he intends next Summer to visit his Irish Estate: may I hope for Notice when he is to set out, that I may be in Dublin to pay early Respects to him. You'll please to direct the Advice of the Rec.^{t} of this Bill to me at Waterford as I mean to begin

9 Change] i.e. the money exchange.

my Journey thither next week —— My best Respects wait on you & Mr Price. I have the Honour to be Madam

Y.^{r} most obed.^{t} hble Serva[nt]
EdmSpencer

[folio 113]

[To Mrs Alice Price
Brynypiece]

Madam

I make no Doubt but you are surprized at not receiving a Bill for Mr Pearde's Rent, and realy I scarce know what to say thereon; In a Letter of his 23^{d} March Past he assures me that I might expect a Payment from him in Easter Week, which made me return to my House from <~~xxx~~> Carlow where my Family were on a Visit to spend some Weeks, but did not hear from him; I still for a considerable Time expected to no purpose, therefore wrote twice, to my Second Letter I received an Answer that he had been from Home & did not receive it till a considerable Time after Date, / but that he did not get my first Letter / that he was obliged to me for my Indulgence, & that I might certainly expect a Payment at Michaelmas, this Letter dated 20th Augt last. As I could not well proceed this Term I acquiesced so far as not to answer his Letter, but Term being now at Stand I have wrote to him that, if he does not clear off the Rent and Arrears before the 10th November / at wch Time I intend to set out for Dublin / I must make Use of the Power the Court has granted & get the Possession, & also Use the proper Methods to make him pay what is due, I realy can't form to myself any Opinion what this Notice may produce, as he $_{\wedge}$^{has} not yet kept touch to any of his Promises; if he does not now clear off, I shall certainly direct

———————

Mr Wallis to renew the Habere & take Possession of the Lands with the Sheriff, & also mark a Writ against him for the Rent & Costs, & extend his Estate for Payment. I beg Leave to assure you that the many Dissapointments I meet with about this small affair of Mohire, give me more Chagreen & Uneasiness / least you might think I am guilty of Remissness / than the whole of my other Agencies,

5 Carlow] a small town roughly fifty miles equidistant between Dublin and Waterford.

14 at Stand] 'at a standstill' (*OED*, n^{I}.5.a), not 'finished' as Michaelmas term would have started at the beginning of October.

20 kept touch] 'acted in faith in relation to'(*OED*, n.24.a).

21 clear off] 'settle or discharge his debt' (*OED*, v.18.a).

26 Chagreen] i.e. 'chagrin', 'trouble, fret, uneasiness' (*OED*, n.3).

tho' very considerable, having lately got an Additional Agency in the County of Kilkenny from Mrs Payne of £600 a year Rent ——
My Family join me in our best Respects to you & Mr Price.
I have the Honour to be Madam

Y.^{r} most obedient Servant
EdmSpencer

Waterford 27.th Octr 1759

28 having lately [...] Agency] again, one wonders how Spencer manages to find the time to conduct all this extra work on top of his revenue job.

[folio 114]

[*from Mr Spencer with a bill on*
*Mr James Folliot <***> in Chester*
To Mrs Alice Price *for £61 – 4 – 9*
*English value. which with R<***>*
fees & exchange is 92 – 12 – 6 Irish
mony Dated Dublin Decr ye 8 –1759
Carleton & Jeuers
Draft Brynypiece]

Madam

A few Days after my last to you, a Messenger came to me from Mr Pearde with a Remittance of £92:12:6 for which I gave a Rec.^{t} there is also a Charge of £2:– for Walsh & 7:6 paid Chiefrent to the day on which he received my Letter to put a Stop to that Paym.^{t} & he assures that shortly he will pay more, as I found that my Affairs would detain me longer than I expected at Home & in Kilkenny, I chose to take Bills from Waterford rather than carry money about with me, & sendt them by Post to a Friend here for Acceptance; if I am rightly informed, a Bill on London is negociable at Chester without any Discount, you'll please to have that askd of some of the Merchants there, & acquaint me thereof, & I can constantly remit you any Paym^{ts} made to me immediately at a lower Exchange from Waterford than from hence. I did not come to Town till 24th Nov.^{r} & was in two days obliged to go to County of Kildare from whence I returnd last Thursday. Above you have Messrs Carleton & Jeuers Bill on Mr Folliot of Chester at twenty one days Sight for Eighty one pounds four shillings & seven pence Exch$^{\partial}$ for Irish Money – – £88:0:0
Fees on receiving – – – – – 4:12:6
92:12:6

I have wrote to Mr Pearde that I would advise his clearing off all Arrear before the first of Term, otherwise he would be proceeded against at Law —

---

3 7:6] there appears to be something written above these figures but it is very faint; it might be an /s/ for /shillings/ over the /7/ and a /p/ for /pence/ over the /6/; this would be 37.5 pence in decimal money.

12 County of Kildare] the county just west of Dublin.

your Observation of being too late I don't think will be of any Consequence against you, for if you mean to preserve the Estate in you[*s*], I think it better that you should have it in your Power to take into Possession when you have a Tenant secured, which might be done by Compact, not to insist on the Term agreed on if your Interest should not last so long. I wish I could see Coun$^{\partial}$ Fazakerly's Opinion, I have had some Conversation with Mr Wallis thereon, & he is still possitive that you have a good Title, as in a Cause tryd at Corke some Time ago / of which I think I formerly told you / the Deed produced on Behalf of Barrymore, was adjudged not be good or valid against a Purchaser, & therefore is of Opinion that I ought to acquaint the Tenant that whatever Quitrent has been already paid by the Prices or their Tenants, was in their own Wrong as the Estate of Mohire is in Mr Price solely by Virtue of a Deed of Sale which Mr Price is determined to support, but this I decline doing untill I have your further Orders thereon, which I hope you'll please to give me when Mr Price returns from London. I shall not set out for Waterford till the 21.st Ins.^{t} and may expect to receive your Commands perhaps before I leave town,

---

I shall continue at Home but a Month and return hither for the next Term. My best Respects wait on Mr Price with the Compliments of the Season to you both I am Madam

Your most obedient Servant
EdmSpencer

Mr Conolly's Mary Street
Dublin 8th Decr 1759

21 you[*s*]] the /s/ may just be a flourish on the /u/, or Spencer may have omitted the /r/ in /yours.

23 by Compact] 'by mutual agreement or understanding', possibly in contradistinction to 'a covenant or contract' (both *OED*, n^{I}.1). The following clause may qualify this word more strongly than the comma would imply, suggesting that this 'compact' would involve an agreement that the tenancy could be terminated by the Prices early if they chose to do so.

[folio 115]

[To Mrs Alice Price
Brynypiece]

Madam

Your Favour of the 21.st Instant, being forwarded from Dublin, I have this Day received, with Advice of the Rec.^{t} of Messrs Carleton & Jeuers bill for £81:4:7 English. I return Thanks for your kind Information of Mr Price's Intention to alter his Condition, our News Papers inform us that he is marryed, & I sincerely wish him and you all the Joy imaginable on the Occasion; as tis some Years since I had the Pleasure of his Correspondence, I take the Liberty to intreat you'll please to present him with my Congratulations & those of my Wife & Daughter, for be assured that none can have your & his and Happiness more at Heart than me, may you live long to see him blessd with many Children to make you both happy: I am convinced his Lady will be so for he who has been a good Son must also be a good Husband & Father. Yet I own I am surprized at your saying you are to quit Brynypiece, for I realy think it will not be to his Advantage to have you removed from him, especially so far as Leverpoole, which I fear you may find too keen a Climate for you to reside in, especially in Winter, give me Leave, Madam, to hope that this Match of my Kinsman's is not disagreeable to you or contrary to your Inclinations, when I knew him he was fond & dutyfull & I hope still remains so, & I should think Brynypiece house large enough, & sincerely wish you may alter your Resolution, which must be of Service to him & comfort to you — I am sorry to find you still complain of a Weakness in your Eyes, mine are often very much enflamed, as I am obliged to write a great deal, and I never found any Ease from any Applications but one, which I send a Recipe for, & hope if you make use of it you will receive the same Benefit by it which I constantly do, two Nights bathing my Eyes with a little of it after I am in Bed eases all Inflamation, 'twill smart a little but is intirely innocent.

I received a Letter from Mr Henry Pearde / in answer to mine to his Father /

———————

acquainting me that his Father had been dangerously ill, and at that Time not fit to be spoken to on Business, but that as soon as he was recoverd he would communicate the contents to him & try to expedite a Remittance, I shall delay giving any further ‸Directions about the ~~Quitren~~ Chiefrent to him, or saying any more to you thereon till I see Mr Wallis, who is now in the County of Corke, & who I expect next Week here, as he has promised to spend a few Days with me in his Return to Dublin & I will not fail to embrace that Opportunity of talking to him at large on Mohire Affair

My Wife & Daughter join me in our best Respects to you
I have the Honour to be Madam

Your most obedient Servant
EdmSpencer

Waterford 31st December 1759

————————

R∂ Aq. Rosar, rub. 3ÿ
Vitriol. alb.
Bol. ver. ãã ∂i
G. Camphor. gr. vi ~~m~~ f.l Collyr.
S. the Eyewater

4 M.r Price's [...] Condition] Richard Price married Dorothea, daughter of Sir John Byrne, Bart, in December 1759; she died in December 1761, having given birth to a son in November of that year (memorial in St Mary's Church, Overton). He then married Anne Puleston in 1765 with whom he had another son. Richard Price died in 1782 aged 45 after 'a very long and lingering illness' (memorial tablet in Birkenhead Priory, quoted by J. H. Hanshall, *The History of the County Palatine and City of Chester* (Chester: printed by John Fletcher, 1817) p. 256).

22–28 I am sorry [...] intirely innocent] recipes for medications were frequently kept and passed on to friends and relatives, as Spenser does here (Kelly, 'Domestic Medication', p. 122).

Recipe] some of the characters in this recipe are too unusual to admit of even approximate reproduction here.

[folio 116]

[To Mrs Alice Price

Brynypiece]

Waterford 12th March 1760

Madam

Your Favour of the 20th February came with the Pacquets due when I was on my Survey, from which I returned last Night. I am sincerely concerned to find, by the whole Scope thereof, that you too much give your self up to Melancholy, the late Disorder you have gone thro', with some Dissapointments / I am heartily sorry you have met with / must have encreased those gloomy Thoughts you so feelingly express; yet Madam please to reflect how much you are answerable to let them prey too much on you; to your self, your Son, the Poor to whom you have ever been a great Benefactor, & to a higher Power than all: I should think my self extreamly ∧^{happy} if I could give any Hint that could induce you to shake off all melancholy Reflections, as it can be so greatly enlarged & animadverted on by one of your extensive & superior Understanding, & this believe me I offer with my whole Heart; How pleasing ought the Thought be, that in a few Months you may have the Satisfaction of fondling in your Arms a little Grand-Child, who may have all the little Smiles of his dear Papa which often made you happy, & which will be all rememberd in him, how agreeable the View thereof must be, & ought it not help to Shake off all disquietudes: Parting with Mr Price to go to South Wales I think need not much trouble you, for I am convinced he will not be on Action there, & the Militia are not to be sent abroad, but the Parting you so feelingly mention, long very long may it be from you; my Reason for thinking there will not be Action for the

---

2 my Survey] at this point Spencer was supervisor of the Wexford hearth tax district (Barnard, *Irish Protestant Ascents and Descents*, p. 297), so this probably refers to his having to conduct a survey of the number of hearths in his district (an apparently unpopular exercise with the householders which would have been part of his duties); the words 'survey' and 'surveyor' have long had a close correlation with taxation, the *OED* 1709 illustration of the latter word including the phrase 'a Surveyor and 16 Tidewaiters [i.e. customs officers]'. In the next letter (ll.14–15) he complains, 'could I have been absent from my Survey I would have gone to Dublin'; as that letter was written nearly six months later than this one it would seem that these surveys were time-consuming affairs.

4 Melancholy] in humoral theory this was believed to be caused by an excess of black bile; by the eighteenth century the term 'melancholy' could be applied to any form of sadness or mild depression and could be used to describe inanimate objects, such as landscapes; it generally was thought more to affect men, who had hot and dry constitutions, than women.

Militia is founded on the low State of the French Marine, so that they can't be able to invade England, nor do I think they will even attempt us, the Fate of Thurot & his Squadron will deter; yet we were greatly alarmd last Week with a Rumour that twenty thousand French were landed in the County of Clare; & realy if there was a Landing I can't see how we could oppose them for some Time, as our Militia is not arrayed nor the Act yet passd, it seems votes of Credit are of greater consequence than arming the Protestants to defend themselves — I write to Mr Pearde this Night to delay his Visit, and will also obey your Orders by detaining Mr Pearde's last Paym^{t} in my Hands to be ready on Occasion, to answer Law Demands —

My Wife & Daughter join me in our best Respects to you & Wishes for the Recovery of your Health

Iam Madam
Y^{r} most obedient Servant
EdmSpencer

Please to present our Respects to Mr Price and his Lady when you write to him ——

25 Militia] the Militia Act of 1757 aimed to create a professional reserve military force.

27 Thurot & his Squadron] François Thurot, a French privateer and naval captain, took three ships into Belfast Lough in February 1760, landed a force of some 600 men near Carrickfergus, took the castle there and held it for several days. He was forced to abandon the action by the arrival of a Royal Navy squadron and was killed in the pursuit that followed (<https://en.wikipedia.org/wiki/François_Thurot> [accessed 3 September 2015]).

31 votes of Credit] votes that were taken in Parliament to empower the administration to borrow in anticipation of expenditure (see *OED*, *credit*, n.11, though the earliest illustration of the phrase is for 1854); in the next letter Spencer notes that 'the present low Ebb of Cash renders Credit also very low' (ll.8–9) so there may have been a particular sense of urgency behind such votes at this point.

32 arming [...] themselves] this is an oddly detached piece of phrasing, suggesting as it does that 'the Protestants' are a group that the writer does not belong to, and that their need to 'defend themselves' is not his need; again, one is inclined to wonder whether this is because, though not identifying with it, he nevertheless has some sympathy with the Catholic faith, and hence feels he has nothing personally to fear from a French invasion.

[folio 117]

[To *From M^{r} Ed: Spencer*
with a bill on Mr Peter Cazalet
merch^{t} in London for
£65–8-4 English value of
Mrs Alice Price the Elder
£70 Irish
Dated waterford
Sepr ye 1 — 1760 Wrexham
~~Brynypiece~~]

Madam Waterford 1..st Sepr 1760

Above you have Messrs Newport's Bill on Mr Peter Cazalet London for £65:8:4 English for £70:- Irish Exch.^{d} at £7:- p Cent 21 days. after Sight payable to you as I suppose Mr Price is with his Command; the above is a remittance lately made by Mr Pearde for December Gale, to my very great Concern I find my self incapable of answering immediately your last Orders, being dissapointed in two places where I had just Reason to expect a Compliance with my Request having often obliged them in more material Sums, but the present low Ebb of Cash renders Credit also very low, I have therefore wrote to the Person who has my little Fortune at Interest to remit me <~~xxx~~> Sufficient thereof to answer this Emergency. / for the Gentleman on whose Acc^{t} I expended great Part of it, I know can't at present answer it / and I expect very shortly to be able to send you a bill for it, could I have been absent from my Survey I would have gone to Dublin & am pritty certain I should not have been dissapointed,

———————————

<**>
closing Months, twas impossible for me to be a day absent from

In line with Spencer's general habit, this letter is written on a sheet folded once to create four sides; the letter is written on the first two sides and the address on the fourth side after the sheet had been folded again, twice horizontally and twice vertically, to make a packet; in this instance, though, the folded half that forms the first two sides has been cut across halfway down so that the whole sheet, when opened out, forms the shape of a step. We can assume that this was done by Spencer because he has started the letter with the address and the salutation at the very top of the first half side.

Address] the address 'Wrexham' is followed by the deleted 'Brynypiece'; in the note she writes on this letter Alice Price refers to 'a vissit from two ladais yester evening — who I had never seen or heard of since I Came to wrexham'; clearly she has moved from the family home to Wrexham after the marriage of her son; in the letter that was written between that one and this and which was addressed to her at Bryn y Pys (12 March 1760: folio 116) Spencer refers to 'some Dissapointments / I am heartily sorry you have met with / [which] must have encreased those gloomy Thoughts you so feelingly express' (ll.5–7). Perhaps, then, the marriage has caused a rupture between Alice Price and her son, or, as all the remaining letters are to Richard Price, it could be ill-health that has caused her retiring to Wrexham.

Duty —— Mr Wallis did not make his Way as I expected being obliged to go home thro' Limerick but will be here before Term, when I will consult him on the Opinion & Letter & will communicate his Sentiments thereon to you. I hope the fine Season has quite establishd your Health, & that Mr Price & his Lady are well. my Wife and Daughter present their best Respects to you & them with those of Madam

Your most obed^{t} Servant
EdSpencer

———————————

pray my dear be so good to enter ~~this~~ this bill pd from m^{r} Peard it was due as you see m^{r} Spencr mentions Decem^{r} ye 4–1759 — but pray first enter the half years Rent pd by young peard last Spring — & is now in m^{r} Spencers hands — owing to my folly — however you must give m^{r} Peard Credit for that half years Rent in your account — as One sinc the 4–1759 — & which if mr Spencer is not able to pay you I will — I Cannot exactly Remember what the Sum was English value — I know it was £70 Irish but the exchange & Receivers fees — had Reduced it — I think to Sixty pound or very little more — the exchange differs but Receivers fees is 1^{s} ye pound — which is 3–10–0

I pray God allmighty Bless & preserve you in health & safety y^{r} affec:' mama
A Price

m^{r} adams voice was much admired yesterday in wrexham Church — & I verily believe accasion'd me a vissit from two ladais yester evening — who I had never seen or heard of since I Came to wrexham — both maiden ladais — the younger a<> a very large fortune — I believe he is gone to Breakfast with them — for it seems they were not strangers to m^{r} adams — tho' they were so' to me — I shall write to m^{r} Spencer to morrow*

16] the top line has been partially erased and hence rendered illegible by the chamfering of the support paper to which this letter has been pasted.

25–47 *pray* [...] *to morrow*] this note, from Alice Price to her son, is written on the third (and whole) page of the oddly shaped folded sheet on which Spencer's letter is written; Alice Price has then forwarded the letter to Richard Price, with the information about the bill Spencer has sent her written around the address. Alice Price's hand has some distinctive features, such as the /c/ which looks like a capital, though often in the middle of a word; other capital usages are odd, such as the lower case initial in some names; the spelling is generally conventional but prone to oddities such as /accasion'd/ in l.20 and /ladais/ in l.21. Superscription is used but is not always clear.

37 *3–10–0*] one shilling in the pound on £70 is 70 shillings in old money which is £3/10/0 (3 x 20 + 10), £3.50 in decimal money.

[folio 118]

[To Richard Parry Price Esqr
With a bill on Messrs Haywoods
in Liverpool for £62–13–1 Eng.^{h}
dated ~~Liv~~ Waterford feb.^{y} 27–1761

Brynypiece]

Dear Sir

Above you have Messrs Newport's Draft on Messrs Heywood in Liverpoole 21 days Sight for £62:13:1 English Exchange at £6 p Cent for £66:8:3½ Irish money, which with £3:12: 8½ the value of Mr Pearde's Cow & Expences attending her being drove, make £70––– for his Gale at June last. And under the same Cover with this Letter I inclose for your Perusal, a Letter I have just received from Mr Wallis relating to the Affair / except the Postscript / — To me it appears the Barry Family are diffident of their Title, or sure they would order their Driver to be supported, which you will see by the inclosed has not been done as we have obtained Judgement without their Appearance, and I am very certain that your Title by the Deed of Sale is a good one, yet I make no doubt but it will be contested as the Concern is too valuable to be peaceably given up. — I have been in a miserable Situation since Michaelmas last with my own, my Wife's & my Daughter's Illness who is not yet well enough recoverd to leave her Chamber. this hinderd my being able to meet in Dublin the Gentleman I so much wanted to settle with to enable me

---

[*to make*] you a [*Remittance f*]or my [*self*], which must [*be done*] as soon as I can fix him; the many Disapointments I have lately experienced will caution me never to make use of any thing belonging to another on

3 £66:8:3½ [...] £3:12: 8½] if these figures are correct the total would be £70.1.0, not £70.

4 drove] i.e. taken by a landlord in the place of owed rent, a common practice in eighteenth-century Ireland (see also 25 April 1748: folio 72, ll.9–10); in this case the cow was driven by a cattle driver working for Lady Barrymore and presumably acting on her instruction (see l.9), this act being an assertion of the Barrymores' right to the rent from Mohire and hence their title to the estate; ll.8–11 make it clear that the poor driver was subsequently hung out to dry by her ladyship as he was the one who was prosecuted for taking the cow, even though he was acting for someone else when he did so; this is confirmed in the letter which Spencer encloses with this one (see l.6) in which Mr Wallis, the lawyer handling the case, states: 'I have obtained Judgment by Default ag.st Lady ––– Barrymores Driver <~~x~~> on the Action I brought ag.st him, for Selling H. Peard Cow' (Puleston 25: NLW MS 3585C, folio 15, ll.2–5; see Appendix I). In the next letter (ll.9–12) we learn that the cattle driver — hardly surprisingly one might think — tries to escape the long arm of this oppressive law which effectively fines him £10 (a very considerable sum of money) for carrying out his aristocratic employer's bidding.

any Acc^{t} whatsoever, nor should I have done so in this, but that I thought I was to apply it occasionally as the Lawyers would require, which I must acknowledge is but a poor Excuse, yet it is the real Truth — You will please to give me advice of the Rec^{t} of the above Bill which I got on Liverpoole, thinking it more convenient to you there than on London, but if not so please to inform me & the next shall be on London —— My Wife and Daughter join me in our best Wishes for & Respects to you, your Lady, & your good Mother

I have the Honour to be

Dear Sir Your sincerely affectionate
Kinsman & most humble Servant
EdmSpencer

Waterford 27th Feb.^{ry} 1761

[folio 119]

[*From Mr Spencer with*
a bill on Messrs C^{r} & [J^{y}] Muilman
To Richard Parry Price Esqr
merch^{ts} in London for £65–14–6
dated Waterford Octr 21–1761

Brynypiece]

Waterford 21st Octr 1761—

Dear Sir

Above you have Messrs Newport's draft on Messrs Muilman London for £65:14:8½ English Ex$^{\underline{ed}}$ at £6½ for £70— Irish which I received from Harry Pearde the 3^{d} Ins^{t} at Clonmell where I had been some Time speeding a Commission, I came from thence the 7th Ins.^{t} but could not get a bill on London till this Day as all the bills here were on Bristol & I chose to delay rather than send one on that Place as I believed it would be troublesome to negociate it at Chester. I know no better way to show you the Reason of this Delay than by sending you the inclosed which I received at Clonmell. I must also inform you that Lord Barrymore's Driver was taken at Castlelyons on an Execution for Damages ab^{t} £10 but I find has made his Escape, I shall know of Mr Wallis what Method must ^^{be} used to retake him / if possible / when I see him, which I expect to do shortly — Youll please to give me Advice when you receive this, directed to me at Churchtown near Charleville, whither I intend to set out to Morrow, my Wife having gone on thither from Clonmell, where we are to spend a couple of Months with my Daughter & her Husband— I am then promised to have some Money paid me ^{in} which I have for some Time past been often dissapointed, which has obliged me to sue for it in order to make a remittance to you — I paid Mr Wallis's Bill of

Cost about £15— some Time agoe — With my best Respects to Mrs Price & your Good Mother I am Dear Sir

Your Sincerely aff^{te} Kinsman
& most humble Servant
EdmSpencer

1 Messrs Newport's] Spencer tell us he has been in Clonmell for some time so this is possibly the banking family of Clonmel, 'a prominent Waterford family of Dutch extraction' (*DIB*).

3 Clonmell] this town is some fifty miles north-east of Cork and twenty five miles west of Waterford.

10–14 Lord Barrymore's [...] do shortly] see note to l.9 of the previous letter.

[folio 120]

[To Richard Parry Price Esqr
Brynypiece]

Dear Sir

I received your Favour, acknowledging the Rec^{t} of the Bill, in due Course --- The inclosed from Mr Wallis came this Day, which I send for your Perusal; I desired him if possible to put off the Record till Spring Assyzes, least the Original Papers might not be sent over Time enough; you see by the inclosed Lord Barrymore means to try the Title and in my Opinion his Agents know nothing of the Deed of Sale, which certainly when brought into the Plea must discontent them; twill be absolutely necessary to send over the Originals as speedily as possible; I need not recommend it to you to take Care to send by a careful Person, as they are of very great Consequence, & please to direct them for Mr Henry Wallis Attorney at his House in Aungier Street Dublin, As ∧$^{fast\ as}$ I receive Acco^{ts} of the Proceedings from him I shall acquaint you therewith.

My Wife joins me in our best Respects to your good Mama & you, & sincere Wishes for little Frank. I am D^{r}Sir

Your very affec^{te} Kinsman
& most obedient Servant
EdmSpencer

Waterford 28th June 1762 ——

2 The inclosed [...] Wallis] for this letter see Appendix 1; despite the episode of the driven cow going against them (see 27 February 1761: folio 118, ll.1–13), and just as Spencer predicted when he said in that letter, 'I make no doubt but it will be contested as the Concern is too valuable to be peaceably given up' (ll.12–13), the Barrymores show that they are determined to press their claim on the Mohire estate.

13–14 Aungier Street] this ran due north-south, just south of Dublin Castle.

17 little Frank] i.e. Richard Price's son, Francis Parry Price who died in 1787 aged twenty six (memorial in St Mary's Church, Overton).

Folio 122: Accounts

The tables of accounts presented on the next two pages are not two separate sheets but a single sheet that has been folded in half and then glued into the archive volume by its spine in such a way that these pages form the outer sides of the folded sheet, i.e. sides one and four. Side one is the first to be seen in the archive volume and hence has the folio number written on it, though in fact it is the right-hand side of the fully opened sheet, as can be seen from the top lines of the two sides reading continuously across the full width of the sheet. Here, the left hand side of the sheet is reproduced on page 216 and the right hand side on page 217. In the final line the word /Errors/ also needs to be read across to connect with the final line on the right-hand side of the sheet: /Errors Excepted 28th Novr 1774 EdmSpencer/.

{*folio 122*}

Deb.^{r} Edmund Spencer's Acco.^{t} Curr.^{t} with R[ic]

1774

	Tenant's Names	Denominations	Y$^{\partial}$ly Rents			Paym.^{ts}			in full of	
1	The King	Parliam.^{t} House . .	240	10	. .	541	. 2	.6	24th June	
2	Mrs Freeman	College Green . .	14	. .	. .	35	. .	. .	Ditto	now her Son
3	Mr Wm Burne . . .	Ditto	9	. .	. .	27	. .	. .	1st Nov^{r} {	John Gillmer Esqr
4	Mr Kingsbury . . .	Turnstile Ally	9	. 5	. .	23	. 2	.6	25th March {	pays once a year
5	the Same	Ditto	3	. .	. .	7	10	. .	Ditto	
6	the Same	Ditto	6	. .	. .	15	. .	. .	Ditto	
7	James Doyle	Ditto	5	. .	. .	15	. .	. .	1st Feb. $^{\partial y}$	Den.^{s} Brett
8	John&Thos Taylor .	Ditto	20	. .	. .	40	. .	. .	1st June	
9	Mr Kingsbury . . .	Mylers Ally	1	10	. .	3	15	. .	25th March	
	M^{r} McCaghran . . .	Ditto	5	. .	. .	12	10	. .	24th June	
	Thos Bourke	Ditto	5	10		12	. 2	10½	On Acco.^{t}	Ann Bourke
	Wm Barrington . . .	Bull Ally	12	. .	. .	30	. .	. .	24th June	
3	Mr Anth$^{\partial}$ Bacon . .	Bride Street	30	. .	. .	75	. .	. .	Ditto	Miss Eliz Bacon
14	Mr Thos Gleadowe .	Ditto	8	. .	. .	16	. .	. .	25th March {	Wm Gleadowe Newcomen Esq
15	Ball's House	Ditto (now set for	16	. .	. .	30	. .	. .	1st May	Thos Conolly
16	Percival Hunt Esqr	Ditto	15	. .	. .	37	10	. .		
17	Mrs Marg.^{t} Church .	Ditto	15	. .	. .	37	10	. .	Ditto	
18	Mr Danl Lawrence	Ballard	45	. .	. .	90	. .	. .	29 Sepr 1773	
19	the Same	Cullentragh	45	. .	. .	90	. .	. .	1st Novr 1773	
20	Saml Stayes Esqr	Clonckeen	4	. .	. .				owes two Y.^{rs}	rent 1st May
	Mr Kingsbury for Taylors Holding . .		. .	. .	. .	14	. 4	. 3	to 1.st June 1772	N° 8
	Part of Arrears of Balls House recoverd		. .	. .	. .	3	19	. 7½		N° 15
	Renewal Fine from Mrs Church		. .	. .	. .	15	. .	. .		N° 17
					£	1171	.6	.9		Errors

[folio 122]

h.^{d} Parry Price Esqr from 4th July 1772 to 28th Novr 1774, Cred.^{r}

		£	s	d
	By Cash paid repairs of Bales Stable in July 1772	1	. 2	. 9
	By Cash to Couns^{r} Wood with a Case for his Opinion in Novr 1772	2	. 5	. 6
	By Mr Gleadowe's Bill on Mr Folliot of Chester sent 14th Decr 1772	200	. .	. .
	By Cash paid register$^{∂}$ Taylor's lease in Jan$^{∂}$ 1773	. .	. 4	. 4
	By Mr Gleadowe's Bill on Mr Folliot of Chester sent 27th Augt 1773	230	. .	. .
	By Cash paid repairs of Mr Caghran's House in Myler's Ally Sep^{r}	.	17	. 2½
	By Cash paid repairs of Ball's House	1	. 4	11
	By Mr Gleadowe's Bill on Mr Folliot of Chester sent 10th March 1774 . . .	220	. .	. .
	By three years Rent of Ballard & Cullentrogh to 29.th Sept.$^{r∂}$ last and 1st Novr Ins.^{t} paid M.^{r} & Mrs Marshall . . . . }	73	16	. .
	By three years Rent of the Chanter's Orchard to 29.th Sept.$^{r∂}$ last paid the Rev.d Doctor Caulfeild . . . . }	36	. .	. .
	By three years Rent of Turnstile Ally to 29.th Sepr last paid Mr Levinge . . . . }	30	15	. .
	By two years Rent of the Bishop of Ossory's Burying Ground to 25th March last paid the Churchwardens of St Audeon's Parish }	4	. .	.
	By Fees at the Auditor General's Office for nine Debentures	2	. 8	. 9
	By Postage paid for Letters to this Day	.	. 8	. 3
	By Poundage of £1171 : 6 : 9	58	11	. 4
Novr 28th	By Balance sent this day Mr Gleadowes Bill on Mr Folliot in Chester £285 : 16 : 4 Exchange for Irish }	309	12	. 8½
	£	1171	. 6	. 9
Excepted	28th Novr 1774 EdmSpencer			

{folio 122 Verso}

Postage
1772

		s	d
June 26th date of a Letter from.	Mr Hayman. . . .	1	: 6
July 24th	. . . . Mr Price	1	: 1
Augt 26th	. . . . Mr Hayman . . .		: 11
Dec.r 11th	. . . . the Same		: 7
24th	. . . . Mr Price		: 7
1773			
Sep.r 6th	. . . . the Same		: 6
1774			
March 22d	. . . . the Same	1	: 1
June 25th	. . . . Mr Hayman . . .		: 7
Augt 4th	. . . . the Same		: 6
Sep.r 14th	. . . . Mr Studley		: 11
	£0	: 8	: 3

[Nb]
Mr Spencers
last Acct sent
to England
of his Rects
in Ireland
tho repeatedly
solicited to ^send th[e]
succeeding one[s]
by Mr Price
in his Life
Time —

This postage account is written on the top left-hand of the verso side of the sheet that forms folio 122. The note in the bottom right-hand corner is in pencil and in a hand other than Spencer's; its being right up against the central fold of the sheet would suggest that it was written after the sheet was folded. The note implies that Spencer stopped, for some reason or other, working for Richard Price in very late 1774 or 1775, even though Richard Price expected him to carry on doing so. The phrase 'in his Life Time' suggests that Richard Price (grammatically the antecedent of the phrase) is, at the date of writing, dead, which would mean the note was written at least eight years later, as he died in 1782.

APPENDIX I: ADDITIONAL LETTERS FROM THE PULESTON COLLECTION

The letters included here are also from the Puleston Collection and they shed an interesting light on Spencer's situation, some of the events and business referred to in the letters, and the social world in which he lived.

The first two are the final letters in the volume in which Spencer's letters are archived and they were written to Francis Price by H. Williams late in 1747 in response to Price's asking for help in finding Spencer a place in the Irish Revenue office — a favour that Spencer notes in his letters of 5 January 1747: folio 65 and 16 January 1747: folio 66. As the second of these two letters was sent under Williams's own frank he was most likely a member of parliament, and the address, Grosvenor Street, would lend support to that idea. The only MP whose name fits is Charles Hanbury-Williams (1708–1759), but he lost his seat (Monmouthshire) in 1747 shortly before the date of the first letter, becoming then envoy to Dresden, where one might therefore have expected him to have been during that year.[1] However, he could easily have been in England at the time these letters were written, could still have been entitled to franks as an envoy, and he did have an interest in Ireland which could explain why Price had written to him. Whoever the writer of these letters is, though, they show how widely Price was casting his net in the hope of obtaining Spencer a position in the revenue, and illustrate neatly, along with Price's draft letter on folio 124, the way the eighteenth-century system of patronage worked when it came to finding employment.

The third letter,[2] from William Pearde (the man Barnard identifies as Spencer's half-brother but whom Spencer himself refers to as his uncle)[3] shows that Spencer's financial situation had become so dire in the early 1740s that he had been incarcerated in the notorious 'Black Dog' Debtors' Prison, near the Cornmarket in Dublin, which ran from *c.*1700–1794.[4] Pearde, as his address shows, lived in Castlelyons where Lord Barrymore had his main Irish estate, and it is possible that he worked for Barrymore there in some capacity. He, like Spencer, had a substantial correspondence with Price, some of it suggesting, as this letter does, that he felt it his job to report to Price on Spencer's behaviour: Barnard quotes from another one

1 <http://www.historyofparliamentonline.org> [accessed 18 February 2016].

2 Letter dated 26 February 1741/2, Puleston 19: NLW MS 3579D, folio 56.

3 Barnard, *Irish Protestant Ascents and Descents*, p. 292.

4 Maurice Curtis, *To Hell or Monto: The Story of Dublin's Most Notorious Districts* (Stroud: The History Press, 2015), ch. 8.

of Pearde's letters to Price in which he suggests that Spencer is living beyond his means and is being led into this reckless expenditure by his wife.[5] However, there are other letters in which he supports 'poor Spencer' in his increasingly desperate search for employment: in August 1741 he told Price that 'his case is melancholy, I don't doubt if there was proper application made to the Duke of Marlborough but he w[ill] get him a civil or Military Employment. I assure you he's a young gentleman of very good parts [...] if Lord Barrymore is intimate with the Duke, I am sure as he has a kindnesse for Spencer and be good natured enough to introduce him'.[6] The letter is interesting for the verbal parallels it has with Spencer's letter of 2 August 1741: folio 4, suggesting that the two of them might have been working in concert to persuade Price to speak to Barrymore about mentioning Spencer's plight to Marlborough.

The fourth letter is from Lord Barrymore to Francis Price and was written the day before he was imprisoned for treason.[7] Barrymore is clearly not referring to the weather when he complains about being unable to get outside and exercise. The comment about 'old Grove' refers to the printer and journalist, Henry Cross-Grove (1683–1744), a well-known Jacobite who was constantly in trouble for his attacks on the Hanoverian establishment, delivered from his base in Norwich. Grove frequently complained that what he regarded as his legitimate criticism of Parliament was taken for treason.[8] Barrymore's letter is easy to decode and its message, to stay indoors and hope for the best rather than rising in open rebellion, would have been obvious to anyone reading it, which we should assume the authorities did. The judgement of Barrymore's *ODNB* biographer is hard to dispute: 'So ill-concealed were his movements and correspondence during the years prior to the 'Forty-Five that the government rightly judged that a public humiliation of "the Pretender's General" [...] would be of more value to the Hanoverian cause than another show trial'.[9]

The fifth and the sixth are from the attorney Henry Wallis and are the letters referenced in footnotes to Spencer's letters of 27 February 1761: folio 118 and 28 June 1762: folio 120.[10] As they were written to Spencer one might think it odd to find them amongst the Price's papers, but they were, of course, forwarded by him to the Prices so that they could read for themselves Wallis's reports and opinions on cases he was handling for them. What is actually more surprising is that there are not more of them, since it is clear from what he says in other letters that Spencer forwarded many similar communications he had with Henry Wallis and other people with whom he was working on behalf of the Price family.

5 Barnard, *Irish Protestant Ascents and Descents*, p. 292.

6 Letter dated 7 August 1741, Puleston 19: NLW MS 3579D, folio 59.

7 Letter dated 22 February 1744, Puleston 22: NLW MS 3582D, folio 87.

8 J. B. Williams, 'Henry Cross-Grove, Jacobite Journalist and Printer', *The Library*, 3rd ser., 5 (1914), 206–24. It is hard to know whether Barrymore's caution had a fatal impact on the progress of The Forty-Five: as Paul Langford comments: '"Now is the time or never", the Prince wrote to Barrymore as he prepared to march south from Carlisle. On the basis of his subsequent experience the answer was clearly never' (*A Polite and Commercial People: England 1727–1783* (Oxford: Clarendon Press, 1989), p. 200).

9 *ODNB*, entry for *Barry, James, 4th Earl of Barrymore.*

10 Puleston 25: NLW MS 3585C, folios 15 & 16.

These two letters are interesting in that they help to fill in the background detail to two of the Price's disputes with the Barrymore family after the death of the 4th Earl, but more than that they illustrate the nature of the relationship between Spencer and Wallis, the diminutive of 'Edmund' that he uses — 'Mon' — indicating a considerable intimacy between the two men. This also reminds us that nicknames, soubriquets, and pet names were a common element of the familiar letter in this period, and that the choice of name can be an important indicator of the nature of the relationship between the named and the namer. Barrymore's affectionate nickname for Francis Price, 'the Doctor', carries a clear valuation of Price's intelligence which seems to acknowledge a levelling of the considerable social distance between the two men.

The last document, given the multiple insertions, corrections, and recorrections, is most likely a draft, not the final copy of a letter.[11] It was written, according to the prefatory note on the first side of the sheet, by John, Bishop of Chester, and Thomas Lloyd of Bangor (who countersigns it on the final side). According to the National Library of Wales catalogue the bishop was John Pearson, Bishop of Chester from 1673 to 1686; no explanation of this ascription is given but presumably there are other documents relating to the separation of Worthenbury from Bangor that support it.[12] Whether Thomas Lloyd is the same Thomas Lloyd as Spencer's 'Trigger' is discussed in the footnote to 8 November 1743: folio 8, l.6, but we might note here that the definition of this Thomas Lloyd as being 'of Bangor' would not necessarily contradict such an identification since Lloyd is here acting in his role as patron of Bangor, rather than as a resident of a particular place. No date is given on the letter, the catalogue suggesting a date of 1683, again without explanation, but again presumably on the basis of supporting dateable documentation.

The letter announces the establishment of Worthenbury, hitherto a chapelry in the parish of Bangor, as a new 'Parish to it Self'. It also confirms Sir Roger Puleston and his heirs as the patrons of this new parish, and states that he has relinquished his and his heir's rights to the tithes of Worthenbury, which will henceforth be used to provide 'a house for ye parson & convenient glebe'. It is the final three lines, however, that are interesting for our purposes, as they seem to make a connection between the Overton curate's stipend (which Francis Price appears to have been responsible for paying through his tithe) and the revenues of the parish of Bangor, of which Trigger (whether the Thomas Lloyd of this letter or a later Thomas Lloyd) was the patron:

> & especially for y^{t} it is no ~~losse~~ for Bangor
> curates stipend of
> in its [*revenue*] hertofore Swallowed up in the [*Overton*] but is now very Consi
> derable [*revenue*] to ye future parsons of Worthenbury.

Whether that has any bearing on the dispute that Francis Price was engaged in,

11 Puleston 15: NLW MS 3575E, folio 1.

12 There were two earlier Johns who were bishops of Chester (John Bridgeman, 1619-1652, and John Wilkins, 1668-1672) but there was no later bishop of Chester named John until the second quartile of the nineteenth century.

though, is impossible to say with any certainty. The payment and ownership of tithes was a horribly complex business, and we have insufficient evidence to assess whether this case has any relationship to the situation in Overton some fifty or so years later.

How the document came to be in this archive is another question. It may be that Francis Price obtained it as evidence in the dispute over tithes in which he appears to have been involved; more likely, however, is that it was in the Puleston family's archive — the draft perhaps having been sent to the Sir Roger Puleston mentioned in the letter for his approval — that archive then being combined with the Price archive when Richard Parry Price (1765–1840) married into that family and adopted its name.

[folio 129]

Dear Sir

I have the favour of your Letter & will certainly recommend the Gentleman in as Strenuous amanner as possible & hope to Succeed, The Charter Petition at presen[*t*] seems to be made a point of I fancy you'll join with me in thinking, Sir Robert Grosvenour ought to be here & endeavour to interpose as far as in his power with the Minister before its too late & certainly the sooner the better we have nothing new ~~here~~ but whats in the Papers, when anything happens

————————

I will give You the trouble of another Letter I beg my Complimts to your Lady & am

Dear Sir

Your most Obedient
humble Servant
HWilliams

Grosvenor Street 24 November
1747

4 The Charter Petition] along with many other major ports of England, Liverpool petitioned parliament in 1749 to have the Hudson Bay Company's charter annulled on the grounds that it interfered with open trade in Canada (*Politics and the Port of Bristol in the Eighteenth Century: The Petitions of the Society of Merchant Venturers 1698–1803*, ed. by W. E. Minchinton (Bristol: Bristol Record Society, 1963), p. 69); Williams's assumption that Price would be interested in this matter supports the suggestion that he had some financial interest in the Liverpool trade (see the Introduction).

6–7 Sir Robert Grosvenour] 1695–1755, MP for Chester (1733–1755) and mayor of Chester (1737); he seems to have had a reputation as a Jacobite, as during the Forty-Five he was 'supposed to be marching to join the Young Pretender in Lancashire', though he was actually at court at the time (<http://www.historyofparliamentonline.org/volume/1715-1754/member/grosvenor-robert-1695-1755> [accessed 28 March 2016]).

[folio 130]

[To
Francis Price Esqr at
Bryn apeace near Overton
Flintshire
Free
Hwilliams]

Dear Sir

I have the pleasure to acquaint you that I am promis'd strong recommendations in behalf of your Friend to the Commissioners of the Revenue in Ireland and have the greatest hopes of his Succeeding. please to let me know how to Direct to him that he may wait upon them. Ishall allways be glad to have it in my power to Oblige you I am Sir

Your most Obedient hble Servt
HWilliams

my Compliments attend Mrs Price

Grosvenor Street 3^{d} Decem. 47

D:^{r} Sir

Since my last to you I rece.^{d} a lett^{r} from Harry Critchley in wch he gave me an acc.^{t} of M:^{r} Spencer, who was taken xmass Eve by two Baliffs as he was paying his way in Order to sett Sail for England y:^{e} next day, it was a debt due to his Aunt Spencer, who was left by her father £500 on y:^{e} lands of Renny as a portion in Case she married, if not, was to have £20 p ann as a support wch last June was not duly paid, so y.^{e} poor Spencer, who she persecuted, in Order to stop her—— Mouth, past her his Bond for £100, wch at her death she left to One Byrne, poor you =ng gentleman was confined along time in y:^{e} black dogg, at last gott Out on giving Baile for his appearance, how hee'l be able to discharge y:^{e} debt I can't tell, but cant stirre from Dublin till some end is put to it, this is an additional misfortune; the poor Secretary, was, last Week taken very ill w.th a Violent trembling they thought he w.^{d} have died, 'tis believd now to be an ague, should anything happen him, I begg you'l use y.^{r} interest w.th <~~x~~> Lord Barrymore in my fav.^{r} [*Carly*] has wed. y.^{r} kind [*Gent*] wch will be a gr[*eat*] Support to him & his poor family, I am w:th best resp:^{s} to you & M:^{rs} Price and Service to Master Price .

Dear Sir

your most affect.
Hum^{ble} Servt
Willm Pearde.

Castlelyons
Feb.^{ry} y:^{e} 26:th 1741–2.

2 Harry Critchley] possibly the 'Mr Critchly' mentioned in 19 July 1755: folio 96, l.30.

6 his Aunt Spencer] Spencer had an aunt called Susanna (the daughter of William Spenser, his grandfather, who had owned Renny) so the bequest Pearde mentions is plausible; his account of the reason for the arrest, however, is not ideally clear: Susanna died in 1737 (Welply, 'The Family and Descendants of Edmund Spenser', p. 257), some three years before this event took place, so the failure to pay 'last June' (ll.9–10) does not make much sense; presumably Pearde is conflating the £20 per year she was to get for not having married with the £100 Spencer agreed to pay her 'in Order to stop her---- Mouth' (ll.11–12), and which she in turn bequeathed to Byrne, who is actually the person responsible for Spencer's imprisonment.

15 y:^{e} black dogg] the Dublin debtors' prison.

{hole}ry Febr: 22^{d} 1744

Dear Price,

This covers the <~~xxx~~> you sent me wch I send to
Maurice Mathers to forward to you, in a <~~xx~~> or
two I will write to the Coll. my thoughts on it
and advise him to make a fair offer for your
Interest in it for he cannot sett it aside and must
pay whatever the kings rent is for you have nothing
to doe wth that, the Continuance off the bad
weather and the Impossibility for me to take
any Exercise almost destroyes mee
our friends that went to petition parliament, as
old Grove, used to phrase it, had much
better have been quiet at home when matters
are dry. perhaps it may rub out
all our services attend Mrs Price you & my
Godson. I Expect Dick soon he has a promise
off a Ship that is as hereafter may bee
I Longe to see you I am

Dear Doctor

y^{rs} Sincerly
Barrymore

10 to petition parliament] before people had a vote petitioning was the most usual form of political action, and numerous petitions were presented to parliament in the eighteenth century (Joanna Innes, 'Legislation and Public Participation', in *The British and Their Laws in the Eighteenth Century*, ed. by David Lemmings (Woodbridge: Boydell, 2005), pp. 102–32 (pp.114–15)); Barrymore, though, may be using the term 'petition' as a code for rather more direct action.

11 old Grove] the Jacobite printer and journalist, Henry Cross-Grove.

11-13 had much … rub out] this passage is obscure, perhaps deliberately so in order to maintain the 'coded' nature of the communication; Barrymore might be continuing the weather metaphor of ll. 7-9, saying that the Jacobite plotters have risked revealing themselves too soon, thereby creating a 'storm' which makes any action on his part too dangerous to pursue; better for them to lie low — keep 'quiet at home' — when their affairs are not progressing well — i.e., are 'dry' in the sense of sterile or unfruitful; the 'perhaps' could equally well introduce a pessimistic or an optimistic conclusion, 'rub out' meaning either 'be obliterated and come to nothing' or 'work out successfully'.

15 Dick] the Hon. Richard Barry (*c.*1720–1787), the second of Lord Barrymore's sons; while a lieutenant in the English navy he negotiated with the French on behalf of the English Jacobites, and became a close friend of the Young Pretender; in January 1744 he was sent by his father to join the French expedition against England; as noted here by Barrymore, he managed to obtain a ship but the expedition was abandoned; in 1745 he went to Derby to offer Charles Stuart the support of his father and Sir Watkin Williams-Wynn but arrived two days after Charles had left; that act apparently ended his naval career (<http://www.historyofparliamentonline.org> [accessed 8 April 2016]).

[To
Mr Edm.^{d} Spencer
Esq
Waterford]

Dublin Feb[*t*]y ye 24th: 1761

Dr Mon

It gave me great pleasure to hear by yr^{s} that yr family are so much better. I have obtained Judgment by Default ag.st Lady — Barrymores Driver <~~x~~> on the Action I brought ag.st him, for Selling H. Peard Cow, & I have Issued a Writ of Inquiry, / in ord.^{r} to Assert the Damages Sustained by H: / wch is to be sped as soon as I go into the Country, and I am pritty Sure that we shall good Damages, I am Dr Mon

y.^{rs} Sincerely
Hen: Wallis

I wish you wo.^{d} let me know how much rent Pole owes for [*Camage*]

2 yr family [...] better] nonetheless Spencer reports to Richard Price in the letter with which this one is enclosed that he has been 'in a miserable Situation since Michaelmas last with my own, my Wife's & my Daughter's Illness' and that his daughter in particular 'is not yet well enough recoverd to leave her Chamber' (27 February 1761: folio 118, ll.14–16), giving this as the reason for his not dealing with some financial difficulty that affects Richard Price.

6 Writ of Inquiry] 'a writ requiring the summoning of a jury to enquire into what damages a plaintiff has sustained as the result of another person's actions' (*OED*, *inquiry*, 3).

6 Assert] 'lay claim to' (*OED*, v.4).

7 sped] 'expedited, prosecuted' (*OED*, *speed*, v.8.b)

9 shall good] presumably Wallis has omitted 'get'.

Dublin June the 26th: 1762

Dr Mon

I arrived here last Thursday morning & I find that Ld Barrymore is Determined to proceed upon the Replevin, he has filed a very Long Avowry wch I have laid before Co Wood with Copys of all the Deeds & the English Opinion you gave me in Ord.^{r} to Draw a Plea in Barr, You must Imediately Write to England to have ∧ ^{all} the Orig.^{l} Deeds relating to the lands of Mohery, sent over as soon as possible, least the record sho.^{d} be brought — down this Assises, to Tryal, wch I will prevent if possible, but you know we must Guard ag.st the Worst., I believe we shall be Oblidged to file a bill for an [*Inj͞on*], but you shall hear further from me Ab.^{t} this Matter by next Post. I am Dr Mon y.^{rs} Sincerely

= Hen: Wallis

3 Replevin] either 'a writ empowering a person to recover goods taken from him or distrained' (*OED*, n.2) or 'an action arising out of a case in which goods have been taken or distrained' (*OED*, n.3).

4 Avowry] 'the answering for or avowal of an act done, especially the plea whereby one who distrains for rent avows the act and justifies it' (*OED*, 5).

7 Plea in Barr] 'a plea either in abatement or in bar of an action or prosecution, alleging some new fact' (*OED*, *plea*, n.2.c).

10 the record] 'a copy of the material points, pleadings, and issue between defendant and plaintiff constituting the case to be decided; a case so constituted or presented' (*OED*, n.4.b); here probably in the latter sense of 'the case itself'.

14 [*Inj͞on*]] i.e. 'injunction', 'the judicial process by which a person is restrained from continuing wrongful behaviour, or is commanded to restore matters to the position in which they stood before that wrongful behaviour' (*OED*, 2).

To all Christian People to whom these p^{r}nts shall
come John by Divine Providence Bishop of Chester
and Thomas [*lL*]oyd of Bangor in the County of Flintshire
and Diociss of Chester Esq Send Greeting

———————————

~~in the Diocese of Chester~~
To all Xstian people John [*says*] greeting. whereas the Parish of Bangor ^ wth the
or Churches within the Diocese of Chester
Parochial Chappels ^ of Overton and Worthenbury ^ are of very great Extent & very
all the ~~Rector~~ Rector
populous, & by the Cure of ^ Souls incumbent upon y^{e} ~~parson~~ ^ of Bangor; & whereas
Worthenbury has its [*known*] ~~Townships~~ [*mesrs*] & bounds, & is remote fr^{m} y^{e} <~~xx~~>
churches of Bangor | also from | of Bangor <~~xxxx~~>
Parish ~~chappel of Bangor~~ & y^{e} Parsonage house, & whereas ~~as~~ also y^{e} ^ tithes in kind
of all y^{e} s^{d} <~~xxxx~~> <~~xxxx~~> ^ belong to Sr Roger Puleston & his hrs under a modus
<~~x~~> of <~~x~~>
of 20$^{\partial}$ p an ~~as hath been <*> ag^{d} by <****> verdicts & Judgem^{ts} given therupon~~, so
Parochial or Church of Worthenbury
as the said ^ Chappell ^ & cure of Soules there hath heretofore been rather a
Rectors
burthen than advantage to y^{e} Parsons of Bangor. And whereas Sr Roger
Puleston afores^{d} in pursuance of his Grandfathers intentions in y^{r} behalf
and Church of Worthen
gr^{t} & Parochial bury
hath declared his willingnesse to ^ confirm to the sd ^ chappell ^ for ever a house
thereof to
for ye parso^{-} & convenient glebe & to relinquish ye p^{r}scripts afores^{d} & ^ leave
Parochial Chappell or Church
the of Worthenbury
<~~x~~> tithes in kind to the parso^{-} these and his Succesors for ever So as this ~~Chappell~~ ^
and seperated
by all ness^{y} Townships & land wthin its known limits be secured ^ for the s^{d}

This document, Puleston 15: NLW MS 3575E, folio 1, is the letter referred to in the second note to l.3 of 8 November 1743: folio 8. Given the multiple insertions, corrections, and re-corrections, it is most likely a draft which was prepared for Thomas Lloyd to countersign and possibly also for Sir Roger Puleston to see and approve (and hence, possibly, its presence in the Puleston archive). For the attribution of the letter to John Pearson, Bishop of Chester (1673–1686) and its date, see the introductory note to this appendix.

1 p^{r}nts] abbreviation of /presents/, i.e. 'the present document' (*OED*, n^{1},2.b).

4 [*mesrs*]] abbreviation of /measures/ (?), possibly in the sense of 'size ascertained by measurement' (*OED*, n.2.a).

5 in kind] 'in the form of goods or produce rather than money' (*OED,* n.15).

10 under a modus] under an arrangement to pay the tithes in money rather than kind (*OED*, modus, 4); the agreed amount of £20 per annum is given in the next line.

and Rectory
parish ^ of Bangor ~~& made a Parish to it Self~~ & have a Distinct Rector to
Sr Puleston
be p^{r}sentable for ever by the s^{d} Roger ^ & his hrs. And whereas also Tho=
aforesaid
lloyd Esq the true & undoubted Patron of Bangor ^ hath in pursuance of a
the said
former agreem^{t} wth^ Sr Roger Pulestons Grandfather declared his consent &
Sr Puleston
be p^{r}sentable for ever by the s^{d} Roger ^ & his hrs. And whereas also Tho=
aforesaid
lloyd Esq the true & undoubted Patron of Bangor ^ hath in pursuance of a
the said
former agreem^{t} wth^ Sr Roger Pulestons Grandfather declared his consent &
desire y^{t} the same should be seperated accordingly. We considering Princi-
pally y^{e} [*promote*˜] of Gods Service & y^{e} benefitt of ye Church & y^{t} ye Cure of
Rector
so many Souls cannot so well be regarded by y^{e} ~~Parso~~^ of Bangor as by
aforesaid <******>
having another in Worthenbury^ & especially for y^{t} it is no ~~losse~~ for Bangor
curates stipend of
in its [*revenue*] hertofore Swallowed up in the [*Overton*] but is now very Consi
derable [*revenue*] to ye future parsons of Worthenbury

———————————

And I the sd Tho. Lloyd doe hereby as farre as in me lyes gr^{t} ratify
and Confirm all the matters [*abouesd*] agst me & my hrs for ever

18 ness^{y}] abbreviation of /necessary/.

27 [*promote*˜]] the main part of this word is clear enough, but the final mark, which looks too small for a letter, is not; there might also be a superscript mark just to the right of that final mark; if this is an abbreviation the whole word would be /promotion/ or /promoting/, which in either case would mean, 'furtherance, advancement or encouragement' (*OED*, *promotion*, 2.a).

30 [*Overton*]] this word is very unclearly formed, but it bears a distinct resemblance to the 'Overton' in l.2.

APPENDIX II: INDEX OF PEOPLE MENTIONED IN THE CORRESPONDENCE

The middle column gives the folio numbers of the letters in which the person is mentioned. The folio numbers are listed consecutively in this column, not in the order in which they appear in the transcription.

Biographical details, if known, are given where relevant in the footnotes.

Francis Price's wife, Alice, and his son, Richard, are referred to in the valediction of nearly every letter to Francis Price, as, usually, is Spencer's wife, Ann; these mentions are not referenced in the following index.

People mentioned in the accounts sent by Spencer to Richard Price (folios 122–23) are not indexed here.

Adam, Mr	117	He sings in Wrexham church and breakfasts the next morning with a young lady of large fortune.
Addis	8	A grocer in Cork whose widow marries Hodder Roberts, a friend of Price.
Alderman, The	12	Spencer expresses concern for this gentleman's health, and fears that the illness could be fatal. (This is presumably a nickname for a mutual acquaintance.)
	15	Spencer congratulates him in the postscript on his wife's pregnancy.
	22	He is involved in an intrigue with a 'gallant' lawyer which appears to have resulted in the birth of some illegitimate children; he is at the time of writing, though, apparently still unwell and confined to his house.
Annesley, Mr (Lord Altham)	10	James Annesley is mentioned as a successful litigant in the Four Courts, gaining an estate worth £400 per annum in Co. Meath, and the recognition of his claim to the title Lord Altham.

Apperly, Dr	10	A doctor and friend of Price, he appears to have had a lawsuit of some kind at Westminster, in which Spencer wishes him well.
	92	Though here called 'Master Apperly', this is quite possibly the same person; Spencer sends his compliments at the end of the letter.
	94	Named here as 'Mr', Spencer sends him compliments at the end of the letter.
Badham, Brettridge	8	He is mentioned as having paid Col. Barry 600 guineas for the parliamentary seat for his borough.
	24	Spencer reports that he has died, providing Col. Barry with another opportunity of raising money by selling the seat for Rathcormuck. Spencer compares him to Trigger, saying that at least he was not a hypocrite.
Barry, Arthur		This is presumably a sibling of either the deceased or the new Lord Barrymore; as the forename is not always used it is sometimes not clear if this is the specific Barry being referred to.
	68(?)	He has arrived in Dublin with the two Lady Barrymores.
	72	He visits Lord Barrymore with his brother, Capt. Barry, but does not stay at the castle.
	102(?)	His estate is referred to, and it would appear that he is sub-leasing some of the Mohire land from Mr Pearde.
Barry, Capt. David John	20	Spencer reports his death and subsequent burial at Castlelyons in March 1744.
Barry, Col.	8	A friend of Price and a land owner who, Spencer says, has made money out of the sale of the parliamentary seat for Rathcormuck to the tune of 600 guineas from Brettridge Badham and £700 from Mr Leeson.
	24	Spencer suggests he has a further opportunity of making money from his borough following the death of Badham
Barry, Lady Ann	60	Spencer reports that she is sick and likely to die.
Barry, Capt. Richard?	72	He visits Lord Barrymore with his brother, Arthur, for some time but does not stay at the castle.
	84	Spencer reports that he has married clandestinely and is staying at the bride's family home, Castle Hyde.
Barrymore, Dowager Lady	67	She is expected to arrive in Dublin soon with her daughter-in-law, Lady Barrymore.
	68	She has arrived in Dublin with her daughter-in-law.
	94	She has been appointed an executor and guardian of the 6th Earl on the death of the 5th Earl.
Barrymore, Lady	67	She is expected to arrive in Dublin soon with her mother-in-law, the Dowager Lady Barrymore.
	68	She has arrived in Dublin with her mother-in-law.
	94	She has been appointed an executor and guardian of the 6th Earl on the death of the 5th Earl.

Barrymore, Lord (4th Earl, James Barry)		(There is sometimes confusion as to which Lord Barrymore is intended in these letters and account of this is taken in these notes; the confusion is increased by the fact that some of the Lords Barrymore were also known by the title 'Buttevant' and Spencer refers to them as such at times without further indication of which one he is taking about.)
	3	Spencer says Barrymore has advised him to sell 'Renny & the Wood'.
	4	Spencer asks Price to speak to Barrymore regarding the commission promised by Baron Wainright.
	11/14	He is seen by Spencer as a possible source of support for his plan to publish his *Works of Mr Edmund Spencer.*
	20	Spencer expresses concern on learning of his arrest.
	22	Spencer sees his removal of certain valuables from Castlelyons as indicating that he will not return to Ireland.
	58	Barrymore returns to Ireland and Spencer says that he intends to pay his compliments to the lord as soon as he arrives at Castlelyons.
	60	He has such a company of grand aquaintances that Spencer is diffident about waiting on him.
	63	Spencer asks Price not to intervene on his behalf with Lord Barrymore with regard to his mortgage arrangements for Renny as Barrymore regards the Powers with favour.
	66	He has died, naming Price one of his executors, and been buried privately. Shortly before his death he had one Dominick Roch arrested for debt.
	67	Spenser expresses his surprise that he has named Col. Jephson as one of his executors.
	114	A deed produced 'on Behalf of Barrymore' was judged not to be valid in a case heard at Cork some time ago. (This may refer to the family in general rather than any specific person.)
	121	Spencer states that Lord Barrymore returned home 'last night'.
Barrymore, Lord (5th Earl, James Barry, Viscount Buttevant)	67	He is expected in Dublin soon.
	68	He has still not arrived in Dublin but is expected soon.
	72	Captain and Arthur Barry visit him but stay nearby rather than at the castle, suggesting a lack of harmony between them; Spencer hints that the new lord will be harsh on his tenants as they had their cattle impounded to pay the March rent.
	94	He has died.

Barrymore, Lord (6th Earl, Richard?)	107	He apparently has a right to collect rents from the tenant of Mohire.
	109	Spencer makes enquiries concerning the guardians of Lord Barrymore.
	119	His cattle driver escapes having been arrested 'on an execution for damages'.
	118	Spencer suspects he may be unsure of his title to Mohire, but also thinks he will contest it.
	120	He intends to pursue the claim for title to Mohire but Spencer thinks he will not succeed.
Barton and Smith	105/ 110	Merchants in London on whom bills are drawn to transfer rental payments to England.
Besbourough, Lord	64	He is mentioned as the father of John Ponsonby, the current first commissioner of the Revenue.
Bligh, Col.	45	The officer who takes over the regiment of Dragoons previously commanded by Col. Whitehead.
Bowen, Mr	62	A gentleman who travels with Spencer to Dublin, lending him a horse on which to ride.
Breley, Mr	90	Spencer tells Mr Buchan in the postscript that money due to a Mr Mathews has been sent to this person.
Brother		See Spencer, Nathaniel.
Brother-in-law		See Crofter.
Brown, Col.	52	The colonel of Spencer's brother Nathaniel when the latter was a cavalry soldier and who helps him find employment on his discharge from the army.
Buchan, Mr	90/91/ 92/93	The addressee of this and the three letters that follow.
Buchan, Mrs	90/91/ 92/93	Spencer sends her his compliments at the end of these letters.
Bulkeley	31	He is mentioned in relation to the property in Mallow in which Price appears to have an interest and concerning which Spencer makes enquiries in 1745. See also Callaghan, Checkley, Chinnery (John), Daniel, Dennis, End (Michael), End (William), End (William?) Hoar, Jephson, Marret, Newman, Noble, Noble (John), Price, Price (Capt.), Roberts, Sullivan (Cornelius), Sullivan (James), and Wrixon.
Burgess, Tom	61	A farmer who died, says Spencer, as a result of drinking milk and water rather than his accustomed strong spirits.
Busteed (also spelled / Busted/)	3	A lawyer who, after the death of Nathaniel Spencer, acted as guardian to Spencer during his minority but failed to look after his ward properly and defrauded the estate.
	124	This repeats the charge made in 6 February 1732: folio 3 that he appropriated the income from the estate, and adds that he died insolvent leaving Spencer with further debts.
	125	Referred to in lines 34–40, but not by name.
Buttevant, Lord	96	One of the Lords Barry (which one is not specified) who sells Mohire to John Price in 1692.

Callaghan, Anthony	34	He is mentioned in relation to the property in Mallow in which Price appears to have an interest and concerning which Spencer makes enquiries in 1745. He might have been Capt. Price's rent collector in Mallow. See also Bulkeley, Checkley, Chinnery (John), Daniel, Dennis, End (Michael), End (William), End (William?), Hoar, Jephson, Marret, Newman, Noble, Noble (John), Price, Price (Capt.), Roberts, Sullivan (Cornelius), Sullivan (James), and Wrixon.
Carey, Miss	94	An acquaintance of Spencer who informs him about the travel plans of her partner at Christmas time.
Carleton and Jeuers	105/110/ 112/114	Spencer arranges bills with them to transfer money to Alice Price.
	115	Spencer receives advice of their receipt of a bill.
Causabon	21	He is reported as having died at Carrick, May 1744, shortly after marrying a daughter of Sir John Rogerson.
Cavendish, Commissioner	71	The leader of a group of Cork merchants who formed themselves into a company to fit out a privateer, *The True Blue*.
Cazalet, Peter	117	A London merchant with whom Spencer arranges for a bill to be cashed.
Checkley, Thomas, Phillip, and Charles	31	This family, that had for several generations had a holding in Mallow, are relevant to the enquiries made by Spencer in 1745 about the property in that town in which Price appears to have an interest. See also Bulkeley, Callaghan, Chinnery (John), Daniel, Dennis, End (Michael), End (William), End (William?), Hoar, Jephson, Marret, Newman, Noble, Noble (John), Price, Price (Capt.), Roberts, Sullivan (Cornelius), Sullivan (James), and Wrixon.
	32	Spencer reports that Philip Checkley died ten years ago.
	34	Spencer reports that the Checkleys' holding is not the one in dispute.
Chesterfield, Lady	39	Spencer observes that she has set a fashion for ladies of wearing Irish Poplins.
Chesterfield, Lord (Lord Lieutenant)	28	Spencer insists that an approach to this lord on his behalf by some of Price's friends would help him to find a position.
	36	Spencer repeats that were someone to speak for him to the lord lieutenant he could get a position.
	37	Spencer again asks Price if he has any acquaintances who could effect a recommendation to Chesterfield whom Spencer praises as an esteemed lord lieutenant and generous man.
	39	Spencer says he is preparing a petition to the lord lieutenant to further his pursuit of a position, and describes how the Irish barristers waited on Chesterfield.
	43	Spencer says that it is not known when he intends to leave Ireland.

Chesterfield, Lord (Lord Lieutenant) (*continued*)	46	He is about to leave Ireland, to general regret; reference is made to his good work in Dublin to discourage gambling.
	47	Spencer asks if anybody could be prevailed on to speak of him to Chesterfield on the latter's return to England.
	50	The Earl's secretary, Mr Liddell, has died.
Chinnery, Dick, and his son	25	An acquaintance of Price who lived in Mallow, and whose son, Spencer suggests in the postscript, would benefit from Price's putting in a word for him to the owners of a Liverpool privateer on which the son had served.
	30	Spencer repeats his request to Price to intercede with the owners of the ship on which young Chinnery served.
Chinnery, John	34	A person from whom Cornelius Sullivan may have taken the lease on the property in Mallow in which Price appears to have an interest and concerning which Spencer makes enquiries in 1745. See also Bulkeley, Callaghan, Checkley, Daniel, Dennis, End (Michael), End (William), End (William?), Hoar, Jephson, Marret, Newman, Noble, Noble (John), Price, Price (Capt.), Roberts, Sullivan (Cornelius), Sullivan (James), and Wrixon.
Chip, Capt.	71	Captain of *The True Blue* privateer, noted for having once sailed from Gdańsk to Kinsale in an open boat.
Chritchly, Mr	96	A relative of Francis Price who, Spencer feels, has treated Alice Price 'indifferently'.
Colclogh, Mr	70	The person for whom Capt. Stannard was bound for the £500 debt which led to the Captain's arrest.
Colonel		See Smith, Mr or Col.
Conolly, Barbara	83	Spencer's sister, to whom he makes (along with his brother-in-law) a payment related to the sale of Renny.
Conolly, Mr	107/114	The owner of a house where Spencer lodges when in Dublin in February 1757 and December 1759.
Coppinger, Mr	121	He, his wife, and son will be on board the yacht Spencer intends to take to return to Ireland from Chester.
Crofter	8	Spencer names him as a brother-in-law with whom he boarded in 1743 at Churchtown.
	83(?)	Possibly the brother-in-law with whom Spencer and his family are lodging at Castletownroche after the sale of Renny.
Daniel	34	A leaseholder of a property in Mallow next to the one in which Price appears to have an interest and concerning which Spencer makes enquiries in 1745. See also Bulkeley, Callaghan, Checkley, Chinnery (John), Dennis, End (Michael), End (William), End (William?), Hoar, Jephson, Marret, Newman, Noble, Noble (John), Price, Price (Capt.), Roberts, Sullivan (Cornelius), Sullivan (James), and Wrixon.
Danny, Col.	9	A politician who supported, to his detriment, Mr FitzMaurice rather than his own brother-in-law Mr Hasset in the election for Knight for Co. Kerry in 1743.
Daughter		See Spencer, Rosamond.

Dean of St Patrick's Cathedral	89	Spencer is trying to see him to discuss the repairs to the house Alice Price owns in the precincts of Dublin Cathedral.
Deane, Mr	23	He is the owner of the winning horse at Carrigtohill in June 1744.
	96	Spencer gives an account of the disputed election for Portrive 'in Mr Deane's Corporation'.
	97	Spencer is attending to some business for Mr Deane concerning property that gentleman owns in and around Dublin.
	108	Spencer tells Alice Price his method for ensuring prompt payment of rent from Mr Deane's tenants in Co. Dublin, but says he is less strict with those in Co. Kilkenny.
	111	Spencer is prevented by ill health from transacting business in Dublin for him.
Deane, Sir Matthew	41	He is mentioned as an old acquaintance of Price who has recently journeyed to Dublin.
	42	Spencer dined with him and reports that he is in good spirits and has left Dublin for Munster.
	57	Spencer reports that he has died.
Dennis	34	A person from whom Cornelius Sullivan may have taken the lease on the property in Mallow in which Price appears to have an interest and concerning which Spencer makes enquiries in 1745. See also Bulkeley, Callaghan, Checkley, Chinnery (John), Daniel, End (Michael), End (William), End (William?), Hoar, Jephson, Marret, Newman, Noble, Noble (John), Price, Price (Capt.), Roberts, Sullivan (Cornelius), Sullivan (James), and Wrixon.
Denny, Edward	96	He is granted a ninety nine year lease on the lands of Mohire in 1666.
Devonshire, 3rd Duke (Lord Lieutenant)	18	He has reconvened parliament because of the threat of invasion; the date of his departure for England is not known.
	19	His date of departure for England is still uncertain.
	64	He is mentioned as the father-in-law of John Ponsonby, the current first commissioner of the Revenue.
	124	Price says that the lord lieutenant of Ireland had promised Spencer a commission in the army but did not follow through on his promise.
Dickens, Mr	121	The nephew of an unnamed doctor; he marries a Miss Houghton against the wishes of the lady's father.
Donnohoh, an eagle	55	Spenser finds a very tame eagle in Co. Limerick and persuades the owner to sell it to him.
	56	Spencer gives instructions for keeping and feeding this eagle which he has obtained for Richard Price, and explains how he will be carried to Wales.
	57	Spencer tells Price that the eagle is on its way, and tells him its name.

Elizabeth, Queen	127	She is stated to have granted lands in Ireland to Edmund Spenser the poet.
Ellis, Mr	15	An acquaintance of Price who lives at Oxford, and who, Spencer hopes, will raise some subscribers for his proposed *Works of Mr. Edmund Spencer.*
End, Michael	33	A quaker of Cork and a son of the End mentioned in 1 July 1745: folio 32, and possibly brother of the one mentioned in 20 August 1745: folio 34 (see following two entries); he is mentioned in relation to the property in Mallow in which Price appears to have an interest and concerning which Spencer makes enquiries in 1745. See also Bulkeley, Callaghan, Checkley, Chinnery (John), Daniel, Dennis, End (William), End (William?), Hoar, Jephson, Marret, Newman, Noble, Noble (John), Price, Price (Capt.), Roberts, Sullivan (Cornelius), Sullivan (James), and Wrixon.
	35(?)	He is possibly the End who is described as 'still alive in Cork & well' (see next entry).
End, William	34	Another son of the End mentioned in 1 July 1745: folio 32 (see next entry, also possibly called William); he is mentioned in relation to the property in Mallow in which Price appears to have an interest and concerning which Spencer makes enquiries in 1745. See also Bulkeley, Callaghan, Checkley, Chinnery (John), Daniel, Dennis, End (Michael), End (William?), Hoar, Jephson, Marret, Newman, Noble, Noble (John), Price, Price (Capt.), Roberts, Sullivan (Cornelius), Sullivan (James), and Wrixon.
	35(?)	He is possibly the End who is described as 'still alive in Cork & well' (see previous entry).
End (William?)	32	He is mentioned in relation to the property in Mallow in which Price appears to have an interest and concerning which Spencer makes enquiries in 1745. At the time of Spencer's writing he is deceased. See also Bulkeley, Callaghan, Checkley, Chinnery (John), Daniel, Dennis, End (Michael), End (William), Hoar, Jephson, Marret, Newman, Noble, Noble (John), Price, Price (Capt.), Roberts, Sullivan (Cornelius), Sullivan (James), and Wrixon.
Eyre, Mr	66	A candidate in the forthcoming Galway election.
Eyton, Miss	10	An acquaintance of Spencer and Price, possibly a neighbour of the latter, who is mentioned in a comment upon an elderly spinster in Price's neighbourhood getting married. (See also Shylock.)
Father		See Spencer, Nathaniel (father).
Fazakerly, Counsellor	114	He gives an opinion on the title to Mohire which Spencer has not seen.

FitzMaurice, Mr	9	He was the successful candidate in the election for Knight for Co. Kerry, November 1743. (See also Hasset and Danny.)
Fitzpatrick, Mr	66	A candidate in the forthcoming Galway election.
Fitzwilliam, Lord	77	He leaves Ireland without remembering his promise to help Spencer find employment.
Fleetwood, Miss	94	A young lady present at the Bryn y Pys Christmas festivities without her partner.
Fleetwood, Mr	96	A merchant who provides the Price family with ale at Christmas.
Folliot, James	112/114	A merchant in Chester through whom Spencer arranges bills for Alice Price.
Francis	121	A person (probably a servant of Price) who accompanies Spencer to Chester on his return from Overton to Ireland.
Freeman, John (father-in-law)	3(?)	He possibly looks into the mismanagement of Spencer's estate by the guardian, Busteed (though this may be the uncle, William).
	124/125	He reneges on the marriage agreement and instead persuades Spencer to borrow money from him, repayment of which is then enforced. He dies in poverty leaving the young couple in dire straits. (In neither of these documents is he referred to by name.)
Freeman, Mr William (uncle)	3(?)	He possibly looks into the mismanagement of Spencer's estate by the guardian, Busteed (though this may be the father-in-law, John).
	26	A hunting companion of Spencer; he is referred to here only by surname.
	31	Described by Spencer as his only remaining friend in Ireland, but one 'who lives so fast, that God knows, he cant long remain'.
	51	Spencer visits him in August 1746, naming his place of residence in this letter as Duhallow.
	83	He is to fix the price to be paid to Spencer for Renny.
Freny, James	78	A famous highwayman who, Spencer notes, 'sometimes visits the Corke road and is greatly dreaded', though some of his gang are now in custody.
George, Sir	10	He is mentioned in the affair of Sir Watkin Williams-Wynn and Middleton.
Gower, Lord	12	He has lost his government position (presumably as lord privy seal).
Grey, Commissioner	52	The head of the Dublin Excise, who appointed Spencer's brother Nathaniel to a post in that department.
Grierson, George	11	Spencer approaches Grierson, the King's Printer, concerning the publication by subscription of *The Works of Mr. Edmund Spencer*, an edition of the complete works of his ancestor, Edmund Spenser.

Harrison, Harry	79	Having lived like a hermit for years Harrison (the vicar of Castlelyons) gives £1,000 to the Society for Promoting Protestant Schools in the hope, Spencer suggests, of wiping out the extortions with which he might be charged.
	82	Spencer tells Price again about his death, adding that Harrison's brother has also died.
	92(?)	A previous lessee of Mohire House who had a lease with a Mr Nason which obliged the lessee to keep the property in good repair. (This is possibly the brother referred to in 21 February 1748: folio 82, or a completely different Harrison.)
Harrison, John	82	The brother of Harry Harrison, he has also recently died.
Harwood	8	He is returned MP for Doneraile, Spencer implying that he purchased it from an unnamed lord.
Hassett, Mr	9	Son of Col. Hassett, and unsuccessful candidate in the election for Knight for Co. Kerry, November 1743. (See also FitzMaurice and Danny.)
Hawksaw, Dr	89	Spencer is told that this man's heir has fraudulently prevented Alice Price from getting the rent from some land in Ireland.
Hayman, Mr	101	He gives advice on the nature of the documents required for a legal procedure.
Hely, Mary	99	An inhabitant of Castlelyons who writes a letter to Richard Price apparently asserting that Spencer had recommended her to Richard Price with a view to marriage, an assertion which Spencer refutes in the strongest terms.
	100	Spencer mentions her in this letter asking Richard Price to assure his mother that he, Spencer, never, on any occasion, suggested her as a suitable marriage partner, or offered advice any other matter.
	109	Though not mentioned by name she is referred to here as apparently likely to visit Alice Price in Wales.
Hennessy, James	83	A man to whom Spencer's father owed £100, which Spencer has now repaid.
Heywood, Messrs	118	A merchant house in Liverpool through which Spencer arranges a bill for Richard Price.
Hill, Mr	38	Spencer thanks Price for an introductory letter to Hill, an influential person who may be able to help obtain a position.
	39	Spencer meets him at last. He says that though he is of little influence at the court he will support Spencer where he can.
	124	Arthur Trevor is asked to recommend Spencer to Mr Hill for a post.
Hoar, Alderman	31	He held at some time a mortgage to the property in Mallow in which Price appears to have an interest and concerning which Spencer makes enquiries in 1745. See also Bulkeley, Callaghan, Checkley, Chinnery (John), Daniel, Dennis, End (Michael), End (William), End (William?), Jephson, Marret, Newman, Noble, Noble (John), Price, Price (Capt.), Roberts, Sullivan (Cornelius), Sullivan (James), and Wrixon.

Houghton, Miss	121	A lady who marries a Mr Dickens against the wishes of her father who is angered by her action.
Hurt, Mr	121	Spencer meets him in Chester before embarking for Ireland.
Hyde, Col. Arthur	57	He puts himself up for election as the member of parliament for Sir Matthew Deane's seat on the death of the latter.
	84	Spencer suggests his avaricious nature will enable him to get on well with his new son-in-law, Capt. Barry.
Ingoldsby, Miss	10	She is mentioned as having eloped to France with a Hugh Massey.
	49	She is mentioned as the lady 'carried off' by Hugh Massey.
Jephson, son of Col. Jephson	21	A young man who married a daughter of Sir John Rogerson and who died shortly after the marriage. (See also Causabon.)
Jephson, Col. Anthony	31	The owner of the property in Mallow in which Price appears to have an interest and concerning which Spencer makes enquiries in 1745. He is regarded by Spencer as an untrustworthy person. See also Bulkeley, Callaghan, Checkley, Chinnery (John), Daniel, Dennis, End (Michael), End (William), End (William?), Hoar, Marret, Newman, Noble, Noble (John), Price, Price (Capt.), Roberts, Sullivan (Cornelius), Sullivan (James), and Wrixon.
	32	Spencer gives an example of the Colonel's dishonest behaviour involving his shirking of a military duty.
	34	Spencer again suggests that Jephson is a slippery and unpleasant character while reporting on Price's property dealings in Mallow.
	67	Spencer expresses his worry on hearing that Col. Jephson has been named by Lord Barrymore as one of his executors along with Price.
Jessop, Mr	88	He was the last tenant of a house in Dublin now owned by Alice Price and which he has so ruined by his carelessness that the house cannot be let and is probably fit only to be rebuilt.
	89	He is named again as the last lessee of the house in the precincts of Dublin Cathedral.
Kane	22	He is referred to as a brother by Spencer, who has asked him to search for an eagle to send to Richard Price.
Kelly, Mallaky	48	One of Price's lawyers in Ireland, whose death Spencer here reports.
Kent, Mr	51	A gentleman of Cheshire who is 'taken up for uttering treasonable Words'.
Kingsbury, Dr	12/13/14	He is spoken of by Spencer as an influential person of wide acquaintance who could help obtain subscribers for his proposed *Works of Mr Edmund Spenser.*
	19	Spencer tells Price that he has delivered the letter Price wrote to the doctor on Spencer's behalf.

Kingsbury, Dr (*continued*)	28	Spencer assures Price that he will write to the doctor about his proposed *Works of Mr Edmund Spenser* 'as soon as priviledge comes in'.
	58	Spencer reports his death and hopes that this will not have an adverse effect on Price's affairs in Ireland.
	73	Spencer expresses surprise that his furniture and household goods have all been auctioned, and that his books were sold rather than being kept for his son.
Kingsbury, Thomas	67	Spencer tells Price that Kingsbury has given him Irish pounds when exchanging a bill.
	88	Spencer has dealings with him over a property in Dublin that Price's widow, Alice Price, now owns and has asked Spencer to look into.
	89	He gives Spencer further advice about the house Jessop had rented and damaged, and about the procedure Alice Price needs to follow to get the rents of the Parliament House.
	93	Spencer says he will check the deeds of Mohire house for the clause about who is responsible for repairs, if Mr Kingsbury has them in his possession.
	94	He sends some books for Spencer to pass on to the Prices in Wales.
	100	Spencer acknowledges that he asked Richard Price to recommend his services to Mrs Price on Mr Kingsbury's moving to the Temple.
	112	Spencer learns from him that Richard Price intends to visit Ireland soon.
Kingston, Lord	24	Spencer reports that he is dangerously ill, and that he has threatened an unspecified 'attack' on 'young Thornhill' who might benefit from Kingston's death.
	53	He and his family leave Ireland to visit England.
Leeson, Joseph (father and son)	8	Leeson, the son of a Dublin brewer, paid Col. Barry £700 for a parliamentary seat.
Lestock, Admiral	53	Spencer reports that his squadron has arrived at Cove harbour.
Lindsay, Justice	124	He is mentioned as having represented Spencer's pursuit of a pair of colours to the Duke of Devonshire.
	125	He is referred to as a friend who had promised Spencer assistance but who is now dead.
Lloyd, Mr	109	A person of some power whom Alice Price is suing.
Loyd	8	A new rector who, Spencer implies, has paid Col. Barry for the living.
Lumbard, Mr	44	The person from whose house in Fishamble Street, Dublin, Spencer writes on 15 March 1745.
Liddell, Mr (*spelled* /Lyddile/ *by Spencer*)	50	The Earl of Chesterfield's secretary through whom Spencer hoped to gain some employment but who has died.

Marlborough, Duke	4	Spencer is convinced that what he believes to be his familial connection with the Duke could lead to patronage, and requests Price to ask his acquaintances to intercede with the Duke on his behalf.
	14	Spencer mentions his intention of dedicating the *Works of Mr. Edmund Spencer* to the Duke.
	18	Spencer asks Price to persuade friends to intercede with the Duke regarding his intention of dedicating the *Works of Mr. Edmund Spencer* to the Duke.
	80	Spencer proposes sending a memorial to the Duke through a suitable intermediary in his search for employment.
	81	Spencer discusses the nature of the memorial he ought to write and send to the Duke.
	82	Francis Price has apparently told Spencer that he has no acquaintance who could intercede with the Duke.
Marret	34	He is the leaseholder of a property in Mallow next to the one in which Price appears to have an interest and concerning which Spencer makes enquiries in 1745. See also Bulkeley, Callaghan, Checkley, Chinnery (John), Daniel, Dennis, End (Michael), End (William), End (William?), Hoar, Jephson, Newman, Noble, Noble (John), Price, Price (Capt.), Roberts, Sullivan (Cornelius), Sullivan (James), and Wrixon.
Marshall, Serjeant	52	He is mentioned as the legal adversary of Price in an unspecified dispute.
Massareen, Lord	94	He has been appointed an executor and guardian of the 6th Earl of Barrymore on the death of the 5th Earl.
Massey, Hugh Fitzjohn	10	He has eloped to France with Miss Ingoldsby a wealthy heiress.
	49	Massey assaults a jockey at Mallow races and is tried the next day.
Mathews, Mr	90	Spencer asks Mr Buchan to tell this person that money due to him has been sent to a Mr Breley.
	94	Spencer sends some books to him for the Prices, along with some poplin.
Mathews, Admiral	20	Spencer reports the celebrations for Mathews's success in the naval battle of Toulon.
Mead, Sir Richard	3	Interest owing to him after the death of Spencer's father was not paid, but the rent of Killcoleman was paid to him.
	22	He is the unsuccessful litigant in a case against Capt. Web, a failure which Spencer considers to be the cause of Mead's death shortly after the case was concluded.
Meade	111	A cousin of Mr Pearde who has died leaving the tenant of Mohire financially better off.
Meath, Lord and Lady	6	They are passengers on the ferry from Chester to Ireland; she and Spencer were the only ones not sea-sick so were much in each other's company for the voyage.

Middleton	10	The person against whom Sir Watkin Williams-Wynn seems to have succeeded (in an election dispute), much to Spencer's satisfaction.
Middleton, Lady	38	A person who may be able to help Spencer obtain a position. (See also Trevor.)
Muilman, Messrs	119	Merchants in London through whom Spencer arranges a bill for Richard Price.
Nason, Mr	92	Mr Pearde has had some correspondence with Mr Nason which he has forwarded to Spencer who tells Mr Buchan that he will try to meet Mr Nason to settle the dispute about repairs to Mohire House.
	93	Further details emerge suggesting that he is the person responsible for the repairs to Mohire House, but is trying to avoid making them.
	99	He is mentioned regarding Spencer's recent connections with Castlelyons and in relation to the letter Mary Hely writes to Alice Price.
Nettervill, Lord	14	Spencer notes that his trial has been postponed, and that it is generally believed that he will not be found guilty of the charges laid against him.
	15	Spencer notes that the trial is now imminent, and that some consider it likely he will be found guilty.
Newman	34	A family mentioned in relation to the property in Mallow in which Price appears to have an interest and concerning which Spencer makes enquiries in 1745; one of them takes up the mortgage on the lease on that property from Cornelius Sullivan, and on Sullivan's death takes over the lease. See also Bulkeley, Callaghan, Checkley, Chinnery (John), Daniel, Dennis, End (Michael), End (William), End (William?), Hoar, Jephson, Marret, Noble, Noble (John), Price, Price (Capt.), Roberts, Sullivan (Cornelius), Sullivan (James), and Wrixon.
Newport, Messers	117	Spencer arranges a bill for Alice Price through them.
	118/119	Spencer arranges bills for Richard Price through them.
Noble	32	A person, no longer alive, who is connected with the property in Mallow in which Price appears to have an interest and concerning which Spencer makes enquiries in 1745. See also Bulkeley, Callaghan, Checkley, Chinnery (John), Daniel, Dennis, End (Michael), End (William), End (William?), Hoar, Jephson, Marret, Newman, Noble (John), Price, Price (Capt.), Roberts, Sullivan (Cornelius), Sullivan (James), and Wrixon.
Noble, John	33	He is a son of the Noble mentioned in the previous letter (see previous entry). See also Bulkeley, Callaghan, Checkley, Chinnery (John), Daniel, Dennis, End (Michael), End (William), End (William?), Hoar, Jephson, Marret, Newman, Noble, Price, Price (Capt.), Roberts, Sullivan (Cornelius), Sullivan (James), and Wrixon.
Old Gentleman of Overton	54	See Trigger

Oliver, Col.		This is probably the same person as the Mr Oliver of the next entry.
	31	Described by Spencer as a dear friend when he reports his death to Price in May 1745.
	47	Spencer laments that had Col. Oliver lived he would have provided for him.
Oliver, Mr		This is probably the same person as the Col. Oliver of the previous entry.
	12	A friend who writes to Lord Talbot to promote the proposed *Works of Mr. Edmund Spencer.*
	26	He is mentioned as a hunting companion of Spencer who has a villa at Kilcummer, near Renny.
Orrery, Earl of	94	Spencer sends his *Pliny* to Alice Price, and makes some critical remarks upon the gentleman.
Parker, Gen.	23	A candidate for Kinsale in the parliamentary election of 1744.
Payne, Mrs	113	Spencer has taken on work as her agent in Co. Kilkenny.
Pearde, (William)	58	Referred to by Spencer as an uncle who sends him some money on Price's order. (He is not the Pearde referred to in the letters from 28 July 1750: folio 90 onwards; see footnote to l.4 of this letter and the following entry).
Pearde, Mr		The tenant or sub-tenant of Mohire House. He is not the same person as the William Pearde of the previous entry; he is nearly always spelled with the final /e/, but Spencer is not completely consistent about this.
	90	He is being dilatory in the payment of rent he owes, though he assures Spencer that he has the money ready to send.
	91	Spencer expresses surprise that he still has not sent the money for his rent, and there appears to be some dispute about repairs to the property.
	92	There has been an exchange of correspondence with Mr Pearde who is apparently being obstructive with regard to the repairs to Mohire House.
	93	He finds and gives to Spencer a letter written by a Mr Nason to Francis Price in which the former agrees to make the repairs to Mohery before handing it over, and Mr Pearde suggests that Mr Nason's avoidance of doing these repairs is founded on his belief that Mrs Price will not take him to court over the matter.
	95	Spencer reports that he has received bills for £100 from him.
	96	Mr Pearde remits £100; Spencer advises Alice Price against giving him a lease in order to keep a legal hold over him and notes that he is obliged only to pay in Irish money, not English.
	97	He fails again to make a payment despite Spencer's having written him letters threatening legal action, but this is because he is ill; his son promises to arrange the payment.

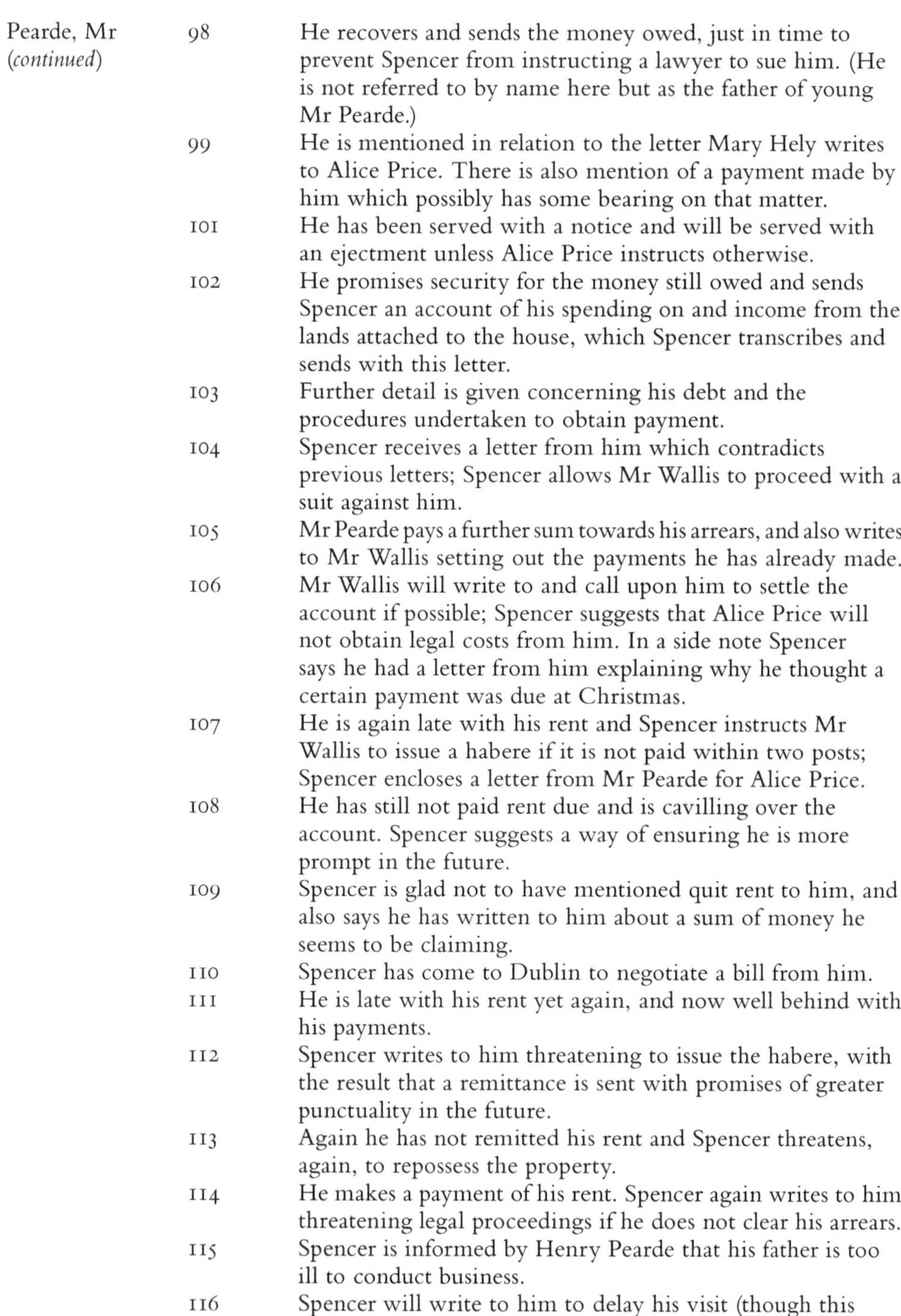

Pearde, Mr (*continued*)	98	He recovers and sends the money owed, just in time to prevent Spencer from instructing a lawyer to sue him. (He is not referred to by name here but as the father of young Mr Pearde.)
	99	He is mentioned in relation to the letter Mary Hely writes to Alice Price. There is also mention of a payment made by him which possibly has some bearing on that matter.
	101	He has been served with a notice and will be served with an ejectment unless Alice Price instructs otherwise.
	102	He promises security for the money still owed and sends Spencer an account of his spending on and income from the lands attached to the house, which Spencer transcribes and sends with this letter.
	103	Further detail is given concerning his debt and the procedures undertaken to obtain payment.
	104	Spencer receives a letter from him which contradicts previous letters; Spencer allows Mr Wallis to proceed with a suit against him.
	105	Mr Pearde pays a further sum towards his arrears, and also writes to Mr Wallis setting out the payments he has already made.
	106	Mr Wallis will write to and call upon him to settle the account if possible; Spencer suggests that Alice Price will not obtain legal costs from him. In a side note Spencer says he had a letter from him explaining why he thought a certain payment was due at Christmas.
	107	He is again late with his rent and Spencer instructs Mr Wallis to issue a habere if it is not paid within two posts; Spencer encloses a letter from Mr Pearde for Alice Price.
	108	He has still not paid rent due and is cavilling over the account. Spencer suggests a way of ensuring he is more prompt in the future.
	109	Spencer is glad not to have mentioned quit rent to him, and also says he has written to him about a sum of money he seems to be claiming.
	110	Spencer has come to Dublin to negotiate a bill from him.
	111	He is late with his rent yet again, and now well behind with his payments.
	112	Spencer writes to him threatening to issue the habere, with the result that a remittance is sent with promises of greater punctuality in the future.
	113	Again he has not remitted his rent and Spencer threatens, again, to repossess the property.
	114	He makes a payment of his rent. Spencer again writes to him threatening legal proceedings if he does not clear his arrears.
	115	Spencer is informed by Henry Pearde that his father is too ill to conduct business.
	116	Spencer will write to him to delay his visit (though this could be the son); his last payment is to be retained in Spencer's hands to pay legal dues.

Pearde, Mr (*continued*)	117	Spencer sends Alice Price his remittance for the December quarter. He is also mentioned in the letter written by Alice Price to her son on this sheet: she tells him how to enter Mr Pearde's recent payments in the accounts.
	118	Spencer transfers rent payments from him, and details expences for the cost of his cow and having it driven.
Pearde, Mr Henry	97	Henry Pearde, the son of Mr Pearde (the tenant of Mohire House), writes to Spencer informing him of the father's illness and promising to send the money owed.
	98	He writes to Spencer to say that his father is now better.
	102	The elder Pearde offers to enter into a bond with his son in order to secure his payments to Alice Price. Spencer suggests that as young Mr Pearde is of age this offer may be acceptable.
	115	Spencer receives a letter from Henry Pearde saying that his father is too ill to attend to business but would send a remittance on his recovery.
	117	He is mentioned in the letter written by Alice Price to her son with regard to his payment of his father's rent.
	119	Spencer receives a payment from him.
Peggy	15	Wife of the otherwise unnamed 'Alderman'; Spencer notes that she is pregnant.
	22	She is mentioned as a possible source of comfort to the Alderman during his illness.
Percivall, Mr	80	A gentleman whose death creates a vacancy in the Customs which Spencer decides not to pursue.
Perry, Mr	76	He is murdered at Cashel races after an argument in a tavern with one Shannahan.
Ponsonby, John	64	The son of Lord Bessbourough and first commissioner of the Revenue (where Spencer is trying to get a place).
Poultney, William	10	The Earl of Bath, whom Spencer supposes to have been the author of a pamphlet he has recently read.
Power	62	Spencer notes that the financial disagreement between himself and the Powers is to be settled soon.
	63	Spencer says the Powers have used him basely; however, as they have the ear of Lord Barrymore Spencer asks Price not to intercede with Barrymore on his behalf.
	74	To Spencer's alarm the Powers force the sale of Renny within the current law term, giving him very little time to obtain a good price for it.
	83	Spencer states that he has paid the Powers £1,309.
Price		This may be the same person as the Capt. Price mentioned in 20 August 1745: folio 34. See next entry.
	31	He is mentioned in relation to the property in Mallow in which Francis Price appears to have an interest and concerning which Spencer makes enquiries in 1745. See also Bulkeley, Callaghan, Checkley, Chinnery (John), Daniel, Dennis, End (Michael), End (William), End (William?), Hoar, Jephson, Marret, Newman, Noble, Noble (John), Price (Capt.), Roberts, Sullivan (Cornelius), Sullivan (James), and Wrixon.

Price, Capt.		This is most likely Price's father, who is named as 'Captain Richard Price' on his son's memorial tablet in St Mary's Church, Overton; he may or may not be the same Price as is mentioned in 23 May 1745: folio 31. See previous entry.
	34	He is mentioned in relation to the property in Mallow in which Price appears to have an interest and concerning which Spencer makes enquiries in 1745. See also Bulkeley, Callaghan, Checkley, Chinnery (John), Daniel, Dennis, End (Michael), End (William), End (William?), Hoar, Jephson, Marret, Newman, Noble, Noble (John), Price, Roberts, Sullivan (Cornelius), Sullivan (James), and Wrixon.
Price, Alice (Francis Price's wife)	33	Spencer is worried that sending Richard Price away to school would cause her great anxiety.
	44	Spencer is sure that she will get the dress materials he has sent her safely.
	59	Spencer asks if she will give Welsh some Jesuit Drops to bring back to Ireland for him.
	83	Spencer sends condolences for an illness she is suffering.
	91	Spencer will enquire for her about who to recommend for doing repairs to Mohire house; he also asks if she has any further commands for him.
	92	Spencer further discusses her options with regard to Mohire.
	93	Spencer asks how Alice Price wishes to proceed with Mr Nason over the repairs to Mohire.
	105	Mr Pearde expresses, through Mr Wallis, his hope that she will withdraw her notice of ejectment.
Price, Francis	90	Spencer encloses a letter from him to Mr Pearde concerning Mohire, a house leased from the Prices by Mr Pearde.
	93	Mr Pearde shows Spencer a letter from Mr Nason found amongst some letters from Price in which Mr Nason promised to effect repairs on giving up Mohire.
	96	Spencer tells Alice Price that he will send her a copy of her late husband's letter to Mr Pearde and regrets that she is not well treated by her relations on his side.
	102	Mr Pearde expresses gratitude for his and his wife's friendship (though the reference here may be to Richard Price, his son).
Price, Frank	120	Spencer sends his good wishes to Richard Price's recently born son.
Price, John	96	Possibly Francis Price's grandfather, he is the person to whom Lord Buttevant sells Mohire in 1692.

Price, Richard Parry (Francis Price's son)	13	Spencer expresses his concern that Richard may catch smallpox, which has broken out in the locality of Overton.
	22	Spencer asks Price to reassure Richard that the promise to find him an eagle has not been forgotten.
	33	Spencer expresses his worry that sending the boy away to school would cause his mother unnecessary anxiety.
	40	He appears to have been ill while at home on holiday from school (though this letter is so badly damaged that it is not possible to make out the cause).
	44	Spencer expresses his pleasure on hearing that he is well.
	51	Dick Welsh is to visit the Price family to train a hunting dog for him.
	55	Spencer reports that he has at last found an eagle for Richard.
	57	Spencer hopes that the eagle will please Richard Price, and passes on the bird's name.
	58	Spencer expresses his pleasure that Richard Price likes the eagle.
	86	Spencer thanks Richard Price for his letter.
	94	There is some discussion of his being enamoured of an unnamed young lady who is at Bryn y Pys for the Christmas festivities.
	96	Spencer advises Alice Price not to start a law suit about the title to Mohire until her son is of age.
	99	Mary Hely asserts in a letter to Alice Price that Spencer recommended her to Richard Price as a wife, an assertion that Spencer refutes, requesting Alice Price to confirm his refutation by asking Richard Price whether it is true.
	102(?)	Mr Pearde expresses gratitude for his and his mother's friendship (though the reference here may be to his father).
	106	Spencer, mistakenly thinking that Richard Price was at Oxford rather than at home, sends a money bill for him to collect in London rather than Chester.
	109	He is owed £10 by Mr Pearde; Spencer hopes he will have an enjoyable tour in the Welsh mountains.
	112	Spencer expresses his pleasure on hearing that Richard Price is well and that he intends to visit his estates in Ireland in the near future.
	114	Spencer says that he has been advised to tell the tenant of Mohire that Richard Price is determined to maintain that he has a full title to ownership of the estate.
	115	He is married.
	116	He has been sent to South Wales with the Militia; Spencer tries to reassure Alice Price that he is in no danger; it is also clear that he is due to become a father. Spencer sends his respects to him and his wife in a postscript.
	117	He is unable to cash a bill as he is with his militia unit; Spencer hopes that he and his wife are well.
	128	Rosamond Spencer thanks him for his interest in her father's illness.

Rider, Parson	24	Someone, possibly known to Price, who is involved with Lord Kingston in the unspecified threat to 'young Thornhill'.
Roberts	31	He is mentioned in relation to the property in Mallow in which Price appears to have an interest and concerning which Spencer makes enquiries in 1745. See also Bulkeley, Callaghan, Checkley, Chinnery (John), Daniel, Dennis, End (Michael), End (William), End (William?), Hoar, Jephson, Marret, Newman, Noble, Noble (John), Price, Price (Capt.), Sullivan (Cornelius), Sullivan (James), and Wrixon.
Roberts, Hodder	8	A resident of Cork and an acquaintance of Price who has married the widow of one Addis, a grocer in Cork, by whom he got £40 a year and some silver.
	71	He has died of an inflammation of the lungs.
Roch, Dominick	66	He has been arrested for debt and sent to gaol at the suit of Lord Barrymore.
Rogerson, Sir John	21	The father of two daughters, both of whose husbands died shortly after their marriages.
Row, Mr		The curate of St Mary's Church, Overton.
(spelled Roe in	8	Apparently he is a great hunter of woodcocks.
parish records)	40	(Here spelled /Rowe/.) He is mentioned as having spoken disrespectfully of Trigger.
[Sandys, Samuel]	12	Probably the name that is blotted out in l.4 of this letter. Spencer notes that he has been made a peer.
Seel, Sam	30	One of the owners of the ship on which the young Chinnery served; Spencer asks Price to write to him on behalf of young Chinnery.
Shakerly, Frances	75	She marries Sir Watkin Williams-Wynn on the death of his first wife.
Shannahan	76	The man who, at the Cashel races, murders a Mr Perry in a tavern after an argument; he is arrested and held for trial.
Shaw, Capt.	43	The captain(?) of the yacht concerning which Spencer makes enquiries on behalf of Price.
Shylock	10	Either the character from *The Merchant of Venice* being used as the archetype of miserliness, or the nickname of an acquaintance of Spencer and Price who has those characteristics and who is wished upon Miss Eyton as a husband suitable to her character.
Sinclair, Gen.	54	Spencer reports on the movement of the troops under his command, and that they have brought a dangerous fever into the country.
	55	Forces under his command march from Cork to Galway and then back to Cork to await embarkation to an unknown destination.
Sister (of Spencer)		See Conolly, Barbara.

Smith, Mr or Col. (sometimes spelled / Smyth/)	7(PS)/ 8(PS)/ 10(PS)/ 11(PS)/ 20(PS)/ 21/ 26(PS)/ 27(PS)/ 29(PS)/ 31(PS)/ 32(PS)/ 33(PS)/ 34(PS)/ 38(PS)/ 41/ 42(PS)/ 43(PS)/ 45/47/ 49/ 50(PS)/ 51(PS)/ 52(PS)/ 53(PS)/ 54(PS)/ 55/56/ 57(PS)/ 58(PS)/ 69/ 72(PS)/ 73(PS)/ 76(PS)/ 80(PS)/ 81(PS)/ 92	Spencer sends his 'service' (or equivalent) to Mr or Col. Smith, a mutual acquaintance who lives near Price
	12	He is congratulated on his good health which Spencer attributes to the use of Elixir Salutis.
	36	Spencer congratulates him on his recovery from an unspecified illness and recommends punch as a means of remaining healthy. (He is referred to here only as 'the Colonel'.)
	44	Named as 'the Old Colonel', he is mentioned as suffering from gout, perhaps, suggests Spencer, the result of too much acid in his punch.
	61	Spencer recommends that he take a lesson from the death of Tom Burgess and not drink 'too cooling liquor'.
	83	Spencer, in a postscript, congratulates him on his 'vigour'.
Southwell, Mr	23	A supporter of Mr Stowell in the Kinsale parliamentary election of 1744.

Spencer, Anne (Spencer's wife)	83	Spencer notes that some money has been put aside after the sale of Renny to provide for his wife should he die.
	93	He tells Alice Price that he will leave some legal documents with his wife so that she can see they are dealt with while he is in Dublin.
	106	As Spencer is ill his wife sends a letter to Mr Wallis.
	115	Spencer sends her congratulations to Richard Price on his marriage.
	118	She has been ill.
	119	She has gone ahead to her daughter's house where the Spencers are to stay for two months.
Spencer, Nathaniel or Natt (Spencer's brother)	50	He obtains employment in Dublin as a 'Coast Officer' through Spencer's good offices.
	52	Having been discharged from the army for being under size he obtains employment in the Dublin Excise.
	53	Spencer reports that he has been posted to Strabane on a salary of £40 per annum.
	81	Spencer is obliged to pay him and his sister(-in-law?) £150 for joining in a fine on a property.
	83	He repeats that he paid his brother and sister(-in-law?) £150 for joining in a fine on a property.
Spencer, Nathaniel (Spencer's father)	83	Spencer has paid off a debt of £100 incurred by his father to one James Hennessy (he is referred to as 'father' rather than by name).
	124/ 125/ 127	His effective destruction of the family estate, inherited from grants to his great-grandfather and father for their services to the monarchy, is rehearsed in all these documents. He is mentioned by name only in 127.
Spencer, Rosamond (Spencer's younger daughter)	63	She has been innoculated against smallpox.
	83	Spencer notes that some money has been put aside after the sale of Renny to provide for his daughter should he die.
	115	Spencer sends her congratulations to Richard Price on his marriage.
	118	She has been, and still is, unwell.
	119	Spencer and his wife are to visit her and her husband for two months.
Spencer, William (Spencer's grandfather)	81	Spencer suggests invoking his grandfather's name to persuade the Duke of Marlborough to help him (referred to here as 'grandfather', not by name).
	124	He helped the Williamite army win the Battle of Aughrim (referred to here as 'grandfather', not by name).
	125	He helped the Williamite army win the Battle of Aughrim.
	127	He was granted lands in Ireland by William III for his services at the Battle of Aughrim.
Spenser, Edmund (the poet)	125	Price notes that Spencer is his great-great-grandson.
	127	The memorial notes that Spencer is the great-grandson [*sic*] of the poet, to whom Queen Elizabeth granted lands in Ireland.

St Leger, Col.	21	He is reported as being very ill and likely to die, a prospect regarded by Spencer with some satisfaction as he has a poor opinion of the man.
Stannard, Capt.	7	A gentleman who farms in Roches Country and who, to Spencer's surprise, has no old corn stacks in his yard.
	70	He is arrested and gaoled for debt, but redeemed by his brother and brought home to Ballyhooly with great celebration.
Stannard, Old	75	Spencer reports his death. (This is possibly Captain Stannard, his father, or another relative.)
Stocah, the	8	Mentioned as perhaps setting out to visit Price in November 1743. The definite article suggests that this is a nickname for a mutual acquaintance.
	23	Spencer notes that he is having very little luck fishing for salmon.
Stowell, Mr	23	A general councillor who puts himself forward for election as Member for Kinsale, 1744.
Stradwick, Mr	7	A mutual acquaintance who is regarded by Spencer and Price as a somewhat incredible raconteur.
Sullivan, Cornelius	34	The leaseholder, sometime in the past, of the property in Mallow in which Price appears to have an interest and concerning which Spencer makes enquiries in 1745. See also Bulkeley, Callaghan, Checkley, Chinnery (John), Daniel, Dennis, End (Michael), End (William), End (William?), Hoar, Jephson, Marret, Newman, Noble, Noble (John), Price, Price (Capt.), Roberts, Sullivan (James), and Wrixon.
Sullivan, James	34	The son of Cornelius Sullivan (see previous entry) who takes over his father's lease on a property in Mallow. He died around 1734. See also Bulkeley, Callaghan, Checkley, Chinnery (John), Daniel, Dennis, End (Michael), End (William), End (William?), Hoar, Jephson, Marret, Newman, Noble, Noble (John), Price, Price (Capt.), Roberts, Sullivan (Cornelius), and Wrixon.
Swift, Jonathan	94	Spencer sends Orrery's *Remarks on Swift* to the Prices, and makes some critical comments on the author of the book for being, amongst other things, 'too severe upon the Deane'.
Sympson, George	96	A public notary who witnesses the deed of sale of the lands of Mohire to John Price in 1692.
Taaf, Mr	75	He is at Castlelyons 'setting the Demesnes' and killing the deer.
Talbot, Lord	12	A person of influence to whom Mr Oliver writes to obtain his help in promoting the proposed *Works of Mr. Edmund Spencer.*
Thornhill	24	The son-in-law of Brettridge Badham and the object of some unspecified threat on the part of Lord Kingston; Spencer implies that Lord Kingston's being carried away by his illness would be of benefit to Thornhill.

Thurot	116	A French privateer and naval captain who led a successful raid on Carrickfergus.
Trevor, Mr	11(PS)	Spencer says he fears that Price has not seen this person since last mentioning him.
	38	Spencer asks Price if he can provide an introductory note from Mr Trevor to Mr Hill and Lady Middleton.
	124	He is mentioned at the beginning of this draft as having been asked to mention Spencer to Arthur Hill.
Trigger		Spencer and Price's nickname for Thomas Lloyd of Gwernheylod, the patron of Bangor parish and hence of St Mary's Church in Overton.
	8	He appears to be involved in a dispute with either the rector of Bangor or the curate of Overton, and this dispute may have some bearing on Price's right to tithes.
	24	He is compared unfavourably with Brettridge Badham insofar as the latter was at least not a hypocrite.
	40	Mr Roe, the curate of St Mary's, Overton, appears to have spoken disrespectfully of him.
	54(?)	Spencer makes a slighting remark about the 'Old Gentleman of Overton' (who is most likely Trigger).
	65	Spencer suggests that he is dying, but holds on to life simply to vex his neighbours.
	75	He dies, much to the relief, Spencer suggests, of all his neighbours.
	82	Spencer suggests that Overton must be quieter following his death, though Price has said nothing to confirm that.
Verling, Coun.	93	He provides the draft of a deed for Mohire House.
	94	Spencer will ask Verling to obtain further opinions about the question of title when in Dublin.
Vernon, Admiral	27	Spencer notes that Vernon had observed, before her loss in 1744, that *The Victory*, a man-of-war, had been badly built, but had no notice taken of him.
Wainwright, Baron (Judge)	4	He promises Spencer a regimental commission but dies before the promise can be honoured.
	5	Spencer is in Dublin to talk to Wainwright's friends about the commission.
	124	Mentioned as having promised the pair of colours because he knew the plight Spencer was in.
	125	Referred to as a friend who had promised Spencer assistance but who is now dead.
Wales, Prince of	41	His birthday festivities in Dublin are mentioned.
Waller, Col.	8	He loses the parliamentary seat for Doneraile to Counsellor Harwood.

Wallis, Henry and John		There are two lawyers named Wallis but the forenames are used infrequently; all references to a Wallis are therefore collected together here and the forename is specified only when given in the letter.
	48	Spencer recommends John Wallis to Price as a replacement for the deceased lawyer Mallaky Kelly.
	83	'Mr Wallis the Attorney' is the purchaser of Renny.
	97	Spencer expected to receive Mr Pearde's payment from Mr Wallis but the money failed to arrive owing to Mr Pearde's being ill.
	98	Spencer is on the point of instructing Mr Wallis to sue Mr Pearde for his failure, again, to pay the rent for Mohire on time.
	101	Mr Wallis will not require payment for the time being; he will serve ejectments on Mr Pearde the following week.
	102	Spencer has written to Mr Wallis to delay serving the ejectments on Mr Pearde.
	103	Spencer has further correspondence with Mr Wallis about obtaining the money owed by Mr Pearde; his father is the owner of a good estate near Castlelyons and hence a man of some local influence.
	104	Spencer says he will not prevent Mr Wallis from proceeding with a suit against Mr Pearde unless he hears to the contrary from Alice Price.
	105	Spencer receives money from Mr Wallis to pass on to Mrs Price, and is also given a summary of a letter sent by him to Mr Pearde; Mr Wallis declines payment for his services so far, saying that he thinks this affair will come to an end soon.
	106	On receiving a letter forwarded to him Mr Wallis replies that he will write to and then call on Mr Pearde. Further detail about his action concerning that gentleman is given.
	107	Spencer asks Mr Wallis to issue the habere if Mr Pearde does not remit his rent within two posts. Mr Wallis decides not to charge Mr Pearde with costs for this business as that would end the suit and then need a fresh service of ejectments if ejectment were required.
	108	Mr Wallis has not received the rent promised by Mr Pearde, and will perhaps obtain it from him when he visits the neighbourhood of Castlelyons in the near future.
	111	Spencer has written asking Mr Wallis to send Mr Wood's further opinion on the Mohire affair.
	112	Spencer has not given Mr Wallis the money to pay Counsellor Wood yet, and has told him to take no further steps regarding the title of Mohire for the time being.
	113	After yet further delays with payment, Spencer tells Alice Price that he will instruct Mr Wallis to act against Mr Pearde if payment of rent is not made by a certain date.
	114	Spencer reports that Mr Wallis maintains that the Prices have a good title to the Mohire estate.
	115	Mr Wallis will stay with Spencer for a few days on his way from Co. Cork to Dublin.

Wallis, Henry and John (*continued*)	117	Mr Wallis does not make the expected visit, but will do at the beginning of the next term.
	118	Spencer encloses a letter for Mr Wallis concerning the title to Mohire.
	119	Spencer seeks advice from Mr Wallis on how to retake Lord Barrymore's cattle driver if he finds him; Spencer has also paid his bill.
	120	Spencer encloses a letter from Mr Wallis and asks Richard Price to send documents concerning the impending court case about the title to Mohire to him in Dublin.
	128	Rosamond Spencer tells Alice Price that Mr Wallis considers it good that Counsellor Wood is looking at the papers she has sent over.
Walsh, Mr	109	Another person with whom Alice Price is having problems concerning rents; Spencer has threatened him with eviction, and thinks she may soon be rid of him.
	114	Spencer mentions 'a Charge of £2:– for Walsh' who has also paid his quit rent and has promised more.
Warburton, Mr	83	A letter from this person is enclosed in the one sent by Price to Spencer; it is unclear whether Price encloses it to demonstrate that he is doing all for Spencer that he can, or that Warburton says this himself in the letter.
Web, Capt.	22	The successful litigant in a case against Sir Richard Mead involving Kilcolman.
Welsh, Mr Richard (Dick) (also spelled /Welch/)	7	He lives in 'Roches Country'; he is in financial trouble having 'lost his house' and wishes to return to Wales, though apparently cannot do so.
	33	He visits Price in Wales; Spencer tells Price that Welsh has recently been ill, and asks that Price give Welsh some seeds for Spencer when he returns to Ireland.
	50	He visits Spencer and tells him that an unknown person is disputing Price's title to some property in Ireland.
	51	He visits Price in Wales to train a dog for Richard Price, and Spencer expresses surprise at his being able to make the journey from Ireland to Wales so often at his age.
	55	He will bring the eagle that Spencer has found for Richard Price the next time he visits Wales.
	56	He is hindered from travelling to Wales with the eagle when expected as he has injured his foot and his wife is about to give birth; Spencer also says he will make a cage that Welsh can carry to convey the bird.
	57	He has set out for Wales with the eagle for Richard Price; his wife has given birth to a daughter.
	58	Spencer asks whether some extra money sent by Price for Welsh should be given to his wife or kept for his return.
	59	Spencer asks that Mrs Price give Welsh some Jesuit Drops to bring back to Ireland.
	67	He returns from Bryn y Pys looking younger, which Spencer attributes to the better food he gets when staying there.

Welstead (?), Major	73	A possible acquaintance of Price who, having recently married a young girl and fathered five children, is now in a dropsy and likely to die impoverished.
Wife		See Spencer, Ann.
William III	124	Spencer's grandfather helps his campaign against the Jacobites at the Battle of Aughrim.
	127	He granted the grandfather, William Spencer, lands for his services at the Battle of Aughrim.
Williams, Mr	65	A person who has some influence in the revenue office from whom Spencer expects a letter; Price has offered advice as to how Spencer should answer him.
	66	His letter has not yet arrived, but Spencer describes how he will respond to it when it does; he asks Price how long he should wait.
Williams, Lady	73	The newspapers reported her death a month ago though she is still alive.
	75	Before her death she entreats her husband, Sir Watkin, to marry Miss Shakerly.
Williams-Wynn, Richard	75	Brother to Sir Watkin Williams-Wynn; Spencer suggests he will be disappointed that his brother has remarried as he had hoped his son would be Sir Watkin's heir.
Williams-Wynn, Sir Watkin	10	He is mentioned as having had a 'success' but in what sphere in not stated.
	11/14	He is seen by Spencer as a possible source of support for his plan to publish the proposed *Works of Mr. Edmund Spencer.*
	60	Spencer is worried that his letters, sent to Price under cover to Sir Watkin, are not arriving.
	61	Spencer explains that he would have sent his last letter under cover had he been sure Sir Watkin had returned home.
	75	His wife entreats him to marry Miss Shakerly before she dies.
Whitshed, Col. (spelled /Witched/ and /Whitchead/ by Spencer)	44	Spencer reports his death.
	45	A Col. Bligh is to take over his old regiment of Dragoons.
Wood, Counsellor	110	Spencer reminds Alice Price that he has sent her this person's opinion on the Mohire affair.
	111	He has provided Mr Wallis with further opinion on the Mohire affair.
	112	He has been dangerously ill and so unable to send his further opinion regarding the title of Mohire.
	128	Papers recently sent over by Mrs Price are now with him.

Wrixon, Henry	31/33/34	The current lease-holder of the property in Mallow in which Price appears to have an interest and concerning which Spencer makes enquiries in 1745. See also Bulkeley, Callaghan, Checkley, Chinnery (John), Daniel, Dennis, End (Michael), End (William), End (William?), Hoar, Jephson, Marret, Newman, Noble, Noble (John), Price, Price (Capt.), Roberts, Sullivan (Cornelius), and Sullivan (James).

APPENDIX III: INDEX OF PLACES MENTIONED IN THE CORRESPONDENCE

The middle column gives the folio numbers of the letters in which the place is mentioned. The folio numbers are listed consecutively in this column, not in the order in which they appear in the transcription.

Generally the spellings used for the first column are those preferred by Spencer; variants and modern spellings are noted in brackets after that.

Places mentioned in the accounts sent by Spencer to Richard Price (folios 122–23) are not indexed here.

Places given by Spencer as his current address are referenced to the letters in Appendix IV and are not generally noted as such in this Appendix.

Ballinguile		Some seven miles south of Charleville, eight miles north of Mallow and just north of Buttevant.
	3(PS)	Spencer asks Price to address any reply to this letter to Ballinguile, describing it as 'near Charleville'.
Ballyhooly		A village north of the River Blackwater and about one and a half miles east of Renny.
	67	The home of Welsh, and where Spencer suggests he does not enjoy such good food as he does when staying with Price.
	70	The village celebrates the return of Capt. Stannard from gaol.
	75	'Old Stannard', a resident of Ballyhooly, has died.
Bandon		A village approximately fifteen miles south-west of Cork.
	20	A recusant priest arrested near Bandon is to be transported.
Bennet's Bridge		A village five miles south of Kilkenny on the River Nore.
	45	A military camp is planned here in 1746.
	48	Named here as 'the Camp', Spencer stays overnight on his way home from Dublin.
Boston	51	The origin or home of someone Spencer suspects of being the 'Mr Kent' of Cheshire who is 'taken up for uttering treasonable Words'. (It is possible Spencer means Bostock, near Middlewich.)

Place	Letter	Note
Bristol	26	*The Terrible* has to take a prize to Bristol to avoid being quarantined in Cove.
	119	Spencer says he is delayed in sending a bill to Richard Price as bills at Waterford are payable only at Bristol and explains that he thinks bills payable at Bristol would be difficult to negotiate at Chester.
Bridgetown		One mile from Castletownroche on the River Blackwater.
	8	It is given by one Roberts to his son.
Brynypiece (spelled with variations by Spencer; it is now spelled /Bryn y Pys/)		Francis Price's house in Overton, near Wrexham.
	13	Spencer expresses his fear on hearing that small-pox has broken out near Price's house.
	33	Welsh is expected to have arrived here by the time this letter arrives.
	36	Spencer asks how far it from here to Wem, where Richard Price has been sent to school.
	51	Dick Welsh visits Brynypiece to train a dog for Richard Price.
	57	It forms part of the address to this letter which tells Price that Mr Welch has set out for his house with the eagle for Richard Price.
	67	Spencer suggests that Welsh enjoys better food here than he does in his own home.
	89	Spencer tells Alice Price that he must defer his proposed visit until he has seen the Dean about the repairs to the house in the precincts of Dublin Cathedral.
	94	Spencer discusses the Christmas festivities that were held here.
	115	Spencer expresses concern that Alice Price intends to move from here on her son's marriage.
Carlow		A village between Dublin and Cork, about fifty miles from the former and 100 from the latter.
	113	Spencer and his family are spending some weeks here on a visit.
Carrick		Lewis gives a Carrig, two miles east of Mallow on the road to Fermoy, but there are so many 'Carricks' in Ireland that it is impossible to identify this one with any certainty.
	21	'Young Causabon' dies at his seat here, May 1744.
Carrigtohill (now /Carrigtwohill/)		A village some ten miles east of Cork.
	23	Spencer reports the result of one of the horse races held here.
Cashel		A town in Tipperary, approximately fifty miles north-east of Mallow
	76	A Mr Perry is murdered by one Shannahan at the races held here.
Castlecorr (now /Castlecor/)		A village some thirty miles north of Cork.
	83	A dwelling place of his cousin Will Freeman, who is to fix the price to be paid for Renny (see also Duhallow).

Place	Letter	Reference
Castlehyde (now /Castle Hyde/)		A village about one and a half miles west of Fermoy; the seat of the Hyde family.
	84	Capt. Richard Barry and his wife stayed here after their marriage.
Castlelyons		A village approximately eight miles south of Fermoy and fifteen miles north of Cork; the seat of the Earls of Barrymore.
	20	Lord Barrymore's house at Castlelyons is guarded after his arrest in London.
	22	Spencer believes that Barrymore's decision to have the plate of Castlelyons taken to England suggests that he no longer intends to visit there.
	58	Lord Barrymore, having returned to Ireland, is expected soon at his house here.
	72	Captain and Arthur Barry visit for some time but stay nearby rather than at the castle.
	75	A Mr Taaf is there 'setting the Desmesnes' and killing the deer in the park.
	80	Spencer asks that Price's next letter be directed to 'near Castlelyons.'
	82	The vicar of Castlelyons has died, as has his brother.
	91	Spencer spoke to Mr Pearde about his rent when here the previous week, and promises to make enquiries about someone he can recommend to settle the dispute about repairs to Mohire House when he returns next week.
	92	Spencer is delayed on his journey here by the illness that had affected horses in Ireland; he later says he is willing to go here again to see Mr Nason about the disputed repairs to Mohire House.
	93	Spencer goes there on legal business connected to the dispute about repairing Mohire House.
	99	Spencer states that he has not been to Castlelyons for many years and so could not have had any conversation with Mary Hely, with whom this letter in mainly concerned.
	100	It is mentioned as the town where Mary Hely lives.
	103	Mr Wallis's father possesses a good estate here, and is hence a man of some local power.
	108	Mr Wallis is to be near this town soon and perhaps able to obtain from Mr Pearde the rent due on Mohire.
	119	Lord Barrymore's cattle driver has been arrested here but escaped.
Castletown roch (now /Castletown-roche/)		A village midway between Mallow and Fermoy, three miles from Renny and roughly twenty miles due north of Cork. (See also Roches Country.)
	83	Spencer is lodging with a brother-in-law here after the sale of Renny.

Charleville		Approximately forty miles north of Cork on the road to Limerick.
	3	Described as near Ballinguile in the postscript.
	19	Price is asked to direct his next letter to Spencer here.
	119	Mentioned as being ‘near to Churchtown.’
Chester		The main port for shipping to Ireland.
	3	It is included as part of the address for this letter.
	5	Spencer suggests he might travel from Dublin to Chester at Christmas to visit Price and his family.
	18	Spencer gives this as the main point of delivery in England for his *Works of Mr. Edmund Spencer.*
	23	A horse bought here by Mr Deane won a race at Carrigtohill in June 1744.
	95	Spencer tells Mrs Price that he will send some money to her by means of bills on Chester.
	106	Spencer sends a money bill to London rather than Chester, thinking that Richard Price was at Oxford.
	112	A bill has been sent to be cashed at Chester.
	114	Spencer says that he believes that bills on London can be negotiated at Chester without discount, and sends Alice Price a bill that can be cashed there.
	119	Spencer explains that he thinks bills payable at Bristol would be difficult to negotiate at Chester.
Churchtown		Presumably the hamlet of that name some four miles south of Charleville.
	8	A hamlet where Spencer's brother-in-law lives, and where Spencer is temporarily lodging at the time of writing.
	119	Spencer asks Richard Price to direct his next letter here where he and his wife are going to stay with his daughter and her husband.
Clare		A county on the mid-western side of Ireland.
	22	The home of Spencer's brother Kane, to whom Spencer wrote asking if he could catch an eagle for Richard Price.
	116	It was rumoured that the French had landed an invasion force here.
Clonmell		A town some fifty miles north-east of Cork and twenty five miles west of Waterford.
	119	Spencer has been here attending to a commission; he collects a payment from Henry Pearde.
College Green		See Dublin, College Green.

Cork — The main port on the south coast of Ireland and a county.

5 Proposing a visit to Price, Spencer says travelling to Chester from Dublin is less fatiguing than to Co. Cork.

8 Col. Barry has given up the idea of quitting Cork; Price's friend Hodder Roberts has married a widow of Cork and moved there

18 Spencer mentions his intention of attending the assizes at Cork in March 1744 in order to solicit subscribers for his *Works of Mr. Edmund Spencer.*

20 Spencer has returned from Cork where a naval victory was being celebrated; he also reports the funeral procession in Cork of Capt. David Barry.

21 No indian grass is to be found in Cork in May 1744.

25 Spencer gives an account of the trial of a naval officer held at Cork assizes in August 1744.

26 Spencer receives an account from Cork concerning *The Terrible* being quarantined in Cove.

28 Spencer is in Cork receiving medical treatment for a 'consumption'.

29 An embargo has been passed on Cork Harbour to prevent covert trading with the French.

31 Spencer refers to the generosity of his friend Col. Oliver who paid off the debt he contracted in Cork for medical bills.

32 It is noted as the place where two people involved in the enquiries into Price's lease in Mallow died; Spencer says he will make enquires about them next month when he goes to Cork assizes.

33 The home town of three people who might have information concerning Price's lease in Mallow.

35 One of the End family concerned in the business about the Mallow property is still living in Cork.

42 The merchants of Cork petition to have butter exempted from a trade embargo.

49 The judges are due to go to Cork in three weeks.

52 The Mayor of Cork is ordered to provide quarters for 6,000 soldiers.

53 The arrival of Admiral Lestock's squadron in Cove and the quartering of his troops in Cork cause the markets there to rise.

54 Only Dublin bills are being accepted as payment in Cork; Gen. Sinclair's forces have left for Limerick and Galway.

55 The forces under the command of Gen. Sinclair that marched from Cork to Galway have returned to Cork to await embarkation to an unknown destination.

71 Spencer sees *The True Blue*, a privateer fitted out by some merchants of Cork, along with its prize, a ship that was bound for Martinique.

83 The price to be paid for Renny is to be fixed at the next Cork assizes.

90 Mr Pearde tells Spencer that he has some money ready to send to Cork.

Cork (*continued*)	91	Spencer has just returned from Cork; he also says it should be easy to buy bills there for large sums to send to anywhere in England.
	112	Counsellor Wood has been dangerously ill here during the previous vacation.
	115	Mr Wallis will stay with Spencer on his way back to Dublin and from Co. Cork.
Cove (now / Cobh/)		A port near Cork to the east of the River Lee where it passes into the sea.
	25	The departure point of one of the ships involved in the trial that Spencer gives an account of in this letter.
	26	*The Terrible*, a privateer, has brought a French prize into Cove; the *Old Noll* takes shelter near Cove after being mauled in a fight with a French privateer.
	32	Col. Jephson takes a draught of soldiers bound for Flanders here but then abandons them and returns home.
	53	Admiral Lestock's squadron arrives with a large contingent of men and some plunder from France.
Dantzick (now / Gdańsk/)	71	A Baltic port in Poland, the point of departure for Capt. Chip's voyage to Kinsale in an open boat.
Dingle		A town in Co. Kerry.
	9	Mentioned in relation to Col. Danny's foolish behaviour during the 1743 election for the member for Kerry.
Doneraile	8	A town in Co. Cork, the parliamentary seat for which changes hands.
Dublin (sometimes referred to as 'Town')	12/13	Spencer plans to go to Dublin in order to find subscribers to his planned *Works of Mr. Edmund Spencer.*
	14	Spencer reports that his *Proposals for Printing by Subscription the Works of Mr. Edmund Spencer* are in process of being printed here.
	23	Spencer comments on the 'military madness' that seems to have seized Dublin.
	24	Spencer says that he hopes to be in Dublin later in the year to put his *Works of Mr. Edmund Spencer* to press.
	25	A privateer called *The Boyne* has been fitted out in Dublin.
	36	Spencer plans to go to Dublin to get his *Works of Mr. Edmund Spencer* printed.
	37	Spencer has been in town three days in hope of being recommended for a position.
	43/44/45	Due to the parliamentary recess few people are in town at this time.
	46	MPs are leaving town on the proroguing of parliament.
	52	Spencer's brother Nathaniel is discharged from the army after a spell of duty in Dublin.
	54	Only Dublin bills are being accepted as payment in Cork.
	61	Spencer surmises that Price's last letter to him had been delayed at the Post Office in Dublin.
	66	Spencer asks Price how long he should stay in Dublin awaiting a response from Mr Williams.
	68	The two Lady Barrymores have arrived in town with Mr Barry.

Dublin (*continued*)	69	He intends to leave Dublin in about a week.
	70	Following Price's suggestion, Spencer sets out from the 'Metropolis'.
	73	The late Dr Kingsbury's books were sold at Dick's Coffee House in Dublin.
	77	Spencer says he must set out for Dublin on 1 November as Renny is to be sold very soon after that.
	81	He tells Price that he wrote from Dublin to say that friends have suggested he apply to the Duke of Marlborough for help.
	86	Spencer tells Alice Price that he proposes going to Dublin the next month to purchase a commission.
	87	Dublin is not mentioned, but it is clear that Spencer has come here to conduct some business for Alice Price.
	92	Spencer says he is due to go to Dublin early in the new year.
	93	Spencer intends going there later in the month to discuss a business trip to London with an unnamed gentleman.
	94	He says he will make further enquiries about Mohire when the lawyers are in town for the new term.
	97	Spencer is staying here and conducting some business for Mr Deane concerning property that gentleman owns 'in & near this city'.
	98	Spencer tells Alice Price that when he came here he had intended to instruct Mr Wallis to sue Mr Pearde for his rent, but then received a bill drawn on Dublin for the due sum.
	106	Spencer's wife forwards a letter from Mrs Price to Mr Wallis in Dublin.
	107	Illness has prevented Spencer from coming to town until three days ago.
	108	Spencer gives this as the place where he wrote his last letter to Alice Price. He also explains his method for ensuring prompt payment of rent from Mr Deane's tenants in Co. Dublin.
	109	Spencer writes to Dublin to enquire who are the young Lord Barrymore's guardians.
	110	Spencer goes to Dublin to negotiate a bill from Mr Pearde.
	111	Spencer is unable to travel there at present as he is still weak after his last illness.
	112	Spencer threatens to issue the habere against Mr Pearde when next in Dublin; he asks for advance notice of Richard Price's visit to Ireland in order to meet him in Dublin.
	113	Spencer intends to set out for Dublin in about two weeks.
	115	Alice Price's last letter is forwarded to Spencer from Dublin; also Mr Wallis will stay with Spencer on his way back to Dublin from Co. Cork.
	117	Spencer is prevented from going here by his working on a tax survey.
	118	Illness prevents Spencer from going here to meet a gentleman about a financial arrangement.
	120	Spencer asks Richard Price to send the Deed of Sale for Mohire to Mr Wallis in Dublin.

Dublin, Aungier Street	120	The address of Henry Wallis, one of the Prices' lawyers in Ireland.
Dublin, Bride Street	48	The address of John Wallis, Spencer's lawyer.
Dublin, College Green	37	The square opposite Trinity College, Dublin, where Spencer lodges with Widow Thornton in November 1745. The Parliament House is also located in this square.
Dublin, Dick's Coffee House	62	Spencer's lodging place in Dublin in November 1747.
	73	The late Doctor Kingsbury's books were sold off here at the end of 1747, somewhat to Spencer's surprise.
	93	Spencer asks for replies to this letter to be sent here as he will be in Dublin.
Dublin, The Eagle Tavern	15	Spencer reports that the tavern is 'shutting up' despite the owner's apparently sound circumstances.
Dublin, Fishamble Street	14(PS)	The location of The Scales and Sugar Loaf, Spencer's lodging place in Dublin in January 1743.
	44/78	The address also of Mr Lumbard the apothecary, where Spencer lodges in March 1746 and November 1748.
Dublin, Mary Street	107/114	The address of Mr Conolly where Spencer lodges in February 1757 and December 1759.
Dublin, Stephen's Green	8	The location in Dublin of the elder Leeson's brewery.
Dunlary (now / Dún Laoghaire/)		A seaport in southern Dublin.
	6	Bad weather forces the boat on which Spencer is returning to Ireland to land here in the winter of 1741/2.
Duhallow		A barony in the northern part of Co. Cork.
	51	Spencer stays here in August 1746 visiting his friend and hunting companion Mr Freeman.
Funcion, River (now / Funshion/)		A northern tributary of the River Blackwater which it joins some two and a half miles west of Fermoy.
	61	Tom Burgess, 'a hearty honest Farmer', who died after drinking milk and water, lived near this river.
Galway		A town in Co. Galway, approximately 125 miles north of Cork.
	54	Gen. Sinclair's forces have left Cork for here.
	55	The forces under the command of Gen. Sinclair which marched from Cork to Galway have now gone back to Cork to await embarkation to an unknown destination.
	72	Ships carrying consumer goods have docked here, as at Kinsale, since the beginning of the war.
Kerry		A county in south-west Ireland.
	9	Spencer gives an account of the 1743 election for the member of parliament.
Kilcolman		The castle at Kilcolman, roughly thirty miles due north of Cork, was once the residence of the poet Edmund Spenser.
	3	Spencer notes that the rent for this property had been paid to Sir Richard Mead for some years.
	22	It is the subject of a law case between Capt. Webb and Sir Richard Mead which the former won.

Kilcummer		A village less than one mile north of Renny, one and a half miles south-east of Castletownroche, and some twenty miles due north of Cork.
	26	Mr Oliver, a hunting companion, has come to his villa at Kilcummer for the winter.
Kildare		A county and a town just west of Dublin.
	114	Spencer says he was delayed in coming to Dublin as he was obliged to go to Co. Kildare.
Kilkenny		A county; also a town on the River Nore roughly mid-way between Dublin and Cork.
	45	A military camp is planned at Bennet's Bridge near here and the town will benefit financially from visitors as a result.
	46	The people of Kilkenny are unhappy that the camp at Bennet's Bridge may not be constructed because the rebellion is waning.
	78	Several members of a gang of highwaymen are being held in Kilkenny gaol.
	95	Spencer intends to visit the county for a few days.
	101	Spencer has been electioneering here.
	104	Spencer has been in Kilkenny collecting rents.
	108	He notes that he is less strict with Mr Deane's tenants in Co. Kilkenny than those in Co. Dublin on account of their poverty and distance from a market.
	113	Spencer has taken on work as an agent for a Mrs Payne in Co. Kilkenny.
	114	He is detained here longer than he expected.
Kill Saint Anne		An area just to the west of Castlelyons.
	72	Captain Barry and his brother Arthur stayed here rather than in the castle at Castlelyons when visiting the new Lord Barrymore.
Kinsale		A port approximately fifteen miles south of Cork on the estuary of the River Bandon.
	23	Two captured ships are brought into Kinsale; Spencer names the candidates for a forthcoming election.
	29	The arrival of the hulks indicates that war is imminent, but it has also meant the raising of rents in that town; also an embargo has been imposed on the harbour to prevent covert trading with the French.
	67	Several prisoners of war are killed by a fire in the house where they are imprisoned.
	71	Capt. Chip arrived here at the end of his voyage from Dantzick (Gdańsk) in an open boat.
	72	Women of fashion are flocking here to buy China goods from two Indiamen that are docked for repairs.
Lab a colly (now /Labacally/)		A hamlet near Glanworth, Co. Cork, situated approximately three miles north-west of Fermoy
	61	The home of Tom Burgess, a farmer, who has recently died.

Limerick		A county of Ireland, and a town sixty miles north of Cork.
	27	Like the countryside around Renny, Limerick is badly flooded, much of the hay harvest destroyed, and many in danger of destitution.
	29	Lambs are dying because of the cold, and heavy snow has destroyed the potato crop.
	30	The county in which Newcastle is situated.
	36	The price of beef is very low here.
	53	The low price of beef is causing losses to Limerick farmers.
	54	Gen. Sinclair's forces have left Cork for here.
	55	Spencer finds an eagle for Richard Price here; the forces under the command of Gen. Sinclair that marched from Cork to Galway have returned to Cork to await embarkation to an unknown destination.
	72	Many ships carrying consumer goods have docked here, as at Kinsale, since the beginning of the war.
	117	Mr Wallis has to return home via Limerick and so does not visit Spencer.
Lismore		A town approximately thirty five miles north-east of Cork and on the River Blackwater.
	23	An acquaintance has little luck fishing because the weir at Lismore is preventing salmon from swimming further up the Blackwater.
Liverpool (Spencer sometimes spells it /Leverpoole/)	25	The home port of two of the ships involved in the trial which Spencer gives an account of in this letter.
	35	Spencer wonders if the recent lack of communication from Price is because the latter has been in Liverpool.
	115	Spencer advises Alice Price against moving here on the marriage of her son as the climate is 'too keen', especially in the winter.
	118	Spencer arranges for a bill to be cashed here by Richard Price.
London	11	Spencer believes that as Lord Barrymore and Sir Watkin are currently in London they could procure a good many subscribers for his *Works of Mr. Edmund Spencer.*
	12	Spencer asks if Price thinks it a good idea to advertise the proposed *Works of Mr. Edmund Spencer* in the London papers.
	15	Spencer decides it will not be necessary to advertise the proposed *Works of Mr. Edmund Spencer* in the London papers.
	18	Spencer says that London subscribers to his proposed *Works of Mr. Edmund Spencer* will have their copies delivered there.
	19	Spencer says he has been advised to go to London in order to solicit subscribers for his *Works of Mr. Edmund Spencer.*

London *(continued)*	93	Spencer says he is negotiating with an unnamed gentleman about accompanying him to London on legal business.
	98	He tells Alice Price that he will send her a London bill for the sum remitted by Mr Pearde.
	105	Spencer sends a bill drawn on merchants in London.
	106	Spencer says he sent the bill mentioned in the previous letter to London rather than Chester, thinking that Richard Price was at Oxford.
	110	Spencer sends Alice Price a bill drawn on merchants in London.
	114	He believes that bills on London can be negotiated at Chester without discount and asks that further instructions be sent to him when Richard Price has returned from there.
	117	Spencer sends a bill on Mr Cazalet of London.
	118	Spencer asks Richard Price if he would prefer for bills to be made payable here rather than in Liverpool.
	119	Spencer arranges for a bill to be paid at London.
Martinique (spelled / Martinico/ by Spencer)		A French Caribbean island.
	25	The destination of a French ship taken by *The Thurloe.*
	71	*The True Blue* has captured a ship that was bound for Martinique.
Mallow		A town approximately seventeen miles north of Cork and eight miles east of Castletownroche.
	25(PS)	The home town of a young sailor whom Spencer asks Price to assist by writing to the owners of his ship.
	31	Spencer has been to Mallow three times to make enquiries about the property there on which Price has a lease.
	32	Spencer goes again to Mallow to make further enquiries about Price's lease; Col. Jephson returns home to Mallow having, on a pretence of illness, left a squadron of men at Cove to be transported to Flanders without him.
	33	Spencer has made several more enquiries about the property in Mallow.
	34	Spencer despairs of getting to the bottom of the 'Mallow affair', concerning which he gives considerable further detail.
	35	Spencer provides more information about the Mallow affair and complains that he has written to Price four or five times without getting a reply.
	49	Spencer reports on the race meeting and the assault of a jockey by Hugh Massey.
	55	500 Highlanders are quartered at Mallow where they are well liked for their good behaviour.
Meath		The county north-west of Dublin.
	10	The county in which lay the estate won by Mr Annesley in the law case he brought against his uncle in 1743.

Mohire (also spelled /Mahiry/, /Mohery/ and /Mohiry/ by Spencer; now /Mohera/)		A house and its associated land in Castlelyons.
	90	Spencer tells Mr Buchan that he has forwarded him some letters and other particulars about this place.
	91	Spencer says he will find a person who can help settle the dispute about the repairs to the house.
	92	Further discussion about the disputed repairs to the house.
	93	Further discussion about the disputed repairs to the house.
	94	Spencer tells Mrs Price that he will make discreet enquiries about the title to the house when the counsellors come to Dublin for the new term.
	96	Spencer states that he has found notes concerning the original lease of the lands of Mohire and a deed of sale of those lands between Lord Buttevant and John Price dated 1692.
	99	Spencer says he will have to defer looking into something Alice Price has asked him about regarding Mohire because he has been distracted by the business of Mary Hely.
	102	Mr Pearde sends an account of his spending on and income from the lands attached to the house.
	103	A statement is provided of the rents due from and paid by Mr Pearde.
	110	Spencer asks Alice Price to let him know her thoughts about Mohire once she has read Counsellor Wood's opinion.
	111	Spencer is unable to give Alice Price a report on this matter owing to illness; Mr Pearde is now three quarter days behind with his rent.
	112	The papers of the Mohire affair are in the hands of Counsellor Wood, but he is too ill to deal with them.
	113	Spencer expresses regret at the many disappointments the affair of Mohire has caused him.
	114	Richard Price is determined to maintain his full title to Mohire.
	115	Spencer will talk with Mr Wallis at length about the affair when the lawyer visits him.
Munster		One of the provinces of Ireland; the poet Spenser held a considerable number of properties here, and it is the home province of Edmund Spencer.
	19	Spencer mentions his intention setting out for Munster in March 1744 in order to solicit subscribers for his *Works of Mr. Edmund Spencer.*
	42	Sir Mathew Deane, an old friend of Price, sets out for Munster.
	47	Spencer intends to leave Dublin for Munster soon.
	48	Spencer is on his way there as he writes this letter.
	72	Spencer notes that he has not had a letter from Price since his return here from Dublin.
	78	Spencer rides to Cork without meeting a highwayman, though the roads of Munster are said to be infested.
	80	Spencer announces his intention to leave Dublin for Munster.

Newcastle		Newcastle West, a town twenty five miles south-west of Limerick.
	30	Hay has risen to eight shillings per hundredweight in the area around this town.
Overton		The village in Wales, some ten miles south-east of Wrexham, where Francis Price lived.
	13	Spencer expresses his fear on hearing that small-pox has broken out in the area where Price lives.
	54	Spencer responds to a story recounted by Price in his previous letter about an unidentified 'old Gentleman of Overton'.
Oxford	15	The home of a Mr Ellis, who, Spencer suggests, might be able to obtain some subscribers for the proposed *Works of Mr. Edmund Spencer.*
	19	Spencer is advised to go to Oxford in order to solicit subscribers for his *Works of Mr. Edmund Spencer.*
	106	Spencer sends a money bill to London rather than Chester, thinking that Richard Price is at Oxford.
Parkgate, Chester		A village and, in the eighteenth century, a port on the Wirral peninsula to the west of Chester; which was a major point of embarkation for Ireland.
	121	Spencer expects to board a yacht here to return to Ireland.
Passage		Passage West, a port on the north-west side of the River Lee as it passes from Lough Mahon into the sea near Cove.
	26	The *Old Noll* takes shelter here after being mauled in a fight with a French privateer.
Rathcormac (spelled / Rathcormuck/ by Spencer)		A small town twenty miles north of Cork on the road between Fermoy and Dublin.
	24	The death of the member of parliament provides Col. Barry with another opportunity for making some money.
Renny		A hamlet close to Castletownroche, just above the River Blackwater and some twenty miles due north of Cork.
	3	Spencer considers selling some of the land at Renny.
	8	Poor prices for produce force Spencer's tenant to surrender this property.
	21	Spencer says he has abated the rent and come to board here for the year in order to assist the tenant.
	36	Spencer states that Renny will soon be sold by court order, and wonders how he will then survive.
	62	Renny is soon to be put up for sale.
	63	Spencer discusses the values of different parts of the estate, and how he will raise money by means of a mortgage.
	69	Spencer asks Price to direct his next letter here.
	74	The Powers push for an immediate sale of Renny to the alarm of Spencer, though he manages to get it put off for a week; a friend promises to bid high for it.
	76	It is to be sold in November and Spencer hopes to get the full value as he expects many will be bidding for it.
	79	The sale is completed and after paying off encumbrances Spencer expects to have £400-500.
	83	Spencer notes that he moved from Renny two years ago.

Ringsend		An area of Dublin on the southern side of the confluence of the River Liffey and the sea.
	50	Spencer obtains a posting for his brother here as a coast officer.
Roches Country		Possibly Castletownroche (see Castletown roch).
	7	Spencer mentions that he stayed here for ten days in September/October 1743.
	10	Spencer mentions that he stayed here in November/December 1743.
	29	Frost damage to crops elsewhere has meant the local corn has raised in price.
Strabane		A town in Co. Tyrone, 100 miles north of Dublin.
	53	Spencer's brother Nathaniel is posted here as a gauger in the Excise.
Tralee		The county town of Co. Kerry in the south west of Ireland.
	9	An inhabitant of the town gives Spencer the account of the 1743 election of the member of parliament provided in the letter.
Waterford		The name of a county and of a substantial port on the estuary of the River Suir, some seventy miles east of Cork.
	25	A prize taken by *The Terrible* is taken into Waterford.
	78	The notorious highwayman Freny has a large gang in the county.
	99	It is mentioned in relation to the business of Mary Hely as the nearest Spencer has been to Castlelyons for many years.
	112	Spencer requests Alice Price to let him know at Waterford that she has received his last bill of exchange.
	114	He negotiates bills here rather than at Dublin and says this can be done at a better exchange rate than in Dublin; he will not be setting out there for a fortnight.
Wem		A small market town in Shropshire, about fourteen miles from Overton.
	36	The location of the school to which Richard Price is sent.
Wicklow		A port some thirty miles south of Dublin, and a parliamentary borough.
	44	The death of Col. Witched (Whitshed) means the parliamentary seat is now vacant.
	97	Spencer tell Mrs Price that he has obtained employment here as a land waiter in the Customs, and asks her to address letters to him here.
	98	Spencer states his intention to return here from Dublin the next day.
	105	Spencer receives this letter at Wicklow, but answers from Dublin; he says in the postscript that he will return to Wicklow the next day.
	107	Spencer says he will set out from Dublin to Wicklow on the following day.
	110	Spencer will return here the next day.

Wrexham		Approximately twenty five miles south of Liverpool, the nearest town to Francis Price's house in Wales; Spencer sometimes includes it in the address when he is not writing under cover.
	94	Spencer refers to Bryn y Pys as Wrexham metonymically in this letter.
	117	Alice Price has moved to Wrexham from Overton; she tells her son that a Mr Adam sang in the church there.

APPENDIX IV: PLACES GIVEN AS ADDRESSES OF ORIGIN

The folio numbers only are given and they are listed consecutively, not in the order in which they appear in the transcription.

Castlelyons (sometimes 'near')	4; 23; 30; (70); (71); 74; 82; 83; 84; 85; 86
Chester	121
Ballinguile, nr Charleville	3(?)
Charleville	7; 8; 9; 10; 11; 12; 13; 20; 91; 92
Dublin	5; 14; 15; 18; 19; 37 (see also 38); 39; 47; 65; 66; 68; 69; 80; 90; 94; 95; 96; 97; 98; 105; 110; 112
Dublin, College Green	38 (see also 37); 40(?); 41; 42; 43; 63; 64
Dublin, Dick's Coffee House	62; 67; 87; 88; 89
Dublin, Fishamble Street	44; 45; 46; 78; 79
Dublin, Mary Street	107; 114
Renny	21; 22; 23; 24; 25; 26; 27; 28; 29; 31; 32; 33; 34; 35; 36; 49; 50; 51; 52; 53; 54; 55; 56; 57; 59; 60; 61; 70; 71; 72; 73; 76
Waterford	111; 113; 115; 116; 117; 118; 119; 120; 128
Wicklow	99; 100; 101; 102; 103; 104; 106; 108; 109

BIBLIOGRAPHY

Manuscripts

Cheshire Record Office, Chester: Marriage Licence Bonds and Allegations, EDC 8 1735 (J) — 1736 (V) (marriage bond between Francis Price and Alice Lloyd)

Flintshire Record Office, Hawarden:

Overton, St Mary, Parish Registers, GB 0208 P/46/1

Bangor Is y Coed, St Dunawd, Parish Registers, P/3

Schedule of Hawarden and Bangor Tithes, 1741, D/BJ/A40

Deed of Covenant to Levy a Fine, 12 Mar 1738/1739, D/LJ/885

Liverpool Record Office, Liverpool: Lease Register for Liverpool Corporation, 352 CLE/Con 3/2, 1672–1767 (transference of a lease from John Cleiveland to Francis Price)

Llyfrgell Genedlaethol Cymru/National Library of Wales, Aberystwyth:

Puleston 15: NLW MS 3575E (miscellaneous seventeenth-century letters)

Puleston 17: NLW MS 3577C (correspondence of Arthur Barry with Francis Price)

Puleston 18: NLW MS 3578E (correspondence of John Buchan with Francis Price)

Puleston 19: NLW MS 3579D (correspondence of William Pearde with Francis Price)

Puleston 20: NLW MS 3580E (correspondence of Edmund Spencer with Francis Price, Alice Price, John Buchan, and Richard Parry Price)

Puleston 21: NLW MS 3581E (correspondence of Dr Apperly and George Dickens with Francis Price)

Puleston 22: NLW MS 3582D (correspondence of James Barry, 4th Earl of Barrymore, with Francis Price)

Puleston 24: NLW MS 3584E (correspondence of Thomas Kingsbury with Francis Price)

Puleston 25: NLW MS 3585C (miscellaneous correspondence of Francis Price)

[NB: the final capital letter in references to the Puleston volumes is that given in the online catalogue of Llyfrgell Genedlaethol Cymru/National Library of Wales]

Welsh Wills, Thomas Lloyd, Overton, 1748, C1748/6

University of Dublin, Trinity College Library: Entrance Books/Matriculation Registers, TCD MUN V 23/1 (1637–1725)

Printed Works

BANNET, EVE TAVOR, *Empire of Letters: Letter Manuals and Transatlantic Correspondence, 1680–1820* (Cambridge: Cambridge University Press, 2005)

BARNARD, TOBY, *A New Anatomy of Ireland: The Irish Protestants, 1649–1770* (New Haven, CT: Yale University Press, 2003)

—— *Irish Protestant Ascents and Descents, 1641–1770* (Dublin: Four Courts Press, 2004)

BARTHOLOMEW, JOHN, *A Gazetteer of the British Isles, Statistical and Topographical* (Edinburgh: John Bartholomew and Co., 1893)

BECKETT, J. C. 'Eighteenth-Century Ireland', in *A New History of Ireland: IV, Eighteenth-Century Ireland, 1691–1800*, ed. by T. W. Moody and W. E. Vaughan (Oxford: Clarendon Press, 1986), pp. xl-lxiv

BERG, TEMMA, 'Truly Yours: Arranging a Letter Collection', *Eighteenth-Century Life*, 35, 1 (2011), 29–50

BEW, PAUL, *Ireland: The Politics of Enmity, 1789–2006* (Oxford: Oxford University Press, 2007)

BOTTIGHEIMER, KARL S., *English Money and Irish Land: The Adventurers in the Cromwellian Settlement of Ireland* (Oxford: Clarendon Press, 1971)

BRANT, CLARE, *Eighteenth-Century Letters and British Culture* (Basingstoke: Palgrave Macmillan, 2006)

BROCKLISS, LAURENCE, 'Religion and Social Mobility in Eighteenth- and Early Nineteenth-Century Ireland,' in *Ireland and Medicine in the Seventeenth and Eighteenth Centuries*, ed. by James Kelly and Fiona Clark (Farnham: Ashgate, 2010), pp. 73–10

BUCHAN, JOHN, *Midwinter: Certain Travellers in Old England* (London: Hodder & Stoughton, 1923)

BURKE, J. BERNARD, *A Genealogical and Heraldic Dictionary of the Landed Gentry of Great Britain and Ireland for 1852*, 2 vols (London: Colburn and Co., 1852)

CARLISLE, NICHOLAS, *A Topographical Dictionary of Ireland* (Bedford Bury: printed for William Miller, by William Savage, 1810)

—— *A Topographical Dictionary of the Dominion of Wales* (London: printed for the author by W. Bulmer and Co., 1811)

CARPENTER, ANDREW, ed., *Verse in English from Eighteenth-century Ireland* (Cork: Cork University Press, 1998)

CICERO, M. T., *On Old Age, On Friendship, On Divination*, trans. by W. A. Falconer (London: Heinemann, 1923)

—— *Selected Letters*, ed. by D. R. Shackleton Bailey (Harmondsworth: Penguin, 1986)

CONNOLLY, SEAN, *Religion, Law and Power: The Making of Protestant Ireland, 1660–1760* (Oxford: Clarendon Press, 1992)

CULLEN, L. M., 'Economic Development, 1691–1750', in *A New History of Ireland: IV, Eighteenth-Century Ireland, 1691–1800*, ed. by T. W. Moody and W. E. Vaughan (Oxford: Clarendon Press, 1986), pp. 123–40

—— 'Economic Development, 1750–1800', in *A New History of Ireland: IV, Eighteenth-Century Ireland, 1691–1800*, ed. by T. W. Moody and W. E. Vaughan (Oxford: Clarendon Press, 1986), pp. 141–58

CURTIS, MAURICE, *To Hell or Monto: The Story of Dublin's Most Notorious Districts* (Stroud: The History Press, 2015)

DAYBELL, JAMES, *The Material Letter in Early Modern England: Manuscript Letters and the Culture and Practices of Letter-Writing, 1512–1635* (Basingstoke: Palgrave, 2012)

DELANEY, MARY, *Letters from Georgian Ireland: The Correspondence of Mary Delaney 1731–68*, ed. by Angélique Day (Belfast: Friar's Bush Press, 1991)

DITZ, TOBY, 'Formative Ventures: Eighteenth-Century Commercial Letters and the Articulation of Experience', in *Epistolary Selves: Letters and Letter-writers, 1600–1945*, ed. by Rebecca Earle (Basingstoke: Ashgate, 1999), pp. 59–78

EARLE, REBECCA, 'Introduction: Letters, Writers and the Historian', in *Epistolary Selves: Letters and Letter-writers, 1600–1945*, ed. by Rebecca Earle (Basingstoke: Ashgate, 1999), pp. 1–12

ELLIOT, MARIANNE, *Wolfe Tone* (Liverpool: Liverpool University Press, 2012)

ELRINGTON BALL, FRANCIS, *The Judges in Ireland, 1221–1921*, 2 vols (London: John Murray, 1926)

FERGUS, JAN, 'Provincial Servants' Reading in the Late Eighteenth-Century', in *The Practice and Representation of Reading in England*, ed. by James Raven, Helen Small & Naomi Tadmor (Cambridge: Cambridge University Press, 1996), pp. 202–25

FOSTER, ROY, *Modern Ireland, 1600–1972* (Harmondsworth: Penguin, 1988)

FRASER, JAMES, *Guide Through Ireland* (Dublin: William Curry, Jun. and Company, 1838)

FRENCH, H. R., *The Middle Sort of People in Provincial England, 1600–1750* (Oxford: Oxford University Press, 2007)

FROUDE, J. A., *The English in Ireland in the Eighteenth Century*, 3 vols (London: Longmans, 1882)

GIBSON, CHARLES, *The History of the County and City of Cork*, 2 vols (London: Thomas C. Newby, 1861)

GOLINSKI, JAN, *British Weather and the Climate of Enlightenment* (Chicago: Chicago University Press, 2012)

GRAY, THOMAS, *The Correspondence of Thomas Gray*, ed. by Frederick A. Pottle, Charles H. Bennett, rev. by Herbert W. Starr, 3 vols (Oxford: Clarendon Press, 1971)

HADFIELD, ANDREW, 'A Mortgage Agreement of Hugolin Spenser, Edmund Spenser's Grandson,' *Spenser Studies*, 27 (2012), 329–35

——*Edmund Spenser: A Life* (Oxford: Oxford University Press, 2012)

HANSHALL, J. H., *The History of the County Palatine and City of Chester* (Chester: printed by John Fletcher, 1817)

HARRIS, ALEXANDRA, *Weatherland: Writers and Artists Under English Skies* (London: Thames & Hudson, 2015)

HASSELBERG, YLVA, 'Letters, Social Networks and the Embedded Economy in Sweden: Some Remarks on the Swedish Bourgeoisie, 1800–1850', in *Epistolary Selves: Letters and Letter-writers, 1600–1945*, ed. by Rebecca Earle (Basingstoke: Ashgate, 1999), pp. 95–107

HISTORICAL MANUSCRIPTS COMMISSION, FIFTEENTH REPORT, PART VII, *The Manuscripts of the Duke of Somerset, the Marquis of Ailesbury, and The Rev. Sir T. H. G. Puleston, Bart.* (London: Her Majesty's Stationery Office, 1898)

HONAN, PARK, 'Eighteenth and Nineteenth Century English Punctuation Theory', *English Studies*, 41:1–6 (1960), 92–102

HOUSTON, R. A., *The Population History of Britain and Ireland 1500–1750* (Cambridge: Cambridge University Press, 1995)

HOW, JAMES, *Epistolary Spaces: English Letter Writing from the Foundation of the Post Office to Richardson's Clarissa* (Aldershot: Ashgate, 2003)

INNES, JOANNA, 'Legislation and Public Participation', in *The British and Their Laws in the Eighteenth Century*, ed. by David Lemmings (Woodbridge: Boydell, 2005), pp. 102–32

JARRETT, DEREK, *England in the Age of Hogarth*, rev. ed. (New Haven, CT: Yale University Press, 1986)

JOHNSON-LIIK, EDITH MARY, *History of the Irish Parliament, 1692–1800*, 6 vols (Belfast: Ulster Historical Foundation, 2002)

KELLY, JAMES, 'Domestic Medication and Medical Care in Late Early Modern Ireland', in *Ireland and Medicine in the Seventeenth and Eighteenth Centuries*, ed. by James Kelly and Fiona Clark (Farnham: Ashgate, 2010), pp. 109–35

LAMMEY DAVID, 'The Irish-Portuguese Trade Dispute, 1770–90', *Irish Historical Studies*, 25, 97 (1986), 29–45

LANGFORD, PAUL, *A Polite and Commercial People: England 1727–1783* (Oxford: Clarendon Press, 1989)

LEWIS, SAMUEL, *A Topographical Dictionary of Ireland*, 2 vols (London: S. Lewis, 1837)

——*A Topographical Dictionary of Wales*, 2 vols (London: S. Lewis, 1840)

MACCULLOCH, DIARMAID, *Reformation: Europe's House Divided, 1490–1700* (Harmondsworth: Penguin, 2004)

MATTHEW, COLIN, and BRIAN HARRISON, eds, *The Oxford Dictionary of National Biography*, online edition (Oxford: Oxford University Press, 2014), <www.oxforddnb.com>

McCracken, J. L., 'The Ecclesiastical Structure, 1714–60', in *A New History of Ireland: IV, Eighteenth-Century Ireland, 1691–1800*, ed. by T. W. Moody and W. E. Vaughan (Oxford: Clarendon Press, 1986), pp. 84–104

——'The Political Structure, 1714–60', in *A New History of Ireland: IV, Eighteenth-Century Ireland, 1691–1800*, ed. by T. W. Moody and W. E. Vaughan (Oxford: Clarendon Press, 1986), pp. 57–83

McDowell, R. B., 'Parliamentary Independence, 1782–9', in *A New History of Ireland: IV, Eighteenth-Century Ireland, 1691–1800*, ed. by T. W. Moody and W. E. Vaughan (Oxford: Clarendon Press, 1986), pp. 265–88

McGuire, James, and James Quinn, eds, *Dictionary of Irish Biography*, 9 vols (Cambridge: Cambridge University Press, 2009)

Minchinton, W. E., ed., *Politics and the Port of Bristol in the Eighteenth Century: The Petitions of the Society of Merchant Venturers 1698–1803* (Bristol: Bristol Record Society, 1963)

New Manual Exercise as Performed by His Majesty's Dragoons, Foot-guards, Foot, Artillery, Marines, and by the Militia, 2nd edn (London: printed for J. Millan, 1758)

Nuki, George, and Peter Simkin, 'A Concise History of Gout and Hyperuricemia and their Treatment', *Arthritis Research & Therapy*, 8, Supplement 1 (2006)

Osbourne, Dorothy, *The Letters of Dorothy Osbourne to William Temple*, ed. by G. B. Moore Smith (Oxford: Clarendon Press, 1928)

Pennant, Thomas, *Tours in Wales*, 2 vols (Caernarvon: H. Humphreys, 1883)

Pollard, Mary, *A Dictionary of Members of the Dublin Book Trade* (London: Bibliographical Society, 2000)

Ray, John, *The Ornithology of Francis Willughby* (London: printed by A. C. for John Martyn, 1678)

Redford, Bruce, *The Converse of the Pen: Acts of Intimacy in the Eighteenth Century Familiar Letter* (Chicago & London: University of Chicago Press, 1986)

Richmond, Sir Herbert William, *The Navy in the War of 1739–48* (Cambridge: Cambridge University Press, 1920)

Riding, Jacqueline, *Jacobites: A New History of the '45 Rebellion* (London: Bloomsbury, 2016)

Rizzo, Betty, 'Banter and Testimony, Supplication and Praise, in the Letters of Christopher Smart', in *Sent as a Gift: Eight Correspondences from the Eighteenth Century*, ed. by Alan McKenzie (Athens & London: University of Georgia Press, 1993), pp. 68–89

Russell, Nicholas, *Like Engend'ring Like: Heredity and Animal Breeding in Early Modern England* (Cambridge: Cambridge University Press, 1986)

Shakespeare, William, *The Riverside Shakespeare*, ed. by G. Blakemore Evans (Boston: Houghton Mifflin, 1974)

Simms, J. G., 'The Establishment of Protestant Ascendancy, 1691–1714', in *A New History of Ireland: IV, Eighteenth-Century Ireland, 1691–1800*, ed. by T. W. Moody and W. E. Vaughan (Oxford: Clarendon Press, 1986), pp. 1–30

Smith, A. D., *The Development of Rates of Postage: An Historical and Analytical Study* (London: George Allen & Unwin, 1917)

Sobel, Dava, *Longitude* (London: Fourth Estate, 1995)

Symcox, Geoffrey, *Victor Amadeus II: Absolutism in the Savoyard State, 1675–1730* (Berkeley: University of California Press, 1983)

Taylor, George, and Andrew Skinner, *Taylor and Skinner's Maps of the Roads of Ireland* (London & Dublin: 1778)

Teltscher, Kate, 'The Sentimental Ambassador: The Letters of George Bogle from Bengal, Bhutan and Tibet, 1770–1781', in *Epistolary Selves: Letters and Letter-writers, 1600–1945*, ed. by Rebecca Earle (Basingstoke: Ashgate, 1999), pp. 79–94

THOMAS, PETER G., 'Jacobitism in Wales', *Welsh History Review*, 1.3 (1962), 279–300

TILLEY, M. P., *A Dictionary of the Proverbs in England in the Sixteenth and Seventeenth Centuries* (Ann Arbor: University of Michigan Press, 1950–1966)

TURBERVILE, GEORGE, *The Booke of Faulconrie or Hauking, for the only Delight and Pleasure of all Noblemen and Gentlemen* (London: by Henry Bynemann for Christopher Barker, 1575)

WALPOLE, SIR HORACE, *Horace Walpole's Correspondence*, Yale Edition, ed. by W. S. Lewis, 48 vols (New Haven, CT: Yale University Press, 1937–1983), <http://images.library.yale.edu/hwcorrespondence>

WARBURTON, J., J. WHITELAW, and R. WALSH, *History of the City of Dublin: From the Earliest Accounts to the Present Time*, 2 vols (London: T. Cadell and W. Davies, 1818)

WELPLY, W. H., 'Edmund Spenser: Being an Account of Some Recent Researches into His Life and Lineage, with Some Notice of His Family and Descendants', *Notes & Queries* 162 (1932), 128–32, 146–50, 165–69, 182–87, 202–06, 220–24, 239–42, & 256–60

—— 'The Family and Descendants of Edmund Spenser', *Journal of the Cork Historical and Archaeological Society*, 2nd ser., 28, 127 (1922), 22–34

—— 'The Family and Descendants of Edmund Spenser (contd)', *Journal of the Cork Historical and Archaeological Society*, 2nd ser., 28, 128 (1922), 49–61

WHYMAN, SUSAN, 'Paper Visits: The Post-Restoration Letter as Seen Through the Verney Family Archive', in *Epistolary Selves: Letters and Letter-writers, 1600–1945*, ed. by Rebecca Earle (Basingstoke: Ashgate, 1999), pp. 15–36

—— *The Pen and the People: English Letter Writers, 1600–1800* (Oxford: Oxford University Press, 2009)

WILLIAMS, GOMER, *History of the Liverpool Privateers and Letters of Marque: With an Account of the Liverpool Slave Trade* (London: Routledge, 2013)

WILLIAMS, J. B., 'Henry Cross-Grove, Jacobite Journalist and Printer', *The Library*, 3rd ser., 5 (1914), 206–24

WRIGLEY, E. A., and R. S. SCHOFIELD, *The Population History of England, 1541–1871* (Cambridge: Cambridge University Press, 1981)

WYLIE, J. C. W., *Irish Land Law*, 2nd edn (Abingdon: Professional Books Limited, 1986)

Online

BBC, <http://www.bbc.co.uk/blogs/wales/posts/jacobites_in_wales>

A Detailed Account of the Establishment for the Collection of Excise at the Port of Dublin, House of Commons, 1823, <http://www.dippam.ac.uk/eppi/documents/9650/>

KALLER, BRIAN, 'Burning the Bones of the Earth: Lime Kilns', <http://www.lowtechmagazine.com/2013/09/lime-kilns.html>

MAC CON IOMAIRE, MÁIRTÍN, 'Coffee Culture in Dublin: A Brief History', website of the Dublin Institute of Technology, <http://arrow.dit.ie/cgi/viewcontent.cgi?article=1139&context=tfschafart>

MURPHY, SEAN, *A Short History of Dublin's Temple Bar*, Centre for Irish Genealogical and Historical Studies, <http://homepage.eircom.net/~seanjmurphy/dublin/templebar.htm>

PRATT, DERRICK, 'A Description of Bangor Parish 1699', <http://bangor-on-dee.co.uk/bangor_parish_1699/>

REDDAN, NICK, IMMIGRANT SHIPS TRANSCRIBERS' Guild website, <http://immigrantships.net/newsarticles/ireland1700_1819.html>

<http://thequackdoctor.com/index.php/walkers-jesuits-drops>

<http://www.atsjournals.org/doi/abs/10.1164/arrd.1961.83.2P2.41?journalCode=arrd#.VrYZXekrzdk>

<http://www.cefnpennar.com/flint/flint_sheriff.htm>
<http://www.cracroftspeerage.co.uk>
<http://www.historyofparliamentonline.org>
<http://www.thepeerage.com>
<http://en.wikipedia.org/wiki/Thomas_Mathews>
<http://en.wikipedia.org/wiki/Daffy's_Elixir>
<http://en.wikipedia.org/wiki/James_Freney>
<https://en.wikipedia.org/wiki/François_Thurot>
<https://en.wikipedia.org/wiki/Inoculation>
<https://en.wikipedia.org/wiki/Irish_Charter_Schools>
<https://en.wikipedia.org/wiki/Privilege_of_peerage>
<https://en.wikisource.org/wiki/Equine_Influenza_Epidemic_of_1872>

INDEX

N.B. For the individual addressees and people mentioned in the letters see 'Appendix II: Index of People Mentioned in the Correspondence'; for places see 'Appendix III: Index of Places Mentioned in the Correspondence'. People and places are indexed here only when there is discussion of them in the text or in a footnote which a reader will not easily find from consulting these two appendices.

Accounts 215–18
Aix-La-Chapelle, Treaty of 147
America 16, 58
Anglican Church (Church of Ireland) 14, 15
Army 96, 97, 107, 114, 123, 124, 125, 143, 155, 166, 220
Army commissions 52, 166–67
Aughrim, Battle of 2, 31, 107, 133, 155, 156
Austrian Succession, War of 17, 147

Balls 19, 108, 110, 111n
Ballyhooly 1, 11
Barnard, Toby 4, 11, 16, 30, 31, 32, 49, 127, 128, 162, 171, 219
Barry family:
  Barry, Arthur 143, 146
  Barry, James, 2nd Lord Barrymore 176n
  Barry, James, 4th Lord Barrymore 5, 7–9, 10, 11, 12, 14, 26, 29, 30, 34, 49n, 50n, 55n, 65n, 78n, 104n, 110n, 128n, 176n, 219, 220, 221, 225, 226, 228
  Barry, Richard, 2nd Earl Barrymore 78
  Barry, Richard 226
  Barrymore, Lady Anne 212, 214
Berg, Temma 38
Birkenhead 1, 6, 37, 99n, 207n
Boyle, Elizabeth 2, 3, 132n
Boyle, Richard 78n
Boyne, Battle of 85n
Boyne The 85
Breda, Treaty of 147n
Buchan, John (politician and novelist) 8
Buchan, John (doctor) 9, 171n, 109
Bulkeley, Rosamund 2
Burke, Bernard 6n, 10n, 181n
Burns, Robert 122n
Burns, William 35
Busteed (lawyer) 4, 36, 49n, 50n, 162n
Buttevant, Lord 6, 14, 173n
Byrne, Dorothea 37, 177n, 207n

Canada 124n, 223n
Caroline, Queen 111n
Castlelyons 5, 6n, 9, 10, 28, 48n, 51n, 53n, 128n, 146n, 150n, 152–53n, 171n, 172n, 174n, 181n, 219
Castletownroche 51n, 85n, 87n, 117n, 132n, 161n
Catholic, Catholicism 13, 14, 16, 27–28, 132n, 150n, 209n
Cattle 79
Cavendish, William, 4th Duke of Devonshire 15, 77n, 135n
Chambers, Ephraim 22n
Channel Islands 17, 89n
Charity 150, 159
Charter Petition 223
Chester 41, 54n, 55n, 64n, 217, 223n, 229
Childe, Maccabaeus 2, 27
China 143–44
Chinnery, Dick 7, 23n, 27
Cicero, Marcus Tullius 20
Cleiveland family 7
  John 6, 99n
Coppinger, Jack 9
Coffee houses 19, 53n, 132n
  Dick's Coffee House 19, 132n, 144, 169–70, 175
Connaught 106n
Cork 1, 2, 9, 11, 16, 17, 18, 35, 50n, 92, 121, 127n
Cricket 111n
Critchley, Harry 181n, 224, 225n
Cromwell, Oliver 27, 77n, 84n
Cross-Grove, Henry 220, 226
Culloden, Battle of 110n, 115n
Customs, *see* Excise
Cycle Club 8, 30, 64n, 65n

Daffy, Thomas 68n
Dates, dating xxi, 90n, 110n, 176
Day, Angelique 29
Deane family 31n
  Deane, Sir Matthew 11
Declaratory Act (1720) 14–15
Deer 146n
Defamation 177–78n
Delaney, Mary 29
Denny, Edward 173n, 189
Derby 8, 18, 110n, 226n
Desmond Castle Fire 138
Desmond Rebellion 2
Dettingen Club 30, 32, 65n, 66n

Dickins, George 23n, 54n
Dogs 120
Doneraile 61n, 79n, 80n
Dragoons 113, 114, 143n
Dublin *xiv*, 1, 6, 7, 14, 15, 18, 27, 32, 36, 53n, 61n, 67n, 71n, 72n, 104n, 117n, 119n, 121n, 167n, 168, 169n, 170n, 181n, 195n
  Dublin Castle 19, 110, 115n
  'Black Dog' Debtors' Prison 219, 224–25
Duelling 147

Eagle 11, 25n, 80, 126–27, 125–28
Earle, Rebecca 19
Economics 15
Edinburgh 18, 102n
Elections 63, 64n, 180, 187
Evelyn, John 57n
Excise and Revenue Commission 27, 61n, 119n, 121, 122n, 129, 135, 142n, 149n, 151, 167n, 178n, 179, 181n, 191n, 201n, 219, 224
Expenses 196

Famine 15, 94n
Farmers, Farming 15, 18, 81, 88, 92, 93, 98–99, 102, 121, 122, 123, 128, 143, 144, 147, 174
Fashion 15, 108, 140, 143
Fishing 80, 81, 82n
Fontenoy, Battle of 96n
Food 24, 83n n, 93, 98, 113n, 121, 138, 147n
Forty-Five Rebellion 8, 13, 19, 220, 223n
France, French 7, 17, 29, 50n, 57n, 66, 77, 78, 84, 92, 93, 96n, 147n, 209, 226n
  French Revolution 16
Freeman, Ann 3, 35, 62
Freeman, William 11, 49n, 86, 96, 120, 160

George II 30, 31n, 66n, 111n, 112n, 150n
George III 16
Gibson, Charles 35–36
Gillespie, Raymond 179n
Grattan, Henry 16
Gray, Thomas 4n, 5n, 18n, 31n
Grierson, George 67
Grovesnour, Robert 223

Hanbury-Williams, Charles 136n, 219
Hanover, House of 7, 28, 30, 31, 66n, 107, 147n, 155, 220
Harris, Alexandra 40n
Harrison, John 99n
Health and Medicine 9, 17, 68, 83, 88, 89n, 90–91, 92, 97, 102, 104, 109, 113, 129, 130, 131, 133–34, 138, 142, 144, 171n, 182–83, 194, 195, 197, 200, 201, 202, 206–07, 208, 210n, 212
Hearth-money 34, 105, 201n
Hely, Mary 185n, 198n
Highwaymen 149
Hill, John 23n

Horses 132, 173, 174
Horse racing 81, 82n, 118, 147
How, James 29n
Hyde, Arthur 11, 23n, 49n, 79n, 162n
Hyde, Jane 162n

Inheritance 4, 6, 36, 48–51, 105–06, 155–56
Ireland 13–16
  Irish Parliament 14–15

Jacobites 7, 8, 18, 29, 30, 50n, 64n, 65n, 66n, 69n, 78n, 82n, 107n, 110–11n, 115, 116, 129n, 132n, 147n, 220, 223n, 226n
Jamaica Expedition 56, 58n
James II 2, 85, 155
'James III' 8n
Jenkins' Ear, War of 17, 89n
Jephson, Colonel 24, 80n, 94n, 95n

Keats, John 40n
Kilcolman Castle 2, 4, 50n, 61n, 80n, 81n, 106n, 133n, 157n
King, William 15
Kingsbury, Thomas 9, 54n

Land, land law 13–14, 94–98, 100, 104–05, 173–75, 180–82, 188–90, 228
Landlords 15, 168–70, 174, 212n
Langford, Paul 17n, 28, 220n
Law, lawyers 116–17, 121, 145
Letters 19–33, 37–38, 101–02n, 103–04n, 150, 179, 181n, 184–85, 210n, 218
Lime 175
  Lime kilns 133–34
Liverpool 1, 6, 7, 99n, 109n, 223n
Lloyd, Alice 6
Lloyd, Thomas (Trigger) 9–10, 30, 221, 229
Longitude 99–100
Lords, House of 103

Mallow 2, 7, 14, 34, 35, 36, 95, 99–101, 118n, 174n
Mann, Horace 99n
Marriage 6, 48, 106, 156, 162, 206
Marlborough, Duke of 128n, 151–52, 154n, 156n, 220
Mead, Richard 157
Medicine, *see* Health
Melancholy 103, 166, 208–09
Militia 28, 81, 208–09
Mohire estate 6, 14, 128n, 171n, 173n, 179n, 189n, 195n, 196n, 212, 214n
Money 17, 19, 27, 60, 108, 109, 110, 124, 138n, 162, 204, 229n
Montagu, George 99n
Montagu, Lady Wortley 134n
Mummers 141
Murder 18, 35, 71n, 147–48
Munster 1, 2, 6, 82n, 152n

Navy, naval matters 17–18, 69, 78n, 84–87, 92, 93, 122, 142, 143, 209n, 226n
Newspapers 68, 69, 72, 81, 86, 128, 144, 146, 148, 174, 206, 223
Netterville, Nicholas 18, 61n, 71

Old Noll, The 17, 84, 85, 86–87, 93
Orange Order 16
Orrery, Earl of 23, 176–77
Osborne, Dorothy 34
Overton 1, 5, 6, 9–10, 12n, 13, 37, 48n, 55n, 59n, 70n, 80n, 101n, 176n, 222, 229–30
St. Mary's Church 5, 58–60n, 62n, 95n, 165, 207n

Parks, parkland 146
Parliament, Irish 10, 14–15, 16, 31n, 60, 64n, 65, 68, 70, 71, 90, 93, 96, 110, 112, 113, 115, 116, 129, 130, 137, 209, 220, 223n, 226
Patriots, Patriot Party 15, 16, 31, 32, 91n, 177, 180, 181n
Pearde, William 2n, 9, 53n, 54n, 181n, 219–20
Pearson, John 221, 229n
Peep O'Day Boys 16
Penal Laws 14, 27, 28, 31, 181n
Pennant, Thomas 80–81n
Petition 71, 108, 111, 121, 223, 226
Petty, William 79
Pliny the Younger 23, 176–77
Ponsonby, Brabazon 135
Ponsonby, John 31n, 135
Population 14, 15, 94n
Portugal 123, 124n
Post, Post Office 11–12, 28–29, 77n, 84 , 129n, 130–31, 166n, 173, 182
Power family 3, 26, 105, 132n
Power, Pierce 3, 4, 132–33n
Prerogative court 170
Prestonpans, Battle of 18
Price family 2, 24–26, 29n, 41, 54n, 55n, 95n, 167n
Price, Alice 1, 5, 9, 10, 14, 17, 27, 31, 32n, 33, 34, 128n, 166n, 167n, 171n, 173n, 176n, 179n, 182n, 186n, 196n, 210n, 211n
Price, Francis 1, 2n, 4, 5–9, 11–13, 14, 15, 17, 18, 22, 23, 25–27, 30, 31, 32, 33, 34, 37, 41, 146n, 156–57n, 171n, 174n, 181n, 182n, 219–22
Price, Francis Parry 37
Price, Mary 5–6
Price, Richard 1, 5–6,
Price, Richard Parry 8, 11, 14, 32, 34, 37, 80, 171n, 176–77n, 186n, 207n, 210n, 211n, 218n, 227n
Printer, King's 67
Protestant, Protestantism 13, 14, 15, 16, 27–28, 84n, 85n, 150, 159n, 209
Pue, Richard 132n, 142n
Puleston, Anne 37, 207n
Crawshay Wellington 37
Roger 221–22, 229–30
archives 1, 7, 8, 9, 37, 219–30

Ray, John 125n, 126n
Renny Castle 2, 4, 27, 48n, 50n, 51n, 57n, 133n, 148n, 150, 157n, 158n, 161n, 224
Rent, Tithes 134n, 144n, 160–61, 168–70, 190, 191, 192, 194, 197, 198, 201, 202, 203, 204, 210, 211, 216–17, 229–30
Revenue Commission, *see* Excise
Riga 98–99, 99n, 127n
Rivers 120, 132n
Rizzo, Betty 40n
Roads xiii, 82n, 117n, 136, 149, 173
Royal Society, The 134

Savoy mines 56, 58n
Schools 8n, 23n, 49n, 85n, 98, 102, 104, 150, 159
Science 18
Seven Years War 17, 35n, 52n
Shakespeare, William 65n, 99n, 114n
Spencer family 2, 3, 134n, 227n
Spencer, Anne 32, 34, 35
Spencer, Edmund 1, 2, 3, 13, 19–37, 39–41, 156–57n, 179n, 196n, 200n, 210n, 219–21, 224, 225n, 227n
Spencer, Rosamond 32n, 33, 35, 41, 91n, 134n, 200n
Spencer, Susanna 225n
Spenser family 3, 27, 28n
Spenser, Edmund 1, 2, 50n, 61n, 62n, 68, 70, 72–75, 76n, 78n, 81n
Spenser, Hugolin 2, 3, 4, 27, 132n
Spenser, Katharine 2, 78n
Spenser, Nathaniel (Edmund's brother) 3, 27, 119n
Spenser, Nathaniel (Edmund's father) 2, 3, 4, 23n, 35, 49n, 133n
Spenser, Peregrine 2, 3, 6
Spenser, Sylvanus 2, 3, 4
Spenser, William 2, 3, 4, 27, 28, 106n, 133n, 225n
Stanhope, Philip, 4th Earl of Chesterfield 15, 90n, 91n, 112n, 113n
Stuart, Charles, The Young Pretender 7, 8, 13, 18, 50n, 102n, 110n, 226n
Swift, Jonathan 15, 23, 57n, 177

Teltscher, Kate 23
Tenants, tenancy, *see* Rent
Terrible, The 85, 86
Textiles 108, 112, 139, 140
Thurloe, John 84n
Thurloe, The 7, 84, 86
Tithes, *see* Rent
Tone, Wolfe 16
Travers, Sarah 50
Trigger, *see* Lloyd, Thomas
True Blue Privateer 142
Turbervile, George 125n, 127n

United Irishmen 16

Vernon, Admiral 18, 58n, 89n
Victory, HMS 17, 89n
Volunteers 15

Wales 1, 5, 7, 8n, 9, 11, 24, 25, 41, 48n, 52n, 53, 54n, 55n, 77n, 104, 125, 208
National Library of 1, 7, 37
Wallis, Henry, lawyer 212n, 214n, 220, 227, 228
Walpole, Horace 4n, 99n
Walsh, Michael 71n
Waterford 34–35, 201n, 214n
Weather 15, 24, 57, 81, 86, 88, 94n, 97, 98, 102, 120, 121, 128, 136, 141, 143
Welply, W. H. 5, 34, 35, 36, 49n, 81n, 106n, 128n
Welsh, Richard 11
Wexford 34, 201n, 208n
Whyman, Susan 17, 23n
Wicklow 19, 32n, 201n
William III 2, 28, 31, 85n, 107n, 133n, 156n
Williamite Wars 2, 13, 107n, 132n
Williams-Wynn, Sir Watkin 7, 8–9, 11, 12–13, 29, 64n, 101–02n, 110n, 129n, 166n, 226n
Wills 49–50, 170n, 184
Woods, woodland 50, 88, 133, 146, 156, 157n

Youghal 11, 49n, 61n, 127n

www.ingramcontent.com/pod-product-compliance
Lightning Source LLC
Chambersburg PA
CBHW080837250626
47160CB00009B/2964